THE
ENCYCLOPEDIA
OF
Fortune-
Telling

THE
ENCYCLOPEDIA
—OF—
fORTUNE-
tELLING

FRANCIS X. KING

HAMLYN

First published in Great Britain in 1988
This updated edition published in 1999 Hamlyn, an imprint of Octopus Publishing Group Limited,
Michelin House
81 Fulham Road
London
SW3 6RB

ISBN 0 600 59761 X

A CIP catalogue record for this book is available from the British Library
Printed in China

ACKNOWLEDGEMENTS

Operations Director: Laura Bamford
Creative Director: Keith Martin
Executive Editor: Jane McIntosh
Design Manager: Bryan Dunn
Editorial Team: A. Jefford, J. Wilkinson, J. Kuhn, M-C. Jerram, L. McOwan, Nicola Hodgson
Art Editor: Pedro Prá-Lopez
Designer: Bob Burroughs
Jacket Designer: Mike Moule
Picture Researchers: Kathy Lockley, Wendy Gay
Production: Eleanor McCallum, Garry Lewis, Trevor Jones, Katherine Hockley

Western Astrology update: Robert Parry

PICTURE CREDITS
ACE PHOTO AGENCY: Mike Tate 74; Vibert-Stokes 125; ALDUS ARCHIVE: Ashmolean Museum, Oxford 15; 104, 114, 116LC, 116TC; ANCIENT ART & ARCHITECTURE COLLECTION: 91, 94; BARNABYS PICTURE LIBRARY: 87, 179; BBC HULTON PICTURE LIBRARY: 31, 64TL, 64TR, 176, 185TR; BRIDGEMAN ART LIBRARY: 77, Gulbenkian Museum of Oriental Art, University of Durham 101; Victoria & Albert Museum 109; 142, 143; National Gallery 145; Nationalgalerie Staatliche Museen Preussischer Kulturbesitz, Berlin 149; 157BL; J. ALLAN CASH PHOTOLIBRARY: 117, 121; C.M. DIXON: 159; E.T. ARCHIVE: British Museum 98, 100; Freer Gallery of Art 102, 103; British Museum 107; National Palace Museum, Taiwan 108; British Museum 113; 122; MARY EVANS PICTURE LIBRARY: 10, 12BR, 13, 14TR, 14CL, 16TL, 18, 27, 28, 50BR, 64TC, 123; FINE ART PHOTOGRAPHS: 70; WERNER FORMAN ARCHIVE: 72, Statens Sjöhistoriska Museum, Stockholm 95; FORTEAN PICTURE LIBRARY: 21, 180, 181; FOTOMAS INDEX, LONDON: 20, 83, 134, 148; JOHN FROST HISTORICAL NEWSPAPER SERVICE: 29; ROBERT HARDING PICTURE LIBRARY: 6, 9, 38, British Museum 40TLC, 41L, 42, 44BL; 44BCL, British Museum 45BR; 47CR, 48TCL, British Museum 48TCR, 49CL, 49CR; Victoria & Albert Museum 49BR; 50TCR, Bibliothèque Nationale 54BL, 56C, 56BR; British Museum 57TR; 73, 75, 80, 157TR, 183TL; MICHAEL HOLFORD: Statens Sjöhistoriske Museum, Stockholm 93BR, 97; British Museum 96; Victoria & Albert Museum 105; IMAGES COLOUR LIBRARY: 76; FRANCIS X. KING: 24; KOBAL COLLECTION: Eon Productions 126; 130, 131, 132, 133, 156; MANSELL COLLECTION: 16BR, William Walker & Son (Otley) Ltd 26; 128, 129; NATIONAL PORTRAIT GALLERY: 19, 23; OCTOPUS PUBLISHING GROUP LIBRARY: 2, 12TC, 22, 25, 40TL, 40CR, 40TR, 41BR, 43TL, 43TCL, 43TCR, 44-45, 46TL, 46TCL, 46TCR, 46TR, 47CL, 47C, 47CR, 47BL, 48TL, 48TR, 49C, 50TL, 50TCL, 51-3, 54TR, 55CL, 55C, 55CR, 57C, 58-60, 82TL, 82BR, 86, 88, 89, 110, 127, 136-141, 146, 147, 155, 162-175; MIRANDA PAYNE: 69BL, 69BC, 78; POPPERFOTO: 8; GILREID: 183BR; TONY STONE ASSOCS, LONDON: 119; WEIDENFELD & NICHOLSON LTD: 32-35; WELLCOME INSTITUTE LIBRARY, LONDON: 111; ZEFA: 1, 182TL, 182BR, 183TR, 184TL, 184BR, 185BL.

The publishers would like to thank Waddington's Games Ltd for permission to use Waddington's No. 1 playing cards for the illustration on page 36.

CONTENTS

1 INTRODUCTION

The lines on the hand, the mystic and entrancing symbols of the tarot, the runic alphabet of the ancient Vikings – these are just some of the materials which fortune-tellers draw on in their endeavours to penetrate the veils of space and time.

Those who learn how to divine character and predict the future by the use of these and other fortune-telling methods are practising ancient techniques whose origin goes back to the dawn of human history and which, in the present century, have attracted the favourable attention of such writers, philosophers and psychologists as Robert Graves, D. H. Lawrence, P. D. Ouspensky and C. G. Jung.

Since prehistoric times mankind has observed the movements of the various elements of the solar system. It has been asserted that Stonehenge and other megalithic structures like it were lunar observatories of considerable sophistication.

If, at some social gathering, word gets round that one of those present has the ability to read palms, to tell fortunes by the use of playing cards or the tarot, or to cast horoscopes, he or she is soon approached with such requests as 'Would you read my palm?' or 'Would you like to come round for a drink and bring your tarot cards?'

The odd thing is that, in spite of the popularity of almost anyone reputed to be able to tell fortunes and predict the future, few people believe in fortune-telling – or so it would seem from the replies which, when questioned on the subject, a majority of people give to opinion pollsters. It would appear that, paradoxically, a great many people don't believe in fortune-telling but are very anxious indeed to have their fortunes told! It is all a bit reminiscent of the answer given by an eighteenth century writer when asked whether he believed in ghosts. 'No,' he said, 'but I am afraid of them'.

In other words, most people of the present day claim to be sceptical about fortune-telling on an intellectual level, but have a strong instinctive feeling – which they are shy about communicating to pollsters – that there 'may be something in it'.

There is, in fact, no good reason to feel that fortune-telling is unworthy of serious consideration. Believers in it are in good company: for thousands of years those who have practised the divinatory arts, from astrology to crystal gazing, have received gratitude from those to whom they have given their advice. These latter have included emperors, kings, great warriors and, at the other end of the social scale, poor peasants who sought the aid of the local 'cunning man' or 'white witch' – in other words an individual skilled in one or more fortune-telling techniques – in finding a lost cow or in tracing some stolen property.

It has sometimes been assumed that 'cunning men' and other peasant fortune-tellers were charlatans or rogues who simply told their clients what they knew those clients would like to hear. No doubt this was true of some of them (every profession includes some villains among its membership), but by no means all. Some of these diviners left manuscript records of their dealings with clients and these demonstrate, quite conclusively, that those same diviners not only believed in their powers of predicting the future but were skilled practitioners of the techniques they employed.

Thus, for example, the manuscript records of one nineteenth century Lincolnshire cunning man, of which the

C. G. JUNG AND THE ARTS OF FORTUNE-TELLING

C. G. Jung, the analytical psychologist and philosopher, regarded the despised arts of fortune-telling with much more respect than most of his intellectual contemporaries. He was particularly interested in both astrology and the Chinese oracle book called the *I Ching* – 'the Book of Changes'. In the latter years of his life he always insisted on seeing a horoscope drawn up for the moment of birth of each of his patients. If a patient was married he also felt it useful to examine the horoscope of that patient's husband or wife. He regularly consulted the *I Ching*, which he revered almost as much as Confucius is reputed to have done, and wrote a lengthy introduction to Richard Wilhelm's German translation of its Chinese text together with commentaries upon it.

present writer has made a detailed study, show that he was an accomplished practitioner of 'horary astrology': a method of fortune-telling which, in the present century, attracted the attention of the great Swiss psychotherapist C. G. Jung, who believed it effective and explained its success on the basis of what he called 'synchronicity' (see below).

An horary astrologer sets up a horoscope ('casts a figure' – a diagrammatic representation of the positions of the sun, moon and planets) for the exact moment he or she is asked a question by a client. On the basis of this horoscope the question is answered, sometimes in great detail. Many of the most successful fortune-tellers of the past have been horary astrologers. Their number has included John Dee, William Lilly and Simon Forman, and more will be related of their activities in Chapter One of this book.

Meaningful Coincidence

But how does it work? Why should processes which depend on chance – the exact moment at which an horary astrologer is asked a question, the way in which dice fall, and tea leaves come to rest in the bottom of a cup – produce accurate predictions of future events? What is the cause – if any – of the fortune-teller's often uncanny success?

The answer to this question given by Jung, one of the most original and important thinkers of modern times, was very odd indeed – but well worth consideration.

There is no cause, said Jung, for the fortune-teller's arts are concerned not with causality – one thing causing another to happen – but with what Jung termed 'synchronicity'. By synchronicity he meant *meaningful coincidence*: two events which take place at the same time, and are relevant to one another, but which have taken place quite independently of one another, i.e. neither event has caused the other. Jung felt that there could be a relationship between events via a web of time, rather than a single line of cause and effect. An example of a synchronistic event would be the interruption of a conversation about Camelot and the Knights of the Round Table by a telephone call from a double-glazing salesman giving his name as Arthur King. Jung believed such a coincidence to be the result, not of mere chance, but of what he described 'a peculiar interdependence of objective events among themselves as well as with the subjective states of the observer'.

Jung expressed this idea of synchronicity in rather simpler language when he said that 'anything done at a particular moment of time has the qualities of that moment of time'. By this he meant that, in relation to fortune-tellers, it is coincidence – meaningful coincidence, not just chance – which causes a question to be asked of the horary astrologer at the time at which the planetary positions are such that the right answer is derived from them or tarot cards shuffled in such a way that the spread derived from them gives an accurate indication of the true nature of a situation.

This may well be the true explanation of why fortune-telling, even by the oddest of methods, can provide an effective diagnosis of a problem and suggest an answer to it. On the other hand it may be that, as some of the diviners and occultists of the Middle Ages believed, invisible spirits influence the fortune-teller in his or her actions – thus ensuring that a correct answer is obtained. These 'spirits', of course, might be elements of the fortune-teller's own unconscious mind rather than supernatural entities.

There are, therefore, many possible explanations of why fortune-telling works. The next chapter recounts the activities and predictions of famous fortune-tellers of the past, thereby indicating something of the scope and provenance of this mysterious art. All that remains then is for you to experiment with the techniques described in this book, so that you can decide for yourself whether or not fortune-telling works for you and your family and friends, as it has for others.

THE MYSTERY OF STONEHENGE

The origin and purpose of Stonehenge, Britain's largest megalithic monument, has been the subject of speculation for almost a thousand years.

The medieval historian Geoffrey of Monmouth asserted that its stones were brought from Ireland by Merlin – King Arthur's court magician. The Jacobean architect Inigo Jones believed that the Romans had built Stonehenge 'after the Tuscan manner', while John Aubrey, author of the enchanting *Brief Lives*, argued that it had been a temple of the Druids, the priest-magicians of Celtic Britain.

The latter view was dominant until well into the nineteenth century. Two fallen stones became known as the 'Altar' and the 'Slaughter' stones – it was believed that the Druids had conducted human sacrifices upon them. They may have done; but in fact, Stonehenge was already over a thousand years old when the first Druids came to Britain, so it is likely that the megalith was as mysterious to them as it is to us.

Modern Theories
By the beginning of the present century most students of prehistory accepted that the oldest parts of Stonehenge dated from before 2000 B.C. and that even its most 'modern' element – the outer circle – was erected before 1000 B.C. The current tendency is to put the completion of Stonehenge even earlier, to around 1400 B.C.

But what was the purpose of Stonehenge? Was it a temple, a meeting place for chieftains, or an observatory? Probably all three, but while there is still a great deal of controversy upon the matter, increasing numbers of scholars believe that the structure had at least some astronomical functions, perhaps connected with the prediction of eclipses.

A Lunar Observatory
The astronomical alignments of Stonehenge were first pointed out before World War One by the astronomer Sir Joseph Norman Lockyer (1836-1920). At the time Lockyer advanced his arguments few archaeologists took them seriously – they respected Lockyer's distinction as a scientist but felt that he was incompetent to judge matters which lay outside his own field – and within a few years Lockyer's theory was almost forgotten.

The theory was revived and revised, however, in the 1960s by scholars such as Professors Hawkins, Hoyle and Thom, all of whom believed that they had produced hard evidence of significant astronomical alignments between the positioning of the megaliths of Stonehenge and the motions of sun, moon and planets in relation to the earth. The arguments put forward by these men were by no means in complete accordance with each other, and are still the subject of much controversy. It does seem, however, that the case put forward by one of them, Professor Thom, is a very strong one, and a number of professional archaeologists now accept his argument that Stonehenge and many other megalithic structures were erected for the purpose of making accurate lunar observations. If so, one can regard the neolithic builders of Stonehenge as being amongst the first astrologers and astronomers.

Temples and Ziggurats
Lockyer was interested in Egyptian temples and Chaldean ziggurats – seventiered buildings which may have been regarded as links between earth and the heavens – as well as in megaliths, and he believed that their orientations had a solar significance. He may well have been right in this contention, for it would seem that the seven tiers of the ziggurat pertained to the sun, the moon, and the five planets visible to the naked eye, and that from the highest of these priest-astrologers observed the heavenly motions and made predictions on the basis of them.

According to the Greek historian Herodotus, however, at least one ziggurat was used for marriages between gods and women – which seem unlikely. This tale of sexual relationships between gods and women was nevertheless recounted as fact by Herodotus, a serious historian who undoubtedly believed it to have been true. Possibly he had been told it by a hoaxer, and the tale was pure invention. It has been suggested, however, that some sort of sexual rite, a symbolic union of the sun and moon, was celebrated in the topmost chamber of a ziggurat.

The ziggurats were built in seven tiers, corresponding with the sun, moon and five planets known to the ancients.

FORTUNE-TELLING'S FAMILY TREE

oday there is something of a craze for family history – for tracing details of one's ancestry, constructing a family tree, and finding out what sort of people were one's forebears. When the researcher has managed to construct a family tree he or she usually finds that his or her forebears include saints and sinners, the vicious and the virtuous, the highly intelligent and the very stupid, and so on. Most ancestors, however, come somewhere between these two extremes.

The 'family tree' of fortune-telling presents a similarly chequered appearance. It has included men and women of great intellectual power and unstained moral reputation, like Nostradamus or Robert Fludd, as well as some rather black sheep, such as the Elizabethan occultist Simon Forman. Most, however, have fallen somewhere between such extremes.

On September 1, 1939 the Panzer formations of the German army crossed the Polish frontier and began their 'lightning war', the *blitzkrieg*, against the republic which, almost alone of the states of eastern Europe, had refused to be browbeaten by Nazi threats. Two days later France and Britain declared war on Germany in accordance with the guarantees they had given to Colonel Beck, the Polish foreign minister.

World War Two had begun.

In spite of heroic resistance, which included its cavalrymen charging German armoured formations, Poland – stabbed in the back by an invasion from the Soviet Union – was within a few weeks under brutal foreign occupation.

At about the same time as the Germans were occupying Warsaw, Magda Goebbels, the fanatically Nazi wife of Hitler's propaganda minister, was reading in bed. The book she was reading was H. H. Kritzinger's *Mysteries of the Sun and the Soul*, published in 1922. Suddenly Frau Goebbels called out excitedly, waking her husband from sleep. The 'crisis of 1939', she said, had been clearly foretold in Kritzinger's book, published seventeen years earlier.

In reality Kritzinger was no prophet; he had merely given an account of cer-

Nostradamus, the sixteenth-century seer, was one of that minority of fortune-tellers who have advised monarchs. The meanings of his cryptic prophecies are still debated today, as they have been for the past four centuries.

tain interpretations of one of the mysterious predictive four-line verses, known as quatrains, written almost four centuries earlier by Michel de

Nostradame, better known as Nostradamus, a French physician, astrologer and seer. The quatrain in question, first printed in 1555, reads as follows:

Sept fois changez verrez gent
   Brittanique,
Taintz en sang en deux cents
   nonante an:
Franche non point par appuy
   Germanique,
Aries doubte son Pole Bastarnan

The quatrains of Nostradamus were written in a curiously mixed-up language of his own manufacture which included the ordinary French vernacular of his own time; anagrammatic variants of that French – Paris, for example, usually appears as *Rapis*; curious puns; and both Latin words and words of his own invention that derive from the Latin. This quatrain, however, is clearer than most and can be translated with reasonable accuracy as:

Seven times you will see
   the British race change,
Stained with blood in the year
   two hundred and ninety;
Not at all free through German
   support,
Aries will fear for his vassal
   Bastarnan.

As long ago as the eighteenth century an English student of Nostradamus published a suggestion that the period of 290 years should be dated from the execution of Charles I in 1649 and that some event of very great importance to Britain would take place in 1939. A century or so later the French writer Nicoullaud arrived, quite independently, at a similar conclusion – the year 1939, he said, would be *taintz en sang*, 'dyed in blood' or 'stained with blood'.

It is true, of course, that 1939 was 'dyed in blood' but the same could be said of a great number of other years between the publication of Nostradamus' quatrain and the date on which Frau Goebbels was made acquainted with it through the medium of Kritzinger's book. What excited the unpleasant Magda Goebbels was that Kritzinger's book, written so many years before, specifically claimed that 1939 would be dyed with blood because of an international crisis involving Britain, Germany and Poland.

Germany and Britain are, of course, specifically mentioned in the quatrain but not Poland (*pole* would seem to mean 'vassal' or 'protectorate'). In fact Kritzinger was merely repeating in his book a suggestion made in 1921 by an occultist named Loog. The Bastarnae, said Loog, had been a tribe which in classical times had inhabited the area which was now Poland, and by the 'Bastarnan' Nostradamus had meant 'the Polish state'. Loog had been quite specific about what he thought Nostradamus was foretelling. He wrote: 'Nostradamus therefore clearly indicates that in 1939 there will be a critical state of affairs in the revived country of Poland, hand in hand with Britain's last and greatest crisis.'

Goebbels was so impressed by what seemed to be Nostradamus' astoundingly accurate prediction of the outbreak of war in 1939 that he ordered that a search should be made for Nostradamus quatrains which could be used for the purposes of Nazi propaganda. The search was made with so little success that Goebbels was reduced to forging quatrains; these were dropped as leaflets over France in the early summer of 1940.

The prophecy discussed above could, of course, have been no more than a lucky hit by Nostradamus and his interpreter, Herr Loog. It would be difficult, however, to make the same claim in relation to another quatrain – one which contains the place name Varennes. This somewhat obscure townlet has once, and only once, featured in any event of real historical importance. The quatrain reads:

De nuit viendra parla forest de
   Reines,
Deux pars vaultorte Herne la
   pierre blanche,
Le moins noir en gris dedans
   Varennes,
Esleu cap, cause tempeste feu,
   sang tranche

This quatrain is not easily translatable, if only because it seems to contain two of the partial anagrams with which Nostradamus filled his verse: *Herne* is possibly an incomplete anagram of the French word for 'Queen' while *noir*, literally 'black', was often used by Nostradamus as a code term for the French word meaning 'King'. It thus seems fairly likely that the quatrain means:

At night will come through the
   forest of Reines,
Two partners, by a roundabout
   way, the Queen *(Herne)*, the white
   stone,
The monk King *(noir)* in grey at
   Varennes,
The chosen (elect) Capet,
   resulting in tempest, fire, or
   bloody slicing.

The only significant historical event to have taken place at Varennes was the capture there of Louis XVI and his Queen, Marie Antoinette, when they endeavoured to escape from Revolutionary France disguised as private individuals. The King, the 'chosen Capet', was dressed in grey and the capture of the two did indeed result eventually in 'bloody slicing', for both King and Queen were guillotined.

Many other of the prophecies of Nostradamus seem to have been fulfilled – although by no means all of them. Some of them may come true at some time in the future. Others were quite wrong. Thus, for example, Nostradamus wrongly foretold the date of his own death – he had said he would meet his end some time in November 1567, whereas he actually did so sixteen months earlier, in July 1566.

Nevertheless a far higher number of Nostradamus' prophetic verses seem to have wholly or partially predicted future events than can reasonably be attributed to chance. How did he achieve his results? Was it, for example, by astrology, an occult art in which Nostradamus was renowned for his skill?

One can be reasonably sure that it was not entirely so – there is no known astrological technique by the use of which a place name, such as 'Varennes', can be derived from the movements of the sun, moon and planets. Almost certainly the predictions which Nostradamus expressed in his barbarously worded and often obscure verses were derived from experiments with scrying (a fortune-telling technique dealt with on pages 70 to 79 of this book).

Scrying has been defined by one of its devotees as a method of 'freeing the mind from the body and letting it roam free through space and time, thus enabling it to see the future'. This freeing of the mind from its physical surroundings, sometimes referred to as 'dissociation of consciousness', can, so it is claimed, be achieved by all of the many different methods of scrying, perhaps the best known of which is crystal-gazing.

A variant of crystal-gazing is gazing at a tumbler or bowl of water (see page 74). There is some reason to believe that this is what was done by Nostradamus. For in two of the quatrains he describes the seer, himself, as follows:

Sitting alone at night in secret study it [a bowl of water] is rested upon a brazen tripod. A little flame comes from the void and makes successful that which should not be vainly believed.

The wand in the hand [of the seer] is placed between the tripod's legs. He [the seer] moistens his foot and the hem [of his robe]. A voice – he trembles within his robes [at the] divine splendour. The god sits close by.

It may be that this description was mere literary fantasy – but the process described bears a strong resemblance to one written about by Iamblichus (c.250-326), a Neoplatonist philosopher and mystic, in his treatise *Of the Mysteries of the Egyptians*. Nostradamus was almost certainly familiar with this book: a Latin edition of it had been published at Lyons in 1547.

Nostradamus may have made some of his predictions on the basis of astrology – for example the quatrain which seems to have foretold the outbreak of bubonic plague in London (1665). His prophecy of the Great Fire of London of 1666, however, must have been based on something other than astrology, for it mentioned a specific year ('thrice twenty and six'), and astrology as such can no more supply an exact date than it can be used to derive a place name from astronomical phenomena.

Nevertheless, both the plague of 1665 and the Great Fire of London which followed a year later are believed to have been predicted in general terms by William Lilly, a seventeenth-century English astrologer whose autobiography, throwing

This is the 'Astrological Hieroglyph' published by William Lilly in 1651, in which he successfully foretold the Great Fire of London of September, 1666.

much light on the occult sub-culture of his own times, still makes entertaining reading.

Lilly's prophecies, expressed in the form of what he termed 'hieroglyphs', meaning symbolic prints from woodcuts, were originally issued in 1651. The first of them showed scenes of unusually high human mortality; the second showed the 'Heavenly Twins' – Gemini, the zodiacal sign traditionally believed to rule London – suspended upside down over flames which men were unsuccessfully trying to extinguish (see above).

Following the plague and the Great Fire, the last widely (although erroneously) believed to have been the result of arson, Lilly was called before a committee of the House of Commons and ordered to explain his supposed foreknowledge of plague and fire. In answer to questions he replied:

Having found [from the study of astrology], Sir, that the City of London should be sadly inflicted with a great plague, and not long after with an exorbitant fire, I framed these two hieroglyphics . . . which in effect have proved very true.

The House of Commons accepted Lilly's astrological explanation and discharged him from further questioning,

exonerating him from involvement in any fire-raising plot. A century or two earlier he would have been lucky not to have been charged with witchcraft; until fairly recent times an ability to predict the future with reasonable accuracy has rarely been looked upon with unqualified admiration and respect. Even today there are people who feel that there is something uncanny, even sinister, about those who are capable of telling fortunes.

In connection with this an interesting personal anecdote has been recounted by Arlene Dahl, actress and beauty expert. In a light-hearted way she had started to 'read the tea leaves' for her friends, using 'cook book' interpretations similar to those given on pages 177-8 of this book. After a time she had ceased to rely entirely upon these, supplementing them by the use of her own intuition – in other words, she improvized whenever she felt improvization rather than sticking to the script was called for. The results were surprising; 'I was right too often and got scared', she said. Others were not scared – but they were certainly impressed by Arlene Dahl's abilities. Thus, for example, her hairdresser jokingly called her 'a real witch' after the hairdresser had unexpectedly become pregnant, a condition she had been hoping for five years to attain,

William Lilly (1602-1681), the English astrologer whose almanacs enjoyed such fame that they were translated into Swedish, also wrote Christian Astrology, a text book which is still studied, and an amusing autobiography.

only five weeks after Ms Dahl had foretold it. The hairdresser's reference to her client as a witch was made admiringly; even today there are those who would make such a remark with dislike tinged with fear.

Prediction and the Individual

Nostradamus' supposed prediction of the year 1939 being dyed with blood, his undoubted prophecy of some incidents of importance taking place at Varennes, and Lilly's mysterious hieroglyphics were all concerned with events of general importance. More usually, however, since the Middle Ages, prediction of the future has been concerned with fortune-telling: attempts to forecast coming events in the life of a particular individual, like Arlene Dahl's successful prediction of her hairdresser's pregnancy.

Originally, however, predictive techniques were probably only used to tell the fortunes of the tribe, the kingdom, or the individual who led one or the other. This is certainly true of one of the best-known fortune-telling techniques: astrology, based upon the observation of the sun, moon and planets in relation to both each other and to the signs of the zodiac.

The very beginnings of astrology – careful observations of the phases of the moon – probably go back to a very remote period, to a time when human beings still lived by hunting and gathering wild fruits and vegetables. Archaeologists have found scratchings on a bone, thought to be 30,000 years old, referring to lunar changes.

However, it was less than 3,000 years ago that astrology as we know it began its development. That was in Babylon, where, by 700 B.C., the priest-astrologers who served its kings had already developed the idea of there being twelve signs of the zodiac. They had also attributed supposedly good and bad significances to the various heavenly bodies and begun carefully observing the planets, specifically their positions in relationship to one another and their apparent colour changes. These last were regarded as being of great importance. For example, it was believed that if the planet Jupiter appeared whitish its influence was good; if it was seen as tinged with red it brought ill fortune to the kingdom and its ruler.

A large number of inscribed Babylo-

nian clay tablets containing reports to the king from his astrologers have survived and been translated. Without exception they are concerned with matters of importance to Babylon and its rulers – wars, prospects of good harvests, and so on. It would seem that astrology was regarded as too important a subject for its experts to concern themselves with the lives of ordinary men and women.

Astrology spread from Babylon to Egypt and Greece. Curiously enough, however, the Egyptians seem to have taken little interest in astrology until the time of the Ptolemies, the Greek-speaking pharaohs of whom Cleopatra was the last representative.

It was the Greeks who really developed astrology as a predictive art applicable to individuals, not just to kings and kingdoms, and from about 200 B.C. onwards Greek-speaking astrologers were not only practising their art in almost all the lands of the eastern Mediterranean but were beginning to produce instructional manuscripts on the subject – 'Do-It-Yourself' books on astrological fortune-telling, in which the main concerns were the horoscopes of persons, not those of kingdoms and empires.

Probably the most important, certainly the most influential, of these was the *Tetrabiblos* of Claudius Ptolemaeus, better known as Ptolemy (c. 102-180 A.D.), a man of remarkable intellect who was not only the greatest astronomer and astrologer of his time but also an outstanding geographer.

Ptolemy catalogued 300 previously unobserved fixed stars and the mathematical tables of planetary motions which he compiled were being used by astronomers and astrologers until the seventeenth century.

By the time at which Ptolemy wrote, almost every citizen of the Roman Empire, from Syria to Britain, accepted the idea that the sun, moon and planets ruled human destiny, and those that could afford it consulted *mathematici* – astrologers. It seems that many Romans knew their 'zodiacal birth sign', regarding themselves as, for example, Gemineans or Pisceans. There was an important difference between the way in which a Roman citizen regarded himself as being born under a particular sign of the zodiac and the way in which someone today regards him or her self as being, say, a Capricornian or a Taurean. Nowadays a person says he or she is 'born under such-and-such a sign' if the sun was in that sign at the date of birth; a Roman citizen would have claimed to be born under that sign if the moon had been in it at birth.

This difference is well illustrated by some of the coins minted in the reign of the Emperor Augustus, who died in 14 A.D. Augustus was a convinced believer in astrology – possibly because at the time of his birth an astrologer named Nigidius had predicted, quite correctly, that the new-born babe would become 'master of the world' – and on the obverse side of the coins in question Augustus had stamped a representation of a 'sea-goat', symbol of Capricorn, bearing aloft an over-flowing horn of plenty. At the time of the birth of the future Emperor it had been the moon, not the sun, which had been in the sign of Capricorn.

With the rise of Christianity the practice of astrology went into a decline as a result of opposition from Church leaders. They felt that astrology's identification of the heavenly bodies with aspects of the deities of Greece and Rome – the moon, for example, with Artemis and Diana – marked it as tarred with a heathen brush. By the time of the fall of Romulus Augustulus (476 A.D.), the last Western Roman Emperor, fortune-telling by means of astrology survived only in Byzantium, now Istanbul, and

An imaginative Renaissance portrayal of Ptolemy, the classical astronomer who flourished in the second century A.D. and whose astrological theories were influential for 1500 years.

the territories ruled by it.

From Byzantium, astrology reached the Arabs, who refined it and attached even more importance to the moon than had the astrologers of ancient Rome. The Arabs were responsible, for example, for developing a technique by which, so they said, they could use the moon's position at birth

to calculate the exact moment at which the individual in question had been conceived. They called this technique 'the Trutine of Hermes' and it is still employed in modified form by some modern astrologers who refer to it as 'the Pre-Natal Epoch'.

Seven hundred years after the fall of the Western Empire, astrology had re-emerged in Europe as the result of scholars translating Arabic treatises into Latin. These Latin translations were at first studied by only a minority of learned men – but they began the process of the popularization of fortune-telling by western astrology which, today, has resulted in every popular newspaper printing a daily astrological column.

By the second half of the sixteenth century astrology had become accepted by almost everybody in western Europe – by peasants, aristocrats and monarch alike. Humble men would pay a small fee to the local fortune-teller, in England usually referred to as a 'cunning man' or a 'wise woman', in order to get an answer to a question concerning a sick cow or some stolen property. Wealthy women would seek advice from well-known astrologers concerning such matters as the health of their children or, sometimes, their extra-marital affairs. Kings and Queens had advis-

A diagrammatic representation of Ptolemy's geocentric ('earth-centred') astronomy, accepted as correct by all astrologers until well into the seventeenth century and still believed in by some, notably 'Zadkiel', 200 years later.

ers who consulted the heavens on matters of state.

Perhaps the best known of the astrologers who advised royalty was John Dee (1527-1608), who was visited at his home by Queen Elizabeth I on more than one occasion. More typical of fortune-tellers of that time, however, was Simon Forman, who only seems to have encountered Dee on one occasion. That was in July 1604, when the two seers had dinner together and talked of the occult. It would be worth knowing exactly what they discussed – all that is certain is that Dee unsuccessfully tried to borrow a rare manuscript from his fellow occultist. Forman may have disliked lending books but he was a skilled and resourceful practitioner of astrology and other predictive arts. So skilled, indeed, that he succeeded in predicting the date of his own death – or so, at any rate, it was widely believed. While he lived, his abilities almost always resulted in his own financial advantage although, on occasion, they led him into danger.

The Remarkable Simon Forman

According to his own account Simon Forman was descended from the minor nobility, his greatgrandfather being 'Sir Thomas of Leeds', though whether of Leeds in Yorkshire or in Kent he did not say. Probably this was untrue – snobbery about social background was even more rampant in Tudor times than it was in the reign of Queen Victoria. All that can be said with certainty about Forman's origins is that he was born on December 30, 1552 at Quidhampton in Wiltshire, the fifth child of William Forman, who appears to have been a yeoman farmer.

Forman's occult abilities seem to have been inborn, for, when he was only six years old he began to see visions. In his own words he would:

> . . . see in visions many mighty mountains and hills come rolling against him . . . he got up always to the top of them and with much ado went over them. Then he should see many great waters like to drown him . . . yet he thought he did overpass them. These dreams and visions . . . every night continually for three or four years space.

Forman's father died in 1564, at which time the boy had received only a broken and desultory education. He had learned to read and write from William Ryder, a cobbler turned priest and schoolmaster; subsequently he had been 'put to the free School in the Close at Salisbury with one Doctor Bowles, which was a very furious man'.

In spite of his short formal education, Forman seems to have acquired enough learning to have been able to teach others. For in 1572 he set himself up as a schoolmaster and continued teaching in various places until June 1579 when he was arrested, following which he spent over a year in prison. Exactly on what charge he was arrested is uncertain, but it was most probably for fortune-telling of some sort. Possibly he was suspected of practising magic. If so, the suspicion was perhaps justified, as would seem to be shown by the following passage written in Forman's own words, concerning events of 1579, and specifically the sentence I have italicized:

I was robbed and spoiled of all my goods and books . . . I had much trouble and defamation without desert . . . I had much sickness and could get no justice nor law . . . till a whole year was past . . . This year I did propesy the truth of many things which afterwards came to pass. *The very spirits were subject unto me* . . . And I had a great name; yet I could do nothing . . .

Forman was released from prison in July 1580 and during the next ten years or so he earned a living in an extraordinary variety of ways – as a carpenter, as a farm labourer, as an unlicensed physician, and as a fortune-teller.

By the early 1590s Forman had established himself in London as a successful fortune-teller, a profession which he continued until his death in 1611. Many of Forman's case books,

John Dee, mathematician, astrologer, and practitioner of 'angelic magic', whose advice was sought by Queen Elizabeth I on such matters as an auspicious date and time for her coronation.

which he kept with all the care of a present-day psychotherapist, have survived and are to be found in the Bodleian and the British Library. He recorded the questions he was asked, the processes he employed to answer them, and the answers he gave, with what seems to have been complete honesty. Thus, for example, he would note his failures – his predictions which proved false – as well as his successes. His casebooks also show the names of his clients, who included men and women from many widely differing social backgrounds. Among them were, for example, a servant to a merchant, a sailor's wife, and the extraordinary Mrs Blague, wife to the Dean of Rochester.

John Dee, sitting at the table, with his crystal-gazer, Edward Kelly – who prophesied the execution of Mary Queen of Scots – attending an alchemical furnace.

the period from roughly 1500 to 1750 fortune-tellers seem to have enjoyed a good reputation for success in this sort of 'occult detection'. Forman certainly seems to have had a talent for it. Mrs Webb's stolen property was recovered with Forman's aid; the fortune-teller reported that 'He who stole it his name was Arnold, a gentlemanlike fellow; he was taken abed with two wenches . . . He is in Bridewell; he hath been burned in the hand afore.' Bridewell was a prison. By 'he hath been burned in the hand afore' it was meant that Arnold had previously been convicted of theft and branded on his palm with a hot iron in such a way that others would know of his conviction.

While Simon Forman seems as a fortune-teller to have been something of a specialist in affairs involving love and sexuality, he was also consulted on such matters as property, lawsuits, lost children, promotion in the Church and stolen property.

On the whole the answers he gave to specific questions were surprisingly accurate, sometimes quite astoundingly so, as illustrated by his forecast of a military expedition to Ireland by

An eighteenth-century print (engraved after a lost sixteenth-century portrait) of Simon Forman, playgoer, astrologer, geomancer, and dedicated fornicator.

Strange Questions

Many of the questions asked by Forman's clients seem understandable enough. For instance, the merchant's servant wished to know whether a fellow servant was trustworthy for the enquirer 'misseth money often in his accounts'; while the sailor's wife wished to know whether her husband would return from his present voyage safely. By no means all of the questions asked were quite so innocent and some of them were very strange indeed, notably many of those asked by Mrs Blague, a lady who seems to have regularly deceived her husband, the Dean of Rochester, and on at least two occasions had sexual relations with Forman himself. Forman had no illusions about the character of Mrs Blague, noting in his casebook that she was:

given to lust and to diversity of loves and men . . . And did in lewd banqueting, gifts, and apparel, consume her husband's wealth, to satisfy her own lust and pleasure . . . And was always in love with one or another. She loved one Cox, a gentleman on whom she spent much. After that she loved Dean Wood, who cozened her of much . . . She kept company with base fellows, such as she was herself of, of lewd con-

versation, and yet would seem as holy as a horse. She was never without one bawd, or cunning woman or other, to keep her company . . .

Dean Wood, a Welshman from Ynys Mon, never seems to have visited his Deanery in Armagh nor contributed to the spiritual welfare of its inhabitants. Instead he seems to have spent his time in intriguing for a better-paid office in the Church, satisfying his own lusts, and extracting the Dean of Rochester's money from his wife.

Not all of Forman's wealthy clients were quite as disreputable as Mrs Blague and her associates. Most of them, however, seemed to have had a rather loose sexual morality. For example, Martha Webb of Canterbury, wife of a certain William Webb, had numerous consultations with Forman concerning her affair with Sir Thomas Walsingham. In spite of the fact that Mrs Webb believed herself to be deeply in love with Sir Thomas, one of these consultations concluded with Forman and herself 'halek . . . plene et volenter'. 'Halek' was a code word used by Forman to signify sexual intercourse while 'plene et volenter' means 'fully and freely'.

Martha Webb consulted Forman on matters other than her love life, on tracing stolen goods for example; in

Elizabeth I's favourite, the Earl of Essex. Most people believed that this would be an outstanding success, that the English army would rout the 'barbarian' Irish and impose order on the over-mighty Irish nobility and the peasants they ruled.

Forman, on the basis of information provided by astrological techniques, thought differently. On March 19, 1599 he cast a horary figure with the object of discovering how Essex's adventure would end. His judgement of the figure was gloomy in the extreme:

There seems to be in the end of his voyage negligence, treason, hunger, sickness and death. He shall not bring much good to bring it to effect. At his return much treachery shall be wrought against him; the end will be evil to himself, for he shall be imprisoned or have great trouble. He shall find many enemies on his return and have great loss of goods and honour; much villainy and treason shall be wrought against him to the hazard of his life, because the moon goeth to Jupiter. Yet he shall escape it with much ado after long time, much infamy and trouble.

This prophecy was so uncannily accurate that one academic historian, A. L. Rowse, has commented that 'with Forman there seems to have been an element of the psychic'. Perhaps – but there is not the slightest doubt that Forman's prophecy was based upon the horoscope he cast and that he interpreted in complete accordance with the rules of horary astrology.

Talismanic Magic
A great many of Forman's clients believed that he had helped them in their difficulties by the use of what is called 'talismanic magic' – the manufacture of a lucky charm for a particular purpose by a process involving the ceremonial invocation of spirit forces. This was a perilous occupation for any person to indulge in during the reign of Elizabeth I. It savoured of black magic and witchcraft and on more than one occasion Forman aroused suspicions by his use of it. In one incident Forman visited Plymouth in order to consecrate a talisman for Sir William Monson, a noted naval commander, but his activities were mis-

taken for an illegal celebration of the Mass, 'or like exercises', and he was arrested. His belongings were searched and were found to contain 'certain wicked books of conjuration'. Such a discovery would have brought most fortune-tellers of the time into danger of imprisonment, even of the gallows. Fortunately for Simon Forman his client, Sir William Monson, was a man of considerable influence; he wrote a mollifying letter concerning the matter to William Cecil, the Queen's trusted adviser, and Forman was released from custody.

The Death of Simon Forman
It was William Lilly who recorded that Forman successfully foretold the exact day of his own death.

On a Sunday, early in September 1611, Forman's wife asked him which of them would die first. Her husband's reply was gloomy: 'I shall die ere Thursday night.' What followed is best told in Lilly's own words:

Monday came, all was well. Tuesday came, he was not sick. Wednesday came, and still he was well; with which his impertinent wife did much twit him in the teeth. Thursday came, dinner was ended, he very well. He went down to the waterside, and took a pair of oars to go to some buildings he was in hand with in Puddledock. Being in the middle of the Thames, he presently fell down only saying, 'An impost, an impost', and so died.

The word 'impost' had two significances in the medical terminology of Forman's time. It usually referred to an abcess or swelling, but it could also be used to refer to the bursting of an aneurism, a swelling in an artery, and it is likely that it was from this cause

A 'Geomantic Shield' of the sort used by Robert Fludd and other devotees of this fortune-telling technique, derived from the Arabic 'raml' (sand divining).

17

that Forman died – there is good reason to believe that he suffered from a condition which often results in the development of an aneurism.

It is possible that Lilly's story was either untrue or much exaggerated – such stories have frequently grown up about well-known fortune-tellers after their deaths – or that Forman died on that particular Thursday because he so strongly believed in his impending demise that he had willed himself to die. But there can be no doubt of the accuracy of many of his other predictions – there is documentary evidence of them and their fulfillment – so this one may also have proved true.

Sand and Sixteen Symbols

Forman had derived the answers to the questions he was asked by his clients not only from astrology but from what is today a much less well known method of fortune-telling, known as geomancy. Literally the word geomancy means 'prediction by means of earth', and it is almost certain that geomancy had its origins in a type of sand divination used in ancient Arabia.

The form in which geomancy reached Western Europe in the twelfth century and the way in which it is still practised today bears a certain relationship to both numerology (see pages 114-133) and to astrology.

Sixteen random numbers are derived by the fortune-teller by any one of a number of methods – for example by throwing dice or picking up sixteen handfuls of pebbles and counting each handful. From these are obtained, by a time-consuming but simple process, a 'geomantic shield', an example of which is reproduced on the previous page.

It can be seen that each individual compartment of the shield contains a figure made up of four lines, each containing one or two dots. There are, for mathematical reasons, only 16 different forms of a figure containing four different combinations of one or two dots (crosses can also be used) and each of these is attributed to either the sun, the moon, one of the planets, or one of the nodes of the moon. These lunar nodes are mathematical points referred to by astrologers as 'the Dragon's Head' and 'the Dragon's Tail'.

By their astrological significance and their relationship to one another in the shield the figures enable those who practise geomancy to give specific answers to questions asked of them.

Sometimes these answers have been amazingly accurate. In this connection a remarkable story was told by Robert Fludd (1574-1637), a physician, occultist and philosopher whose ideas influenced, among others, the astronomer Kepler.

Fludd, then only 26 years old, had gone to Avignon – in France geographically, but then part of the Pope's dominions – towards the end of 1601 and had taken lodgings with what he called 'other young men of good background and sound education'.

One evening when the young men were drinking together the conversation turned to the subject of the truth or falsity of geomancy. Some believed it to be nonsense; others, including Fludd, argued that it was a viable method of foretelling the future.

Fludd defended geomancy with such skill that it became apparent to his companions that he had some practical knowledge of the subject. Later on that night one of the young men came to Fludd and asked him to find out by means of geomancy 'whether a girl with whom he had vehemently fallen in love returned his love with equal fervour with her entire mind and body, and whether she loved him more than anybody else'.

What followed is best told in Fludd's own words:

> Having drawn up the chart I . . . described to him the stature and shape of the girl's body . . . I said also that the girl loved vineyards and this detail . . . was confirmed by him with pleasure. Finally I gave the answer to the question: that his beloved was unfaithful and by no means steady in her

Robert Fludd, intellectual, occultist and geomancer, who was deeply influenced by the mysterious Rosicrucian Order.

love of him, and that she loved someone else more than him. At which he said he had always much suspected that this was the case . . . He left my room . . . then related to his companions with some admiration the truth and virtue of my art.

There was a curious sequel to Fludd's demonstration of his abilities as a fortune-teller. Two Jesuits who heard of the affair approached the Papal Legate who ruled Avignon and suggested that Fludd should be arrested for practising forbidden arts. The Legate's reply to this suggestion showed both that he was a man of common sense and that, at the time, even princes of the Church were prepared to consult fortune-tellers. 'Truly', he told the Jesuits, 'this is not so serious an offence as you are trying to make out. Is there, indeed, a single Cardinal . . . who does not possess an interpretation . . . after the astrological or geomantic method?' The Legate followed this tolerant reaction to Fludd's activities by inviting the young man to a meal and discussing fortune-telling with him.

The years in which Simon Forman and Robert Fludd flourished, and the two or three decades that followed, marked the height of intellectual belief in astrology, geomancy, crystal gazing and other forms of fortune-telling. In England, for example, there had been almost an epidemic of fortune-telling in the years 1641-58; during the Civil War astrologers had been used to make suitably favourable interpretations of the stars in both the Cavalier and Roundhead interests.

After the Restoration of the Stuarts in 1660, however, there was a slow but steady decline in upper class belief in all the fortune-telling arts, from astrology to palmistry – a similar process was also taking place throughout western Europe.

Decline and Revival

A paradoxical fact about the general decline in upper class belief in fortune-telling in the 200 years or so after 1660 is that it was accompanied by what seems to have been an *increase* of interest in the subject in all its aspects, but particularly astrology, among those members of the population who were 'literate in the vernacular'. That

is to say, among those people who could read and write their own language, English or French for example, but not Latin, the language both read and written by all European scholars at that time.

The popular concern with fortune-telling and associated subjects was, in England, reflected in steady increases in the sales of almanacs – annually produced calendars for the coming year which included not only astrological forecasts but articles on such subjects as palmistry and the interpretation of dreams.

Mr Ellic Howe, a distinguished historian in the fields of both printing and the occult, has given some figures for the print-runs of one of the few annuals of this sort, *Old Moore's Almanac,* which has survived to the present day. Exact figures for the publication are not available before 1768, when almost 107,000 copies were printed. However there cannot be much doubt

Jonathan Swift, author of Gulliver's Travels, *who satirized astrology and made personal attacks upon its exponents – but was ignorant of the theory and techniques of the ancient art.*

that for seventy years previously the popularity of this almanac (originally named *Vox Stellarum,* 'Voice of the Stars') had been growing. By 1803 almost 400,000 copies were being printed, and in 1837 when Queen Victoria came to the throne sales were well over half a million.

The increasing popularity of almanacs with ordinary people caused annoyance among the university-educated who, from the beginning of the eighteenth century, attacked the almanac makers and other fortune-tellers as 'ignorant charlatans' and indulged in a series of practical jokes at their expense. The charge of ignorance was, in most cases, ill founded; the practical jokes were sometimes rather funny.

The best known and most deftly accomplished was carried out by Jonathan Swift, author of *Gulliver's Travels*, and took place in 1708, its victim being John Partridge – who was, in fact, an accomplished fortune-teller and mathematician.

Shortly after Partridge had issued his almanac for 1708, another almanac was issued purporting to be by 'Isaac Bickerstaff Esquire' – really Jonathan Swift. The first prediction in this work concerned the coming death of John Partridge:

I have consulted the star of his nativity by my own rule, and find he will infallibly die upon 29 March next, about 11 at night, of a raging feaver; therefore I advise him to consider of it and settle his affairs in time.

Partridge is unlikely to have been concerned by this forecast – the astrological references in Swift's spoof almanac clearly showed the great writer's total ignorance of the subject – and the morning of March 30, 1709 found the fortune-teller in good health, not dead 'of a raging feaver'.

Within a few days, however, Swift had issued a pamphlet which purported to have been written by 'an officer of the Revenue' and to be 'an account of the death of Mr Partridge

John Partridge, cobbler turned astrologer and unlicensed physician, was the subject of cruel practical joking from Swift and his friends.

. . . upon the 29th inst.' This was a brilliant forgery. It described the agonies of Partridge in his 'burning feaver', the closeness of the room, and the dying fortune-teller's confession – quite imaginary, of course – that he had always been a fraud.

The astonished and undoubtedly healthy John Partridge must have been very annoyed to read this graphic account of his own death. He was even more annoyed by a continual stream of callers at his home. These included other fortune-tellers offering their condolences to the 'widow', mourning coaches and hearses, coffin makers in search of work, and messengers from the sexton of the parish asking when the funeral would take place.

Swift kept the joke going by anonymously issuing a broadsheet of a mourning *Elegy*. This, black-bordered and adorned with woodcuts of skeletons, concluded with a mock epitaph:

You that die your Fortunes seek,
Step to this Grave but once a
    Week,
The earth which bears his body's
    Print
You'll find has so much Virtue in't
That I durst Pawn my Ears, 'twill
    tell,
Whate'er concerns you full as
    well,
In Physick, Stolen Goods, or Love
As he himself could, when above.

Swift's mock-elegy had begun with a sneer at the social origins of Partridge, who had started his working life as a cobbler. In snobbish eighteenth century England it seemed ludicrous to members of the upper classes that men who had been to neither Oxford nor Cambridge should have any pretensions to learning. Yet the publications of John Partridge, Francis Moore and other eighteenth century fortune-tellers show that they were not only skilled in their own occult arts but had a considerable knowledge of fairly advanced mathematics. Thus, the predictions made in the almanacs of John Partridge, Vincent Wing and other fortune-tellers were based on the use of an astrological technique called 'primary directions', which involves the use of spherical trigonometry – a subject Jonathan Swift is unlikely to have known much about, however great his

knowledge of the literature of ancient Greece and Rome.

Even amateur fortune-tellers were often men of some learning, notably in mathematics and mechanics. Thus George Wichell (1720-1785), who studied all the occult arts, had started his working life as a watchmaker's apprentice but had taught himself enough mathematics and astronomy to become Master of Portsmouth's Royal Academy (roughly the equivalent of a grammar school specializing in mathematics, navigation, and other technical subjects). This city was then, as it is now, a centre of naval activities, and it is interesting to note that some of Wichell's researches were of relevance to the science of navigation – so much so that they received the favourable attention of the British government's 'Board of Longitude'.

Wichell's knowledge of astrology and associated fortune-telling techniques was acquired from Ebenezer Sibly, who flourished in the late eighteenth century and whose activities were responsible for a beginning of a revival of serious interest in occultism. Sibly's description of the satisfaction he felt at teaching Wichell shows, in the passage italicized below, the disrepute into which fortune-telling had fallen by the end of the eighteenth century. He wrote:

This was a task I performed with the greater satisfaction . . . because his conviction and approbation of it would stamp new recognition upon a science *which having few or no real advocates, has long been borne down by popular prejudice and obstinate declamation.*

Sibly was primarily interested in fortune-telling by astrology, particularly in relation to health matters – he was a qualified physician – but he also concerned himself with other aspects of occultism. In 1788, he issued a work devoted to a 'general Display of the Mysteries of Witchcraft, Divination, Charms and Necromancy Compiled from a Series of Intense Study and Application and founded on real Examples and Experience'.

Necromancy literally means 'foretelling the future by means of the dead', and from classical times until as late as the seventeenth century it was believed that certain disreputable for-

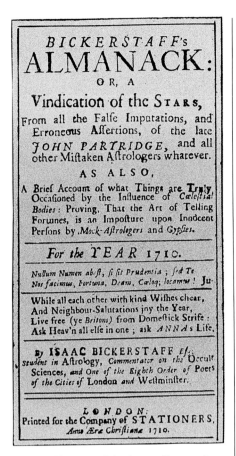

BICKERSTAFF's
ALMANACK:
OR, A
Vindication of the STARS,
From all the Falſe Imputations, and Erroneous Aſſertions, of the late *JOHN PARTRIDGE*, and all other Miſtaken Aſtrologers whatever.

AS ALSO,
A Brief Account of what Things are Truly Occaſioned by the Influence of *Cœleſtial Bodies*: Proving, That the Art of Telling Fortunes, is an Impoſture upon Innocent Perſons by *Mock-Aſtrologers* and *Gypſies*.

For the YEAR 1710.

Nullum Numen abeſt, ſi ſit Prudentia; ſed Te Nos facimus, Fortuna, Deam, Cœloq; locamus! Ju.

While all each other with kind Wiſhes chear, And Neighbour-Salutations joy the Year, Live free (ye *Britons*) from Domeſtick Strife: Ask Heav'n all elſe in one; aſk *ANNA*'s Life.

By *ISAAC BICKERSTAFF* Eſ; *Student* in Aſtrology, *Commentator* on the Occult Sciences, *and One of the Eighth Order of* Poets *of the Cities of* London *and* Weſtminſter.

LONDON:
Printed for the Company of STATIONERS, *Anno Æræ Chriſtianæ* 1710.

The title page of the bogus Almanack *written by 'Isaac Bickerstaff', i.e. Jonathan Swift, which prophesied the exact time of the death of John Partridge.*

tune-tellers, practitioners of black magic, went so far as to dig up corpses, restore the bodies to temporary life by means of spells, and then ask questions of them. By Sibly's time, however, he and other fortune-tellers used the word necromancy in a much less sinister sense – the use of a clairvoyant medium to communicate with supposedly departed spirits. This was done in very much the same way as it is done at a present day spiritualist seance, except that a medium of Sibly's time saw his or her visions in a crystal ball or a black mirror.

A concern with fortune-telling in all its aspects was also apparent in what was probably the world's first occult periodical, *The Conjuror's Magazine*, which was published in London from 1791 to 1794.

At first this magazine was largely concerned with conjuring in the ordinary modern sense of the word, as in 'conjuring tricks' with puzzles, tricks and games. With each successive

issue, however, the fortune-telling preoccupations of the editor became more obvious. Not only were there regular articles on occult subjects but fortune-tellers began to advertise their services in its pages. Some of those who advertised seem to have been rather disreputable representatives of their profession. Take, for example, William Gilbert, who manufactured talismans (see page 17) of the same sort as those sold, two hundred years earlier, by Simon Forman. Clearly he was not only boastful but greedy. He wrote:

> . . . The manufacture of talismans is a great art, which I have completely mastered after many struggles and oppositions . . . I will therefore be PAID, and paid HANDSOMELY . . . I will stop the operation of all those which are made save through my own direction or by myself.

While *The Conjuror's Magazine* was not a profitable enterprise and ceased publication in January 1794, its very appearance showed that there was an occult revival in the England of 1780 – 1800. In France there was a similar resurgence of interest at about the same time.

Cartomancy, Raphael and Zadkiel

By the middle of the eighteenth century, perhaps much earlier, cartomancy – the use of playing cards for fortune-telling purposes – was being employed in England. The cards which were used were of the type with which we are all familiar – the 52 card pack used for such games as bridge and poker. At that time the 78 card tarot deck was unknown in England although, interestingly, it had been used in gambling games during the reign of King James I of England (VI of Scotland).

In France cartomancy seems to have been practised at a much earlier date than it was in England and it was the tarot deck that was used, particularly by gypsies.

Not many years before the Revolution of 1789 the curious symbols of the tarot trumps began to attract the interest of French scholars and it was suggested by one of them, Court de Gébelin, that the crudely printed and brightly coloured versions of the 'tarot

of Marseilles' (see page 40) used by fortune-tellers were degenerate, but still understandable pictorial representations of the secret wisdom of the ancient world. While in the strict sense in which he expressed his ideas Court de Gébelin was undoubtedly wrong – he thought the designs of the trumps had been the work of the priests of ancient Egypt – in a more general sense he was right. That is to say, the symbolism of the tarot, although not the origin of the cards which express it, is of enormous antiquity. More is said of this on page 41. However, as far as the *history* of fortune-telling is concerned, as distinct from the ideas which are the foundations of its techniques, what was important about de Gébelin's ideas was not their truth or falsity, but their *influence*.

A substantial number of French men and women who were interested in mysticism and the occult in general, and fortune-telling in particular, were so impressed by Court de Gébelin's arguments that they began to study the hitherto despised tarot and to use it for serious fortune-telling. They found it effective, as did those whose fortunes they told. So much so that for most of the two centuries that have elapsed since Court de Gébelin first published his theories, French fortune-telling has been dominated by the tarot – far more than by astrology, the most widely used fortune-telling technique employed in the English-speaking world.

This dominance was perhaps at its height during periods of major social upheaval – the years from the 1780s until the final fall of Napoleon in 1815, the years between the revolution of 1848 and the accession of Napoleon III in 1852, the years following on the fall of France in 1940, and so on.

The first of the periods mentioned above was one in which, as was said earlier, there was a substantial revival of French interest in fortune-telling, mysticism, seership and prophecy, and a considerable number of amazing stories, true or false, have been told about some of the seers and fortune-tellers of that time.

One of the most astonishing of these concerned a prophecy supposedly made by Jacques Cazotte, a minor French poet who is reputed to have had clairvoyant abilities and, in the autumn of 1784, to have predicted

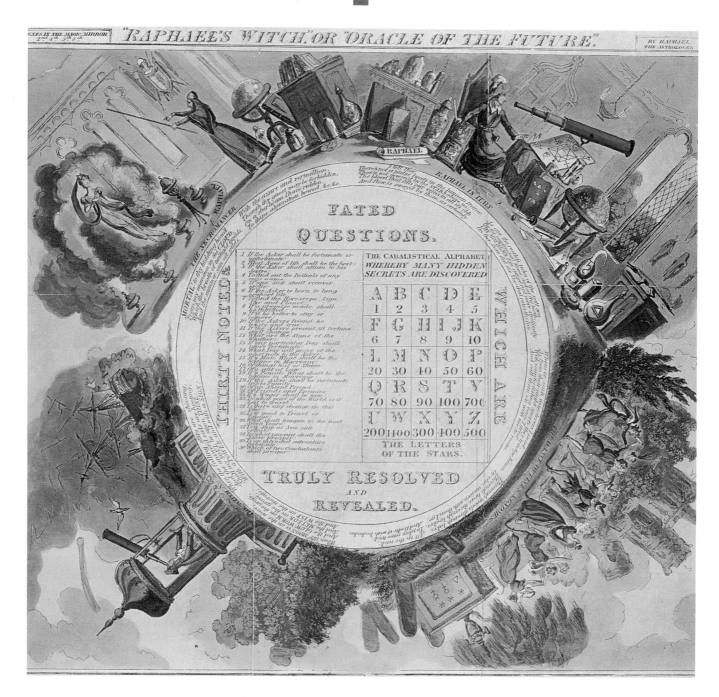

An illustration from an early edition of Raphael's Witch, *an oracle book compiled by Robert Cross Smith, who was an extremely important figure in the nineteenth-century fortune-telling revival.*

some of the events which followed upon the Revolution that took place five years later.

There are several versions of this tale. One of the earliest tells how Cazotte was present at a social gathering at which his fellow guests included Malesherbes, one of the King's ministers, who gave a toast to a future 'Age of Reason' which, he said, he felt sure

was coming, although it would be after his lifetime. 'No,' said Cazotte, 'it will be in five years time and result in your own execution.' Chamfort, another guest and a favourite of the King, would also be executed, he added. As for Cazotte's hostess, the Duchess of Gramont, she would 'be carried to the place of execution in a woodcutter's cart'.

The forecasts seemed ludicrous. 'What of me,' enquired La Harpe, another guest, a notorious atheist, 'shall I too be executed?'

'No,' replied the poet, 'you will have an even more surprising fate –

you will become a devout Christian.' This last prediction seemed even more unlikely than the previous ones – and yet, like the others, was fulfilled.

Whether Cazotte did, in fact, make the prophecies attributed to him is unclear. What is certain is that he and some of his contemporaries became convinced that it was possible for those living to see into the future, and that a growing number of people who had once been sceptical, regularly consulted fortune-tellers.

The best known, although by no means the most reputable, of these cartomantic fortune-tellers of the revolutionary era was Madame Lenormand, who had not only designed her own variant version of the tarot but was believed to have been, on more than one occasion, consulted by Napoleon himself. It was said that when the Emperor had been rude to her after she had predicted military disaster for him, she had thrown her tarot cards in his face.

Whether or not she really did this, there is no doubt that Madame Lenormand had an international reputation as a fortune-teller; her name was one to be traded upon, and a good many stories were told about her that probably related to others of her kind. She survived the fall of Napoleon with an enhanced reputation and was claimed as a contributor to the *Straggling Astrologer* (June-October 1824), a curiously named fortune-telling production which was edited by Robert Cross Smith, better known as 'Raphael', a fortune-teller specializing in astrology but practising other occult predictive techniques, who founded an almanac which is still published today.

Raphael (1795-1834) had a wide acquaintance among the occultists, fortune-tellers, and assorted mystics of late Georgian London and among his friends and associates were G. W. Graham, a pioneering balloonist who was also a student of alchemy (mystical chemistry), astrology and other 'secret sciences'; William Blake, poet and painter; and a woman who combined fortune-telling with campaigning to be recognized as a member of the Royal family – she asserted that she was the daughter of the Duke of Cumberland and styled herself 'HRH Princess Olive of Cumberland'.

Raphael's *Straggling Astrologer* contained much besides astrology. There were articles on such subjects as ghosts, witches, palmistry, magic and – a particular interest of Raphael – geomancy, the predictive art which had been so successfully practised by both Simon Forman and Robert Fludd (see pages 18-19). It seems likely that there was a certain amount of controversy caused by some of the articles Raphael thought fit to publish in his magazine, for in its twelfth issue the publisher apologized for 'several objectionable articles' which had 'crept into the preceding numbers'. To this was added an assurance that, in future, 'nothing offensive to the dignity of the Fair Sex

will ever be inserted'. What, so it must be supposed, had been found offensive was a description in the preceding issue of a fortune-telling technique designed to 'discover if the female you are about to wed be a virgin'.

Raphael seems to have been fairly radical in his politics and he used fortune-telling techniques in an endeavour to find out what would be the final outcome of political initiatives of which he approved. An example of such a political prediction has been provided by Stephen Skinner in his book *The Oracle of Geomancy*, in which he reproduces a 'geomantic figure' cast by Raphael in Kensington Gardens with the intention of discovering the fate of a proposed law to improve the conditions of the impoverished

silk workers of Spitalfields.

While his articles in the *Straggling Astrologer* were written very seriously, Raphael was also capable of writing highly popular books on fortune-telling, such as *Raphael's Witch, or the Oracle of the Future* (1831), which was advertised by its publisher as being 'adapted to lay about in *drawing rooms* . . . to ornament the *boudoir* . . . it removes *ennui* and low spirits . . . alluring to virtue, happiness and bliss'. Besides this production, a slightly revised version of which was still being printed in the 1950s,

The poet and artist William Blake, who claimed to see angels and certainly knew many of the intellectual occultists of late Georgian London.

A design, dated 1800, symbolizing the Mansions of the Moon, painted by Francis Barrett, and here reproduced for the first time.

Raphael also published a popular fortune-telling pamphlet, *The Philosophical Merlin, Being a Valuable Manuscript Formerly in the Possession of Napoleon Buonaparte, Being Fate: by the Rules of the Ancient Geomancy*. The manuscript of this, Raphael asserted, had once belonged to Napoleon but had been lost after the Battle of Leipzig. In his introduction to this work Raphael stated that it is 'a singular . . . fact' that after Leipzig the Emperor never won a battle: 'So that the loss of his manuscripts, and victorious fame went hand in hand.' It is, in fact, very unlikely that Napoleon ever owned the manuscript of *The Philosophical Merlin* – but if he did it is hard to see how the information it gives on lucky days, lucky colours and so forth, could have been applied to military matters.

Raphael was a member of a small society of fortune-tellers that called itself the *Mercurii of London*. One of the members of this group did even more to popularize fortune-telling than did Raphael himself. This was R. J. Morrison (1795-1874), who had served as a naval officer but had been retired on half pay when only 22 years old, as a result of naval cut backs following the peace of 1815.

Morrison seems to have taken up amateur fortune-telling almost as soon as he had left the navy and in 1830 he turned professional, publishing a best-selling almanac and other fortune-telling books under the pseudonym of 'Zadkiel'.

Zadkiel was primarily an astrologer, but he was also a man of wide, if eccentric, interests. He published at his own expense, books designed to disprove the theories of Isaac Newton; he endeavoured to manage both a coal mine and a life insurance company on 'occult principles'; and he had a deep interest in crystal-gazing which eventually involved him in an expensive libel action.

The Prince Consort and Crystal-Gazing

The libel action resulted from a curious series of events which included the death of the Prince Consort, husband of Queen Victoria and father of the future Edward VII, comments made by a London magistrate, and the activities of Rear-Admiral Belcher, a man who regarded all varieties of fortune-telling as 'humbug'.

In his almanac for 1861, which was undoubtedly written in 1860, Zadkiel had expressed gloomy forebodings about the Prince Consort's health. Commenting on the position of Saturn in the zodiac during 1861 he remarked that its effects would be 'very evil', adding that 'among the sufferers I regret to see the worthy Prince Consort of these realms' who should pay 'scrupulous attention to health'. For good measure Zadkiel also examined the horoscope of the Prince of Wales, reporting to his readers that the Prince would go through a period of suffering shortly after the end of November 1861.

On December 14, 1861 the 42 year old Prince Consort died of typhoid fever and his son, the Prince of Wales, did indeed go through a period of suffering. Not just because he was in mourning for his father, but because Queen Victoria held that worry about the Prince's loose morality had lowered her Consort's resistance to disease.

Not long afterwards a city magistrate, Alderman Humphery, hearing a case which had no connection with fortune-telling, commented in open court on the remarkable success of Zadkiel's prediction.

His remarks gave great offence. In a pompous editorial the *Daily Telegraph* denounced 'aldermanic folly', referred to 'Alderman Humphery's ill-advised escapade' and rhetorically asked 'Who is this Zadkiel, and are there no means of ferreting him out, and hauling him up to Bow-street [Magistrates' Court] under the statutes as a rogue and a vagabond?'

The inoffensive if eccentric fortune-teller, who had after all done no more than make an unlikely but accurate prediction concerning the destiny of the Queen's husband, was almost immediately assailed by Rear-Admiral Belcher in a letter to the *Daily Telegraph*.

The Admiral, bursting with rage, asserted that Zadkiel 'is the celebrated crystal-globe seer who gulled many of our nobility about the year 1852', going on to add that Zadkiel had taken money from those present at crystal-gazing sessions, 'made a good thing of it', and bribed the crystal-gazer to describe fake visions.

Zadkiel sued Admiral Belcher, calling as witnesses many of those individuals to whom Belcher had vaguely referred as 'our nobility'. These had included the Countess of Erroll, Admiral Fitzclarence – a relation of the Royal Family, the Bishop of Lichfield, and the novelist and politician Edward Bulwer-Lytton. Zadkiel's witnesses affirmed that they had indeed been present at crystal-gazing sessions arranged by Zadkiel, but that they had never paid him a penny. Rear-Admiral Belcher's lawyer, realizing that his client had no real defence to Zadkiel's action for defamation, simply delivered a speech to the jury which was little more than a denunciation of the fortune-teller for having had the impertinence to make an accurate prediction about the Prince Consort. The judge's summing-up was almost as odd – he more or less said that they might feel they had to give a verdict in Zadkiel's favour, but that they could then award him only nominal damages.

This is exactly what the jury did. They awarded Zadkiel only £1 damages, and the unfortunate fortune-teller was left to pay his own costs. On the bright side, all the publicity had a favourable effect upon Zadkiel's *Almanac*, the circulation of which rose dramatically, and its compiler went on practising his art for another ten years or so.

Zadkiel's admirers were drawn from all classes of society – from those members of the aristocracy who were brave enough to dare the ridicule of their friends by appearing as witnesses for him in his libel case, to the coalminers of North Wales. The miners came out on a one-day strike on

May 11, 1873, refusing to go down the pits because Zadkiel had predicted the possibility of a disaster that day. Oddly enough, there *was* a mining explosion two days later, but it took place in Canada, not North Wales. Perhaps the ageing Zadkiel had made a minor error in his calculations . . .

Zadkiel was unquestionably the best known of the fortune-tellers of his day, as witness the surprisingly lengthy article devoted to him in that monument of Victorian scholarship, the *Dictionary of National Biography* – but there were a host of others, from learned astrologers to semi-literates who read teacups, interpreted dreams, or read palms for a small circle of clients. Some of these obscure fortune-tellers, both in Britain and the United States, combined various forms of fortune-telling in a very odd way. Thus, for example, in the United States W. H. Chaney toured the country combining fortune-telling by astrology with interpreting character by phrenology, the study of the bumps on the head, and sometimes working in co-operation with Flora Wellman, a clairvoyant and medium who bore him an illegitimate son. In later life his son was to win fame as a novelist and short story writer under the pen-name of 'Jack London'.

Tarot Readers
By the 1870s a number of English-speaking students of the occult had begun to take an interest in the tarot both as a supposed repository of 'Egyptian Wisdom' and as a device for predicting the future. Most of these were at least half-scholarly individuals who were capable of reading languages other than their own. For they owed their knowledge of the tarot to the writings of the Frenchman Eliphas Levi (1810-75), a trainee for the Catholic priesthood, who had turned occult writer and teacher; curiously enough one of his pupils seems to have been Bulwer-Lytton, the novelist who had appeared as a witness for Zadkiel.

Levi, who accepted Court de Gébelin's theory that the tarot had originated in ancient Egypt, argued that it was of great significance that the tarot of Marseilles – the 78-card deck with which de Gébelin and the fortune-tellers who followed him had used – had 22 trumps. He correlated these with the 22 letters of the Hebrew alphabet, traditionally regarded as being of great mystic significance, and with other arcane symbols.

Notable among the English-speaking students of Levi's writings was a Scotsman, K. R. H. Mackenzie, who was, so it would seem, of a solemn disposition. He visited Levi in Paris and, reading between the lines of Mackenzie's account of this visit, was the subject of various Levi hoaxes – Levi had a sense of humour, often a rare com-

The title page of a 'book' made up of surplus copies of Raphael's strangely named periodical The Straggling Astrologer.

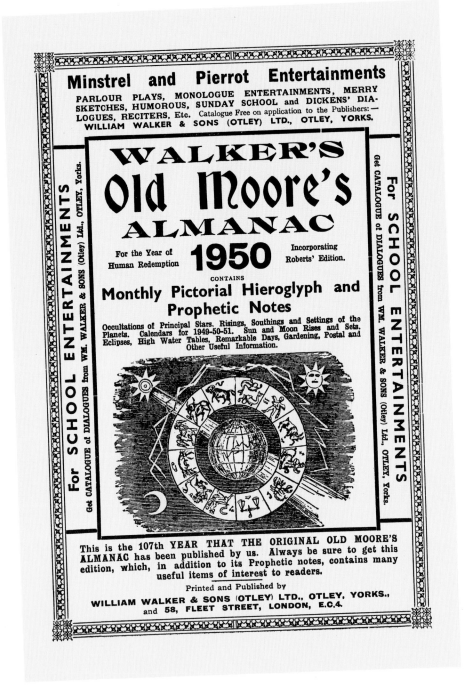

The cover of one of the several rival almanacs calling themselves 'Old Moore's'. Each of them claims authentic succession to the original.

modity among those inclined to occultism generally and fortune-telling in particular. Thus, for example, Levi told Mackenzie that one medieval mystical work, the *Book of Splendour*, was of such extraordinary length that several ox carts had to be employed in order to move the many volumes making up a single copy. Mackenzie seems not to have taken offence at the

joke, nor to have been embarrassed by a ludicrous error which had been made by him – mistaking Levi's tobacco jar for a valuable antique. He returned from Paris an ardent admirer of Levi and an enthusiast for tarot divination, a subject which was quite new to him and the other British fortune-tellers, both amateur and professional. Oddly enough, however, it may have been practised at the Court of Queen Elizabeth I. There is a story that Henry Cuffe, an associate of the Earl of Essex, drew three cards from a tarot pack shortly before he took part in an abor-

tive rebellion against the Queen. The cards drawn were, so the tale goes, *Justice*, the *Hanged Man* and *Death* – an accurate prophecy of Cuffe's future, for he was hanged for treason in March 1600/01.

Among those who knew Mackenzie was S. L. MacGregor Mathers (1854-1918), a man who would not have called himself a fortune-teller but a 'diviner' – in fact it is impossible to draw a sharp distinction between fortune-telling and divination, but Mathers disliked the former word because of its association with fortune-telling for money, of which he disapproved.

Mathers shared Levi's belief that with the aid of the tarot it was possible:

> . . . to open the sepulchres of the ancient world, to make the dead speak, to behold the monuments of the past in all their splendour, to understand the enigmas of every sphinx, and to penetrate all sanctuaries.

It seems unlikely that Mathers did all, or even most, of these things. What he unquestionably did do was to produce the first English account, aimed at the popular market, of how to tell fortunes by the use of the tarot. Mathers' booklet, first published in 1888, sold quite well, as did tarot decks imported from France by booksellers specializing in occult material.

By 1900 the tarot had become almost as popular a method of fortune-telling in the English-speaking world as it had been for so many years in France. Many professional fortune-tellers ceased to be specialists in only one form of predictive technique and were prepared, according to the wishes of a client, to read palms, tarot cards, or even crystal-gaze. Some of these professionals led lives of the utmost obscurity, practising their arts in seedy 'consulting rooms' for a poverty-stricken clientele. Others moved in rather more exalted circles, having clients who were writers, artists, actors, or even society hostesses. In the early years of the 1890s Oscar Wilde, then at the height of his success as a dramatist, regularly consulted a fortune-teller of this sort, a lady whom he referred to as 'the sibyl'. He seems to have made a most unfortunate choice of occult adviser – the 'sibyl' urged him to take action for criminal libel against the Marquess of Queensberry, assuring him of success. In actuality Wilde was not only unsuccessful in his action but, as a direct result of it, was sentenced to two years imprisonment and died in exile as an undischarged bankrupt.

Others of the 'society fortune-tellers' of the time seem to have been more accurate in their forecasts than Wilde's 'sibyl'. The best known of these was 'Cheiro', Louis Hamon, a palmist and numerologist who claimed that he had specifically warned Wilde that if he took 'precipitate action' in 1895, the year of the case against Queensberry, he would be ruined. Whether Cheiro did or did not make his particular forecast is uncertain, but there is no doubt that he enjoyed a reputation for accuracy.

On occasion this was put to the test. During a visit to New York he was given the palm prints of a man and, without being told the identity of the man in question, was asked to foretell his future. Cheiro looked at the print and said that:

> As he enters his forty fourth year he will be tried for murder and condemned to death. It will then be found that for years he has used his intelligence and whatever profession he has followed to obtain money by crime, and has stopped at nothing to achieve his ends. He will be sentenced to death . . . but will not end his life in this manner. He will live for years, but in prison.

The palm print was that of a medical man, Dr Meyer, who had been sentenced to death for murder and was awaiting execution. Shortly afterwards he was reprieved, and lived on as a prisoner for fifteen years.

While this story is reasonably well-authenticated there is something very odd about it. No palmistry technique which is generally known can provide such very specific predictions, whether or not they prove to be right or wrong. Cheiro, it is true, was also a numerologist and practised what he claimed was an ancient Greek method for correlating the years of an individual's life span with the lines upon the palm, but even so it is difficult to believe that he could have been so precise upon the basis of no more than a palm print. Either the story, however well authenticated it seems to be, is a hoax or Cheiro had clairvoyant or psychic abilities.

Cheiro and The Barrister
A remarkable story of Cheiro's abilities was told by Marshall Hall, an English barrister who was perhaps the greatest defence lawyer of all time, a man renowned for his ability to secure acquittals in seemingly hopeless cases.

In a libel case in which Marshall Hall had represented – quite unsuccessfully – the defendants, a witness for the plaintiff had been Cheiro. Impressed by the way in which Cheiro had given his evidence, Marshall Hall decided to consult him professionally.

Cheiro's reading of Marshall Hall's future career proved, so the barrister said, completely accurate. But what impressed him most of all was a very minor prediction made by Cheiro towards the close of the consultation. 'I see you', said Cheiro,

The arrest of the notorious poisoner Dr Crippen, whose life was perhaps dominated by the numbers 4 and 8.

ARRESTATION DU DOCTEUR CRIPPEN ET DE MISS LE NEVE
SUR LE PONT DU «MONTROSE»

standing on a balcony of what looks something like a large country house with a large garden below and big trees all in front ... the grounds seem lighted up with a very vivid electric light ... there are thousands of people trampling down the flower beds, and looking up to the balcony, and you are either trying to speak or actually speaking ... the faces of the crowd are very white in the strong light. Beside you on the left, is a woman, much shorter than you are, waving a white handkerchief in her left hand, and the people below are shouting. This is what I see, but what it means is more than I can tell you.

Sixteen months later Marshall Hall was elected as M.P. for Southport. In the late evening, just before the result was to be announced, Marshall Hall, together with his wife and other supporters, went out on the balcony of the Town Hall with the Returning Officer, the man responsible for announcing the result. The successful candidate looked down at the huge, cheering

Cheiro, the society palmist and clairvoyant who, according to his own account, warned Oscar Wilde of disaster if he sued the Marquess of Queensberry for criminal libel.

crowd, their faces glowing almost ghostly white from the powerful arc lights which illuminated the scene. Marshall Hall had a curious sense of *déjà vu*, a sense that he had already witnessed what was happening. He glanced around, saw his wife waving a handkerchief to the crowd – and remembered Cheiro's clairvoyant prediction.

Clearly Cheiro's accurate description of an event which lay sixteen months in the future was made on the basis of a 'psychic flash', and not on the basis of the palmistry which he so successfully practised. For, as readers of the palmistry section of this book will discover for themselves, the palmist's art provides indications of an individual's character and destiny, not detailed pictures of the future.

Crime and Numerology

Cheiro took an almost obsessive interest in crime and criminals, and it was with respect to these matters that he applied many of his numeralogical analyses. For example, Cheiro discerned numerological significance in the dates on which particular crimes had been committed. Thus he asserted that the numbers 4 and 8 were the keys, as it were, to the life of the infamous Dr Crippen, who had murdered his wife, and then dismembered her body. Crippen, Cheiro pointed out, had been born in 1862 which can be reduced to 8 as follows:

$$1 + 8 + 6 + 2 = 17$$
$$1 + 7 = 8$$

He murdered his wife on the 31st day of a month ($3 + 1 = 4$); her remains were found on the 13th of a month ($1 + 3 = 4$). He tried to escape justice by sailing for the United States with his mistress, who was disguised as a boy, using the name 'Robinson', which has eight letters. The ship the fugitives sailed on was the *Montrose*, again eight letters; after their arrest in New York they were taken back to England on the *Megantic* – another eight letters. And so on, and so on. It would be unwise to take this sort of thing too seriously; one can find numerical coincidences far too easily for it to be possible to argue seriously that they are significant. No one could have been more opposed to this sort of thing than the 'initiate fortune-tellers' who have flourished during the last hundred years or so.

The Initiates

S. L. MacGregor Mathers, the author of the first English popular study of the tarot, was a very serious student of its mysteries, which as far as he was concerned went far beyond what he referred to as 'vulgar fortune-telling'. MacGregor Mathers regarded the symbols of the tarot as keys which would enable their users to unlock the mysteries of life and death.

Together with his wife Moina (a sister of the philosopher Henri Bergson) and Dr Wynn Westcott, a distinguished physician who was also an occultist, Mathers pondered the mysteries of the tarot and their supposed relationship to almost every other aspect of western occult technique, from astrology to geomancy.

The results of the researches of Mathers and his associates, all of whom were initiates of an occult society named the Hermetic Order of the Golden Dawn, were recorded in a remarkable series of documents which were not published until the late 1930s. These documents had been compiled almost fifty years earlier and widely circulated in manuscript form among fortune-tellers who had been initiated into various occult societies.

To give a detailed account of the exact nature of the teachings contained in these manuscripts would be outside the scope of this book. It is sufficient to say that they so convinced some of those who studied them of the reality and importance of the links between the tarot trumps and, for example, the symbolism of astrology and mystical alchemy, that it permanently influenced their attitudes.

Those affected in this way included A. E. Waite, who incorporated astrological and alchemical symbolism derived from Mathers' manuscripts into his own tarot designs, and, rather more surprisingly, both the poet W. B. Yeats and the novelist Charles Williams.

While, as was said earlier, the instructional manuscripts which contained the full results of the investigations made by Mathers and other initiate fortune-tellers did not begin to be published in complete form until the 1930s, from about 1910 onwards they began to exert an influence upon general fortune-telling. That is to say, upon those fortune-tellers, amateur and professional, who were not initiates of occult societies such as the Golden Dawn and the many small groups derived from it.

This was because of various 'leakages' of one sort or another. For example, a considerable amount of information, theoretical and practical, derived from the manuscripts was included in books published by such popular writers on mysticism and the occult as Dion Fortune, A. E. Waite, and Paul Foster Case. Thus any fortune-teller who read Case's excellent book *The Tarot* was, probably without being aware of it, studying aspects of Mathers' system.

An organization founded by Mr Case, the 'Builders of the Adytum', usually referred to as BOTA, has done a great deal to popularize the esoteric teachings of Mathers and the Golden Dawn. The 'Adytum' was the most sacred inmost sanctuary of a classical temple and it is clear that the late Mr Case and those who have succeeded him in the direction of BOTA have looked upon the tarot as being, metaphorically speaking, the inmost sanctuary of the western occult tradition. They have made it clear that, in their opinion, the tarot transcends ordinary fortune-telling and that it provides a method by which the ordinary man or woman can attain that type of consciousness normally considered the domain of the visionary artist or poet.

In reality it seems that almost any form of fortune-telling – not just the tarot – can be the basis of a similar expansion of consciousness if it is approached with the requisite seriousness and determination.

It was not only the inner secrets of the Golden Dawn's manuscripts which began to change the face of popular fortune-telling in the period 1919-39. Two other factors became of major importance – the rise of what has been termed 'newspaper astrology' and the introduction into Europe and the United States of divinatory techniques derived from the ancient cultures of the Far East.

At the present day we more or less take it for granted that tabloid newspapers and mass circulation magazines should carry regular daily, weekly or monthly horoscopes classified according to the twelve signs of the zodiac. The regular publication of such predictive material dates, however, from only shortly before the out-

The Message of the Stars!

By ANN MARITZA

HERE are Ann Maritza's forecasts for to-day and to-morrow:—

SATURDAY, December 5.

Not a very promising business morning.

You may find yourself bustling and hustling, and when midday comes very little will have been achieved.

The tea-time hour should be the happiest. It is good for making new social contacts, especially with those artistically-minded.

In the evening there are certain adverse aspects which could quite easily cause a quarrel with your best friend, so do not be hasty or jump to conclusions.

✦ ✦ ✦

IF TO-DAY IS YOUR BIRTHDAY.—Make up your mind as to what you want, and adhere to your plan, otherwise you will incline to be influenced in many directions, and then find that nothing will go right.

Engineers and inventors will find this an excellent year for putting into operation their ideas and new inventions.

The fair sex have all the luck this year as far as love affairs are concerned. Health should be fairly good, only you are warned to take precautions against internal chills.

To-day's ruling number is 9.

To-day's colour vibration is red

are not of a serious nature, however, and are not necessarily due to any fault of yours.

* * *

—Between December 23 and January 21.— Thursday next should be the beginning of greater happiness and success for you. Be prepared for sudden happenings of a pleasing nature.

* * *

—Between January 22 and February 19.— Changes for the better are about to take place in your life. They will not come through your own seeking or through business circles, but through friends in rather an unexpected way. Make the most of your opportunities.

* * *

—Between February 20 and March 21.—More harmonious conditions should prevail this week, though you will still have a few obstacles to overcome. Contracts and business deals may be held up, but it is only for a time.

* * *

—Between March 22 and April 20.—Take a firm stand in all business affairs. Partners and

This Will Happen...

World interest has centred in the German-Japanese Pact, ostensibly made to combat "Communism."

A study of the heavens for noon at Berlin on the day of the signing of the pact shows that there is undoubtedly a secret military agreement underlying it.

And the heavens likewise proclaim that the parties thereto are like to rue the day they put their hands to it, as it will prove a veritable millstone round their necks.

This Will Happen – *an accurate prediction made in the 1930s. The Anti-Comintern Pact ('the Axis') did indeed contain secret military clauses and led both Germany and Japan to disaster.*

break of World War Two.

The first British newspaper to publicize astrology was the *Sunday Express* which, on August 24, 1930, published a detailed horoscope of the three-day-old Princess Margaret Rose, younger sister of the present Queen Elizabeth II. This horoscope had been prepared by R. H. Naylor, an expert astrologer, who became a regular weekly contributor to the paper after the airship R101 crashed on its maiden voyage in October of the same year – an event which Naylor seems to have predicted in an article which was almost certainly printed prior to the disaster.

Not to be outdone by the *Sunday Express* other mass-market newspapers were soon imitating it – *The People*, for example, running a regular feature by the astrologer Edward Lyndoe. From then on newspaper astrology snowballed and, today almost everyone knows his or her astrological Sun Sign and takes at least an occasional glance at what is predicted for him or her.

By their very nature such predictions tend to be rather vague – indeed, it is best for the newspaper astrologer not to be *too* precise. In the 1950s a

Daily Express astrologer was sacked for prophesying that a certain day would be 'propitious for stock exchange investments'; on the day in question the Stock Exchange was, alas, closed.

The eastern forms of fortune-telling which have become popular in the west are Chinese Astrology – which, strictly speaking isn't astrology at all (see page 158) – and the consultation of the oracle book known as the *I Ching*, which has a reputation of giving extremely accurate answers, sometimes enigmatically expressed, to questions asked of it.

Any reader of this book who uses it to ask a question of *I Ching*, to read a spread of tarot cards, or to employ any other of the methods described is a fortune-teller, however amateur a one. He or she becomes a twig on the family tree of fortune-telling, some of whose many branches have been described in this chapter.

CHAPTER
2
CARDS OF FORTUNE

he number of playing cards contained in a standard deck is 52 – the same number as there are weeks in a year. The suits are four in number, each made up of 13 cards; and there are four seasons in the year, each made up of 13 weeks. Some fortune-tellers have thought fit to attach much occult significance to these and other numerological considerations pertaining to ordinary packs of playing cards.

These supposed significances may be purely coincidental – but there is no doubt that telling fortunes by playing cards is simple, can be great fun, and often produces forecasts which prove to be uncannily accurate.

Cartomancy, the art of using playing cards for fortune-telling purposes, has been practised since the eighteenth century and was probably in use a century or two earlier.

It can be a very serious procedure, using complicated techniques which supposedly give very detailed 'readings' for an enquirer – the person whose fortune is being told – in respect of the past, present and future. Alternatively, it can be a very simple process, designed to answer the question 'Will my wish come true?' Most usually it is something in between these two extremes.

Most cartomancers practise all the techniques, from the simplest to the most complex, choosing their method to fit the circumstances. At a party they might only half-seriously use a simple 'Will my wish come true?' technique – everyone has a favourite wish and wonders whether or not it might come true, however unlikely its fulfilment – and the man or woman who can supply an answer by manipulating playing cards is always popular with friends and acquaintances. On the other hand, cartomancers might, for trusted friends and in complete privacy, carry out a complex 'cartomantic divination' (a fortune-telling session involving the use of cards).

Most (but not all) of those who tell fortunes seriously with the aid of playing cards prefer to use the tarot deck of 78 cards (56 suit cards and 22 'major trumps') rather than the ordinary deck of 52 cards (plus one or two Jokers). So it is likely that if you become a serious cartomancer, you will concentrate your attentions on the tarot, which is dealt with on pages 38 to 69.

Nevertheless, a perfectly adequate fortune can be told with ordinary cards. They are best suited for use in a half-serious context, such as at a social gathering; you may not have easy access to a tarot deck and think it would be best not to invest in one until you have experimented with ordinary cards. In any case, even if you do own a tarot pack, or can get hold of one easily, it is not a bad idea to learn to walk before you try to run – to use ordinary playing cards in fortune-telling before involving yourself in the complex and, at first, often confusing symbolic richness of the tarot.

Will My Wish Come True?
The simplest fortune-telling technique for answering the above question uses the entire pack, but only two cards, the Nine of Hearts and the Ten of Spades, are given any divinatory significance. The first of these is called the 'Wish

Card'; the second, the Ten of Spades, is termed the 'Disappointment Card'.

The person whose wish is the subject of enquiry shuffles the pack, all the time thinking strongly of the wish, but not communicating it to the cartomancer (i.e. the fortune-teller). After the cards have been shuffled they are handed to the fortune-teller who first cuts the deck and then deals it, face upwards.

If the Wish Card comes up in the dealt cards before the Disappointment Card, it is prophesied that the wish will come true; if the Disappointment Card, the Ten of Spades, is the first to appear, the position is reversed. Nothing could be simpler, and the method is basic to the point of inanity – but nothing makes an amateur fortune-teller more sought after. Oddly enough, the method is said to be an effective one, usually giving an accurate indication of whether or not a wish will come true. If you use this method, it is perhaps as well to be discreet about how exactly you arrived at your accurate conclusions about your friends' wishes. Thus you will gain a reputation as one possessed of arcane wisdom and the gift of prophecy.

Three Wishes

This is a method of knowing whether three wishes will be granted to a particular enquirer. Only 32 cards are employed, so remove from the deck all the cards save the Aces, Kings, Queens, Jacks, tens, nines, eights and sevens.

The enquirer shuffles the reduced pack (32 cards) while thinking of his or her three wishes, mentally placing them in order of preference. The shuffled deck is handed to the fortune-teller who cuts it and deals three rows of cards face upwards. The first row, which is taken as corresponding to the first wish, should be made up of three cards; the second and third rows, taken as corresponding to the second and third wishes, should be made up of five and seven cards respectively.

If the first row contains an ace, the wish to which it corresponds will quite certainly, so it is said, come true. If the row is made up of three Court Cards, the wish, equally certainly, will not come true. If neither of these circumstances apply, count up the numerical value of the first row (that of three cards), counting the pip cards as their numbers indicate and the Court Cards in accordance with the following values:

King = 13
Queen = 12
Jack = 11

The lower the total numerical value of the three cards in the row the more likely the enquirer will get his or her wish. Thus, for example, if the row consisted of three sevens, the probability of the wish being granted would be extremely high. If, on the other hand, it consisted of two Court Cards and a ten the probability would be very low. A simple rule-of-thumb is

to take any count below 28 as an indication that the wish will come true.

If the second row, that of five cards, contains either two aces, or an ace and a seven, the wish that it corresponds to will come true. If it is made up of five Court Cards, the wish will definitely not come true. In any other eventuality, count up the numerical value of the row, by the same method as that given in the preceding paragraph; count a single ace as one. Once again, the lower the total the greater the probability of the wish coming true – four sevens and an eight would show a very strong probability; four Court Cards and a ten would indicate an extremely low probability. The rule-of-thumb is that if the count is below 44 the wish will come true.

If the third row, that containing seven cards, contains two aces, the third wish will come true. If it contains either six or seven Court Cards, it will definitely not come true. In other cases count up the numerical total of the row by the usual method; once again, the lower the total the greater the probability of the wish coming true. The rule-of-thumb is that if the count is below 63 the wish will come true.

Try Your Luck

This is a simple method by which a number of people (up to a total of ten) can, firstly, ascertain which of them will enjoy the most good fortune in the coming month, and, secondly, investigate the likelihood of their favourite wishes coming true. Once again a reduced 32-card pack is used.

This time it is the fortune-teller who, after removing from the pack the 20 cards not used in this technique, shuffles and cuts the cards. He or she then hands the shuffled deck to the individual sitting immediately at his/her right hand. This individual then deals three cards, face upwards, and hands the pack to the right where that person deals three cards – and so on, moving always to the right, until whatever cards remain are handed back to the fortune-teller.

The numerical values (as above) of the three cards in front of each participant are then added up by either the fortune-teller or the person concerned. The lower the total (it will vary between 3 and 39) the greater the amount of good luck which will be experienced over the next calendar month. It is then time to ascertain the likelihood of the enquirers' wishes

An elaborately painted fifteenth-century card – the Ace of Swords. This card is the direct ancestor of the present day Ace of Spades.

coming true. Any participant whose three cards contain either two aces, or one ace and a seven, will have his or her wish fulfilled. Anyone who has three Court Cards will not have his/her wish granted. In other cases the probability of the wish being fulfilled is proportionate to the numerical total. The rule-of-thumb is that if the count is below 23 the wish will come true.

The Full Pack Wish Method

This technique is still a very simple one although the entire deck save for the Joker is used. The fortune-teller shuffles the pack, cuts it, and deals out the entire pack face downwards upon a large table or other flat surface of sufficient size. The enquirer, bearing his or her wish in mind, selects seven cards, quite at random and without looking at their faces, and hands them to the fortune-teller. The total numerical value of the seven cards is then totalled up according to the following rules:

Ace	= 1
King	= 0
Queen	= 0
Jack	= 0
Ten	= 0

Suit cards, two to nine inclusive = pip value of the card.

If the numerical total is either nine or seven, or is an exact multiple of either of these numbers (for example 21, which is 3×7, or 18, which is 2×9), the enquirer will certainly get his/her wish granted.

The Sevenfold Triangle

This is a rather light-hearted technique for discovering whether an enquirer will be lucky in love and romantic matters over the next calendar month. All the cards except the Joker are employed.

The enquirer shuffles the deck and hands it to the fortune-teller who cuts it and then deals, face downwards, seven rows of cards in the shape of a triangle. The first row consists of only one card, the second of two cards, and so on, with the last row containing seven cards.

Take the top card of the triangle and the right-hand card of each of the six succeeding rows – seven cards in all – and divide them into suits. See which

EGALITE DE COULEURS

In the Revolutionary France of the 1790s the figures of Kings, Queens and (above) Jacks were replaced by those of republicans.

suit has the largest number of cards among the seven, and interpret the significance of that suit as follows:

Hearts Over the next four to five weeks you are going to have a somewhat hectic love life. Try to avoid crises and ruptures by making an effort to relax with your partner. Overall, this could be a very happy time – and one which will permanently affect the rest of your life.

Diamonds Your love life is likely to become fuller than it has been of late, but it is also likely to be interrupted by quarrels and disagreements. Try to be as calm as possible – don't burn yourself out in flaring rage or flaming passion.

Spades Romance is in the air – but it will probably stay in the air for most of the month. Things will seem to be going well and will then fall apart or not conclude in the way you had anticipated. Not a month to take love too seriously.

Clubs Not a month to think of love at all; all your luck is concentrated in the field of finance over the weeks ahead.

Sometimes no suit will be prominent and there will be either a double or a triple tie. In other words, your seven cards will either include three cards of two different suits or two cards of three different suits.

In either of these cases pick up all the cards which remain in the triangle, shuffle them, and deal the top card face upwards. If its suit matches one of the two or three suits which have tied, take that suit as being the predominant one. If it doesn't, pick it up and put it with the cards first selected from the triangle. Reshuffle and deal the top card again, continuing this process until the card dealt is a tie-breaker.

Getting Serious
All the cartomantic techniques that have been described so far have an element of play in them. Seriously approached they can, although extremely simple, be used as rough-and-ready methods of prognostication, telling the future of an individual. On the other hand, it is possible to use these methods lightly, as games at a party or a family gathering.

There are techniques, however, for correlating ordinary playing cards with every aspect of human existence: the dullnesses, the joys, the emotions, the hopes and aspirations, and so on. Really talented cartomancers build up, on the basis of their intuitive faculties, their own meanings for the individual cards. These are not necessarily in accordance with standard rule-of-thumb interpretations of those same cards. Nevertheless, such intuitive or subjective meanings are usually built up by experience on a foundation of standard interpretations.

There are a very large number of these interpretations. All, however conflicting they may seem to be, make sense – provided that those who use them don't keep chopping and changing, applying one set of arbitrary meanings and interpretations one day and another the next. However odd it may seem, any set of card interpretations can provide a satisfactory basis for fortune-telling so long as the individual fortune-teller sticks to it as the foundation of his/her own insight until he or she is a cartomancer of some experience.

The reason for this is that the fortune-teller's, or the enquirer's, shuffle of the deck will adapt itself to the meanings that are going to be attributed to the cards and the pattern in which they are going to fall. Shuffling the deck of cards for the purposes of

fortune-telling involves the principle of synchronicity as described on page 8. There is a meaningful but non-causative relationship between the arbitrary significances that have been attributed to the cards and the 'mix' that is given to them by shuffling and cutting. Consequently, the pattern of the cards in a specific fortune-telling layout takes on, as a result of meaningful coincidence, a diagrammatic relationship to the enquirer's life, past, present and future. A card layout provides, as it were, a rough sketch map

A charming representation of the Jack of Hearts as youthful lover, from a Bavarian pack of the eighteenth century.

of the enquirer's life. It is not an altogether accurate map – some of the roads that are shown upon it may have fallen into disrepair or have not yet been opened and, furthermore, the scale is not always quite correct. Nevertheless, it provides a better guide than no map at all.

The meanings given to the cards are, as has been said, arbitrary. Some sets of interpretations, however, seem to be more workable than others. Here is one such set of meanings that has proved satisfactory to many serious cartomancers.

MEANINGS OF THE CARDS

HEARTS
Ace This card is taken as your 'base' in both the literal and the metaphorical senses of the word. It is your physical base – your home and what has happened, is happening, and is likely to happen within it. It is also your emotional base – the seat of your feelings about love, friendship and affection.

Two A partnership of some sort; usually a partnership between lovers, close friends, or relations, rather than a primarily financial one.

Three Friends and, more generally, sociability and enjoyable encounters with others.

Four Solid emotional relationships – love and friendship that endures, that stands up with rock-like hardness to all the storms of life.

Five Unsure love, emotional disturbances, love that turns to its opposite, love that is 'honey in the mouth but sickness in the stomach'.

Six Established affection, also offers of love and pleasant invitations generally.

Seven Love fulfilled, Venus triumphant – passionate and happy sexual relationships.

Eight Calm, reasoned and rather intellectual love – the influence of Mercury upon the sphere of Venus. Also love letters, telephone calls from loved ones, and communications about romantic matters generally. Can also indicate books, fiction or non-fiction, concerning love and the human emotions.

Nine The Wish Card which, in company with the favourable cards in a layout, indicates that the enquirer will have his/her wish fulfilled. The fortune-teller can usually decide the area of the enquirer's life to which the wish relates by noting the preponderant suit in the cards around the Wish Card. Hearts, an emotional matter; Clubs, a matter concerned with money and/or property; Diamonds, 'getting on in life', relations with bosses and workmates, etc.; Spades, matters in which there is a large element of chance involved, and travel and adventure generally. Apart from its Wish Card significance, the Nine of Hearts can also be an indicator of 'fruitful love' and children – in other words, fertility. Surrounded by cards with a baleful or negative significance the card can indicate the exact reverse of fertility, i.e. sterility in its both literal and metaphorical meaning.

Ten Solid emotion based on material happiness and financial prosperity.

Jack Can represent either the ideas associated with Cupid – 'love at first sight', impulsive affection, and so on – or a young person of either sex who regards the enquirer with much affection, not necessarily sexual in nature.

Queen A mature woman possessed of strong emotions.

King A man, young or old, with an affectionate nature, desirous of love and being loved.

CLUBS

Ace Wealth and prosperity. Also the beginning of a series of events that lead to the achievement of material success.

Two Material losses, a division between business partners, quarrels and disputes over money and property.

Three Slowness, sluggishness, inertia. Events, particularly those

A nineteenth-century astronomical deck, published in 1830, equated the Nine of Clubs with the constellation of Scorpio.

concerning financial matters, moving slowly and causing annoyance. The irritating and unhelpful intervention of others in matters that do not concern them. Legacies.

Four Financial success and prosperity. A stroke of good luck, probably unexpected, but certainly well-deserved.

Five Disputes about money and property. Disharmony and quarrels. Families divided. Upsets and unexpected obstacles of all sorts, particularly in relation to the enquirer's business and financial concerns.

Six Great prosperity and material happiness. The sun shining on financial matters. A run of good luck.

Seven Financial losses and worries over money matters. Money wasted on idle pleasures. Money frittered away on needless luxuries, foolish speculations or pleasure jaunts.

Eight Money acquired as a result of careful planning or investment. Important documents or letters relating to business and money matters. Money gained or lost by theft and swindle.

Nine Financial matters, involving parents, children or sexual partners.

Ten Material success. Solid and well-established prosperity. A stable and comfortable situation.

Jack A young man or woman with a strong interest in money matters who is not always reliable or trustworthy.

Queen A mature and secure woman, probably comfortably off and notable for her sound common sense.

King A prosperous, secure and thoroughly reliable man. Can also indicate the enquirer's employer, male or female.

SPADES

Ace New and exciting adventures, the end results of which cannot as yet be decided with any certainty. The significance of the cards on the right and left of the Ace indicates the likelihood, but not the certainty, of a particular matter developing in a satisfactory or unsatisfactory way. If the Ace of Spades has a large number of hearts around it, the new beginning concerns, or will concern, love and romance. If Clubs are pre-

In a nineteenth-century French pack the Jack of Clubs was transformed into a foppish gallant of the reign of Louis XIV.

dominant, the venture concerns money, property or the enquirer's career or investments.

Two A dynamic development of some sort. A general moving forward. Ideas, hopes and aspirations beginning to take concrete form. A hopeful start.

Three A meeting or a conference. A sharing of, or transmission, of ideas. Airy concepts being solidified. Prudent and careful consideration of future plans.

Four Solid progress in putting an idea into effect. Good luck and prosperity resulting from foresight.

Five Rows, quarrels and disputes. Turmoil and disorder. Plans going wrong. Partings, temporary and permanent. Unexpected ill fortune.

Six Steady progress in the aspect of life which is, at the moment, of most concern to the enquirer.

Seven Quarrels with partners. The end of a romance. The breaking up of relationships. Accidents and misunderstandings.

Eight Fortunate communications of all sorts – letters, telephone calls, etc. Journeys that end happily. Unexpected arrivals and departures. Something surprising is likely to take place.

A mannered nineteenth-century portrayal of the Jack of Spades which owed much to theatrical portraiture of the time.

Nine Family disputes, usually between parents and children, that cause a great deal of annoyance but have no permanent ill-effects.

Ten This is the Disappointment Card. If the surrounding cards are good omens for the enquirer, it indicates that the good fortune indicated will not be quite so lucky as expected – the ripe apple may contain maggots. If the surrounding cards have unfortunate significance, the strength of these is increased.

Jack A bright and thoroughly agreeable young man or woman who is full of interesting and exciting ideas which are often rather impractical.

Queen A mature woman who is noted for her charm, liveliness and sociability.

King An exciting live-wire even in maturity: a man who is self-confident, popular with most of those he knows, and prepared to take a certain amount of risks.

DIAMONDS

Ace Splendid but erratic good luck. An extraordinary event. A new and rather surprising factor manifesting itself in a situation. An energetic and good beginning to a course of action or a series of events.

Two An increase in prosperity is indicated, but a note of warning is sounded. Action that is imprudent should be avoided. Look before you leap. Try to relax occasionally.

Three Good luck through the co-operation and help of friends and associates. Steady progress with life's problems.

Four Established success, steady good fortune, much happiness and prosperity. Things go so well that there is a danger of complacency.

Five Troubles and conflicts resulting from a clash of ideas or a profound difference of opinion. If this card occupies a strong position in a layout, the enquirer would be strongly advised to keep his/her temper at all costs and on no account to act rashly.

Six Positive happiness – not the happiness of mere satisfaction, but the happiness in which almost any activity seems worthwhile and pleasurable. A very fortunate card.

Seven A passionate relationship; strong bonds between partners. Physical satisfaction and comfort of every sort.

Eight Exciting news. Messages from afar. Adventurous holidays. Eventful journeys. Change. In some contexts can indicate study and academic work, particularly if the physical sciences are involved.

Nine A birth or a marriage. An eventful relationship in which things are always happening. Prosperity. Change for the better. Productive disagreements.

Ten A happy end to turmoil. A well-earned holiday. A substantial sum of money earned with much effort and now being gladly used.

Jack A pushy young man or woman, often rather impulsive but, nevertheless, possessed of considerable courage and tenacity.

Queen A mature and forceful woman, rather a bossy one.

King An extremely energetic and mature man who finds it difficult to relax.

As was said before, these meanings are largely arbitrary, and you may well come across articles or books which give quite different interpretations. This does not mean that one list is wrong and the other one right. What is interpreted in a playing-card divination are the *relationships* between the cards, the pattern in which they fall. As long as you stick to it until you are an accomplished fortune-teller, almost any set of interpretations will provide a basis for a satisfactory divination.

To tell a fortune using cards one has to use a layout or spread, i.e. a particular pattern in which some of the shuffled cards are put down on a table in order to be interpreted. A good, simple layout to begin experimenting with is as follows.

Sixfold Rulership Spread
Shuffle the pack and cut it or, if you are telling someone else's fortune, get him or her to cut it.

From left to right deal three rows of six cards face downwards (18 cards in all) and put the remainder of the deck aside. Now look at your three rows of cards vertically rather than horizontally – in other words, see them as six vertical rows each made up of three cards.

Turn face upwards the three cards making up the vertical row on the extreme left and put them in front of you. Now read them in relationship to yourself, or the person whose fortune you are telling, as an indication of your current general situation and how it is likely to develop.

A nineteenth-century educational card designed to instruct children as well as to be used by them in games.

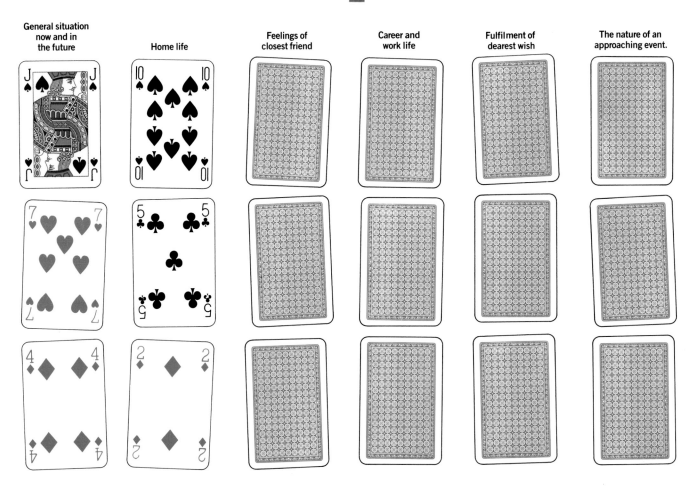

| General situation now and in the future | Home life | Feelings of closest friend | Career and work life | Fulfilment of dearest wish | The nature of an approaching event. |

As an example, let us suppose that the three cards in question are the Jack of Spades, the Seven of Hearts and the Four of Diamonds. The meanings of these, as given on pages 33 and 35, can be summarized as follows:

Jack of Spades An agreeable younger person whose ideas are exciting.
Seven of Hearts A passionately happy relationship; 'Venus triumphant'.
Four of Diamonds Success, good fortune, and a danger of complacency.

The Jack of Spades could indicate either the person whose fortune is being told – the enquirer or the fortune-teller – or, if the description does not fit the enquirer, someone with whom he/she has a close relationship. The Seven of Hearts indicates that the enquirer is enjoying a temporary or permanent passionate relationship with another and, probably as a consequence of this relationship but not necessarily so, is enjoying such good fortune that he or she is in some danger of adopting a complacent atti-

tude towards life and its problems.

Having interpreted the cards in the first (the extreme left) vertical row of three, turn face upwards the second vertical row. Interpret these as relating to your home life or that of the person whose fortune you are telling. If, for example, the three cards were the Ten of Spades, the Five of Clubs and the Two of Diamonds you would first note their 'cook-book' meanings as given on pages 34 and 35. These can be summarized as follows:

Ten of Spades The Disappointment Card.
Five of Clubs Obstacles. Quarrels and disputes, particularly over money and allied matters.
Two of Diamonds An increase in prosperity – but also a warning to be cautious.

The first thing to take note of in interpreting these three cards is that one of them, the Ten of Spades, is the Disappointment Card. As this card makes the meaning of negative cards even more negative, and the meaning of good cards less positive, the interpretation of the other two cards must be

The above sample layout for the Sixfold Rulership Spread would be read by a fortune-teller applying both 'cook book'-style interpretations, and his or her own intuitive faculties to the six vertical rows of three cards – in isolation and in their relationships to one another.

adjusted accordingly. Take the 'good' card, the Two of Diamonds, first. Clearly, the increase in prosperity is going to be a very limited one, or one of very short duration. Equally clearly, a strong note of warning is sounded in relation to money matters – extreme caution is called for. The Five of Clubs has its unpleasant meaning accentuated; home life is now, or will be in the near future, extremely difficult, and there are, or will be, bitter financial disputes.

Putting these interpretations together, the most probable situation would be something like this: 'In spite of some recent increase in prosperity, or one that will shortly come to pass, there is a strong likelihood that a lack of caution where money matters are concerned will cause the home life of the enquirer to be disrupted by bitter disputes over finances.'

You are now left with four vertical rows of three. Running from left to right these are taken as indicating a) your (or the enquirer's) closest friend and his/her feelings; b) the career and work life of the person whose fortune is being told; c) your, or the enquirer's, dearest wish and the likelihood of its being fulfilled; and d) the nature of an approaching event in your life or the enquirer's. The cards should therefore be interpreted in relation to the appropriate aspect of the enquirer's life.

Another useful layout employing interpretations of three cards at a time is as follows.

Past, Present and Future

This spread, or layout, is designed to give readings concerning a) the enquirer's general situation; b) his or her material prosperity, finances, etc., and c) the enquirer's love life and close relationships with others.

The deck should be shuffled and then cut three times. Nine cards are then dealt face upwards in three rows of three; these are interpreted as indicators of the enquirer's general situation in life, past, present and future.

The topmost row is taken to represent the past. The three cards are first read in relation to one another to indicate the overall nature of the enquirer's previous life. They are then interpreted separately. The card on the left of the row symbolizes the distant past; that in the middle of the row represents the situation as it was five to seven years ago; that on the extreme right symbolizes the immediate past.

The second row of three cards relates to the enquirer's current general situation. The cards are read in relation to one another, their individual meanings not being considered in isolation.

The last row of three cards is then read in relation to the future development of the enquirer's general situation. They are first read in relation to each other in order to give a general picture of the enquirer's future, and then individually, the card on the left of the row being taken as an indication of the immediate future, that next to it the medium-term future, that on the right the distant future.

Having finished an analysis of the general situation of the enquirer, past,

PAST	distant past	past 5-7 years ago	immediate past
PRESENT			
FUTURE	immediate future	medium-term future	distant future

This specimen layout for the Past, Present and Future Spread illustrates both its simplicity and its suitability for the use of the novice cartomancer. The top three cards are read individually, the second three together, and the bottom three both in isolation and in combination.

present and still to come, the fortune-teller gathers up all the cards, reshuffles the deck, and again cuts it three times. A further nine cards are dealt in three rows of three. These are interpreted in relation to the past, present and future of the enquirer's financial position.

In using the meanings of the cards as given on pages 33 to 35 for a reading that relates exclusively to money matters, a certain amount of adaptability is called for as some of these meanings have no direct relationship with those affairs. Suppose, for example, that one of the cards symbolizing the enquirer's financial past is the Seven of Hearts, the 'triumph of Venus'. Clearly, this card has no direct relevance to finance. The fortune-teller has therefore to interpret it in relationship to the other two cards in the row. If these were favourable, the interpretation would probably be that 'in the past the enquirer enjoyed considerable prosperity as a result of his/her relationship with another'; if they were unfavourable, the interpretation would be exactly reversed.

After the money reading has been completed the whole process is repeated, and this time the cards are interpreted in relation to the emotional life of the enquirer. Once again, bear in mind that a certain adaptability when using 'cook-book' interpretations is called for.

After you have become really adept at telling playing card fortunes by the layouts described above, you will probably want to go further. In this case it is usually best to start experimenting with the tarot (see pages 38 to 69) rather than using increasingly complicated layouts involving ordinary cards. This is because the symbolic richness of the tarot symbols enables most fortune-tellers to go much deeper into general and specific situations than they find possible with ordinary cards.

THE TAROT

The tarot trump cards usually known as the High Priest and the High Priestess depict two of the most powerful symbols in the strange – almost uncanny – collection of 22 pictorial images which are included among the 78 cards of the standard tarot deck. They show a man and a woman possessed of superhuman power.

Any person who becomes a really accomplished tarot diviner is transformed, in a sense, into one of the archetypes symbolized by these trumps. He or she has the collective wisdom of humanity at his or her disposal.

A selection of cards from three eighteenth-century Florentine tarot decks. Florentine packs of this period normally contain 97 cards, having 19 more trumps than are included in the decks used by most fortune-tellers of the present day.

If you buy, beg or borrow a tarot deck of cards and spread them out before you, face upwards, you will probably – if this is your first encounter with the tarot – feel bewildered, almost dazzled, by the multiplicity of symbolic images which flood your field of vision.

The nature of the pictorial images you will be faced with depends, to some extent at least, on the design of the particular deck you have acquired. You may see, for example, the picture of a naked child plucking roses with one hand while, almost casually, holding a leashed wolf in check with the other; or a portrayal of Perseus, hero of ancient Greek legend, about to engage in battle a monstrous sea dragon who clearly threatens to devour a naked maiden chained to a rock nearby. Alternatively, the concepts expressed pictorially in the two cards described above may be conveyed in quite different images in a different deck. The wolf-leading child becomes a gorgeously dressed young man about to step over a precipice; Perseus and the maid he is about to save are transformed into two children who embrace within a fairy ring.

Whatever the nature of a particular tarot deck, there are very few people who do not find that at least some of the images in the design of individual cards seem to speak to the mind on a deeper level of consciousness than that which is involved in everyday life. Somehow or other the cards seem to be trying to communicate with the person who is looking at them – even to enter into a 'wordless conversation' with him or her.

All the tarot images which impinge upon an aware imagination are striking. Some of them are almost sinister. One card – the usual design of which shows, beneath a night sky, a stagnant pool in the foreground from which a path winds between two lowering towers towards a dark horizon – is sometimes found particularly disturbing in what it hints at rather than what it openly expresses.

The card that features the two towers, usually called the *Moon*, may well have inspired T. S. Eliot to refer to the tarot, in his poem *The Waste Land*, as a 'wicked pack of cards'. The young and then almost unknown Eliot was, of course, striving for literary effect, and was well aware that there is nothing particularly wicked about the tarot cards in themselves. A tarot deck can, it is true, be used for evil purposes – but so can any other material object, from the kitchen knives used by muggers and murderers to the typewriter

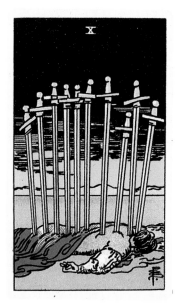

on which a libeller taps out his or her malicious poison.

At one period of his life T. S. Eliot was so fascinated by the symbols of the tarot that, quite arbitrarily, he came to mentally identify the tarot card called the Three of Wands ('the man with three staves') with the wounded Fisher King of the legends of the Holy Grail. The appeal that the tarot symbols had for Eliot has been felt by many others, from the poet W. B. Yeats to the novelist Charles Williams, from the painter Frieda Harris to the philosopher P. D. Ouspensky. The strange imagery which captured the attention of these and many other men and women has led students of the hidden side of things to assert that the tarot deck, while it has and can be used for complex card games, usually involving gambling, is far more than an enlarged pack of playing cards. On the other hand, there can be no doubt that the tarot deck is closely related to the ordinary pack of 52 cards and one or two Jokers; it is, so to speak, an eccentric and rather flamboyant cousin of the dull fellow that players of bridge and poker know so well.

As almost everyone is aware, the ordinary pack of cards is largely made up of four suits, each consisting of ten pip cards, from ace to ten, and three Court Cards, King, Queen and Knave. As well as these 52 suit cards a deck contains either one or two Jokers, usually depicted in the cap, bells and motley jerkin and leggings worn by the Court 'fools' of the late Middle

In 1909, under the guidance of A. E. Waite, the painter Pamela Colman Smith produced pictorial versions of the pip cards of the tarot. As shown by the example reproduced above (Ten of Swords, third from left), these cards displayed an art nouveau mannerism that contrasted sharply with the simplicity of tradition.

Ages. In its way the Joker is quite the most interesting of the standard playing cards. It is a degenerate version of the tarot trump named the Fool which, so some students of the tarot insist, is a pictorial image of the quality of 'divine folly' – the innocent wisdom which the wordly and cynized look upon as foolish childishness.

Besides the Fool, which in most tarot decks is numberless or numbered 0, there are 21 other tarot trumps (sometimes rather pompously termed 'the major arcana') in the standard tarot deck which is used for fortune-telling purposes. These are usually numbered in Roman numerals from I (1), the trump named the Magician, to XXI (21), the trump most often called the World but sometimes known as the Universe or the System. Besides the 22 trumps a tarot deck has, like standard packs of playing cards, four suits of pip and Court Cards. These are:

The Suit of Wands (sometimes called the Suit of *Batons* or the Suit of Staves)
The Suit of Cups (sometimes called the suit of Chalices)

The Suit of Swords
The Suit of Pentacles (sometimes called the Suit of Coins, *Deniers* or Discs)

Each suit contains 14 cards, one more than in a suit of ordinary cards; besides the ten pip cards, ace to ten, there are four Court Cards:

King (in some decks called the Emperor)
Queen (in some decks called the Empress)
Knight (in some decks called the Prince)
Page (in some decks called Princess or Valet)

In the tarot deck which is used in fortune-telling there are, then, a total of 78 cards: the major arcana of 22 trumps plus the minor arcana of 56 cards, made up of four suits of 14 cards.

The 78-card tarot decks used in fortune-telling are all derived from, or identical to, what is most usually termed the Marseilles tarot, but is sometimes called the Venetian tarot or the Piedmont tarot. This is because this pattern of tarot deck was manufactured in these places during the eighteenth and nineteenth centuries in very large numbers. It was also manufactured, although not to such a considerable extent, in other places, which is why there exist eighteenth-century Marseilles decks which were actually printed in what is now Belgium.

Besides the 78-card Marseilles tarot deck, and the fortune-telling and occult packs which derived from it, there are versions of the tarot which contain either more or less cards. One deck, widely used in Sicily and southern Italy, contains no less than 97 cards; such decks are rarely, if ever, used for fortune-telling and in this book we shall only be concerned with the 78-card tarot.

The origins of the mysterious and haunting imagery of the 22 trumps is, in spite of many confident assertions to the contrary, still uncertain. In the eighteenth century the French writer, Court de Gébelin, claimed that the trumps were *The Book of Thoth*, a pictorial expression of the secret wisdom of the priests of ancient Egypt. A century later another theorist saw them as embodying elements derived from Hindu

In Revolutionary France pages were out of fashion so the Valet de Batons (Page of Wands or Staves) was renamed Egalité (Equality) de Batons.

mythology. Today there are those who claim that the tarot originated in legendary, now drowned, Atlantis.

Scholars who have concerned themselves with the history of playing cards in general, and those of the tarot in particular, have tended to reject such stories as myth-making. In the present day all that most scholars are prepared to say with any certainty is that the oldest surviving complete tarot packs, dating from around the mid-fifteenth century and painted for wealthy Milanese noblemen, seem to have derived much of their imagery from the 'actors', images and banners of Italian street festivals of that time. Thus, for example, a version of the Magician trump, almost certainly painted by Bonifacio Bembo at some time after 1450, is thought to represent the Carnival King in the pre-Lenten street procession. Similarly, Bembo's Pope and Emperor trumps are thought to portray those actors who played these parts in the same procession.

The fact that the enchanting symbols of the tarot may well have been derived from the semi-secular festivals of late medieval Italy, not from the mystic broodings of the initiate rulers of long-lost Atlantis, the priest-magicians of ancient Egypt, or – another suggestion – a college of wise men who at one time flourished in the North African city of Fez, does not mean that they are valueless for fortune-telling or other occult purposes. For the imagery of the tarot trumps appears to result in what some students of the great psychologist C. G. Jung, term 'an awakening of the archetypes'.

The theory of unconscious archetypes is a re-expression, in terms of Jungian depth-psychology, of an ancient idea which some of the alchemists and occult philosophers of old expressed by the phrase 'the world has a soul'. They called the world-soul by its Latin name, *anima mundi*.

Anima mundi, so it has been said, is a sort of super-memory in which are recorded all the experiences undergone by the myriads of living beings who have ever dwelt on our planet. In this memory are retained not just events but concepts – religious, philosophical and mystical theories, for example. The planetary memory, then, contains, besides much else, the totality of the collective wisdom of humanity, past and present.

This means that *anima mundi* contains within it enormously powerful images, the archetypes, which represent various aspects of humanity's experience and wisdom in much the same way as an accurate, large-scale map represents a landscape.

It is argued that anyone who wishes to do so, and is prepared to make the effort, can directly experience the rich imagery of *anima mundi* and learn from the traditional wisdom stored within it. For at the very deepest level of the unconscious the minds of all of us are linked up to the super-memory of *anima mundi*. The relationship between the individual mind and the planetary memory can be compared to that between a low wattage electric lamp and the enormously powerful electricity-generating system to which it is linked.

The archetypes of *anima mundi* are partially expressed, so it is claimed, in the symbolism and imagery of the tarot trumps. Thus, by merely looking at them in contemplative mood, the fortune-teller establishes a link with *anima mundi* – he or she has switched on a low wattage lamp and so can draw on the power of the central generator. Once a fortune-teller has 'switched on', that is, brought the archetypes to life in the unconscious self, the entire collective wisdom of

The Queen of the suit of Cups, associated by fortune-tellers with love and pleasure, as shown in an eighteenth-century Marseilles deck.

humanity is at his or her disposal.

But how, it might be asked, did the archetypes come to express themselves in the symbols of the tarot if the cards were not originally designed by wise initiates expressing universal and eternal truths in pictorial form, but by fifteenth-century painters? One answer to this question relates to the nature of the personality of the genuine artist. A creative artist, it is asserted, is by definition an individual who has the capacity to sink voluntarily into the 'inner space' of the unconscious mind and come into contact with the archetypes of *anima mundi*. That is what was done by those who first designed the tarot trumps.

Whether or not this is the right explanation of the way in which the tarot designs came to reflect the powers of the archetypes no one can be sure. There is no doubt, however, that regular use of a tarot deck stirs up strangely powerful (but not unfriendly) forces in the lives of those who use the cards for divination. The first step in reading the cards is always to shuffle them in the correct manner.

Shuffling the Cards

It is usually necessary to shuffle a tarot deck used for fortune-telling by a different method from that used when shuffling ordinary playing cards. The reason is a practical one.

An ordinary playing card is always the right way up. It will always look the same, even if you turn it upside-down by turning it through half a circle. Very few tarot decks share this characteristic. Unless the tarots to which you have access are very unusual indeed, you will find that if you look at any individual card it has a clearly defined top and bottom – it can be either the right or wrong way up.

When tarot cards are used for divination their meanings are not the same when they are reversed, upside-down, in a spread (a fortune-telling layout) as they are when they are the right way up. It is not that the meaning (or 'divinatory significance') of a reversed card is the opposite of its right-way-up meaning, although that is sometimes the case, but that its meaning is different.

When shuffling a tarot deck it is therefore vital that the shuffle is carried out in such a way that roughly half the cards will be upside-down.

The suggested way of doing this is as follows:

1. Cut the deck into roughly equal halves.
2. Turn one half of the deck upside-down and put it on top of the other half.
3. Shuffle the cards thoroughly.
4. Twice repeat 1 to 3.

You should shuffle your tarot cards in this way each time you use them. Otherwise you will either have the same cards reversed each time you tell a fortune or, if you hold the deck in the opposite way to that which you held it previously, the relationship between the ordinary/reverse meanings of two cards will remain the same.

The Genius, in the sense of 'Spirit', of the suit of Deniers *(Discs or Coins) – a French Revolutionary transformation of the King of that suit.*

If you become really absorbed in the study of symbols of the tarot and their use in fortune-telling, it is likely that you will find yourself acquiring several packs of different design. If you become the owner of one of the unusual decks in which the cards have no obvious tops and bottoms, you will

have to put some arbitrary symbol on each individual card so that you know if the ordinary or reverse meaning of that card applies when it features in a fortune-telling spread. You could, for example, write 'top' or put a 't' at one end of each card.

After shuffling your tarot deck as the essential preliminary to an experiment in fortune-telling you must choose a significator – a card which is to represent you or, if you are telling someone else's fortune, the person on whose behalf you are acting.

The Significator

One eighteenth century fortune-teller and writer of books on the tarot suggested that if a woman's fortune was being told, the significator should always be the tarot trump called the High Priestess (sometimes termed Pope Joan or the Popess). Similarly, if the enquirer was a man, the significator should be the High Priest (also called the Pope and the Hierophant).

To follow this course has the advantage of simplicity – but it has the unfortunate effect of removing the possibility of two of the most significant cards in the deck appearing in a spread. Most of those who tell fortunes by the tarot find it preferable to use a Court Card as the significator.

The simple (and non-traditional) method of choosing which Court Card should be the significator is as follows. Cut the pack and observe to which suit the card you have cut belongs. If you cut, not a suit card but one of the 22 trumps numbered from 0 to XXI, simply shuffle and cut the pack again; continue doing this until you *do* cut a card belonging to one of the four suits. Take as significator the King of the suit to which the card you have cut belongs if the enquirer is a man, the Queen if a woman.

Alternatively, you can look through the divinatory meanings of the four Court Cards of each suit as given between pages 44 to 50, and decide which of the 16 Court Cards best signifies you or the person whose fortune you are telling.

Having chosen a suitable significator it is used in or, more usually, along with a tarot spread. There are dozens of tarot spreads: some old, some new, some simple and some very complex. As you become more and more expert at reading the cards for yourself and

Four of the 'major arcana': the 22 trumps (numbered from 0 to XXI) of the standard tarot deck of 78 cards normally used for fortune-telling purposes. These eighteenth-century Marseilles versions of, from left to right, the Empress, the Lovers, the Devil, and the Sun, were first printed in outline and then hand-coloured.

your friends it is likely that you will wish to experiment with the use of fairly complicated spreads such as the Hairdresser Spread and Inner Order Method (see pages 63 to 67). At first, however, it is best to get to know your tarot cards by employing the simpler spreads (pages 61 to 63) and interpreting the patterns in which they fall by the divinatory meanings of the cards as given on pages 44 to 60.

A word must be said about these meanings. As far as the 56 suit cards are concerned these are given very fully and should prove satisfactory until you become a very accomplished tarot reader – although, of course, you must always interpret the meaning of any individual card in the context of the meanings of the cards that it falls among.

The situation as regards the 22 trumps of the major arcana, those symbolic expressions of the archetypes, is somewhat different. The imagery of these cards is so rich, and speaks to the mind of the diviner on such a deep level, that it is very difficult to ascribe to them any hard-and-fast divinatory meanings. On the other hand, it is almost impossible to start telling fortunes by the tarot without using cook-book style interpretations of the trumps.

The following approach has been adopted. For each individual trump there is a Description, a section termed Mystic Significance and, finally, a section called Divinatory Significance. The last section gives short, cook-book meanings for the trumps in their normal and reversed positions. These will suffice until you have become skilled at using the simpler spreads and begin to master the more complex ones. At this stage you will find it worth reading through, referring to, and perhaps thinking about, the contents of the 22 sections headed Description and Mystic Significance.

The first of these gives descriptions of:

a) The trump as it usually appears in the standard Marseilles tarot deck (see page 40). There are plenty of local variations between different versions of the Marseilles tarot, so if you have one of these decks, don't worry if one or more of the trumps is not quite as described.

b) The trump as it appears in the Waite deck. This deck, originally published in 1910 by the London firm of Rider and Co., is very widely used in the English-speaking world. It was painted in accordance with the instructions of A. E. Waite, a mystic who had a vast knowledge of the literature of the tarot, and his trump designs are often startlingly different from the standard ones.

Thus, for example, one Waite trump shows a child riding a horse, whereas usual versions of the same card show two children either holding hands or embracing. While Waite's images frequently vary from the standard ones, what they intend to convey is the same. It is quite probable that you yourself own a Waite deck – it is the most popular of modern tarots. If so, you will see that not only the 22 trumps and the 16 Court Cards have pictorial designs, but also the 40 pip cards of the suits. These, while they incorporate much mystical symbolism, are completely non-traditional. Some tarot students consider this symbolism to be of some significance; others find it tiresome.

c) The trump as it appears in the deck used by members of the Order of the Golden Dawn in the last century. This has never been commercially produced in its original form but its symbolic richness, which has influenced the design of many more recent decks, throws much light on the hidden meanings of the trumps.

d) The trump as it appears in what is here termed the Felkin/Wang deck. In the last ten years or so before World War One a Dr Felkin and his associates produced their own revised version of the Golden Dawn deck. This is now available, as painted by the American artist Robert Wang, under the name of 'the Golden Dawn Tarot' which, strictly speaking, it isn't.

The sections, one for each trump, which are headed Mystic Significance give details of what some tarot students have felt about the inmost meanings of the cards. Once you have got to know the ordinary divinatory meanings of the trumps thoroughly, and are able to apply them easily to a spread, you may find these sections helpful in enabling you to read a spread intuitively, rather than by fixed rules. Before you attempt to do this, however, you must master the art of reading a spread in accordance with the meanings given in the list which follows.

THE DIVINATORY MEANINGS OF THE SUIT OF WANDS

Ace: The beginning of something. A renewal or a birth, real or metaphorical. Activity and energy leading to success. A strong probability that aims will be achieved. **Reversed:** Failure, often as a result of over-ambition. A failure to exert enough effort.

Two: Power, wealth and good fortune – but not always resulting in lasting happiness. **Reversed:** The unexpected is likely to happen in pleasure or in suffering.

Three: Lasting success in material affairs, notably those connected with partnerships and/or the arts. **Reversed:** Depending on the other cards in the spread can indicate either that difficulties will be overcome or that excessive ambition will result in failure.

Four: A successful conclusion to some situation or course of activity. A contented home life or, if the enquirer is elderly, a happy retirement. **Reversed:** Very much the same, but perhaps more so.

Five: Arguments, trials and struggle; success achieved only after much striving. **Reversed:** Disputes and quarrels which may be turned to the advantage of the enquirer.

Six: Success through hard work. Sometimes indicates the nearness of important news or happenings. **Reversed:** Disloyalty among friends or colleagues. A warning to beware of treachery.

Seven: A serious threat which can only be overcome by self-reliance and inner strength. **Reversed:** Indecision could be dangerous in the enquirer's situation.

Eight: Rush, speed – everything is hurrying, perhaps too quickly, towards a conclusion. Urgent messages that must be answered. In the case of a married enquirer sometimes indicates domestic disagreements and/or an infatuation with an outsider. **Reversed:** Disputes and jealousy in the home. Alternatively a theft or a swindle, in the past or still to come.

Nine: Reserved strength, resistance, persistence. In spite of irritating delays the objectives and desires of the enquirer will eventually be achieved. If the divination is concerned with someone suffering from a severe illness, this card is often an indication that there will eventually be a complete recovery. **Reversed:** Irritating delays will be experienced; obstacles may prevent a matter coming to a satisfactory conclusion.

Ten: A misuse of energy. Materialism and selfishness. Injustice. Sometimes indicates 'honey that tastes like ashes', in other words material success that proves not to provide the expected satisfaction, or material failure resulting from an attitude of 'Pull up the ladder, Jack, I'm all right'. **Reversed:** Material loss, perhaps the result of deceit.

Page: As significator, an attractive, daring and enthusiastic young man or woman. Can indicate either a likeable stranger coming into the enquirer's life or, particularly in the case of a female enquirer, a faithful lover. Sometimes, in a spread, this card symbolizes the receipt of reliable information. If found in a spread next to the Page of

Four versions of pip cards from the suit of Wands (Batons, Staves), associated by some with the fiery elements of human personality. From left to right: two 300 year-old Italian cards, Waite and Marseilles designs.

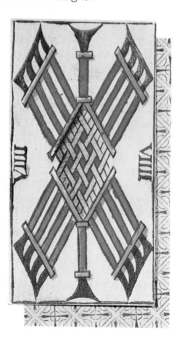

The Valet *(Page),* Cavalier *(Knight) and* Queen of *Batons (Wands or Staves) from a French eighteenth-century deck. Occultists have thought that the Knight's hat signifies infinity.*

Cups, however, the card represents a dangerous rival to the enquirer. **Reversed**: A gossiper, an unreliable and unstable young man. Or, more generally, the receipt of unreliable information concerning matters symbolized by the cards to the left and right of it in a tarot spread.

Knight: As significator a man who is decisive, generous but somewhat unpredictable. In divination symbolizes a man who has bouts of furious energy in all his activities, but tends to lack staying power. As well as representing a person in a tarot spread it can stand for over-hasty decisions and actions. In this case it gives a warning to the enquirer to think carefully before making a definite move. The cards to the left and right of it in the spread symbolize the general background to a contemplated decision. **Reversed**: A narrow-minded and sometimes cruel person. Or, more generally, rows, disruptions, partings and finding life rather disagreeable.

Queen: As significator any mature woman. In divinations represents a woman in whom calmness and a capacity to deal with practical matters are accompanied by considerable charm and a dislike of opposition. She may be snobbish and rather mean – the occultist S. L. MacGregor Mathers

rudely referred to 'the Lady of the Manor' as being typical of the type of woman represented by this card. When in a tarot spread this card does not refer to a particular person, it represents financial success. **Reversed**: When this card represents a person in a spread, it stands for a virtuous woman who is, nevertheless, likely to act on impulse, to take offence over small matters, and suddenly to take either a dislike to a friend or a liking to someone she has previously regarded with disfavour.

King: As significator a mature or elderly man who has a strong character. In divination he represents an honest, generous man possessed of all the old-fashioned virtues and a strong sense of humour. Such a man takes time to make important decisions affecting the life of himself or others. More generally, when not symbolizing a particular person, the card indicates a fortunate love partnership or receiving an inheritance. **Reversed**: A man of intolerant virtue, unwilling to give others the benefit of the doubt or to refrain from imposing his own morality on them. Can also indicate receiving useful advice.

THE DIVINATORY MEANINGS OF THE SUIT OF SWORDS

Ace: This card is particularly associated with male sexuality and can indicate the beginning of a relationship that will be powerful in either

good or evil terms. It is a symbol of stress, tension and the manifestation in the enquirer's life of forces outside his or her control. The tension indicated can result in success, in spite of all obstacles, or utter failure. **Reverse**: The significance is the same but stronger and more usually malefic.

Two: A symbol of balanced force; the tensions represented by the Ace are in a state of equilibrium, and harmony reigns. In a spread this card often indicates an end to pain, physical or emotional, and an end to disagreements or quarrels. **Reversed**: Trouble and treachery are indicated, probably as the result of the activities of someone who enjoys rows and causing personal discord.

Three: A card of disruptions, disequilibriums and separations. It can represent almost any discord, from a lovers' tiff to a divorce. The separation its appearance indicates in a spread is sometimes merely temporary, such as that resulting from a long journey. **Reversed**: Confusion, strife and trouble. Sometimes indicates that someone's mind is very confused.

Four: An end to conflict, the restoration of harmony or the slackening of

A 1709 Ace of Swords. It may be that the sword penetrating the crown is symbolic of male/female relationships.

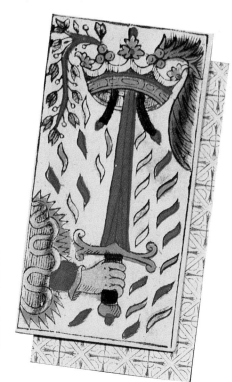

tensions. The card does not indicate death, but has a curious connection with cemeteries and tombs and sometimes seems to foretell an event connected with these. **Reversed**: An indication that the enquirer should be cautious. Sometimes foretells coming events involving a legacy.

Five: The occultist S. L. MacGregor Mathers, perhaps the most profound of modern students of the tarot, termed this card 'the Lord of Defeat'. It has a connection with the ideas that, in astrology, are associated with the planet Mars in its malefic aspects – failure, defeat, anxiety and depression. In a tarot spread it often indicates that some trouble-maker is working against the interests of the enquirer. **Reversed**: The same, but perhaps even more so.

Six: Success through effort. An improving situation. A happy journey, perhaps to foreign countries. Can sometimes symbolize the imminent arrival of an important communication. **Reversed**: A surprise of some sort, most usually connected with the enquirer's emotional life.

Seven: A fluid situation or an unreliable person involved in the enquirer's affairs. A warning that one can only succeed in a particular undertaking if one shows persistence and does not make hasty compromises. **Reversed**: Good advice from someone or prudence on the part of the enquirer.

Eight: A crisis, often one that imposes restraints and limitations. A warning to examine all the implications before entering into binding agreements. **Reversed**: A surprise, usually an unpleasant one, or an unforeseen frustration.

Nine: Misfortune, desolation, failure and general ruin – or so said some tarot authorities of the last century. A good many more recent writers on the tarot, including the eccentric Aleister Crowley, have seen this card as also having a more positive aspect. In this case it implies self-sacrifice, personal suffering voluntarily undertaken for the sake of other people or some great cause. **Reversed**: Can indicate either an unreliable – even criminal – person, or feelings of justified suspicion. Also suggests the onset of isolation and extreme loneliness.

Ten: In popular fortune-telling with an ordinary pack of 52 playing cards the Ace of Spades is usually regarded as 'the worst card in the pack'. The Ten of Swords has a similar reputation among many of those who use the tarot. It usually signifies hopes blasted and/or grief. It is worth remembering that this does not always mean the hopes of the enquirer; it can, according to the nature of the other cards in the spread, indicate that it is the opponents and rivals of the enquirer who will come to grief. Sometimes it symbolizes a 'psychological death' – the enquirer's loss of a set of false

Four Sword cards, from left to right signifying success through effort (Six); a sharp young person (Valet, Page); a dominant man bending others to his will (Cavalier, Knight); and power and responsibility (King).

beliefs. In association with the Ace of Swords it indicates that severe limitations and restraints are imminent. **Reversed**: Temporary advantages. Success followed by failure.

Page: As significator a sharp young man or woman. In a tarot divination indicates a subtle-minded young man (or, sometimes, a sporty young girl) who is graceful, physically well coordinated, tactful and conscious of the feeling of others. **Reversed**: A devious, frivolous young person whose stories cannot be relied on. More generally, unexpected news or a surprising turn of events.

Knight: As significator a dominant man. In divination a forceful man who tends to bend others to his will – a good friend but a dangerous opponent. More generally the card indicates that personal enmity is involved, or will become significant, in the matter the enquiry is being made about. **Reversed**: Either a dominating but very foolish person who is constantly changing or, if the enquirer is a woman, a rival who will be overcome.

Queen: As significator any mature woman, particularly if she is separated, divorced or widowed. In divination can indicate either a woman of this sort or general unhappiness, particularly that caused by loneliness. **Reversed**: Can symbolize either a treacherous and malicious woman who likes making trouble or, more generally, attitudes of prudishness, notably in relations to the sex lives of other people.

King: As significator a man who is elderly and occupies a position of some responsibility. In divination it can be a man of any age who occupies a similar position – perhaps a physician, a clergyman, a barrister or a government official. Often a man who regards himself as very practical, but is quite mistaken in this belief and behaves unreasonably or makes foolish decisions. **Reversed**: A selfish, calculating and rather wicked man who is not to be trusted, particularly in relation to legal matters.

THE DIVINATORY MEANINGS OF THE SUIT OF CUPS

Ace: A very lucky card, its meaning is well conveyed by the phrase 'my cup is overflowing'. It represents abundance and fertility, either real (motherhood or a good harvest) or metaphorical, as in 'a fruitful enterprise'. In a tarot spread in which the enquirer is concerned with his or her emotional life it can symbolize a decla-

ration of love, the opening of a new phase in the enquirer's emotional life or marriage. **Reversed**: Unfaithfulness, the unwelcome ending of something, or the beginning of something new which may end unhappily.

Two: Symbolizes marriage, deep love or friendship and sympathetic understanding and kindness from others. More generally, anything enjoyable not connected with work – holidays, games and so on. **Reversed**: Extravagance and self-indulgence. Alternatively, the possible ending of a friendship or the break-up of an emotional relationship.

Three: Good fortune and abundance. A favourable conclusion to any

Four Cup pip cards: the Ace, below left, one of the luckiest of tarot cards; and (above, left to right) Waite's Three, 'easy success'; the Four, signifying tension; and the Ten, predictive of success on all levels.

matter about which enquiry is being made. Easy success. The pleasures of the senses without harmful after-effects. **Reversed**: The pleasures of the senses to an excessive extent. Or the speedy and reasonably fortunate ending to the matter about which enquiry is being made.

Four: A card of tension between good and bad fortune – the good luck of the past may not continue. More generally, stagnation and boredom in spite of the fact that the personal situation is a happy one. Or, sometimes, a difficult situation created by others

who thought they were acting for the best. **Reversed**: The approach of novelty – a great change is about to take place.

Five: Disappointments in friendship and love. In astrological terms, Mars is intruding into the sphere of Venus. Pleasant activities end in sadness – tears follow laughter and smiles. More generally, unexpected reactions in response to the enquirer's activities – for example, rudeness and unkindness from those to whom the enquirer has been generous. **Reversed**: Things unexpected, plans that go awry, sudden arrivals and departures.

Six: A card of polarity. In other words a card that, depending on cir-

cumstances, can convey quite opposite meanings and is thus difficult to interpret in any tarot spread. In its first meaning it is concerned with looking backward and nostalgia. In its second it indicates a future situation. Sometimes it symbolizes both. Its future significance is happiness or success after struggle. **Reversed**: Something that is going to happen very shortly. The exact nature of the coming event is indicated by the card that was dealt immediately after it.

Seven: The meaning of this card is very roughly equivalent to the astrological significance of a malefically aspected Venus. It symbolizes vice, particularly sexual vice, and a misuse of talent. It is a card of illusion and false glamour – success which is neither real nor lasting. **Reversed**: A symbol of any plan, undertaking or

wish. When occurring next to or close to the Three of Cups the card indicates that desires and ambitions will be fulfilled.

Eight: An indication of repletion, a certain laziness and immobility and, perhaps, unjustified dissatisfaction with past achievements. Sometimes it indicates a new path in life – a sudden realization by the enquirer that he or she has been devoting him or herself to something (or somebody) which is hardly worthwhile. **Reversed**: General happiness, social gaiety and carefree behaviour.

Nine: Good luck, particularly in matters concerning finance and possessions. Success and the fulfilment of desires. Excellent health and/or a complete recovery from illness. A particularly fortunate card if the enquirer's occupation involves physical activity of an energetic nature. **Reversed**: Mistakes and miscalculations. Effort not producing the success that is deserved.

Ten: This card has similar qualities to the Nine of Cups, but on all levels of existence, not just the physical plane. Thus it indicates not only physical well-being but psychological stability and spiritual advancement. Similarly, its appearance in a tarot spread foretells not just material success but intellectual triumphs and the attainment of what could be called 'spiritual wealth'. More generally, it symbolizes a fulfilling home and community life.

Reversed: Foretells the probability of quarrels, disputes and angry outbursts. A definite warning to tread slowly and carefully.

Page: As significator a good-looking young man, perhaps of the type sometimes referred to as 'a Ganymede', or a pretty young woman. In divination it symbolizes a gentle dreamer, often a bit vague about practicalities, of either sex. Someone who is helpful but is to some extent dependent on those he or she helps; not a strong character, but a reliable one. More generally, can indicate thinking at length about some situation, or the reception of some piece of news, good or bad. **Reversed**: An unfaithful subordinate or lover – 'the smiler with the knife'. A lying deceiver who tries to seduce, literally or metaphorically, those with whom he or she feigns friendship, loyalty and love. Can also mean deception generally.

Knight: As significator a gentle and romantic young man. In divination indicates the same sort of man who is liable to temporary enthusiasms but lacks staying power and dogged determination. More generally, the appearance of this card in a spread indicates the recent arrival, or the coming arrival, of some sort of message or proposition, the general nature of which can be gathered from the significance of the cards dealt immediately before or after it. **Reversed**: A totally unreliable person, one who continually changes his or her mind and whose

From left to right: Page (Valet) of Cups, a pretty youth; the Knight, a romantic young man; the 'Liberty' (a republican Queen), a good-natured mature woman; and the King, a man of ambition and responsibility.

statements can never be accepted at face value. More generally, deception and fraud.

Queen: As significator any good-natured woman past her first youth. In divination indicates a woman who is generally kind and helpful as long as she doesn't have to go on being so for too long. Can also represent an artistic, imaginative and dreamy woman whose emotions aren't very deep – the sort of woman who may encourage a host of admirers but rarely commits herself to any of them. More generally, the Queen may represent flirtatiousness and teasing. **Reversed:** A woman who won't make up her mind or, sometimes, an evil woman. More generally cunning, malice and cattiness.

King: As significator a mature man with an ambitious nature. In divination just such a man, usually in a position of responsibility, who is admired by his subordinates but who nevertheless fears disapproval. A man who is only helpful to those who are, or may be, useful to him. More generally, the card is an indication that a superior is hostile to the enquirer. **Reversed:** An evil and dishonest man in a position of power. More generally, dishonesty and deceit.

THE DIVINATORY MEANINGS OF THE SUIT OF PENTACLES

Ace: A most fortunate card when it appears in a tarot spread, particularly when the divination is undertaken to ask questions about, or to find the factors relevant to, a matter which concerns money, property, shares and other securities, and material possessions. In general, indicates prosperity, security and a successful career. **Reversed**: Much the same, but unpleasantly so: greed, putting too great a value on worldly possessions, ruthlessly pursuing a successful career, etc.

Two: The material opposites: successful and unsuccessful projects, particularly those concerned with financial matters; alternating good and bad fortune. Also the psychological opposites: swings of mood from highs to lows, and so on. Often an indication of forthcoming abrupt change. **Reversed**: Things are not what they seem: something looks good is really the opposite, or vice versa. For example, a person's jolly exterior may mask inward misery or depression.

Three: A general improvement in the situation. A very fortunate card in any divination that concerns a project either just started or about to commence. In career matters sometimes an indication of an imminent promotion or an increase in income. **Reversed**: More or less the opposite, although the significance is less emphatic. Staying put in a dull job, for example.

Four: A card of material success and achievement. Security in all matters concerned with money, status and career. Sometimes indicates that good news will be heard from, or through, a woman or feminine influence. **Reversed**: Delay, uncertainty, a fluid situation in which one cannot be sure what will happen next.

Five: Worry about material things, particularly those concerned with career and financial matters. Sometimes actual loss of money, job or home, but which may prove only temporary. A card that, in a tarot spread, indicates the advisability of making financial economies. **Reversed**: Indicates the danger of heavy financial losses through extravagance, self-indulgence, gambling or unwise speculation of all sorts.

Six: Prosperity, often as a result of help received from others. **Reversed**: Financial reverses, probably caused by the envy and greed of either the enquirer or others.

Seven: Something wrong financially – perhaps an unwise speculation, a failure to obtain an expected profit, a failure to get promotion or a gambling loss. **Reversed**: More or less the same, but causing still more worry and disappointment.

Eight: Small profits and small improvements in the work life of the enquirer. Can indicate that the enquirer pays too much attention to matters of minor importance. **Reversed**: A danger from the dishonest tendencies of either the enquirer or those with whom he or she has financial dealings.

Nine: Material good fortune. Large profits or a large increase in income. Sometimes indicates the prospect of a large inheritance. In general, the achievement of prosperity, comfort and the approval of others. A rapid coming to pass of what is foretold by the fortunate cards on either side of it in a tarot spread. **Reversed**: Deceit on the part of others resulting in material loss.

Ten: Great material success, but achieved only after many years' efforts and therefore not altogether satisfactory. Sometimes indicates the inheritance of land or property from a close relation. **Reversed**: Losses resulting from theft or dishonesty. Sometimes indicates disputes over property or ownership matters.

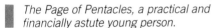

The Page of Pentacles, a practical and financially astute young person.

The Ace, Two and Eight of Pentacles, the 'money suit', signifying (from left to right) financial good fortune; material ups-and-downs; and both small successes and minor details.

Page: As significator any young man or woman with an earthy, practical type of personality. In divination represents a hard-working, methodical person who is careful with money but not miserly. More generally, it can symbolize the qualities associated with prudence and good management. **Reversed**: Can represent either a person who, in money matters, is careless to the point of foolishness or, more generally, the vice of extravagance. It can also indicate imminent bad news.

Knight: As significator a rather clumsy man. In divination a man who is hard-working and conscientious, but lacking in sparkle to the point of dullness. More generally, the qualities of utility – say a gift or a task to complete that is useful but boring. **Reversed**: Either a lazy, careless person or the general characteristics of such a person.

Queen: As significator represents a practical, mature woman. In a divination represents the same sort of woman: sensible, understanding and warm-hearted, but lacks sparkle. More generally, symbolizes the qualities of generosity and warm sincerity. **Reversed**: Either an unreliable woman or the qualities of unreliability and unpredictability.

King: As significator a practical man in late middle or old age. In divination a similar man, unemotional and somewhat impassive in appearance, but in reality far less dull than his outward appearance would suggest, and often

The Knight, Queen and King of Pentacles, signifying (from left to right) a sometimes rather clumsy younger man; a methodical mature woman; and a prosperous older man.

very successful in business or administration. A devoted friend or lover, although rarely a demonstrative one, he is capable of being a vigorous opponent of those things and people he dislikes. Can also indicate the qualities associated with such a man – quiet energy, steadfastness of purpose and implacability. **Reversed**: A cruel and corrupt man or the feelings of terror such a man arouses.

THE TAROT TRUMPS

0 THE FOOL
(in some decks called the Jester)

Description

Marseilles designs show a Renaissance fool, i.e. a jester, clad in comic multicoloured and somewhat tattered garments; over his shouder is propped a pole from which is slung an improvised bag. A dog (or dogs) snarls at his heels. The Waite Fool is a gorgeously dressed young man, carrying a rose in one hand, and with a friendly dog bounding along beside him; both seem about to step happily over a precipice. The Golden Dawn design shows an ancient Fool striding along with, instead of dogs, a lion and a dragon at his feet. The Felkin/Wang Fool is a naked child simultaneously plucking yellow roses and holding a grey wolf in check.

Mystic Significance

Many occultists link the Fool with the Parsifal of Holy Grail legend, i.e. the Pure Fool, the holy innocent who succeeds where the worldly-wise fail. The Fool is seen, by this interpretation, as a madman or simpleton who is in truth closer to the divine realities than the rest of us. (In this connection it is interesting to note that the English word 'simple' originally meant 'blessed'.) Occultists who follow the attributions of the tarot trumps taught in what is sometimes called the Western Esoteric Tradition see the Fool as symbolizing the Air of the alchemists, the breath of spiritual life. This ties in with the fact that the word fool is derived from *follis*, a Latin word meaning windbag.

Divinatory Significance

Oddity, eccentricity, foolishness, even madness. The unexpected and the surprising event. Particularly something 'out of the blue' which has astonished, or will astonish, the enquirer. **Reversed**: Procrastination – putting things off until tomorrow. Carelessness, laziness, and an inability or unwillingness to make decisions.

A Marseilles version of The Fool, one of the most meaningful of the tarot trumps. In a spread it can indicate either foolishness or wisdom.

LE FOU

I THE MAGICIAN
(in some decks called the Juggler)

Description

Marseilles decks show the sort of trickster or illusionist who might have been found performing in the open air at any country fair or market in pre-Revolutionary France. Before him is a small table on which are placed a knife and other small objects towards which he points with a small baton or wand. His immense hat is somewhat suggestive of a figure eight lying on its side. In the Waite deck the Magician wears no hat but above his head floats the mathematical symbol of infinity – an elongated figure of eight lying on its side; the table has been transformed into something very like an altar, and upon it are the symbolic magical emblems of Earth, Air, Fire and Water. A cup for Water; a wand for Fire; a dagger for Air: and a disc, bearing a five-pointed star, for Earth. The Golden Dawn design is similar although the Magician wears a winged hat – a symbol of the Greek god Hermes. The Felkin/Wang Magician wears the ordinary figure-of-eight hat, but has the caduceus, the wand of Hermes/Mercury, embroidered upon his jerkin.

Mystic Significance

A common occult interpretation of this card was expressed by a tarot student of almost a century ago who claimed that it represented the union and balance of the elemental powers controlled by the mind. According to the same student the colours predominant in the 'initiated version' of this trump symbolize the mysterious Astral Light surrounding the great Adept. All this seems rather vague; perhaps the card is best mystically interpreted as both a symbol of the creative will and of those things or forces which link men and women with the higher powers.

Divinatory Significance

Risks taken and also risks manifesting themselves in everyday life. Initiative, skills and general adaptability. This card in a divinatory spread is often indicative of the appearance of something new (or somebody new) and of major importance in the enquirer's life. **Reversed:** Uncer-

A Marseilles portrayal of Le Bateleur: the Juggler, or Magician. This card is said to symbolize the elemental powers controlled by the human will.

tainty, confusion, conscious or unconscious deception and trickery – even swindling or confidence tricks. Can also indicate a deceiving individual, usually a fairly young man.

II THE HIGH PRIESTESS
(in many decks named the Popess or Pope Joan)

Description

The Marseilles version of this card is based upon a legend of the Middle Ages. At some time during an unspecified earlier period a woman named Joan so successfully masqueraded as a man that she was ordained as a priest, consecrated as a bishop and was eventually elected Pope. According to many versions of the legend the imposture was discovered when Pope Joan went into labour and gave birth to a child in the middle of a religious ceremony. The Marseilles card is faithful to the legend, showing a woman in ecclesiastical garb wearing the triple crown of the Papacy and holding an open book, presumably a missal. The

Waite High Priestess is the goddess Isis, enthroned between two pillars, a crescent moon at her feet and a scroll of the law in her hands. The Golden Dawn design is much the same save that the High Priestess is shown reading an open book intently. The Felkin/Wang High Priestess bears a silver chalice and is crowned with a silver crescent moon.

Mystic Significance

Most Western occultists identify this tarot trump with the higher aspects of the feminine principle – woman as the gateway to the world of the spirit.

La Papesse, the 'female Pope', today more usually called the High Priestess and identified with the higher aspects of the feminine principle.

This ties up with both the original legend of Pope Joan, a woman not only carrying out all the sacerdotal functions, but acting as Supreme Pontiff. As the feminine archetype of things beyond the world of matter the High Priestess is looked upon as a symbol of the lunar forces as were Artemis and Isis, particularly the latter. On this interpretation the pillars between which the priestess sits are not only the white and black pillars, Jachin and Boaz, of occult and masonic significance (as they are shown in the Waite card), but the Pillars of Set, the Egyptian god who murdered Osiris, consort of Isis.

Divinatory Significance
Intuition and intuitive feelings. Secret and hidden things. The prospect of something new as well as the barriers that hinder approach to the new. Change generally. Some tarot students interpret the appearance of this card in a divinatory spread as a warning against over-enthusiasm, 'getting carried away'. **Reversed**: Sexual passion, particularly of the type which leads to reckless actions and the establishment of difficult and perilous relationships.

III   THE EMPRESS

Description
The Marseilles Empress is crowned, sceptred and enthroned – usually out of doors, as a small shrub seems to be growing nearby – and clad in a appropriately imperial robe. She carries, or has placed beside her, a shield emblazoned with the eagle symbol of the Holy Roman Empire. In the Waite card the shield has become heart-shaped and upon it is the astrological sign of Venus. The love-goddess aspect of the card is emphasized by having the Empress, seemingly pregnant, lolling on cushions amid a fertile landscape. The Golden Dawn version shows a winged goddess crowned with stars, standing on the moon, and bearing a shield displaying a dove – the bird of Venus – and holding a sceptre. The Felkin/Wang Empress has no shield but bears an ankh, a symbol of Venus in her highest aspect.

Mystic Significance
Students of the Western Esoteric Tradition tend to look upon the Empress as the 'Isis of Nature' as distinct from the 'Isis of the Mysteries' – the High Priestess. In other words, the Empress is a pictorial representation of the archetypes of fertile love. As such she can be regarded as the forces that are represented by Aphrodite and all love-goddesses, by Ishtar (Astarte), the great goddess

of ancient Babylon, by Ceres and Demeter, and by the Mother Goddess revered by modern pagans.

Divinatory Significance
Generally, real happiness and much good fortune. Creative actions leading to pleasurable experiences and sensations, and the reverse – pleasure resulting in creativity. **Reversed**: Inaction, conflict, quarrelling and disagreement, effort without result, unproductive actions or a negative, unproductive person, usually a woman.

IV   THE EMPEROR

Description
The Marseilles Emperor is seated in profile, a six-pointed crown upon his

THE EMPRESS.   THE EMPEROR.   LE ·PAPE

The tarot trumps numbered III, IV, and V – the Empress, the Emperor, and Le Pape, 'the Pope', at the present day often termed the High Priest. The Empress and the Emperor are from the tarot deck painted under the direction of A. E. Waite. On the shield of the Empress is the astrological symbol of Venus, on the Emperor's throne are symbols of Aries. The High Priest is associated with Taurus.

head, a sceptre in his right hand, a shield, upon which an eagle is delineated, propped against the left-hand side of his throne; in some Marseilles cards there is an orb in his left hand. The Waite Emperor is full face, has a sceptre bearing some resem-

blance to the astrological symbol of Venus, has the zodiacal sign of Aries on his crown and has ram's-head decorations (more symbols of Aries) carved upon his throne. The Golden Dawn Emperor is clad in a robe of flame, and is enthroned, in a posture reminiscent of the symbol of the alchemists' Sulphur principle, upon a cubical stone, its visible sides showing a green lion and a white eagle. The Felkin/Wang Emperor is enthroned full face and bears an orb and a sceptre crowned with a ram's head; his feet rest upon a young ram.

Mystic Significance
As the Empress is the positive and creative feminine energy so the Emperor is the positive and creative masculine energy, as suggested by his connections with both the zodiacal sign of Aries and the combustible, fiery principle (Sulphur) of alchemical philosophy. According to one profound student of the tarot, the Emperor is *Ho Nike*, that is Mars as a divine principle, a conqueror in both love and war. On another level the Emperor is seen as a pictorial representation of pure reason – like Mars, a destructive conqueror.

Divinatory Significance
Success, authority and creativity. Ambition or ambitions – usually the ambition(s) of the enquirer but, according to what other cards are in a divinatory spread, may be the ambitions of others. **Reversed**: Obstructions and limitations of every sort. A lack of real progress in spite of effort.

Hasty and ill-considered actions. Over-confidence, and the dangers and difficulties resulting from it.

V THE HIGH PRIEST
(in many decks called the Pope or the Hierophant)

Description

The Marseilles Pope shows just what its name suggests – an enthroned Pope, wearing the triple crown, holding a sceptre (or, sometimes, Peter's key) in his right hand. Before him are two acolytes or sacerdotal attendants. Waite's equivalent card, the Hierophant, is still quite definitely a Pope and is not much more than a prettified version of the Marseilles card, although some commentators have claimed to discern phallic symbols in decorative details of the Papal throne. Significantly, however, the number three is emphasized – Waite's Hierophant wears a triple crown, bears a three-armed cross as a sceptre, and is raising three fingers in blessing. This demonstrates Waite's indebtedness to the Golden Dawn, whose High Priest card is identical to his save that it also shows the four Kerubs (Cherubs) – the heads of a lion, an eagle, an ox and a man. The Felkin/Wang variant eschews the Kerubs but the High Priest's throne is decorated with the carved heads of bulls.

Mystic Significance

Many occultists look upon this tarot trump as having a strong relationship to the zodiacal sign of Taurus. As such it is also equated with Apis, the sacred bull of Memphis in ancient Egypt; interestingly enough, some fifteenth century paintings identified the then Pope, Alexander VI, with Apis. Some devotees of the Western Esoteric Tradition view the High Priest as a personification of the guidance of the Masters, the super-human beings believed to preside over the spiritual evolution of humanity.

Divinatory Significance

Helpful advice and assistance from a friend, perhaps one in a position of some authority. Marriage or a close partnership based upon mutual interest and, often, affection. Religious, mystical and esoteric interests and inclinations. **Reversed**: Bad advice received from others. Deceitful behaviour. A disloyal friend.

VI THE LOVERS
(in some decks called Vice and Virtue or the Two Paths)

Description

The design of the Marseilles Lovers is of a pleasing simplicity. It shows a man standing between an older and a younger woman while above his head Cupid, clothed in the sun, aims an arrow from his bow. The Waite Lovers is very odd indeed and totally untraditional. It shows Adam and Eve naked in the Garden of Eden. On Adam's left is the Tree of Life; on Eve's right is the Tree of Knowledge

The Waite version of trump VI, the Lovers. Some have seen this card as symbolizing spiritual love and physical passion in opposition to one another. Waite seems to have thought of the lovers as Adam and Eve.

of Good and Evil, with the Serpent coiled around it. Cupid has been transformed into an archangel. The Golden Dawn Lovers are similar to those of the Marseilles card, the two women being taken as 'a priestess and an harlot' – symbols of sacred and earthly love. The Felkin/Wang version is different from any represented in other decks. It shows the Greek hero Perseus coming with drawn sword to the aid of the chained virgin Andromeda, who is about to be eaten by a dragon.

Mystic Significance

Some interpreters have tritely taken the Perseus and Andromeda version as signifying the sword of inspiration striking off the fetters of materialism and spreading enlightenment. This seems to be a rather guarded expression of the old dualistic belief that matter is evil and that, therefore, any true love must be exclusively spiritual. The Marseilles/Golden Dawn versions seem both less heretical and in closer accordance with the experience of most of us – that physical love can inspire as well as degrade, lead human beings to the heights as well as draw them down to the depths.

Divinatory Significance

Love and sexual attraction generally – for either good or ill. A choice to be made by the enquirer. This choice is usually, although not always, connected with the emotional life. **Reversed**: Separations and partings, particularly those concerned with the emotions. The breakup of alliances, friendships, partnerships and even marriages. An inability, or an unwillingness, to make a decision – the Hamlet syndrome.

VII THE CHARIOT
(in some decks called the Sphinxes)

Description

The Marseilles Chariot shows the King of France – his crown bears the fleur-de-lis of French royalty – in a typical sixteenth century, canopied open carriage drawn by two horses. Waite, following French occult examples, replaced the horses by sphinxes and indulged in much muddled symbolism; for example, the King's kilt displays the dot symbols of geomancy, a mode of divination which esotericists attribute to the Element of Earth. The Golden Dawn Chariot is also drawn by sphinxes, the King's crown being surmounted by three pentagrams and the front of the chariot being decorated with a winged globe and a phallic object – as a symbol of the creative power of the universe. The Felkin/Wang variant is curiously Teutonic; it shows a Viking-like King, wearing a horned helmet, standing in a light chariot which is pulled by two horses, one white and one black. Beneath the horses' feet is not solid earth but clouds.

Mystic Significance

According to some mystic interpretations of the Chariot, the black and white horses (or sphinxes) represent all the 'pairs of opposites' – that is, all the positive and negative (which does not mean evil) aspects of reality on the physical, emotional, mental and spiritual planes of existence. These opposites draw the charioteer along to a rapture in which he is released from the bondage of earthly things. A somewhat similar interpretation is placed upon the Felkin/Wang variant; the card supposedly symbolizes the spirit of humanity

A magnificent fourteenth-century version of the Chariot, trump VII; in some packs the horses are portrayed as sphinxes.

controlling the worlds of matter and the lower levels of consciousness, rising above the clouds of illusion, and entering a higher sphere.

Divinatory Significance

Success in spite of all difficulties encountered. The overcoming of hindrances and limitations. Travel to new places. New friends and acquaintances. The unexpected change. **Reversed:** Unpleasant news arriving or, more generally, an unexpected piece of bad luck.

VIII JUSTICE
(Note: in some decks Justice is number XI)

Description

This card is normally numbered VIII (8) in the Marseilles deck; it is numbered XI (11) in many esoteric decks, the Waite for example. The Marseilles Justice is a conventional figure of that virtue – sword in one hand, scales in the other. The Waite version is little more than a prettified version of this, although there are some numerologically significant additions. Thus, Waite's Justice – numbered XI of course – wears a tri-turreted crown with a four-sided jewel. This suggests Venus, whose number is 7, which is 3+4, and Venus rules the zodiacal sign of Libra; the astrological symbol of Libra is the balance, or scales, which Justice holds in her hand. The Golden Dawn version of Justice is also a conventional one. In the Felkin/Wang version Justice has been given an Egyptian cast; she wears a black and white nemyss (Egyptian headdress) and sits between black and white pillars.

Mystic Significance

This card is sometimes interpreted as a symbol not only of justice and fairness in the ordinary senses of the words, but as the virtue of discrimination. By an extension of this interpretation Justice also indicates conscience, the natural laws, and the essential 'rightness' of things. An alternative point of view sees his card as representing justice in its ancient meaning – the balance of opposites such as male and female, ebb and flow, darkness and light, sowing and reaping, and so on.

A Marseilles depiction of the trump card Justice. In most tarot decks Justice is numbered VIII, but in some occult packs it is numbered XI.

Divinatory Significance

A time in which the enquirer is put to the test and/or must make decisions. **Reversed:** Unfairness, injustice, things going wrong.

IX THE HERMIT
(also called the Hunchbank, the Old Man and the Capuchin)

Description

The Marseilles Hermit is an old man holding aloft a lantern, which is partially shielded by his enormous cloak, and supporting his weight upon a stout staff. Waite's card is fairly similar, but his Hermit is hooded and a glowing 'Seal of Solomon', a six-pointed star, is within the lantern. This seems to be more or less identical with the Golden Dawn version, which the Felkin/Wang variant closely resembles, the only important distinction being that the 'Eye in the Triangle', usually signifying the Egyptian god Horus, is embroidered on the Hermit's cowl.

Mystic Significance

According to many occultists the Hermit is the wise man looking for truth and illuminating the gloomy world of matter with the lamp of 'Occult Science'. This interpretation seems obvious to the point of silliness. A number of contemporary commentators have therefore discerned – or at least thought they have discerned – male sexual symbolism in the design of the Hermit. This supposed symbolism is concerned with what may be called 'self-reliance on one's own inner powers'. On a higher level the Hermit can be seen as the aspirant to wisdom who finds his teacher at the central core of his own personality.

Divinatory Significance

Prudence and tact. A place from which the enquirer can obtain the guidance and help he seeks; or possibly a person who will supply this assistance. Old age or a particular elderly person. **Reversed**: Secrecy and excessive carefulness resulting

the wheel is frequently surmounted by a sphinx. Waite's Wheel of Fortune shows the Kerubs (the heads of a lion, an eagle, an ox and a man) at the four corners of the card, and the creatures on the wheel include not only a sphinx, but two other figures from Egyptian mythology; additionally the symbols of the alchemical principles of Salt, Sulphur and Mercury are inscribed upon three of the wheel's eight spokes. The Golden Dawn wheel is very similar, but six-spoked. The Felkin/Wang Wheel of Fortune has twelve-spokes, symbolic of the signs of the zodiac. Below it is an ape, above it a winged sphinx.

> *The trumps of the 'major arcana' named the Hermit, the Wheel of Fortune and Strength (La Force). In most decks they are numbered, respectively, IX (VIIII), X, and XI. In some packs designed by esotericists (including the Felkin/Wang and A. E. Waite decks) the numbering of the last is changed to VIII.*

Richard Cavendish, is reminiscent of a well-known passage in William Blake's *The Marriage of Heaven and Hell*: 'Without Contraries is no progression. Attraction and Repulsion, Reason and Energy, Love and Hate, are necessary to Human existence. From the contraries spring what the religious call Good and Evil. Good is the passive that obeys Reason. Evil is the active springing from Energy.' While one might conceivably exchange the opening words of the last two sentences, the whole passage is significant in the context of the ethical teachings implied by the symbolism of the Wheel of Fortune.

Divinatory Significance

Good luck and much success in financial matters. The impact of fate and chance on the enquirer, usually for the improvement of his/her situation. Favourable changes. **Reversed**: Unfavourable changes in a situation or a way of life. An unfortunate happening or a run of bad luck.

in a failure to make decisions. Delay and inactivity.

X   THE WHEEL OF FORTUNE

Description

The Marseilles Wheel of Fortune shows a six-pointed wheel on which men and women ascend and descend. Sometimes animals – usually donkeys and/or monkeys – are substituted for the human figures, and

Mystic Significance

According to some esotericists, the Wheel of Fortune is the revolution of experience and progress, the steps of the zodiac, held in place by the counter-changing influence of light and darkness, time and eternity. The axle at the centre of the wheel marks the still heart of the changing world, while forward (and backward) movement comes about through opposites moving in opposite directions. This, as has been pointed out by the writer

XI   STRENGTH
(sometimes named Force; in some decks Strength is number VIII)

Description

The Marseilles Strength, which is numbered VIII (8) not XI (11), shows a woman (wearing a hat shaped something like that of the Marseilles Magician) either forcibly opening or forcibly closing the jaws of a lion. In the Waite Strength the hat is transformed, like that of the Magician, into the mathematical symbol of infinity, an elongated figure eight lying on its side. The lion is wreathed in roses – flowers in which Waite seems to have taken a near obsessional interest. The Golden Dawn version is similar, but the lion's mouth is being opened, while in Waite's Strength it is being closed. In the Felkin/Wang variant of Strength the lion's jaw is not being manipulated. The animal is simply being gently led by a woman who carries roses in her hand.

Mystic Significance

This card is sometimes held to symbolize the control of the lower by the higher faculties of humanity; more specifically, the earthly passions directed by the powers of the soul. On this level the lion is the unpleasant Mr Hyde who lurks beneath the saintly exterior of every Dr Jekyll. In Freudian terms it is the seething id which lies beneath the conscious mind, always endeavouring to burst forth in its might. There is another, quasi-alchemical, interpretation according to which the lion is a creative force that can be controlled so that it enables the lead (or base matter) of everyday life to be transmuted into the precious gold of ecstatic bliss.

Divinatory Significance

Courage, inner strength and self-control. Can also indicate the influence of a woman who is well-disposed towards the enquirer.
Reversed: Bad temper, illness, a lack of control resulting in self-indulgence. Sometimes indicates an ill-disposed woman or one who exerts an unfavourable influence upon a person or a situation.

XII   THE HANGED MAN

Description

The Marseilles Hanged Man is suspended by his ankle from the cross-piece of a crude gibbet consisting of three roughly shaped beams, two vertical and one lateral. He seems unconcerned by this and there is a happy expression – or, at least, an expression of indifference – upon his countenance. The Waite Hanged Man is suspended from a tau-shaped cross, that is, a cross in the shape of the letter T. The Golden Dawn gibbet is also tau-shaped. The Felkin/Wang Hanged Man is dressed in something which resembles a 1920s bathing costume and is suspended from what is either a curious rock formation arising out of the sea or a strangely deformed stick of seaweed.

Mystic Significance

The Hanged Man and its symbolism have attracted the attention of a very large number of tarot students and commentators from the poet and critic T. S. Eliot to the occultist W. Wynn Westcott. Eliot saw the Hanged Man as the slain-and-risen god who is the subject of much of the world's myth and legend. Westcott

mysteriously wrote that no persons save those who have pronounced clairvoyant or intuitive powers can understand the real meaning of this card. It is the slain-and-risen complex of ideas that has appealed to most of those who have meditated and brooded upon the hidden meanings of the Hanged Man, and it is more than likely that Westcott was hinting at the fact that in certain

Exquisitely painted versions of trump XII, the Hanged Man (above), and trump XIII, Death (right). It was once thought that this pack, of which only 17 cards survive, had been painted to amuse Charles VI of France when he was mentally ill, but this is no longer believed to have been the case.

groups who practise ceremonial initiations, one of the key rites involves the symbolic death and rebirth of the would-be adept.

Divinatory Significance

Eccentric behaviour, setbacks and suffering. Sacrifice and self-sacrifice.
Reversed: Pain and suffering. Sometimes an indicator of a crowd of

unfeeling and thoughtless people – 'the mob', the 'vulgar herd', the uncaring mass.

XIII   DEATH
(in many decks this card is numbered but not given a name)

Description

In the Marseilles version a conventionalized figure of Death – an animated skeleton wielding a scythe – is shown mowing a crop of hands and feet which thrust out of the earth, together with two heads, one male and one female, the male head crowned. Waite's Death is quite untraditional: an armoured skeleton, mounted on horseback, bearing a rose-banner as its emblem. The Golden Dawn Death is similar to the Marseilles version and is reproduced with only very minor symbolic variations in the Felkin/Wang deck.

Mystic Significance

This card perhaps symbolizes both the transience and permanence of human life. In the words of a commentator of 70 years ago, Mrs Felkin, the skeleton may be regarded as the type 'which persists through the permutations of time and space . . . the transmuting power of nature work-

ing from above downwards'. In other words Death symbolizes not death, actual or metaphorical, but renewal through death and after death. According to some students of the tarot an understanding of the inmost nature of this card requires prolonged contemplation of the processes of transformation and transmutation in life: the great sea-changes each one of us undergoes from time to time.

Divinatory Significance
Failures, disappointment, partings and leave-takings without happiness. The loss of friends and friendship. The cessation of help. **Reversed**: Long life or a desired transformation of the nature of life. A birth or a regeneration. Can sometimes indicate a partial or complete withdrawal from the problems of everyday life.

XIV TEMPERANCE
(in some decks called precisely the opposite, Intemperance)

Description
The Marseilles Temperance displays a rather primitively depicted angel pouring a liquid from one vase-shaped container to another. The Waite angel is more prettily drawn. One foot is on land and one in water from which flowering irises sprout. On the angel's breast a triangle, apex upwards, is depicted within a square. The sun blazes from behind the angel's head and light radiates from its brow. The Golden Dawn Temperance is quite different in its design and seems to have been evolved from sketches produced by the French occultist, Eliphas Levi. It shows a crowned angel pouring fire from a torch in her left hand upon an eagle, and with her right hand pouring water from a horn upon a lion. Between the angel's feet a lunar cauldron gives off the smoke of incense. The Felkin/Wang variant shows, like the Waite Temperance, an angel with one foot in water, one on land. On the angel's breast is a yellow square. In the background a volcano is in violent eruption.

Mystic Significance
This card seems on one level to

equate symbolically with the zodiacal sign of Sagittarius. However, it also has certain alchemical implications concerned with the mingling of opposites. These are made fairly explicit in the Golden Dawn version of Temperance, with its eagle and lion, its fire and water; and have certain links with the concepts expressed in the oriental cult of Tantra. The Waite and Felkin/Wang

Temperance, trump XIV, as shown in an eighteenth-century Marseilles deck. Some believe this card mystically signifies the 'mingling of opposites'.

cards, in both of which the angel is neither on land nor in water, hint at similar things – a bridging of the gaps between conscious and unconscious, spirit and matter.

Divinatory Significance
Good management, successful partnerships. Good health or recovery from illness. Sometimes indicates a happy outcome to a difficult situation. **Reversed**: Disagreements and disputes of all sorts. Bad management. Getting involved in a difficult situation. A problem that proves to be insoluble.

Trump XV, the Devil, as depicted in a deck based on the unusual tarot interpretations of M. Alliette.

XV THE DEVIL

Description
The Marseilles Devil is the bogyman about whom stories were told around the peasant firesides of Western Europe three centuries ago. A horned and winged nastiness, he stands on a pedestal holding a flaming torch. Two creatures, half-demon and half-human, are tied to the pedestal. Waite's Devil has a human torso and head, the latter surmounted by horns; a goat's legs, but the feet and talons of a bird of prey. It is not surprising that his expression is a disagreeable one, reminiscent of a diner who has ordered pheasant and been served a portion of fast-food chicken. He squats on a pedestal to which are chained a boy and a girl, their heads horned, their feet cloven. The Golden Dawn Devil is an exact replica of the card as drawn by the French occultist Eliphas Levi. The Felkin/Wang variant is a simplified and attractive version of this original card.

Mystic Significance

According to some commentators the Devil is the exact converse of the Magician and represents the powers of the occultist – intelligence, application and creativity – turned to evil ends. The Devil is seen by others as a trump that should be studied in conjunction with XIII, Death, for together they form a pair of opposites: the destructive and the creative, the static and the dynamic. Curiously enough, there are symbols of each in both cards. This card is often linked with the Greek god Pan. It is also seen as symbolic of the resistance of matter to spirit, form to force.

Divinatory Significance

Temptations and obsessions, particularly those concerning physical sexuality, money matters and material possessions. Male sexuality generally. An inevitable and usually materially advantageous event. Can sometimes indicate a will or a legacy. **Reversed**: Stupidity, malice, materialism and miserliness – or a miserly person. An unfortunate, but inevitable, happening or experience.

XVI   THE TOWER
(sometimes named the Blasted Tower, or the House of God)

Description

The Marseilles Tower shows a castellated tower being struck by lightning. From it are falling two human figures and a number of circular blobs which may be drops of molten lead or gobbets of flaming pitch. The Waite Tower is perched amid mountainous peaks, and its castellations resemble those of an elaborate crown. One of the two figures falling from it is also crowned, and the vague blobs of the Marseilles Tower have become stylized versions of the Hebrew letter *yod*. The original Golden Dawn Tower is more or less identical to this but the position of the falling figures resembled the form of the Hebrew letter *ayin*, which is associated with trump XV, the Devil. The Felkin/Wang version shows the cabalistic diagram termed 'the Tree of Life' on the right of the tower which also has, on its left, a diagram of the 11 *qlipoth*, the evil and adverse forces of cabalistic lore.

The Marseilles trump XVI, 'the House of God', more often known as the Blasted Tower; it is associated with the astrological attributes of Mars.

Mystic Significance

Obviously enough the Tower symbolizes the overthrow of something or other. But what? According to one occult authority the tower represents inertia while the destroying lightning is energy impetuously ejecting those souls who would lock themselves away from life behind the stone walls of habit and tradition – perhaps bad habit and outmoded tradition. In other words, the Tower symbolizes the destruction of false values and ways of thinking which are no longer of relevance to either the life of the individual or that of humanity as a whole. In this connection it is worth bearing in mind a passage quoted by Richard Cavendish from the writings of the Russian occult philosopher, P. D. Ouspensky: 'If only men could see that almost all they know consists of the ruins of destroyed towers perhaps they would cease to build them.'

Divinatory Significance

Everything traditionally associated with war gods and the planet Mars – fires, conflicts, quarrels, accidents, losses of money and possessions, etc. **Reversed**: Much the same, but to a less unpleasant extent.

XVII   THE STAR

Description

The Marseilles Star shows a kneeling nude woman on the banks of a pool, pouring water from two containers. Above her flames a huge eight-pointed star girdled by seven smaller ones. The Waite card is clearly derived from this, although the woman has one foot on the land, and one foot in, or on, the water. The land/water theme is emphasized by the fact that one container is being emptied upon the earth, the other into the water. Waite's Star, like that in the Marseilles deck and in Italian trumps dating from as early as the fifteenth century, is eight-pointed. The Golden Dawn version has only seven points; the naked woman is in a posture suggestive of the shape of the swastika – an ancient nature symbol which originally had nothing at all to do with the Nazis or anti-semitism – and she pours liquid over her head as well as into the pool. In the Felkin/Wang variant both vases are being emptied into the pool and a dove hovers in the air to replace the butterflies which featured in the Golden Dawn card.

Mystic Significance

Many students of the tarot have pointed out that the nude woman can be regarded as the feminine principle, sometimes personified as the Mother Goddess, which pours out the waters of life upon the world of matter. The eight- or seven-pointed star can be interpreted as guidance from above, illuminating the soul during its immersion in the ordinary affairs of worldly life. This is emphasized by the depiction of butterflies in the Golden Dawn Star; the butterfly, emerging as it does from its dry chrysalis, has long been seen as an analogue of the spirit within a fleshy husk.

Divinatory Significance

Unexpected help, often from someone in a position of power or responsibility. Surprise gifts or, rarely, legacies. A coming run of good luck or an especially fortunate happening. **Reversed**: More or less the opposite of the above; unexpected hindrances and expense, sudden reversals of fortune, and so on.

XVIII   THE MOON
(in some unusual decks termed the Crisis)

Description
The Marseilles Moon shines balefully over a landscape dominated by two sinister towers in the background. In the foreground a crayfish crawls from a stagnant-looking pool besides which two dogs (or are they wolves?) stand baying at the sky, which drips liquid, perhaps blood or dew. The Waite Moon closely resembles the Marseilles card, as do the Golden Dawn and Felkin/Wang versions.

Mystic Significance
The significance of this card is in accordance with both its name, the Moon, and its usually, although not invariably, sinister appearance. Dogs and wolves were sacred to

Below, trump XVII, the Star and, below right, trump XVIII, the Moon, as they are usually represented in Marseilles decks. According to some the Star depicts the feminine principle, while the Moon portrays the worlds of matter and spirit.

Hecate, moon-queen of the witches of ancient Greek belief, and it has been the dark side of the lunar forces that has inspired most of those who have drawn or painted this tarot trump. According to one student of the Western Esoteric Tradition, the path which is usually delineated as running between the two towers towards the horizon is that of spiritual toil, effort and possible failure. It is the path of blood and tears upon which fear and wavering must be overcome. The two towers, according to another interpretation, mark the gateway between the worlds of matter and spirit.

Divinatory Significance
Risk and, more particularly, risky situations and adventures. Puzzlement, and even fear, as to the real nature of a situation or the true motives of others. Sometimes indicates a major change in the enquirer's life, past or present, according to the nature of the spread and the card's position. **Reversed:** The minutiae of life: other descriptions, little mistakes, somewhat insignificant changes in life and life style.

XIX   THE SUN

Description
The Marseilles Sun shows a wall before which two children embrace beneath a blazing sun. A radically different Sun is featured in the Waite

A. E. Waite's unusual variant of trump XIX, the Sun. More usually the card shows two naked children playing or embracing beneath a blazing sun.

deck. While the sun still blazes, and the wall still stands, the two embracing children are replaced by a single child riding a bare-backed horse. Sunflowers bloom beyond the wall. In the Golden Dawn Sun the children, naked, embrace in a fairy ring. In the Felkin/Wang variant they hold hands, the boy standing on land, the girl with her feet in a pool.

Mystic Significance
According to some commentators, the wall which featured in almost all versions of the Sun is a symbol of the zodiacal belt through which the moon, planets and sun itself move, radiating, as it were, their influences through the mediations of the 12 signs from Aries to Pisces. The children are, at one level, the 'pairs of opposites', force and form, light and darkness, and so on. They are probably best considered, however, as symbols of the joy of innocence and liberation.

Divinatory Significance
Prosperity and success. Happiness on all levels of being and consciousness. Happy and successful love affairs and marriages. Everything that is encapsulated in the phrase 'the sunny side of life'. **Reversed:** As the right way up, but not to the same extent – a full cup, but not an overflowing one.

XX THE LAST JUDGMENT

Description

The Marseilles version of this card gives a crudely literal interpretation of its name. A conventional angel at the top of the card is blowing the last trump. Below, the earth gives up its dead, who look somewhat surprised at being restored to life. The Waite Last Judgment is basically an elaboration of the primitive design, although the tombs from which the dead arise seem, very oddly, to be flooded or, even more oddly, to be afloat. The Golden Dawn Last Judgment contains a certain amount of Egyptian and other occult symbolism. The angel's trumpet has suspended from it a golden banner emblazoned with a silver cross. Below, a youth rises from an elaborate tomb, his arms extended, palms upward, slightly above his head, as though he were supporting the heavens – a posture in which the Egyptian god Shu was frequently depicted. On the right of the youth stands a naked dark man who formulates, with the aid of fingers and thumbs, the triangle of Fire upon his forehead. On the youth's left is a fair

A French version of trump XX, the Last Judgement. This card is associated with the concept of 'new beginnings'.

woman formulating the inverted (apex downwards) triangle of Water upon her breast. The Felkin/Wang Last Judgment also has the central figure, who stands in a floating coffin, in the posture of Shu, but neither the couple on its right side nor the man on its left are formulating symbolic triangles.

Mystic Significance

Esotericists associate the Last Judgment with the alchemical Element of Fire and its impact on humanity. Thus, this trump is sometimes interpreted as showing the cosmic forces descending on the aspirant to illumination, and giving him or her the power to 'transcend the sepulchre of environment and cast aside the trammels of desire'. In a sense, the 'fire' of this trump is that which burns the legendary phoenix to the ashes from which it is reborn – the fire that destroys form in order that it may come to a new birth.

Divinatory Significance

The settlement of some long-standing problem and/or a fresh start. Doors both opening and closing – leaving one job and starting another, for example. An important decision or a reunion. **Reversed**: Delay, confusion caused by lack of clear thinking, indecision and muddle. An unsatisfactory or inconclusive end to some situation. A problem half-solved. A tooth 'patched up' when an extraction is required.

XXI THE WORLD
(often named the Universe or, less commonly, the System)

Description

The World of the Marseilles deck depicts an almost naked woman dancing in the frame of an oval wreath. In her left hand she bears a wand. At the corners of the card are the Kerubs (heads of a lion, an eagle, an ox and a man). The Waite World is very similar, but the dancer bears two wands, one in each hand. The same is true of the Golden Dawn dancer whose framing oval was made up of 400 small circles – 400 being the number of significance in the Golden Dawn version of the cabala. In the Felkin/Wang variant

The World, trump XXI, as depicted in a Marseilles deck. In a tarot spread is considered very fortunate.

these are transformed into 12 coloured globes, symbolic of the zodiac, linked by a rope of 72 glistening pearls.

Mystic Significance

This card symbolizes not one world but two – the world of matter and the world that lies beyond the physical. In the latter aspect the oval that the woman (who has been indentified with the Egyptian goddess Hathor) is dancing in must be identified with the 'cosmic egg', and the dance she is engaged in is the establishment of the harmony of the universe. In the former aspect the card is a gloomy one, associated with the planet Saturn, the great malefic influence of the old astrologers, and the concepts linked with it include death and the decay of all things subject to time dominion.

Divinatory Significance

Certain success. Happy journeyings, real or imaginary, to the objects of desire, be they persons, things or events. **Reversed**: Failure, boredom and being 'stuck in a rut'. General stagnation. Much effort leading to inadequate rewards.

TAROT SPREADS AND THEIR INTERPRETATION

The very simplest tarot spread involves only two cards besides the significator. Simple as it is, it often gives an adequate answer to a simple question.

Remove the significator from the deck and place it on the table before you. Shuffle the remainder of the pack and place the top two cards on first the right and then the left of the significator. The card on the right is traditionally taken to represent the past, while that on the left represents the future – but it doesn't matter if you take the past/future significance as being the opposite way round as long as you always stick to doing it that way. What you must never do, after looking at the cards, is to change the relationship so that you get the answer you would like, rather than the one you have been given.

As an example of how this ultra-simple spread can be used to answer a straightforward question, let's suppose that you have asked 'Will my financial position improve over the next year or so?', and that the two cards in the spread, apart from the significator, are

Left-hand card – Eight of Swords
Right-hand card – The World (the trump numbered XXI)

The World, which is here being taken as the card representing the past has (see opposite) meanings that imply success and journeyings, real or metaphorical, to those things that are desired.

The Eight of Swords, which is here taken as the card representing the future, has the meaning (see page 46) of 'A crisis, often one that imposes restraints and limitations...'

Putting these meanings together we get something like, 'In the past it has seemed certain that financial success was to be yours and that you were going to get things you wanted in life; but over the next year you are going to go through a severe financial crisis which will impose limitations on your freedom of action.

It is worth noting that if before laying out the two-card spread you had decided that the left-hand card should represent the past, and the right-hand

one the future, your interpretation would have been very different and the answer to the question would have been, 'In the past you have suffered a financial crisis, but over the next year things will improve; you will move closer to achieving your desires and obtaining financial success in life.'

You can extend this basic spread by using three cards, representing past, present and future, besides the significator. Even then, however, the information at your disposal can only be very limited, being based on only three cards, and is likely to be insufficient to give an adequate answer to anything but the simplest questions. Nevertheless, it is not a bad thing to start your tarot experiments with two- and three-card spreads; by doing so you will soon learn the technique of combining the meanings of cards into a coherent whole. Once you can easily cope with this, you can try to give more general readings for yourself and your friends by the use of the following spreads.

The Horoscope Spread

Put the significator on the table before you and shuffle the remaining 77 cards in the usual way. Deal the top 12 cards face up round the significator as though they were the numerals of a clock, but do not deal them in a clockwise direction. Deal the first card at the 9 o'clock position and deal the other 11 anti-clockwise, the last being dealt on the 10 o'clock position.

The meaning of each individual card is then interpreted in accordance with the attributions of the Houses in astrology. That is to say:

The meaning of Card 1 (at 9 o'clock) is to be interpreted as indicating the enquirer's personal character, temperament and general disposition.

As is suggested by its name, the Horoscope Spread is an application of the system of 'House division' used by astrologers to the tarot. It will be noted that the order of the Houses goes 'from east to west', like the sun.

The Horoscope Spread

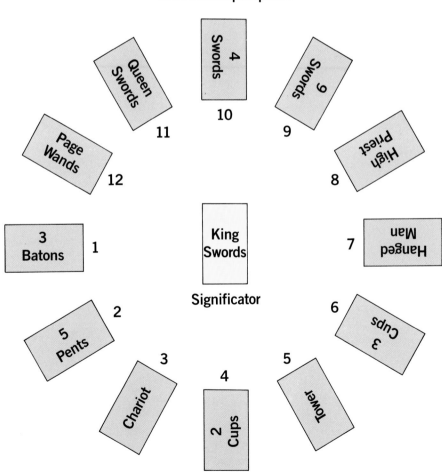

The meaning of Card 2 (at 8 o'clock) is to be interpreted as indicating the enquirer's future financial position.

The meaning of Card 3 (at 7 o'clock) is to be interpreted as indicating the enquirer's capacity for self-expression and communication with others. This card also indicates his/her mental capacities and, so some assert, unconscious desires.

The meaning of Card 4 (at 6 o'clock) is to be interpreted as an indication of the nature of the enquirer's background, home life as a child, etc.

The meaning of Card 5 (at 5 o'clock) is taken as indicating the satisfactoriness or otherwise of the sensuously pleasurable things in the enquirer's life. It also relates to the enquirer's love life and his/her likely success or failure in gambling, speculation and chancy enterprises.

The meaning of Card 6 (at 4 o'clock) indicates the physical constitution of the enquirer, health problems, etc. This card can also be taken as the likely nature of the enquirer's relationships with those from whom services are received or to whom services are rendered.

The meaning of Card 7 (at 3 o'clock) is to be applied to the enquirer's close relationships and associations, particularly those with partners in marriage and business.

The meaning of Card 8 (at 2 o'clock) can be interpreted as an indication of – to use a gloomy phrase – the way in which all things connected with death are likely to influence the enquirer's future life. For example, legacies the enquirer is likely to receive. The card that falls in this house also has a curious connection with personal renewal and ceremonial initiation into certain obscure societies.

The meaning of Card 9 (at 1 o'clock) should be interpreted as an indication of the enquirer's 'ideology' – his or her deepest beliefs in relation to religion and philosophy. The ninth card also gives some indication of the enquirer's dreams and longings – what is wanted out of life apart from material success and a happy love life.

The meaning of Card 10 (at 12 o'clock) can be interpreted as an indication of how others do and will regard the enquirer. In other words, the enquirer's status and reputa-tion, particularly in matters concerned with career or public activities.

The meaning of Card 11 (at 11 o'clock) is interpreted as an indicator of the enquirer's social life, friends, and worldly ambitions.

The meaning of Card 12 (at 10 o'clock) is interpreted as an indication of the limitations upon the enquirer – restraints that are imposed by others and/or by the limitations of the enquirer's own character. It is also an indicator of the enquirer's secret self – the aspects of his or her personality, or activities, that are hidden from others.

A similar-looking spread to the above, although one intended for quite a different purpose, is:

The Clock Spread

Place the significator before you, shuffle the cards and deal the top 12 in a clockwise direction around the significator; the top card goes at the 1 o'clock position, the twelfth card in the 12 o'clock position.

The purpose of this spread is to give a general, month-by-month indication of events in the enquirer's life over the coming year.

The meaning of the card at the 1 o'clock position is interpreted as showing the nature of the dominant influences and likely events of the month immediately following the divination. That at the 2 o'clock position is taken as an indicator of the succeeding month, and so on.

Thus, if you carried out the divination on, say, September 24th the significance of the first card would expire on October 24th, that of the second card on November 24th, and so on round the clock to the twelfth card, the significance of which would expire exactly one year after the date of the divination.

Another good method of asking the tarot about the nature of the major influences in the coming month or the coming year of your life is the following very simple spread:

The Question Spread

This is used as a means of obtaining an answer to any question concerning the influences at work in a particular situation or chain of events.

Remove the significator from the deck and place it on the right-hand side of the table at which you are sitting. Shuffle the cards, thinking of the nature of the question you are asking, and making certain you have formulated it quite clearly.

Deal the top five cards to the left of the significator in the pattern below:

Card 3

Card 1   Card 5   Card 2   Significator

Card 4

Card 1 is the influence just coming into play. Card 2 is the influence just beginning to make itself apparent. Card 3 is the dominant influence at the time the divination is performed. Card 4 indicates the nature of any hidden influence at work – the unconscious motives of others, for example, or the activities are going on behind the scenes. Card 5 shows how the influences indicated by Cards 1 to 4 combine and gives an indication of the real nature of what is happening and its likely ending.

If Card 5 is a Court Card it is an indication that the problem or question you are concerned with, or asking, can only be satisfactorily resolved, or answered, with the aid of an individual whose personality is symbolized by that Court Card.

The identification of the person concerned may be obvious to you. If not, take the Court Card that has appeared as Card 5 and use it as the significator in another Question Spread. This should give you enough clues to enable you to make a satisfactory identification.

Another layout which is often employed for the purpose of analysing a particular situation or answering a specific question is:

The Horseshoe Spread

Place the significator on the table, shuffle the deck, and deal seven cards around the significator in the shape of a horseshoe, its open end towards you. From right to left the horseshoe's seven cards are attributed as follows:

Card 1   The Past
Card 2   The Present
Card 3   Hidden Factors
Card 4   Obstacles

Horseshoe Spread

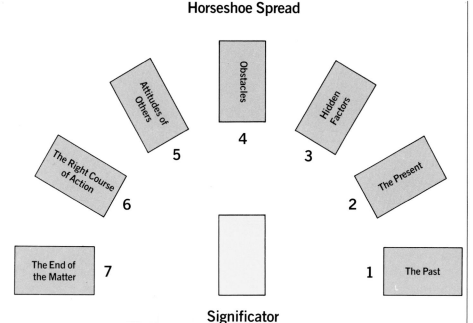

Significator

Card 5   Attitudes of Others
Card 6   The Right Course of Action
Card 7   The End of the Matter

A spread employing a much larger number of cards is:

The Hairdresser Spread

A. E. Waite described this as the best spread for giving a general tarot reading, that is, one in which the enquirer is not asking a specific question but is desirous to know the realities of his or her present situation and what the future is likely to hold in store.

While Waite did not say so, he derived this spread (with a pointless modification) from one of the books written by Etteilla, a French fortune-teller of whom Waite had a low opinion and whom he described, rather snobbishly, as an 'unsuccessful hairdresser'. In fact there is no evidence that Etteilla (whose real name was Alliette) was ever a hairdresser, although he did at one time lodge in the house of a wigmaker. Even if he had been, however, it would not have made him any the worse as a fortune-teller. There seems no reason to assume that being a hairdresser (or a lawyer, a soldier, a dustman) should disqualify anyone from being an expert tarot reader. I have therefore thought fit to call this general tarot layout, sometimes referred to as either the 'Forty-Two Card Spread' or the 'Six Times Seven Spread', the Hairdresser Spread, thus expressing my belief that a man or woman's everyday job is of no relevance whatsoever to his or her talents as a diviner.

The Waite version of this spread calls for the significator to be the Magician if the cards are being read for a man, and the High Priestess if they are being read for a woman. If you wish to follow this course you will be following tradition. For the reasons given on page 42, however, I feel it inadvisable to use either of these trumps as significator, and I suggest that the significator be chosen in the usual manner as described on page 42 below. Whatever the significator chosen, leave it in the deck, shuffle and cut it, and deal seven cards, face down, into a single pile. Repeat the process a further five times, giving you a total of six piles, each containing seven cards. After dealing the six piles, put the rest of the deck aside.

Take the first pile, shuffle it, and deal it face upwards in a row of seven from right to left. Take the second and third piles, shuffle them, and deal them again from right to left, in two rows of seven below the topmost row. Take the remaining three piles, shuffle them together, and deal a further three rows of seven, running from right to left.

You will now have six rows, each of seven cards. Look at them and see if the significator is one of the 42 cards laid out in front of you. If it is, remove it and place it to the right of the topmost row. Fill the empty space by cut-ting the pile of undealt cards you have put aside and removing the card you have cut. If the significator is not among those cards in the six rows of seven, simply remove it from the deck and place it to the right of the top row.

Now read the cards on the table from right to left, top to bottom, starting at the extreme right of the top row and ending at the extreme left of the bottom row.

Normally you would take all the rows as referring to your own future or that of the person for whom you are carrying out the reading. The first row would be taken as the immediate future, the second as indicating the situation in two or three years time, and so on, the last row indicating your life in the very distant future.

If, however, you decide that you want a reading of past, present and future – and you must decide that this is the sort of reading you want before shuffling and dealing the cards – you can take the top row as the past, the second row as the present, and the remaining rows as the future. Alternatively, you can take the two topmost rows as the past, the next two rows as the present, and the bottom two rows as the future. It is essential, however, that you decide which of these alternatives you will follow before shuffling and dealing the cards at the beginning of the divination. If you make the decision at a later stage, after the six rows of seven have been dealt, you will find yourself unconsciously cheating – putting an unpleasant card, or cards, in the past when really it, or they, may apply to the present or the future.

When you are reading past, present and future with this spread remember that reading from right to left, time is presented in its proper sequence. Thus, when you are reading the first two rows as the past, the first one or two cards read – these will be on the right of the topmost row – will symbolize the origins and the family background of the enquirer during early childhood. Similarly, the two or three cards at the extreme left of the second row of seven will represent the nature of recent events in the enquirer's life.

With a layout of cards as that employed in the Hairdresser Spread, in which 42 cards are used excluding the significator, diviners have to develop their intuitive powers if they are to tell fortunes accurately. Just looking

The Irish poet and dramatist W. B. Yeats (above) was deeply versed in the tarot and its mystical significance. His own hand-drawn tarot trumps still survive.

Constance Wilde, shown above, was also a tarot devotee. She studied under the tuition of the occultist S. L. MacGregor Mathers, shown above right.

up the divinatory meanings of the tarot cards as they are given in a book such as this, and then trying to 'tell a story' by combining the meanings of all the cards in a spread works very well – in spreads of up to about 18 cards. As the numbers of cards in a spread increases, however, the task gets progressively more difficult. None the less, one has to start in this way, even when using spreads in which large numbers of cards are involved. For, as Richard Cavendish has pointed out, 'making up a story' by using the different cook-book meanings of the cards is a necessary stage in the development of the individual fortune-teller.

Eventually, however, such mechanical techniques become a hindrance to further progress. There comes a time when conscious reasoning must be replaced by an intuitive understanding of the significance of the relationships between the cards in the pattern they have fallen in a particular spread. Sometimes these patterns are such that, as you will find out for yourself by the time you have become an accomplished tarot reader, a particular card takes on a completely different meaning from any recorded in books on the tarot.

Your intuitive abilities will become of great importance when using the advanced and demanding method of tarot divination which is sometimes called the Opening of the Key but is here termed:

The Inner Order Method

Details of this method of tarot divination were once among the most closely guarded secrets of the 'inner order' of an occult society that included among its members the poet W. B. Yeats; the actress Florence Farr; Constance Wilde, the wife of Oscar Wilde; and such noted occultists as R. W. Felkin, S. L. MacGregor Mathers and W. Wynn Westcott. Something over 75 years ago one of the members of the inner order broke his oath of secrecy and published details of its techniques of tarot divination in a limited edition of 500 copies.

Since then the original manuscript instructions for the use of the Inner Order Method have been printed and reprinted over and over again, often with little consideration for ordinary readers. The latter have usually found them rather impenetrable, largely because a great deal of prior knowledge was taken for granted by those who compiled them.

What is given below is a modernized and simplified version of the Inner Order Method. Nevertheless, while the technique is presented in the simplest possible form, it must be held in mind that this method demands much of the fortune-teller and should not be experimented with in an idle fashion. It is almost certainly best to have completely mastered a number of simple spreads before attempting to use the Inner Order Method. Those who disregard this advice may find themselves suffering from a bad attack of psychic indigestion.

Ideally one should not begin an Inner Order tarot divination until one is in a state of complete calm. J. W. Brodie Innes, a distinguished Scottish lawyer who was also a lifelong student of the mysteries of the tarot, gave some interesting advice on this point. He said that it was advisable to begin by trying to enter a psychological state in which one felt 'no feelings of joy or sorrow at any event, no hope and no fear, neither feelings of like nor dislike for any individual'. What the diviner should aim at, he said, was a desire to know for the sake of knowledge itself – not for idle curiosity about what the future held in store.

It seems improbable that most of

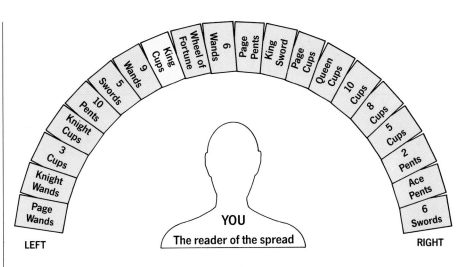

Step Three

those who use the tarot can achieve quite the state of utter detachment and freedom from emotion urged by Brodie Innes. What we can all do, however, is try to be as calm as possible and to interpret the fall of the cards without letting our own preconceptions, prejudices and emotions influence our readings of the spread. No one who reads a tarot spread can be *un*interested in what it portends, but we can all adopt a *dis*interested attitude, one of impartiality, such as that which is adopted by all good judges. In as detached a mood as you are capable of reaching, take the following steps:

Step One: Choose the significator but do not remove it from the deck. Shuffle the cards in the usual way, thinking about the question that the enquirer is asking or the situation or problem about which he or she is concerned. Place the deck on the table before you and cut it into two roughly equal piles, placing the top pile roughly 15 centimetres (six inches) to the left of the remainder of the deck. Cut first the left- and then the right-hand pile to its left, leaving you with four roughly equal-sized piles.

Step Two: The four piles of cards before you are symbolic of the four elements (Earth, Air, Fire and Water) with which the alchemists and occultists of the past concerned themselves. These Elements are not, of course, elements in the sense in which the word is used by a present-day scientist. They represent various aspects of existence and the temperamental qualities which are present in each and every

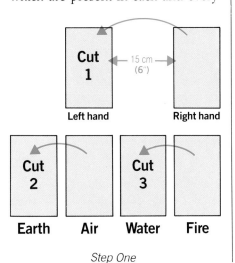

Step One

one of us. Usually an individual shows, by his or her behaviour, that one element is psychologically predominant: we speak of someone being 'a wet', or 'full of airy ideas', or 'having a fiery temper', or even being 'over-fond of earthy jokes'.

From right to left the four piles into which the deck has been divided are attributed to Fire, Water, Air and Earth.

The Fire Pile (that furthest to the right) is taken as representing the work, business or career interests of the enquirer (but not money matters connected with them).

The Water Pile (that second from the right) is taken as representing love, marriage and pleasure of every sort – but only the positive aspects of these. In other words, problems or questions concerning say, divorce, marital breakups or lovers' quarrels do not pertain to this pile but to the following pile (Air).

The Air Pile (that second from the left) is taken as representing discords, losses, quarrels and upsets of every sort.

The Earth Pile (that on the extreme left) represents 'earthly' matters – property of all sorts including money, stocks, shares, bullion, house and other real property, and so on.

Look through the four elemental piles to see if the significator is in one of them. When looking through each pile take great care not to disturb the order of the cards contained in it.

If the significator is not in the pile that pertains to either the aspect of life that you, or the person whose fortune you are telling, is most concerned with

at the moment or to the specific question that is being asked, *do not go any further for the time being*. For the absence of the significator from the relevant pile is an indication from the depths of your own mind that the time is not yet suitable to carry out a tarot divination by the Inner Order Method. Try again not less than two hours later. If, once again, the significator is not in the appropriate pile, do not make a further attempt until at least 12 hours have elapsed. Continue trying, but not at less than 12-hour intervals, until the time is ripe and the significator is, at last, found in the correct pile. Then take:

Step Three: Deal the pile containing the significator into an arch running from right to left. That is, place the top-most card of the pile as the 'foundation stone' of the right-hand side of the bridge and deal to the left so that the bottom card of the pile becomes the 'foundation stone' of the left-hand side of the arch. The spread will then look like the sample illustration above, which is based upon the original instructions, written almost a century ago, for the use of the Inner Order Method.

See which way the significator is looking, that is, whether its head is inclined towards, or profiled towards, left or right as it lies in the arch. If the significator is reversed, it will be, so to speak, gazing in the opposite direction to that in which it would be looking if it was the right way up. It is just possible that you are using one of those tarot decks, very infrequently encountered, in which the cards normally used as

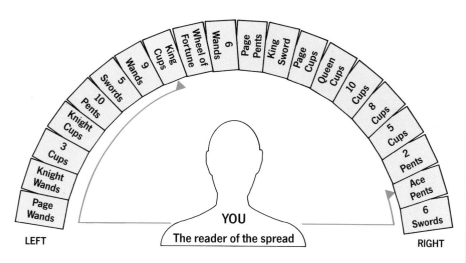

Step Four

significators are in full face, so that it is impossible to decide which way they are looking. In this case just toss a coin to decide in which direction your significator is directing his or her eyes.

Step Four: Taking the significator as card number one, count from it, in the direction in which it is looking, ten cards for a King, Queen or Knight, seven cards for a Page.

On a piece of paper note down the card on which the count of ten or seven has fallen. Count from the card whose name you have just marked down, counting that card as one, in accordance with the following rules:

Court Cards as above
count ten from any card but a Page from which count seven

Aces
count five

Any **suit card** from two to ten
count the number of the card

The **Fool**, the **Hanged Man** and **Judgment**
count three

The **Magician**, the **High Priestess**, the **Empress**, the **Wheel of Fortune**, the **Tower**, the **Sun** and the **World**
count nine

For any other trump card
count twelve

Remember that you must always count in the same direction as that in which the significator is looking. When you reach the end of the arch just carry on counting from the other end.

Step Five: Make a note of the name of the card on which your second count has ended and then carry out a third count in accordance with the procedure described in **Step Four**. Note down the name of the card, do another count, and continue with successive counts until one ends up on a card whose name you have already noted down. The counting process is such that you may conclude the successive counts with the names of only two or three cards noted down, or you may have noted the names of a very large number of cards – sometimes every card in the arch.

Step Six: Develop an interpretation on the basis of the cards whose names you have noted down, i.e. the cards that concluded each successive count. If you are telling your own or someone else's fortune in a general sense, you should interpret these cards as being concerned with your own past or that of the individual on whose behalf your divination is being carried out. If you are trying to get an answer to a specific question, the cards should be taken as indicating the origins of the particular matter about which the enquiry is being made.

In making your interpretation don't be misled by the diagram on page 65 (which, for simplicity's sake, shows no reversed cards) into thinking that the Inner Order Method does not take account of reversed meanings. These

are taken into account in the usual way.

Step Seven: If further information is required concerning the past of the enquirer and his/her associates, or about the origins of the problem being enquired into, read the cards making up the entire arch in pairs; pair the extreme left-hand card with that on the extreme right of the arch, and so on, moving inwards until you have no cards left to read or the only remaining card is the one at the topmost point of the arch. In the case of the sample spread on the left, you would thus start by pairing the Page of Wands with the Six of Swords and continue pairing inwards and upwards, your last pair being the Six of Wands and the Page of Pentacles.

A pair is interpreted in accordance with the significances of its two cards in relation to one another. Thus, for example, the last pair mentioned, the Six of Wands and the Page of Pentacles, could be interpreted as an indication that important news (which pertains to the Six of Wands) will be received from the hard working, methodical person represented by the Page of Pentacles.

Step Eight: Gather together the entire tarot deck, including the cards that made up the arch, shuffle and deal into 12 separate piles.

Step Ten

Step Nine: Look through the piles and find the one with the significator in it, being careful not to disturb the order of the cards. Deal the relevant pile, which will contain either six or seven cards, into another arch.

Step Ten: Repeat **Steps Four to Six** with the new arch. Interpret the cards whose names you have noted down as indicating the present circumstances in the enquirer's life, or the present situation regarding the matter being enquired about. If, as will probably be the case, more information about the present is required, carry out a process of pairing like that described earlier in **Step Seven**.

Step Eleven: Shuffle the whole deck and deal it into ten piles. Take the pile containing the significator and deal as a third arch. Repeat **Steps Four to Six**, this time taking the cards as indicating the enquirer's general future or 'the end of the matter' if a specific question is being asked. For further information, once again carry out the pairing process in **Step Seven**.

Such is the Inner Order Method of tarot divination, otherwise known as the Opening of the Key. The instructions are not quite as complicated as they sound as can be shown by taking the sample arch on the opposite page and working out the relevant counts starting from the significator. Remember that the counts start from the significator, are made in the direction he or she is looking, and end when an individual count concludes on a card whose name has already been noted down. We will suppose that the King of Cups is the significator and that he is looking to his left.

As the count is started from a King we count ten, taking the significator, the King himself, as the first number of the count. Thus:

Nos 1 King of Cups
2 Nine of Wands
3 Five of Swords
4 Ten of Pentacles
5 Knight of Cups
6 Three of Cups
7 Knight of Wands
8 Page of Wands – so, over to the extreme right and
9 Six of Swords
10 Ace of Pentacles (the first card to be noted down)

From the ace we count five, so

Nos 1 Ace of Pentacles
2 Two of Pentacles
3 Five of Cups
4 Eight of Cups
5 Ten of Cups (the second card to be noted down)

From a suit card from two to ten we count the number of the card, in this case ten, so

Nos 1 Ten of Cups
2 Queen of Cups
3 Page of Cups
4 King of Swords
5 Page of Pentacles
6 Six of Wands
7 Wheel of Fortune
8 King of Cups
9 Nine of Wands
10 Five of Swords (the third card to be noted down)

We count five from the Five of Swords, it being a suit card, so

Nos 1 Five of Swords
2 Ten of Pentacles
3 Knight of Cups
4 Three of Cups
5 Knight of Wands (the fourth card to be noted down)

We count ten from a Court Card other than a Page, so

Nos 1 Knight of Wands
2 Page of Wands – over to the extreme right and
3 Six of Swords
4 Ace of Pentacles
5 Two of Pentacles
6 Five of Cups
7 Eight of Cups
8 Ten of Cups
9 Queen of Cups
10 Page of Cups (the fifth card to be noted down)

From a Page we count seven, so

Nos 1 Page of Cups
2 King of Swords
3 Page of Pentacles
4 Six of Wands
5 Wheel of Fortune
6 King of Cups
7 Nine of Wands (the sixth card to be noted down)

We count nine from this, of course, so

Nos 1 Nine of Wands
2 Five of Swords
3 Ten of Pentacles
4 Knight of Cups
5 Three of Cups
6 Knight of Wands

7 Page of Wands – over to the extreme right and
8 Six of Swords
9 Ace of Pentacles

This count has now ended on the Ace of Pentacles, a card whose name we have already noted, the first count having ended with it. This means that the counting is now over as far as this particular arch is concerned, and that the cards to be interpreted are:

Ace of Pentacles
Ten of Cups
Five of Swords
Knight of Wands
Page of Cups, and
Nine of Wands

This, of course, is the first arch of a particular divination, the arch that concerns the past and, being obtained from a pile containing roughly a quarter of an entire deck, has rather a lot of cards. The two subsequent arches will be built of six, seven or eight cards, and with them the counting process is much less burdensome.

Two further points concerning the countings are worthy of mention. Firstly, if you want to be completely traditional you should count four, not ten, for each Court Card other than a Page. The number four was used in the original version of the Inner Order Method for abstruse numerological reasons connected with a Hebrew name of four letters. For reasons too complex to enter into here, many contemporary students of the tarot have decided that a count of ten is preferable to one of four. The second point is that some contemporary users of the Inner Order Method count eleven, not five, from an ace.

The Inner Order method, if correctly carried out, is perhaps the best of all methods (or spreads) for divining the general circumstances of somebody's life and glimpsing the patterns that the future might hold for this person. Although particular questions can also be answered by the Inner Order Method, its scope is likely to overwhelm the interpreter looking for a clear response to a specific problem. This purpose is much better answered by the next spread which, though complex, circumscribes every aspect of a question precisely, often pointing to a practical move forward.

Even when a fortune-teller is using the tarot in order to get a general picture of an enquirer's situation, together with some indications of likely developments, it is usually the case that one particular detail of the overall life-picture is uppermost in the consciousness of the enquirer. It will usually be some aspect of matters which concerns us all, such as health, love, or money, but sometimes it can be an affair of great obscurity about which the fortune-teller can know little or nothing. Even in such cases, however, it is said that the following spread provides accurate information, advice and prediction.

The Grand Cross Spread

This spread was strongly approved of by A. E. Waite, who referred to it as 'an ancient Celtic method'. Quite what he meant to imply by this is not clear, as the ancient Celts were unacquainted with the tarot. Perhaps he learned it from his Welsh friend, Arthur Machen, who would, I suppose, have qualified as a Celt. The Grand Cross Spread, whatever its origins, is considered by many tarot specialists as ideally adapted to answering a specific question, often with a wealth of helpful detail.

Choose the significator in the usual way and place it in the centre of the table. Shuffle the remainder of the deck and deal ten cards as follows:

Card 1 is placed on top of the significator. As it is put down, it is customary to say to oneself 'This covers him'.
Card 2 is placed across Card 1 at right angles, saying 'This crosses him'.
Card 3 is placed above the significator, saying 'This crowns him'.
Card 4 is placed below the significator, saying 'This is beneath his feet'.
Card 5 is placed on the left of the significator, saying 'This is behind him'.
Card 6 is placed on the right of the significator with the words 'This is before him'.

(In the above instructions the word 'him' should, of course, be replaced by 'her' when the significator represents a woman or girl.)
Cards 7-10 are placed in a column of four which is placed to the right of

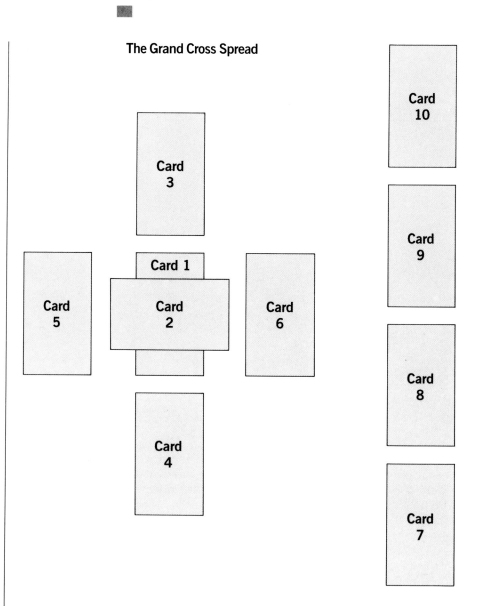

The Grand Cross Spread

the rest of the cards in the spread. This column is built upwards – that is, Card 7 is the bottom card of the column, Card 10 is the top card.

The meanings of the cards in the spread are then interpreted as follows:

Card 1 shows the general factors involved in the matter that is being enquired into.
Card 2 shows the 'crosses' – the obstacles and hindrances – that lie before the enquirer in relation to the matter.
Card 3 represents the enquirer's desires, both conscious and unconscious, in relation to the subject of the enquiry.
Card 4 indicates the background to the matter – to some extent the origins of the situation which concerns the enquirer.

Card 5 is an indicator of influences that are becoming less apparent and important.
Card 6 is a signifier of influences just coming into play.
Card 7 is the enquirer's position at the present time.
Card 8 is the indicator of influences that arise from the nature of the enquirer's personal situation.
Card 9 symbolizes the enquirer's hopes and/or fears in relation to the subject of the enquiry.
Card 10 is the key card; it gives an indication of how a matter will end, how a problem will be resolved.

If Card 10, the key card, is a Court Card, the same considerations apply, and the same course of action should be followed to make an identification, as when Card 5 is a Court Card in the Question Spread (see page 62).

A SAMPLE TAROT QUESTION

Sometimes a fortune-teller wishes to ask a question of the tarot, rather than to 'tell a fortune' in the general sense of the phrase, that is, to give a full analysis of the past and present of an individual and to make some predictions concerning his or her future. There are some quite complex spreads which can be used for answering questions, such as the Question Spread described on page 62, but for simple questions the two- or three-card spread described on page 61 will usually suffice. As an example we will suppose that a three-card spread is being used and that the question asked is 'What will be the future of my love affair with so-and-so?'

We will suppose that the three cards dealt in order to obtain an answer to the question are, from left to right, The Star, Temperance (reversed), and The Sun. These represent, respectively, the past, present and future of the situation about which the question has been asked. In the context of the question which has been asked – 'What will be the future of my love affair with so-and-so?' – The Star signifies the origins of the love affair, Temperance is a pictorial indicator of the emotional situation as it is at the present time, and The Sun gives the answer to the question, for it signifies that future about which the question has been asked.

The divinatory significance of The Star has been described on page 58-59 as:

> Unexpected help, often from someone in a position of power or responsibility. Surprise gifts. . . . A coming run of good luck or an especially fortunate happening.

That of Temperance (reversed) – page 57 – as:

> Disagreements and disputes of all sorts. Bad management. Getting involved in a difficult situation. A problem that proves insoluble.

And that of The Sun – page 59 – as:

> Prosperity and success. Happiness on all levels of being and consciousness. Happy and successful love affairs and marriages. Everything that is encapsulated in the phrase 'the sunny side of life'.

It looks as though the love affair began as the result of the lovers being introduced to each other by 'someone in a position of power or responsibility' – perhaps an older and materially successful mutual acquaintance. It seems likely that the introduction was followed by 'surprise gifts' made by one or both parties, a standard feature of most love affairs, and that the encounter of the two lovers was an 'especially fortunate happening'.

So much for the past. What of the present, signified by a reversed Temperance?

Clearly its appearance as the card indicating the present is a sign that the relationship is going through a difficult patch. Either the enquirer or his or her lover is managing things badly. There seem to be quarrels all the time. The situation is difficult; presumably all sort of problems have arisen. One particular problem will prove insoluble – either the lovers will have to learn to live with it or they must part; nothing that one or other of them could do would make the problem go away. Will the two lovers have to part, or is their love strong enough to cope with the stresses imposed upon them at present?

The answer to this question is provided by the card on the extreme right of the three, The Sun, symbolic of the future. The divinatory meaning of this card is quite explicit. It is obvious that the present extreme difficulties will be overcome, save for the insoluble problem – which the two will probably have learned to live with on the principle 'that which can't be cured must be endured' – and as the result of this affair, the enquirer will achieve both prosperity and emotional happiness.

In practice the accomplished amateur fortune-teller would be able to read such a simple three-card spread almost as soon as he or she had dealt the cards and would sum up the reading in a few simple sentences.

The enquirer would probably be quite happy with this interpretation, but might feel that he or she had so many problems at the moment that it would be desirable to know exactly which of them was insoluble so that attention could be concentrated upon the others. In this case the fortune-teller would mentally ask the nature of the difficulty prior to shuffling the cards and obtain an answer by dealing another three-card spread.

Two of the tarot trumps painted by Miranda Payne in accordance with the pre-1900 'esoteric designs' of MacGregor Mathers. In divinations The Sun is taken as an indicator of great happiness, 'the sunny side of life', while the Star often predicts good luck and surprise gifts.

CRYSTAL GAZING & SCRYING

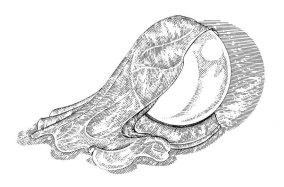

There is a technique used by some occultists of the present day who believe in reincarnation which is termed 'watching the fire of Azrael'. A fire made of cedar and juniper logs, sometimes with the addition of sandalwood chips, is lighted and allowed to burn down until only glowing embers remain. These embers are then stared at until they begin to suggest mental pictures: these, so it is said, are visions of the past lives of those who behold them.

This is a specialized form of scrying – the induction of an inner vision, 'clairvoyance'.

A nineteenth-century portrayal of a dramatically clad professional fortune-teller in consultation with a young client. The latter's expression as she looks into the crystal ball conveys interest mixed with bewilderment.

The cartoonists of the Western world have long made crystal-gazing a standard butt for ribald jokes. It was over eighty years ago that the first drawing was published of a poster inscribed with the words 'Salon for Crystal Gazing and Palmistry', over-printed with the words 'Closed Owing to Unforeseen Circumstances'.

It is not surprising that crystal balls have been a subject of humour, for there is something inherently comic in the sight of someone gazing fixedly into what appears to be no more than a rounded, polished lump of transparent rock.

However, the use in fortune-telling of crystal balls and other objects employed in a very similar way – polished black mirrors and bowls of water, for example – goes back almost to the dawn of human consciousness. It is far older, for example, than the use of tarot cards in divination, or the technique of turning written names into their numerical equivalents in order to find Key Numbers. There is reason to believe that, long before the invention of writing, tribal shamans (the wise men and priest-clairvoyants of primitive societies) used methods of inducing vision and trance which were identical with those employed by crystal-gazing occultists of today.

A real crystal ball – a polished globe of the semi-precious mineral known as rock crystal or clear quartz – is an expensive luxury, particularly if it is flawless, and most of the so-called 'crystal balls' which are commercially available are not made of real crystal but of moulded glass. Even these tend to be surprisingly expensive and anyone who wants to experiment with what is usually termed scrying – entry into 'inner space' by staring fixedly at external objects – would be well advised to begin by using not a crystal ball, glass or otherwise, but items which cost almost nothing.

Some of the latter include a wine glass filled to the brim with clean water; a flat or convex piece of glass, such as that incorporated in most electric torches, painted black; and, simplest of all, either a piece of stiff white pasteboard or a pool of ordinary black ink.

In order to find out whether you are one of the substantial minority of individuals who have an inborn talent for scrying, it is best to know something of the results which, so it is claimed, can be achieved by scryers. More importantly, it is essential that you should appreciate that there is nothing occult or supernatural about the implements used in scrying: even the most expen-

The so-called crystal, in fact highly polished 'cannel coal', in which the scryer employed by John Dee saw prophetic visions of the Spanish Armada of 1588 and the execution of Mary, Queen of Scots.

sive rock crystal ball is no more than a means to an end. That end can either be called 'visionary experience' or, if one prefers to use psychological terminology, 'a voluntary dissociation of consciousness'.

External and Internal
'Dissociation of consciousness' means that the mind is detached from the outer world, from its everyday concerns and the sense impressions – tastes, sounds, shapes, colours, and so on – which pour in upon it from the surrounding environment, so that it turns inwards. In this way, the scryer discovers 'inner space', the riches of the strange states of consciousness of which all men and women are capable, and which, so it is said, allow the scryer's mind (or part of it) to wander freely through time and space.

To describe this dissociation and its effects, real or imaginary, is easy enough. To achieve it is considerably more difficult. The trouble is that when you try to switch off the inputs into the mind (the signals constantly received from the outside world

through sight, hearing and the other senses) even the smallest signals become amplified in the most remarkable way.

For example, you are sitting calmly, eyes shut, in a room you have always looked upon as the quietest in the house. Almost immediately you become conscious of the fact that the 'silent' room is quite extraordinarily noisy. Every now and then a floorboard creaks. Creaks? It makes a noise like an exploding firecracker! As you wait for the next so-called creak, wondering uneasily if your home is subsiding into an ancient and long-abandoned mine-shaft, you suddenly realize that the carriage clock your grandmother left you, a timepiece you always thought notable for its silent operation, is making a noise like a demented death-watch beetle. And so on, and so on. It is as though the mind reacts to a reduction of inputs by perversely exaggerating the nature and importance of those it is still receiving.

The situation is comparable to that of looking carefully into a looking glass before setting out for an important meeting and suddenly noticing that you have a small pimple on your nose. You examine the pimple with care. Surely it is not very noticeable? After a minute or two of peering into the mirror from various angles the thing seems to have grown alarm-

ingly; it has become – as far as your consciousness is concerned – a huge spot, a most unpleasant blemish. If you look in the mirror long enough, your entire consciousness will become dominated by the pimple and, when you leave your home, you will find yourself having to fight off the conviction that passers-by are unable to keep their eyes off it. You decide that the only way to get your mind off the subject is to 'think of something else', but the image of the miserable pimple soon reasserts itself. The most effective technique in these circumstances is to submit your consciousness to boredom – you make it count your footsteps or the cracks in the pavement, for example.

The scryer adopts a similar 'boredom technique' to switch off the signals which flood into consciousness via the senses. He or she bores the mind or, rather, the brain (through which the mind interacts with the world around it) by staring fixedly at whatever external aid is used – crystal ball or pool of black ink, for example – with as blank a mind as possible. The effect of this is to 'inhibit the cerebral cortex'. Part of the brain takes, as it were, a refreshing and well-earned rest, and the mind turns in upon itself to explore within, and perhaps to discern the patterns of the future.

Pictures in the Fire
The mind of the scryer, then, turns away from its immediate surroundings and enters a state in which the scryer experiences, at the very least, interesting and curious day-dreams and sometimes, if the detachment from the outside world is profound, enters strange realms of consciousness in which he or she ventures into another world.

Most of us who have stared into the embers of a glowing fire have, whether we appreciated it or not, engaged in the simplest sort of scrying. We have looked into the hot coals, have become relaxed and dreamy, and have begun to see 'pictures in the fire'. One piece of coal or charcoal, mottled with red and black and surmounted by a veil of grey ash, seems to resemble a human face; another begins to take on the appearance of a boat or a deformed teapot. This is the beginning of a process which, when fully developed, is believed by some to afford glimpses of past and future. It is said that at first these are seen dimly, as 'through a glass, darkly', but can in time assume an almost terrifying reality in which the scryer not only 'sees pictures', but feels that he or she is within the picture. Just how extraordinary such an experience can be is illustrated by a story told by an American journalist, the late W. B. Seabrook, concerning a woman named Nastatia Filipovna, a Russian expatriate living in New York.

Nastatia, who seems to have been convinced that she had psychic powers, and was certainly possessed of either a stronger imagination or a more easily dissociated consciousness than most of us, had for some time been experimenting with scrying, using the classic crystal ball as her external focus. She would stare into the crystal ball until she reached a stage of what was probably self-hypnosis in which she had what were, at the least, intensely vivid dreams. These were uniformly unpleasant. She almost invariably found herself dressed in skins and in some sort of primitive, nomadic camp where she was engaged in skinning and gutting freshly slaughtered game.

Seabrook suggested to her that she might receive a more interesting experience if she used one of the hexagrams of the *I Ching* (see pages 98 to 113) instead of a crystal ball as a means of achieving the mental boredom which can turn the mind inwards.

Nastatia accepted the idea with some enthusiasm. A hexagram was chosen at random by the use of 'sticks' made of tortoiseshell and, in a semidarkened Greenwich Village studio, she carried out the experiment in the presence of Seabrook and two other observers. Interestingly, the hexagram which was generated pertains to ideas associated with the word 'transformation'.

For no less than three hours she concentrated her mind upon the relevant hexagram, strongly imagining it painted upon a door, but with nothing further happening at all. Then – at last – the imagined door swung open and Nastatia felt herself moving through it. As she did so she spoke aloud, reporting her feelings to the observers. She was wearing a thick fur coat which covered her completely; she was first standing, then running, on all fours in thick snow . . . it was so

enjoyable. And then, to the astonishment of Seabrook and his two companions, the beautiful Nastatia suddenly began to 'slaver at the mouth and bay like a wolf'.

Alarmed, one of the observers tried to restore her to a normal state of consciousness by slapping her face. She reacted with snarls and tried to bite her would-be helper . . .

Eventually, with the aid of smelling salts, Nastatia was brought back to normal consciousness, remembering nothing of the experience save its beginning. She had been transformed, psychologically speaking, into a wolf.

Or had she? Perhaps; but Seabrook was a man who was always capable of turning a fairly ordinary account of an interesting experiment into an astounding story. I strongly suspect that his Nastatia account falls into the category of fantastic exaggerations of the truth. The existence of Nastatia and her interest in scrying is well authenticated, but I have little doubt that she either merely 'saw' a wolf in her vision or, if she really felt herself to be a wolf, was simultaneously aware of her own everyday consciousness.

For, without exception, all reliable reports from those whose scrying experiments have reached the stage where they are not just watching what's going on, as though watching a television set, but actually participating in it, aver that the scryer never completely loses touch with everyday consciousness. It is as though he or she were an actor in a play, always fully aware that it was a play and that the audience – everyday consciousness – was sitting on the other side of the footlights.

So, if you want to carry out experiments with scrying, whether with the aid of crystal balls, *I Ching* hexagrams, or anything else, you need have no real fears that you may, feeling that you have been turned into a wild animal, attack your nearest and dearest. Anyone who genuinely believes – as Nastatia may have done – that they have experienced animal transformation as a consequence of scrying would be well advised to seek psychiatric help rather than to consider him or herself a psychic genius.

Flames 'seen' by a scryer in a crystal, a pool of ink, or a glass of water usually have to be interpreted symbolically – perhaps as an indicator of rage, quarrels or burning passion.

Patience and Experiment

The real problem encountered by the novice scryer is not excessive involvement in what is seen, let alone being obsessed by it to the point of delusion, but in seeing anything at all. Even some who have persistently and patiently worked at achieving the state of mind required for successful scrying find that at the end of several months all they have seen with the mind's eye is 'clouds in the crystal', that is, the crystal has seemed to have lost its transparency and turned a milky grey.

If you want to engage in crystal gazing, or any other form of scrying, there are two very important points to bear in mind. The first, even more important in scrying than in other fortune-telling techniques, is that a great deal of patience is required. It is impossible to run before you can walk, and if you expect your first attempt at scrying to produce rich visions containing symbolic indications of your future destiny, you are doomed to disappointment unless you are a natural psychic genius. (These are very rare if, indeed, they exist at all.)

The second thing to remember is that however rich you are, you cannot buy the ability to be a successful scryer. So don't spend large amounts of money on purchasing expensive equipment unless you have first made quite sure by preliminary experiment with, for example, a wine glass filled with water, that you have at least some natural talent which can be developed. The history of scrying is full of well-authenticated instances of would-be seers who have fruitlessly spent small fortunes upon needless 'shew-stones' and other items which they believed would help them to attain psychic powers.

A shew-stone is a much smaller, and even more expensive, version of the crystal ball. It is often made from a cabochon (round-cut) piece of beryl, a stone of which both aquamarines and emeralds are transparent varieties. According to John Aubrey, the seventeenth-century antiquary who wrote the enchanting *Brief Lives* and was friendly with such scryers as William Lilly, the type of beryl best suited to scrying is lightly tinged with red. Not all shew-stones have been made of such rare substances; one of those used by the great Dr John Dee, the sixteenth-century mathematician, astro-

Many scryers 'see' only clouds in the crystal which is being used as the focus of concentration. White clouds are commonly taken as indicators of coming good fortune.

loger and clairvoyant who was consulted by Queen Elizabeth 1, was made of what was called 'cannel coal', which seems to have been an anthracite of almost equal hardness to jet.

A crystal or shew-stone can be given a mounting of some grandeur by any scryer who thinks fit to spend the money. John Melville, who lived in the last century, but whose book *Crystal Gazing* has recently been reprinted and who has a surprisingly large number of admirers at the present time, urged that a crystal or shew-stone should be mounted within a frame of polished ivory on which certain Names of Power should be inscribed in gold lettering. The whole thing should, said Melville, be further mounted upon a glass pedestal and this, in turn, should stand upon a circular table on which more Names of Power were inscribed. The mounted crystal should, during scrying, be illuminated by two wax candles standing in holders engraved with yet more mystic symbols. It was essential, added Melville, that the room in which scrying was to be conducted should contain a fire or an open brazier in which 'perfumes' (that is, different varieties of incense) could be burned as a preliminary to scrying.

If you want to engage in such prac-

tices, there can be no possible objection provided that your bank account will stand the cost and your family don't mind the smell of incense. However, while your scrying room may have an appearance which impresses your friends with your occult knowledge and/or eccentricity, it is unlikely that the results you achieve will be superior to those attainable with a pool of black ink or a glassful of water.

The Practice of Scrying

Ink is messy, so the best 'crystal' with which to begin experimenting is probably a glass of water. Go to a quiet room. The light should be fairly dim and indirect. There is no mystical significance in this romantic gloom – it is simply that if bright sunshine is coming in from the outside world, or the room is lit by spotlights, it will be very difficult to concentrate your attention on something so intrinsically dull as a glassful of water. Provided that you have the required dim lighting, you probably needn't worry about the time of day at which you carry out your experiments. If you want to be thoroughly traditional, however, following the same set of rules as some of the scryers of three or four centuries ago, you should only commence a 'working' at sunrise, at noon, or at sunset – preferably when the sun is in a northern declination and the moon is in the zodiacal sign of either Taurus or Libra. If you want to follow these rules for 'astrological scrying', you should perhaps go the whole hog and drink herbal teas made from the plants supposedly ruled by Libra and Taurus – wormwood, for example. According to Melville, these purify the body of the scryer and increase his or her psychic abilities.

If you don't want to bother with all this, simply ensure that there is not likely to be a great deal of noise and that, as was said above, no bright light is shining into the room.

Gaze fixedly into the depths of the water from above, trying to keep your mind as blank as possible and endeavouring not to let yourself be disturbed by the things which intrude upon your consciousness. As was pointed out earlier, this is not as simple as it sounds, and you will at first find yourself very easily distracted. Thoughts of all sorts will flash into your consciousness which have nothing to do with the matter in hand. If, when you first start trying to scry, you can keep your mind upon the glass of water, and the glass of water alone, for as much as 20 seconds, you have a quite exceptional capacity for concentration, for bringing your mind to 'onepointedness'.

Whether you are good or bad at the beginning, the time that elapses before your mind starts wandering will, if you persist, steadily increase until you can concentrate for several minutes at a stretch with your mind slipping only occasionally into outwardly diverted thought. This sounds a slightly pointless achievement, but remember that the whole object of the exercise is to 'bore' your mind, forcing it to turn in upon itself.

If you have any natural talent for scrying, indications of the inturning will begin to make themselves apparent. These usually take the form of visual illusions – clouds of whiteness seem to drift around the interior of the glass or the water turns, or appears to turn, a mildly opaque yellowish white. Some scryers find that they never get much beyond this first stage and all

that they ever see are clouds – white, black, silver, gold, and the seven colours of the rainbow. Some attach their own meanings to these colours; others use one or other of a number of colour-interpretation conventions. One of the most commonly used of these conventions employs the following interpretations:

White Clouds:
Coming good fortune.

Silver Clouds:
Great good fortune, possibly after difficulties.

Golden Clouds:
Coming happiness and enormous prosperity.

Grey to Black Clouds:
Coming ill fortune; the blacker the clouds, the worse the portents.

> *Some scryers interpret a vision of red clouds as a warning of peril, an indication that great care must be taken. Others associate them with sexual passion.*

Green Clouds:
Coming happiness, particularly in the emotional life.

Blue Clouds:
Promotion, success in career or business, etc.

Yellow Clouds:
There are difficulties ahead.

Orange Clouds:
There are difficulties ahead, particularly emotional ones.

Red Clouds:
Danger! Take great care about everything.

All this is rather vague, and most scryers find that, given time and patience, they begin to see more than coloured clouds, fogs and mists. The scrying vision begins to develop and in the glass the 'mind's eye', sometimes called 'creative visual imagination', will discern pictures. Sometimes these will take the form of images of the scryer and/or people known to him or her. These may represent in a factual

A vision combining gold (as here) and red clouds might be interpreted as an indication that dangers lie ahead but that these will eventually be overcome and great prosperity experienced.

way the nature of some past or future event, or they may be symbolic expressions of the same event. The scryer might see, for example, the image of a friend juggling unsuccessfully with gold coins, spilling them on the ground – perhaps a symbolic indication that the friend in question was in danger of losing money through unwise speculation or gambling.

The Intuitive Glimpse
More commonly, the scryer does not see 'moving visions' of people engaged in actual or symbolic activities. He or she merely has glimpses of objects which briefly impinge upon the inner vision. Perhaps a skull, a blazing sun disc, or a heart, penetrated by an arrow, upon which initials are inscribed.

There are no hard-and-fast rules by which such symbols can be inter-

preted. In such fortune-telling techniques as cartomancy or palmistry there are cook-book techniques which can be applied by rule-of-thumb and which can be used by even the least intuitive person. In scrying, however, you have to use your intuition, interpreting symbols in accordance with your own feelings.

For instance, the flash-vision of a globe might indicate to one scryer 'worldly wisdom' but to another the probability of travel. Similarly, a vast eye could be an indication to one scryer of impending good luck, to another one of spiritual progress – the opening of the interior eye of clairvoyant vision – and to a third a warning to be cautious ('Keep your eyes open, watch out').

The fact that the visions seen by the scryer have to be interpreted intuitively means that crystal-gazing and allied techniques are among the most erratic methods of fortune-telling and attempting to foresee the future. On occasion they can be productive of the most accurate prophecy. Thus, for example, the manuscript diaries and records of Dr John Dee show that,

beyond a doubt, Dee's scryer Edward Kelly reported visions of both the execution of Mary, Queen of Scots and the Spanish Armada's abortive attempt to invade England long before either of these events took place. Equally notable examples of scrying precognitions were recorded by the Society for Psychical Research as the result of a survey undertaken in the 1880s: a Mrs Bickford-Smith had a crystal vision of the death of an old friend, which came about a few days later, and other accurate precognitions were put on record.

On the other hand, scryers can, on the basis of misinterpretation of symbolism and wishful thinking, come up with prophecies, pleasant or unpleasant, which are uniformly incorrect or misleading.

Fortune-telling techniques which call for a large amount of intuitive interpretation on the part of the diviner rely on what are known as 'wild talents'. That is to say, not only are some people possessed of much more innate talent in this respect than others, but those who do possess great talent can be on or off form. A fortune-teller can be on form one day, when even the most unlikely statements or predictions will subsequently prove to be true; while on another day he or she can be outstandingly off form, telling, for example, a lifelong bachelor that he is married with a large family.

The erratic nature of all fortune-telling based on intuitive faculties is so pronounced in the case of scrying that it is probably best to make two rules. Firstly, do not scry for any other person save yourself until you are absolutely certain that you have strong intuitive abilities; and, secondly, however pronounced your talent, scry only on days on which you are confident that you are on form.

Scrying with the aid of a glass or a bowl of water, a crystal, or a similar device for dissociating consciousness is largely uncontrolled – almost anything may appear to the inner vision.

John Dee, the sixteenth-century mathematician and occultist who was consulted by Queen Elizabeth I, employed a professional clairvoyant, Edward Kelly, who predicted the sailing of the Spanish Armada of 1588.

Sometimes this can be productive of worthwhile experiences. Sometimes quite the reverse. I have met an amateur scryer who claimed always to view the same scene, the Victorian Lord Mayor of some industrial city laying the foundation stone of a worthy municipal building. Very interesting the first time, no doubt, but somewhat tedious at the twenty-third repetition.

Tattwas and Symbol-Scrying
A more controlled form of scrying involves the use of symbols, geometric or pictorial, as subjects of the scryer's gaze. These symbols become 'astral doorways' which the scryer opens, as it were, and travels beyond into new dimensions of the consciousness.

The most commonly used symbols are coloured geometrical forms which are usually referred to as 'tattwas', a name of Indian origin. Altogether there are twenty-five tattwas, five of which are simple, being one uniformly coloured geometric shape, and twenty of which are compound, being two-coloured and made up of two geometric shapes. All twenty-five are illus-

trated on page 78. The simple tattwas, those with which it is customary for the novice symbol-scryer to experiment, appear in a row of five at the top of the illustration – a red triangle; a yellow square; a silver crescent, its horns turned upwards; a blue circle; and an indigo ovoid.

These represent the Elements (which in this case means 'psychological factors present in the human mind') of, from left to right, Fire, Earth, Water, Air and the 'fifth element' (the occultists of old called it the *quintessence):* the most subtle aspect of the mind.

If you want to endeavour to symbol-scry, choose one of the five simple tattwas and either paint a copy of it upon a piece of blank paper or cut out its shape from an appropriately coloured piece of paper and stick it on a piece of white, grey or black pasteboard.

Take your chosen tattwa to a room which is quiet and dimly lit, place it on a table, and contemplate it as you would any other material object used as the focus of an experiment in scrying. Endeavour to fill your conscious-

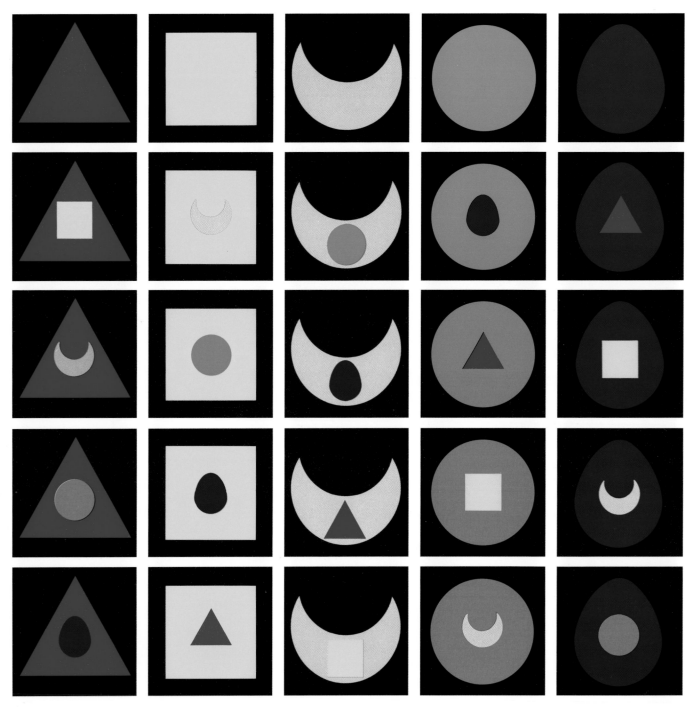

The tattwas – geometric symbols of various aspects of the four 'Elements' of Earth, Air, Fire and Water and the 'quintessence', the 'Akasa', which is considered to be metaphorically beyond or above the elements. These symbols are used as the focus of consciousness by clairvoyants who practise advanced forms of scrying. The tattwas are of Indian origin, and were first introduced into European occultism in the 1880s by Rama Prasad, translator of an obscure Bengali treatise on the tattwas entitled Nature's Finer Forces.

ness with the coloured shape of the chosen tattwa so that when you half- or fully close your eyes you still see it in your mind's eye. When you have reached this stage you may find that you see your tattwa either in its complementary colour or some other colour – the red triangle is imagined, for example, as a green triangle, or the yellow square is imagined indigo.

There is nothing in the least supernatural about such subjective changes in colour – they result from purely physiological and psychological fac-

tors – but their manifestation is a favourable indication, signifying that you have been properly concentrating your vision upon the chosen tattwa and not letting yourself become distracted by your surroundings.

When you reach the stage at which your consciousness is filled by a visual image of the tattwa, try to think of the design as being painted upon a huge door or embroidered upon a vast curtain (either door or curtain should be imagined as completely filling your entire field of vision).

Then comes what is usually the most difficult part. In your imagination, let the door swing open, or the curtain be pulled aside, and 'see' what lies beyond it. Almost invariably you will see either a dramatic landscape or the interior of a room. Most usually the scene is rather vague, flickering in and out of focus in the mind's eye, rather like the picture on the screen of a badly-tuned television. Some scryers, however – those possessing a rare quality termed 'eidetic vision' – see the scene as though it was actually before their eyes. This can, at first, be rather frightening. If so, the important thing for the scryer to remember is that all that he or she is experiencing is a sort of controlled day-dream in which archetypal images and symbols are flooding up into consciousness from the depths of the unconscious mind. (In this connection see the description of *anima mundi* on pages 41 to 42.)

For a time most scryers are content simply to observe what is beyond the door – some of the symbolic imagery that wells up from the inmost depths of their own minds. In time, however, they usually visualize themselves as stepping through the door and exploring what lies beyond. There, in imagination, they encounter other beings and learn much concerning their own natures and destinies. In time they may extend their activities to what is often called 'rising on the planes': they visualize themselves rising above the landscape beyond the astral doorway, and exploring its higher levels.

Tarot and Symbol-Scrying
A step beyond this form of symbol-scrying using tattwas is to substitute the images of the tarot trumps for the simple coloured shapes.

This, in fact, is a very advanced form of symbol-scrying and should not be undertaken lightly. Indeed, some who are highly skilled and practised symbol-scryers assert that it is certainly foolish and possibly dangerous to experiment with it before one has become adept at entering the astral doorways inscribed with the simple and complex geometric symbols reproduced on page 78. The danger, it is said, arises from the extreme complexity and subtlety of the symbols that rush up into consciousness from the realms of vision. Their richness is such that they can be overwhelming to

the inexperienced scryer, cutting him or her off from the realities of the everyday world in which we all have to live for most of the time.

An example of this richness, and the nature of the interior worlds of consciousness which can be reached by symbol-scrying, are the following extracts from an account written almost a century ago by a clairvoyant who went on a voyage of interior exploration in the company of a fellow student. The words enclosed by square brackets are not part of the original account, but are explanatory comments written by me.

The Tarot Trump known as the Empress was taken; placed before the persons and contemplated upon, spiritualized, heightened in colouring, purified in design and idealized.

In vibratory manner pronounced *Daleth*.

[*Daleth*, the fourth letter of the Hebrew alphabet (Hebrew is the 'sacred language' of Western occultism as Sanskrit is that of the yogis of India) is regarded by some students of the mysteries of the tarot as having a special relationship with the trump called the Empress (see page 52). By 'vibratory manner' was meant a particular mode of enunciating words of occult significance which was one of the secrets of the occult order of which both symbol-scryers were initiates.]

Then, in spirit, saw a greenish-blue distant landscape, suggestive of a medieval tapestry. Effort to ascend was then made; rising on the planes; seemed to pass up through clouds and then appeared a pale green landscape [green is the colour of both the planet and the goddess Venus, to both of which the tarot trump the Empress is attributed by some esoteric schools] and in its midst a Gothic Temple of ghostly outlines marked with light . . . Opposite the entrance perceived a cross with three bars and a dove upon it. And beside this were steps leading down into the dark, by a dark passage. Here was met a beautiful green dragon [green, remember, is the colour of Venus] who moved aside, meaning no harm, and the . . . vision passed on. Turning a corner and still passing on

in the dark emerged from the darkness on to a marble terrace brilliantly white, and a garden beyond, with flowers, whose foliage was of a delicate green kind [again the Venusian symbolism] and the leaves seemed to have a white velvety surface beneath. Here there appeared a woman of heroic proportions, clothed in green with a jewelled girdle, a crown of stars on her head, in her hand a sceptre of gold, having at one end a lustrously white, closed lotus flower; in her left hand an orb bearing a cross.

She smiled proudly, and as the human spirit [one of the symbol-scryers] sought her name replied:

'I am the mighty Mother Isis; most powerful in all the world. I am She who fights not but is always victorious. I am that Sleeping Beauty whom men have sought for all time; and the paths which lead to my castle are beset with dangers and illusions . . . I am lifted up on high and draw men unto me, I am the world's desire, but few there be who find me. When my secret is told, it is the secret of the Holy Grail.'

This odd statement did not conclude this fantasy adventure of the mind. The 'astral voyagers' were taken in imagination to the turrets of a lofty castle where the Empress, whom the seers identified with 'the Lady Venus', gave them further instructions.

It is perhaps worth adding that one of the two female symbol-scryers who recorded this curious voyage into the world of myth and symbol was Florence Farr, a leading avant-garde actress of her time who was on very close terms with both the playwright Bernard Shaw and the poet W. B. Yeats.

Finally, it is worth remembering that throughout their adventure the consciousness of both women was, in a sense, dual. They were always conscious that their bodies were sitting in a London room, although their minds were engaged in visionary experiences involving a castle, a dragon and the Lady Venus. No well-balanced person using symbol-scrying has ever confused physical and psychological realities, believing that they have literally become a wolf (as did the psychotic Nastatia Filipovna) or encountered a dragon.

CHAPTER
5

PALMISTRY

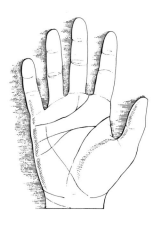

Palmistry, more properly called chiromancy, has been practised for thousands of years: ancient Indian and Chinese hand-reading techniques, still much in use in the present day, were already highly developed some three thousand years ago.

It was the most popular method of fortune-telling employed in the later Middle Ages, and at least some people saw a scriptural warrant for its use in an Old Testament text which asserts that God 'sealeth up the hand of every man; that all men may know his work'.

Modern palmists make no such claims – but they are able to give accurate delineations of character and indicate future probabilities.

Chinese palmistry, already practised some 3,000 years ago, still flourishes in Macao, with its curious blend of peoples and its unique culture: a strange blend of Portuguese Catholicism with elements derived from traditional Chinese Taoism.

Sir Richard Burton, who died almost a century ago, was a most untypical Victorian. He translated into English such classics of oriental eroticism as *The Perfumed Garden*; he journeyed to Mecca disguised as an Indian pilgrim; he visited Brigham Young, the Mormon leader, in Salt Lake City; and he was a total sceptic as far as religion was concerned. Nevertheless his wife was a pious Catholic who had married her unbelieving husband because, so she said, she had been destined to do so: long before her marriage a gipsy palmist had told her that she was fated to marry a man named Burton.

The gipsy's prophecy must have been based on something other than the rules of the ancient art of palmistry, for no palmist, past or present, has ever claimed that the study of the shape of an enquirer's hand and the form of the lines upon its palm can give an indication of the name of a future partner.

Nevertheless almost equally surprising assertions are made by many chiromancers (palmists). Thus, for example, it is argued that the lines on the left hand indicate the genetic inheritance of an individual, the qualities which he or she was naturally endowed with at birth; while those on the right hand show what that indivi-

dual has made, and will make in times to come, of that inheritance. More is said of this in relation to the lines upon the palm on page 89; but before concerning ourselves with lines, crosses and other marks upon the wrists, palms and fingers, let us see what is traditionally believed by professional palmists about the significance of the overall shape of the hand.

THE SHAPE OF THE HAND

Palmists (or chiromancers) look upon the shape of the hand as being just as important as the lines upon it. There are several methods of classifying hand shapes, some extremely simple, some of great complexity. The method used by many present-day palmists divides hands into seven categories, and is a development of a system derived from traditional sources by Casimir D'Arpetigny, a French chiromancer of the last century.

The seven hand shapes developed from D'Arpetigny's system are:

1. The Elementary Hand
This, so it is said, is an indication of an animal nature. It is clumsy, short-fingered to near deformity, and very large palmed – in other words, a

A romanticized eighteenth-century portrayal of a gipsy fortune-teller reading a client's palm. Gipsies seem to have acquired their palmistry from Arab sources.

branches; the hand has pronounced knuckles. As its name suggests, this type of hand is thought to indicate an intellectual cast of mind in its owners, who are 'quiet in their lives and moderate in their pleasures' according to a palmist of the last century – who himself happened to have such a hand.

5. The Conic Hand
This vaguely cone-shaped hand can be sub-divided to indicate three personality types. The first of these, supple, with a thumb which is small in relation to the fingers, is sometimes called 'the artistic hand,' a name which is self-explanatory. The second is large, the palm firm and fleshy, and is believed to indicate a sensual temperament. The third sub-division is like the 'artistic hand', but the hand is usually some-

hand which is disproportioned. People with hands like this are alleged to be coarse-minded, caring for nothing but the satisfaction of their brutal appetites, unintelligent and devoid of any sort of sensitivity of thought and feeling.

2. The Square Hand
Almost as broad as it is long, this 'practical hand' (its appearance is somewhat spade-like) indicates an unimaginative individual with a logical mind and a capacity for bringing order out of chaos.

3. The Spatulative Hand
This category has two sub-divisions: the 'firm' and the 'flabby' spatulative hand. In both cases the shape of the hand displays a certain crookedness, and the fingers are blunt, like a spatula as used by cooks and pharmacists. The firm spatulative hand is taken as an indicator of an enthusiastic and energetic personality. The flabby spatulative hand indicates a personality which is also energetic, but is quite incapable of directing energy to a single aim; in other words, a restless nature which finds it difficult to concentrate.

4. The Philosophical Hand
This is 'knotty', vaguely suggestive of a tree trunk sprouting gnarled

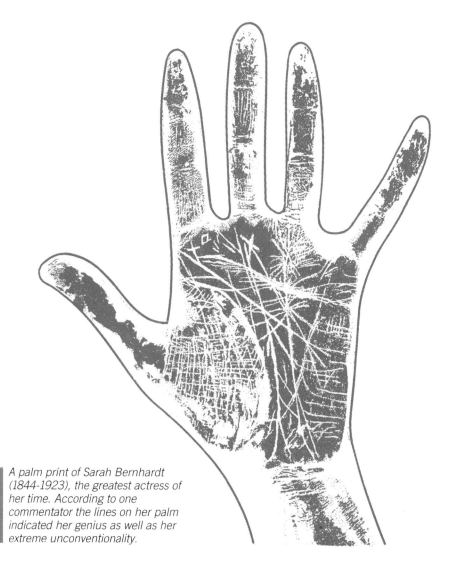

A palm print of Sarah Bernhardt (1844-1923), the greatest actress of her time. According to one commentator the lines on her palm indicated her genius as well as her extreme unconventionality.

what broader and always with the thumb proportionate to the size of the fingers. Such a hand indicates a strongly ambitious nature and a desire for wealth and fame.

6. The Psychic Hand

Long, slim and usually with a slightly crooked little finger, this hand indicates a dreamy and idealistic nature. In some people, so it has been claimed, this type of hand can indicate psychic abilities and/or a tendency to neurosis.

7. The Mixed Hand

This, as its name suggests, combines elements of two or more of types 2 to 6. Its owners will have personality characteristics which are mixed in the same way. For example, a hand combining some of the characteristics of both the psychic hand and the philosophical hand might indicate that its owner was a thoughtful psychic – or a neurotic who spent a great deal of time analysing and trying to understand his/her neurosis.

A more ancient system of classification, but one which is popular among present-day palmists, is the Elemental Classification, which divides hands into four types corresponding to Earth, Air, Fire and Water.

1. The Earth Hand

This hand is short, squarish, spade-like, strong, with lines upon the palm that are very powerfully and deeply marked, though sometimes few in number. It is thought of as a 'practical hand' and its bearers possess characteristics traditionally associated with masculinity: forthrightness, adventurousness, courage, a desire to dominate, and so on. It can sometimes, so it is said, be an indicator of an 'inner rage', usually concealed by a phlegmatic exterior, but sometimes breaking out in a rather violent way.

2. The Air Hand

This hand is strongly built with a squarish palm, on which the lines are usually deeply etched, and long fingers of the sort sometimes referred to as 'artistic'. People with this sort of hand are believed to have many of the qualities which astrologers associate with the planet Mercury. That is, they are quick-witted, good at communicating with

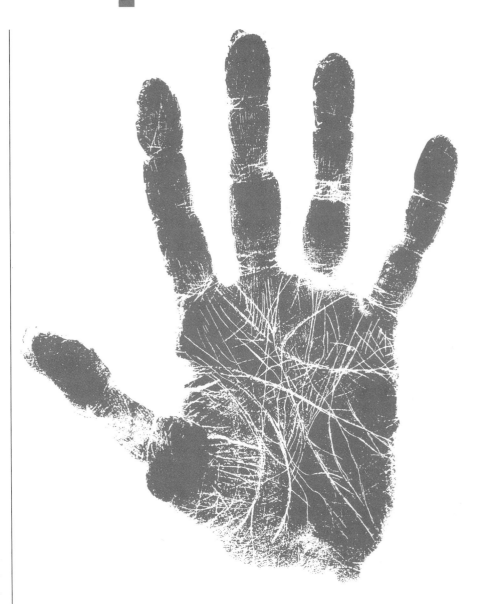

The strongly-etched palm print of William Gladstone (1809-1898), the nineteenth-century British Prime Minister, who annoyed Queen Victoria by – so she complained – addressing her 'as though she were a public meeting'. It has been said that almost every aspect of Gladstone's complicated psychology, from his religious devoutness to the desire to rescue 'fallen women', was clearly indicated by the lines upon his hand.

others, act on the basis of thought rather than feeling and are sometimes a little devious.

3. The Fire Hand

This hand is characterized by short fingers and a long oblong palm with less prominent lines than on the Earth and Air hands. It is sometimes referred to as either 'the intuitive hand', which sounds rather pleasant, or 'the impulsive hand'. It is the latter term which provides the best description of the characteristics associated with this type of hand: a tendency to act without thinking of the consequences, to be restless and changeable, and to fall victim to irrational likes and dislikes. It is, like the Earth hand, believed to be a masculine hand and people who have it are supposed to display, whatever their sex, some of the characteristics traditionally associated with masculinity – an outgoing, extrovert temperament, for example.

4. The Water Hand

This hand is slim and long in both the fingers and the palm, which usually displays a mesh of very fine lines. Those who have this hand are believed to have some of the characteristics traditionally supposed female – a tendency to be moody and introspective being the most notable. It is said that some of those whose hands are of a Water type reflect their surroundings in much the same way that a calm pool reflects the vegetation that surrounds it. Others have psychological characteristics more analogous to a running stream which is sometimes shallow, sometimes deep, and is never quite the same from one day to another.

FINGERS AND PLANETS

The four fingers of the hand and their 'mounts' (the fleshy pads where they join the palm) are attributed to four of the planets. The little finger and its mount are attributed to Mercury; the ring finger and its mount to the Sun; the middle finger and its mount to Saturn; and the index finger and its mount to Jupiter.

The little finger and its mount (the finger and **Mount of Mercury**) are seen as having a particular connection with the individual's capacity to communicate with others. A strong little finger and a prominent Mount of Mercury indicate a good capacity for communication; if these are weak, the opposite applies. A well-developed Mount of Mercury is also considered to reinforce the other features of the hand, 'good with good and evil with evil'. In other words, a prominent Mount of Mercury strengthens both the positive and the negative significance of all the other features of the hand.

The ring finger and its mount (the finger and **Mount of the Sun**) relate to a person's emotional life. A strong, long and well-developed ring finger indicates emotional stability and strength; a weak ring finger has the opposite significance. A prominent Mount of the Sun is a sign of a strong interest in music, the arts, poetry, and so on. A flattened Mount of the Sun is an indication that aesthetic feelings play no great part in the inner life of the person concerned. An excessively prominent mount of the Sun has sometimes been thought to indicate an excessive love of pleasure.

A well-developed middle finger and **Mount of Saturn** are seen as characterizing a prudent and practical personality with a strong sense of order and a capacity for hard and careful work. If finger and mount are weak, the opposite is indicated. An excessively long middle finger, and/or an overdeveloped Mount of Saturn, are looked upon as signs of a temperament that is excessively concerned with practical matters and is inclined to gloom and depression.

A strongly developed index finger and **Mount of Jupiter** are associated with a drive for success and riches. The opposite is an indication of a lack of ambition. If the Mount of Jupiter is exceptionally prominent on a hand, its owner is likely to be overambitious and ruthless in dealings with others.

The large, fleshy pad on the palm at the base of the thumb is known as the **Mount of Venus.** If well-developed, it shows a warm, sympathetic and loving nature which attaches considerable importance to the sexual and emotional aspects of life. It also goes

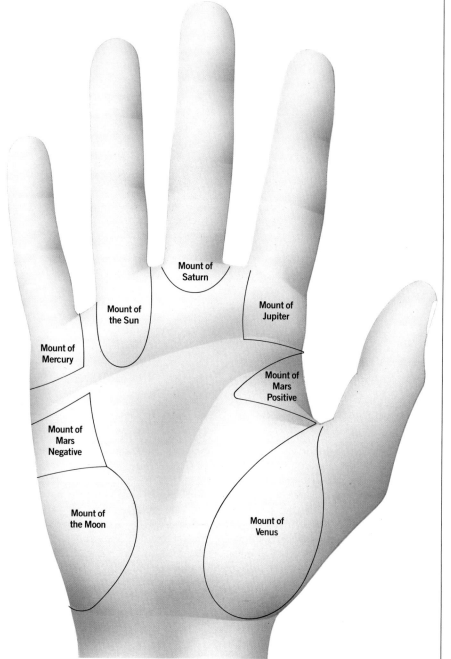

Mount of Saturn

Mount of the Sun

Mount of Jupiter

Mount of Mercury

Mount of Mars Positive

Mount of Mars Negative

Mount of the Moon

Mount of Venus

The fleshy pads known as the 'Mounts' of the Sun, Moon and planets. It is noteworthy that Mars has two quite distinct Mounts, the Mount of Mars Positive and Negative.

with a love of physical pleasures. Overdeveloped, it indicates an excessive love of luxury and a somewhat obsessive concern with the physical aspects of sexuality. If the Mount of Venus is flattened and underdeveloped, its owner is likely to be of a cold and ascetic temperament.

There are several other mounts around the palm. Most of these can be disregarded by all but the most experienced palmist, but the Mounts of the Moon and Mars are believed to be of considerable importance. The **Mount of the Moon** is the fleshy pad which is found near the wrist and below the little finger, i.e. on exactly the opposite side of the palm to the Mount of Venus. A well-developed Mount of the Moon signifies an imaginative and romantic mind with a liking for fantasy. If the Mount is overdeveloped, this indicates that the owner's imagination is dominant – he or she may be unrealistic and unable to cope with real life. An underdeveloped Mount of the Moon would belong to a dull and excessively practical person.

The **Mount of Mars** is really two mounts. The first, the Mount of Mars Positive, is immediately above the Mount of Venus, i.e. it is the small fleshy pad immediately above the fork between thumb and hand. The second, the Mount of Mars Negative, is on the opposite side of the hand, immediately above the Mount of the Moon. Strongly developed, these Martian Mounts show a quarrelsome and aggressive temperament. Underdeveloped or absent, they indicate a timid and withdrawn nature.

THE LINES ON THE HAND

Almost any sort of line can be found on the human hand, but those either invariably or commonly found can be divided into three groups:
A. The three Key Lines
B. The four Major Lines
C. The five Minor Lines

THE KEY LINES
The three Key Lines, which are found on every human hand (with one exception, described below), are:

1. **The Head Line,** which crosses, more or less diagonally but

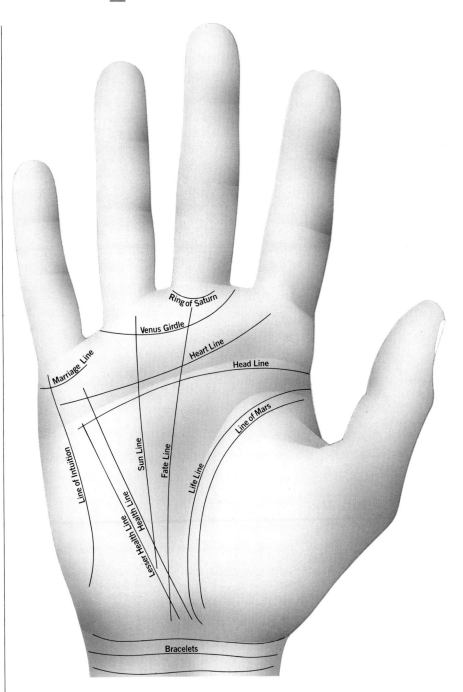

usually with some slight curvature, the centre of the palm.
2. **The Heart Line,** which is roughly parallel to the Head Line but nearer the fingers.
3. **The Life Line** which surrounds and outlines the Mount of Venus, the fleshy pad at the base of the thumb, and the Mount of Mars Positive.

As was said before, these three Key Lines are found in every human hand with one exception. On occasion, the Head and Heart Lines are so close together that it is difficult to be sure

The lines of the human palm. It is most unusual for all of these lines to be found on any individual palm; some of them (e.g. the Ring of Saturn) are very rarely present.

which is which; in a minority of hands these two lines actually blend into one and there is a single Heart/Head Line. When this happens, the palmist has to be tactful in the way he or she explains the situation to the person whose palm is being read, as its significance is mixed. It can imply a most impressive capacity for 'drive', for moving forward remorselessly towards the desired goals in life – mind and emotions were harnessed together in the service of personal ambition. Alternatively, it can indicate a one-sided and unbalanced personality: an individual who so concentrates on his/her ambitions that, psychologically speaking, he or she 'wears blinkers'; everything and everybody are sacrificed to a ruthless pursuit of one desired aim. If the single Heart/Head Line is seen in only one hand (see page 89 for the significance of the right and left hands), this single-mindedness will be mitigated to a greater or lesser extent.

The fortune-telling significances of the three Key Lines are as follows:

The Head Line

If the beginning of the Head Line coincides with the beginning of the Life Line, and if both lines originate at the top of the Mount of Venus, roughly half way between the thumb and the index finger, the person concerned has a shrewdly practical mind, and his/her physical health and vitality will be strongly connected with his/her mind. Such a person will feel physically ill if he/she is worried by emotional or financial problems and bursting with vitality if the mind is untroubled by anxiety. The characteristic shrewdness can dominate; those whose hands display this configuration must guard against letting practical considerations always outweigh emotional ones. In certain rare cases, the Head Line originates even lower on the hand, within the Mount of Venus itself, in which case the individual concerned has a tendency to let his/her emotions outweigh more rational considerations.

If the Head Line originates from within the area above the base of the thumb, the Mount of Mars Positive, a worrying, obsessive and rather quarrelsome temperament is likely.

If the Head Line originates in the Mount of Jupiter (the pad at the base of the index finger), an ambitious, energetic personality is indicated. Such a person is likely to be extremely successful in life.

When the Head Line is hardly curved at all, the individual concerned is likely to be shrewd, rather money-conscious and a little unimaginative.

When it begins straight but then curves downwards in the direction of the Mount of the Moon, a well-balanced mind, combining practicality and imagination, is indicated.

When it curves downwards very strongly throughout its entire length, an extremely imaginative and rather unorthodox personality is indicated. This is particularly so if the line extends down into the Mount of the Moon – this sort of Head Line is often associated with poetry and the arts.

The Head Line sometimes sends out a branch, or branches, to one of the mounts:

a) A branch to the Mount of the Moon has a similar, but lesser

A woodcut from an early edition of Chyromantie ac Physionomie Anastasis *by Bartolommeo della Rocca ('Cocles') (1467-1504), an Italian barber turned fortune-teller.*

significance to the Head Line itself extending into that mount.

b) A branch towards the Mount of the Sun indicates an ambitious and success-orientated mind.

c) A branch towards the Mount of Jupiter has a similar significance, but one in which power, rather than fame, is the goal.

d) A branch towards the Mount of Mercury indicates a powerful mind with a great talent for communication – writing, speaking, performing, etc.

e) A branch towards the Mount of Saturn shows a mind which is

intensely practical, but is interested in religious and philosophical matters.

In certain rare circumstances the Head Line is made up of two lines, running side by side and very close together. A mind of formidable powers, capable of exerting itself in a variety of ways, is indicated by this.

The Heart Line

This should be read in conjunction with the Head Line in order that the balance between emotions and intellect can be clearly discerned.

The line usually originates from either:

a) On, or very near, the Mount of Jupiter.

b) Between the Mounts of Jupiter and Saturn.

c) On, or very near, the Mount of Saturn.

The first formation indicates a person who takes a very idealistic view of love and marriage – he or she tends to idolize the loved one, seeing no faults in his/her partner. If the idol turns out to have feet of clay, the lover feels extremely disillusioned and bitter.

The second formation is associated with a balanced attitude towards the emotions. The individual concerned will display strong emotions, but will always keep practical considerations in mind.

The last formation tends to go with a strongly sensual temperament in which love and sexuality almost always go together. The physical passions are of major importance and Platonic love is an almost meaningless concept.

The Heart Line sometimes originates from the Head and/or the Life Line. A rather cold and unemotional outlook is the usual interpretation of this. A very faintly delineated, or very short, Heart Line is of similar significance. The emotions of the person concerned are far too tightly reined for his or her own good.

An important point in considering the significance of the Heart Line is the extent of its curvature. The more curved, the stronger the need for affection, to love and be loved. A straight line is associated with a cold and unloving personality.

The Life Line

The length of this line does *not* correlate with the probable length of life. It does, however, indicate the general physical vitality of the individual – the longer the line, the greater the vitality. Breaks in the line were at one time taken by palmists as indications of life-threatening injury or disease. In the present day they are more commonly seen as correlating with abrupt changes in career or life-style.

The Life Line usually originates from one of three points:

a) Coinciding with the beginning of the Head Line (the significance of this has already been outlined opposite).

b) On the Mount of Jupiter, in which case the life of the person concerned is dominated by ambition and a desire for success.

c) Above the Head Line but below the Mount of Jupiter. Here the individual concerned is likely to live life in a way which will require physical vitality.

THE MAJOR LINES

The four Major Lines are lines which are usually, but not invariably, found on palms. The absence of a line on your palm or palms may have positive connotations, as described below.

1. **The Fate Line,** running up roughly the centre of the palm from near the wrist to the Head Line and sometimes beyond, to the Mount of Saturn.
2. **The Health Line,** running up from roughly the centre of the wrist towards the Mount of Mercury.
3. **The Sun Line,** running up the palm from the little finger side of the Fate Line towards the Mount of the Sun.
4. **The Venus Girdle,** a crescent-shaped line, nearer the fingers than the Heart Line, and usually running from between the index and second fingers to between the ring finger and the little finger.

The Fate Line

This is sometimes found doubled: if so, the individual concerned will experience good fortune and success in more than one sphere of activity.

There are five points from which the Fate Line usually originates. These are:

a) From the Life Line. This is an indication of a highly successful career resulting from hard work and personal merit. Success, however, will probably not be achieved until the second half of life.

b) From the wrists. A sign of material good fortune and a successful and enjoyable career. Luck and success in work will be particularly notable if the line extends to, or fairly near, the Mount of Saturn.

c) From the Mount of the Moon. An indication that the favour of others will be largely responsible for any career success. Any person with this formation will do best in a career in which he/she has a lot of contact with the general public.

d, e) From the lines of the Head or Heart. This suggests that success, if it comes at all, may be at a fairly late stage in one's career.

The point at which the Fate Line ends is as significant as where it begins. Normally, as was said above, the line extends towards – or even on – the Mount of Saturn. If it ends on, or in the vicinity of, the Mount of Jupiter, it indicates a strongly ambitious personality – a man or woman who will achieve considerable success, probably quite early in life. If it ends similarly, but in relation to the Mount of the Sun rather than that of Jupiter, a successful but rather showy career is indicated; such a career reaches its peak (which may be maintained for a very long time) in middle life. When the Fate Line ends on or near the Mount of Mercury, success is most like to be achieved in a career involving books, communications, science or (rather oddly) deceit.

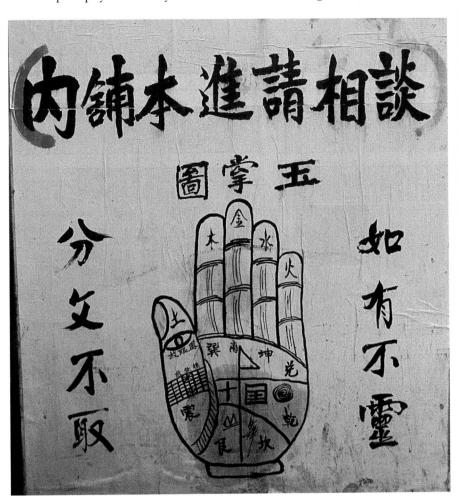

A fortune-telling diagram of the palm from Hong Kong, where (as in Taiwan) Chinese palmistry survived, despite its suppression in the People's Republic.

The Health Line

This line, which the palmists of the Middle Ages termed the 'the hepatic line' (they believed it had a connection with the liver), is, as has already been stated, quite often completely absent from one or both palms. This is associated not with unhealthiness but with an extremely tough and resilient physical constitution. If the Health Line is present in one hand only, the individual concerned should take care of his/her health. If it is present in both hands, care should be taken to follow a healthy way of life. This is particularly the case if the lines are strong, long and deeply etched upon the palm.

The Sun Line

This can originate from:

a) The centre of the palm – an area referred to by the palmists of old as 'the plain of Mars'. This configuration is regarded as a sure sign that the person concerned will eventually achieve the recognition that he/she deserves, although probably not until the second half of the individual's life.

b) The Life Line. This indicates an artistic and slightly showy personality.

Another woodcut from the treatise by Cocles (see illustration on page 86), who successfully foretold 43 violent deaths – including his own murder.

c) The Mount of the Moon. This formation is associated with a person who will achieve success in life largely as a consequence of the help he or she receives from others.

d) The Head Line. Such a formation is associated with a personality with strong artistic interests controlled and held in check by a rational and common-sense attitude.

e) The Fate Line. This is an indicator that success will be achieved in a field connected with the arts – but probably not until a fairly late stage in life.

f) The Heart Line. This indicates a strong interest in the arts, but unfortunately little likelihood of success in a career associated with them.

The Venus Girdle

The palmists of three centuries ago believed that the mere presence of this line upon the palm was a sure sign of a sensual and somewhat lascivious temperament. Most present-day palmists believe that this is only the case if the palm is exceptionally fleshy and the line is very strongly marked. The usual interpretation of the presence of the Venus Girdle upon a palm is that it denotes an intellectual, sensitive and rather moody temperament.

THE MINOR LINES

These are, firstly, the **Line of Mars** – a curved line upon that part of the Mount of Mars immediately above the Mount of Venus. It lies within, and roughly parallel to, the Life Line and has sometimes been called 'the Inner Life Line'. Its presence is very favourable: it indicates an immense constitutional vitality. On the negative side, it does sometimes indicate a truculent, quarrelsome and rather overbearing personality.

The second of the minor lines is that of **Intuition** – a curved line around the Mount of the Moon to beneath the Mount of Mercury, i.e. from the fleshy pad near the wrist, on the little finger side of the palm, to the fleshy pad at the base of the little finger. Its presence, as its name implies, shows an intuitive personality which is strongly receptive to emotional atmospheres.

The **Marriage Line** usually runs or curves horizontally beneath the Mount of Mercury, the pad at the base of the little finger, towards the area beneath the Mount of the Sun. This line is concerned with all close relationships with other people, not just with marriage.

The Marriage Line is not taken too seriously by most present-day palmists. Traditionally, however, it was believed that when this line ran alongside the Heart Line, without actually joining it, a very happy and long-lasting marriage or other permanent relationship was indicated.

The **Lesser Health Line,** which the palmists of old called the 'Via Lasciva', is found in only a minority of hands. When it is present it runs parallel to and outside the Health Line. It indicates a strong personality of forceful – sometimes violent and even uncontrollable – passions.

The **Bracelets** are, strictly speaking, not lines on the hand at all. They are found on the front of the wrists, are usually one, two or three in number, and look rather like strands of wool which are being unravelled. When strongly and depply marked, the Bracelets indicate a very powerful and strong constitution – a body capable of coping with a lot of stress, worry and physical hardship. According to chiromantic tradition, if the Life Line is strongly marked, and so long that it, or a branch from it, reaches the bracelet nearest the wrist, this is as infallible a sign of a long, healthy, happy and successful life as it is possible to have.

A marking so rarely found on the hand that it is hardly even considered a minor line is the **Ring of Saturn**, a half circle outlining the Mount of Saturn. Some present-day palmists attach no significance at all to the Ring of Saturn. Others see it as being associated with a tendency to be unwilling or unable to 'see things through', to have the patience and energy to stick at a problem or an enterprise until it is solved or brought to a satisfactory conclusion. A minority of palmists have interpreted the presence of the Ring of Saturn on both hands (if it is present at all it is usually apparent on only one hand) as an indicator of a mystical temperament inclined to occult studies and possessed of often extraordinary psychic abilities.

The Flemish painter David Teniers (1610-1690) and his wife consulting a gipsy palmist. Unlike Cocles, who irritated his clients by predicting doom, gipsies have usually, if dishonestly, foretold nothing but good.

Left and Right Hands

The three Key Lines, four Major Lines, five Minor Lines, plus the Ring of Saturn are very seldom all present in a hand. On the rare occasions when they are together, it is unusual to find them also present in the other hand of the person in question. This brings us to the subject of the significance of the right and left hands.

There is an old saying, popular for two centuries or more among palmists, that: 'We are born with the lines on our left hand; we make those on our right by the way in which we live our lives.' In a strictly literal sense, this is nonsense. We are all born with lines on both our hands, and throughout the entire course of our lives some changes can be noted in both the right and left hands of each and every person. (Unlike fingerprints, the patterns on the hand are subject to slow changes as the years roll by.)

Nevertheless, most present-day palmists assert that there is an element of truth in the old saying. The left hand, so it is said, indicates the character we are born with, the personality traits which naturally belong to us as the result of genetic inheritance; the changes which take place in that hand indicate how our own efforts and struggles have modified the likely effects of that inheritance. Thus, for example, someone born with a rather feeble physical constitution who has made great efforts to live a healthy life might find that his/her left-hand Life Line slowly deepened, strengthened and lengthened to the point at which it stretched right back to the lowest of the Bracelets – a formation associated with a long and healthy life.

The right hand is taken as an indicator of what we have done and what we will do with our 'natural characters', our genetic inheritances.

It is worth adding that a lot of palmists believe that in left-handed people these indications are reversed – the right hand indicates the natural character of a left-handed person, the left what has been achieved, and what will be made of it.

Telling Your Fortune

Perhaps the greatest problem encountered by the palmist (amateur or professional) is sorting out the multiplicity of fortune-telling indications which are present in even a fairly characterless palm with only a few lines. The difficulty arises from the fact that in any hand there are almost always some contradictory indications. Thus, for example, a strongly developed Mount of Jupiter, suggesting that the person concerned will want to make an impression on the world by being in the public eye, will be contradicted by the appearance in the same palm of an overdeveloped Mount of Saturn, usually associated with a withdrawn disposition.

This, in fact, is a problem which arises in almost any form of fortune-telling that is of any complexity. The fortune-teller has to use his or her intuition in order either to reconcile the contradictions or to decide which indicator is of greater importance and which can be largely disregarded in a particular context.

In the hypothetical case described above (the contradiction between the indications given by the Mounts of Jupiter and Saturn) the palmist might come to the conclusion that the person concerned was subject to changes of mood, alternating between periods of extreme jollity and extroversion and periods of gloom and despondency in which life seemed hardly worth living. On the other hand, he or she might decide that the Mount of Saturn was so overdeveloped that the individual in question was basically extremely depressive, but that the depression never reached a pathological level, amounting to mental illness, because of the jovial (in its literal meaning) element in the temperament indicated by the development of the Mount of Jupiter.

The palmist's use of his or her intuition becomes easier as he or she becomes more experienced. In time, the palmist is able, almost without conscious thought, to decide which indicators must be taken with great seriousness, which must be considered as only modifying these, and which can be virtually disregarded.

CHAPTER

6

CASTING THE RUNES

There is still a popular belief that the Vikings were little more than a set of Dark Age thugs – brainless blond beasts who spent their time in pillage, rape, murder and drunken roistering.

They were, it is true, indomitable warriors. But they were also a great trading and colonizing people, among the principal founders of modern Russia, the explorers of North America half-a-millennium before Christopher Columbus was born, and the guardians of a rich artistic culture.

They, and the other Germanic peoples, divined the future by the symbols of the runic alphabet.

Many people have either read *The Casting of the Runes*, M. R. James's classic tale of the supernatural, or seen the story's filmed adaptation, *Night of the Demon*, which has frequently been shown on late-night television.

James's story tells of the attempt made by a sinister black magician to murder a scholar, who had aroused his wrath, by 'casting the runes'. In order to do this, the black magician placed in his enemy's possession a slip of paper inscribed with mystic Nordic symbols, intending that these would attract a demon to drive his scholar victim to madness and death.

The process of 'casting the runes' with murderous intention seems to have been born of James's imagination, but runes themselves are real enough and are frequently cast today for fortune-telling purposes.

There is nothing particularly mysterious or occult about runes as such. They are merely the letter symbols of an ancient alphabet that originated among the Nordic peoples of Europe, probably two or three centuries before the beginning of the Christian era.

From the earliest times, however, the use of the letters of the runic alphabet was associated with mysterious secret techniques connected with magic and fortune-telling. Indeed, the word 'rune' comes from an old root-word meaning 'hidden' and 'mysterious', and the modern German verb *raunen*, to whisper, is derived from the same source.

Runes were used to carve cursing inscriptions, designed to defeat the wiles of tomb-robbers, upon stones erected in memory of the honoured dead whose bones lay beneath. Thus, part of the inscription upon one Swedish stone reads, '. . . I hid here magic runes undisturbed by evil witchcraft. He who destroys this monument shall die in misery by magic art.' Runes were even credited with the ability, when used by one gifted with occult powers, of restoring the dead to life. The *Havanal*, an old Norse poem, has verses which translate:

A twelfth magic I know,
When I see on high
A corpse swinging from a rope,
Then I cut and paint runes,
So that the man walks and speaks
  with me.

Runes were also used to predict the future. In his *Germania*, the Roman historian Tacitus told how the priests of ancient Germany would carry out this process. A branch was torn from a fruit-bearing tree and sliced into a number of strips. On each of these the form of one of the runes was painted, and then the whole lot was thrown into a white cloth. The fortune-teller, a priest of Wotan (Odin), would pick these up three at a time and, from the particular combination of the three runes, would foretell the future.

So strong were the associations between the letters of the runic alphabet and pagan magical and divinatory techniques that long after the conversion of northern Europe to Christianity, runes were regarded with superstitious awe by the general population. As late as the seventeenth century people were condemned to death in Iceland for the mere possession of objects on which runes were carved or papers upon which they were written.

Carved runic inscriptions have survived over a very large area of Europe. They have been found in places as widely separated as Ireland and Northern Sweden, Iceland and the Ukraine. It is not surprising that inscriptions from different places, carved at different times, show variations in both the physical shapes of runic letters and the actual number of them. One version of the runic alphabet contained only 16 letters; that used to write some Old English inscriptions contained no less than 31.

The form of the runic alphabet used by most present-day diviners who cast the runes in order to predict the future has 24 letters (see pages 92-93). Each letter has not only a name, but that name has a meaning of its own. For example, the eighth letter of the alphabet has the name WUNNA, which not only refers the letter to the Nordic god Wotan, but has a meaning roughly equivalent to the English words 'ecstatic happiness'. There are many methods of using these runes (or a greater or lesser number of runic symbols) for fortune-telling. Most of them seem to be reasonably suitable for that purpose, and some of them outstandingly so – the rune symbolism seems to speak to the diviner's mind on a very deep level. It has to be admitted, however, that none of these methods is entirely traditional. We know that the ancient Germanic and Nordic peoples used runes for divinatory purposes, but no scholar is quite sure of exactly how the runes were

cast or what meaning was given to them, either singly or in combination with one another.

What has happened, in fact, is that some present-day occultists have cast the runes by methods they claim to have derived from an ancient secret tradition of which they are the sole heirs; by their very nature such claims are unproved and unprovable. Other modern rune casters have stated, with the utmost honesty, that they have a) given the rune symbols divinatory meanings which are ultimately derived from the names of the symbols and which, more importantly, work very well in practice, and b) devised methods of casting the runes which

A Swedish monolith dating from late pagan times (circa 1000 A.D.), carved with well-preserved runes which survived attempts at mutilation.

are, while not totally traditional, extremely effective.

The method given in this book for runic fortune-telling is one of the latter. It is not claimed that this method is derived from ancient and secret pagan traditions. It is no more than a simplified version of a technique devised by modern esotericists that has proved itself effective in giving meaningful and useful guidance to those who wish to consult the runes.

Runecards

The first step in using this method is to make runecards. These are simply 24 one-inch squares of light card, on one side of each is inscribed in ink the form and name of an individual runic letter. For example:

It is perhaps worth adding that the SIG rune illustrated above has, in modern times, acquired an extremely sinister reputation. This is the result of the evil activities of the Nazi leader Heinrich Himmler and the black-uniformed SS which he led. Himmler had a cranky interest in runes – he dabbled in a form of yoga that involved devotees distorting their bodies into approximations of the shape of runic letters – and adopted a doubled form of SIG (⚡⚡) as the insignia of his SS. There were, no doubt, two reasons for this. Firstly, ⚡⚡ is the precise runic equivalent of the letters SS, and, secondly, SIG's pronunciation approximates that of the German word *Sieg*, victory.

Himmler has long been consigned to the dustbin of history and his misuse of the SIG rune is best forgotten. Certainly, there is no reason to think that the SIG rune, or runes in general, have an evil import because of Nazi perversions of runic lore. It is also worth remembering in this context that swastika decorations can be seen today in most Hindu temples. The fact that Hitler misused this Hindu symbol of cosmic energy is not considered a good reason for abandoning it.

Runic Castingboards

After you have made your 24 rune cards, a process which should not take more than an hour or so, you must make a 'casting cloth', or a castingboard, on which to place your cards.

If you want to make an elaborate casting cloth on which to spread your runes, you can do so. Such a cloth, either heavily embroidered or painted in the 'elemental colours' (black for Earth, yellow for Air, red for Fire and blue for Water), certainly adds atmosphere to casting the runes and interpreting their positions. However, a simple castingboard made from the

The 24 runic letters used in divination are:

Number	Form of Runic Letter	Name of Letter	English Meaning of Name
1.	ᚠ	FEOH	cattle
2.	ᚢ	UR	ox
3.	ᚦ	THORN	thorn, giant
4.	ᚨ	ASS, sometimes OSS	one of the Aesir, the Teutonic gods
5.	ᚱ	RIT	sun chariot
6.	ᚲ	KAON	literally a flaming torch, but also means 'life force'
7.	ᚷ	GIFU	gift or luck
8.	ᚹ	WUNNA	ecstatic happiness
9.	ᚺ	HAGAL	health, well-being
10.	ᚾ	NAWT	need
11.	ᛁ	IS	ice, heavy frost
12.	ᛃ	YER	year, also the product of the harvest year – crops

side of a large cardboard box should prove perfectly adequate and, indeed, better for the particular method described below.

Take either a piece of cardboard or a sheet of drawing paper, at least 18 inches square, and carefully draw upon it a one-foot square divided into four quarters, thus:

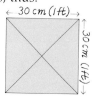

With a compass set at six inches, describe a circle within the square. If you haven't got a compass of sufficient span, you can use a piece of string with one end tied to a drawing pin stuck in the middle of the square and the other to a pencil. When you have drawn your circle the resulting figure will be:

Number	Form of Runic Letter	Name of Letter	English Meaning of Name
13.		YR	a yew-tree
14.		PEORTH	a mountain or large hill, a small enclosure
15.		AKZI	an axe or, sometimes, stone club
16.		SIG	the sun
17.		TIW	Mars, a war-god
18.		BIRCA	primarily a birch-tree but sometimes a large hill
19.		EOH	a horse for riding
20.		MAN	humanity or 'Middle Earth'
21.		LAG(U)	a lake
22.		ING	relations, particularly children and grandchildren
23.		ODAL	native soil
24.		DAG	day

Letter the four segments of the circle as follows:

If you want to give your casting circle a more dramatic appearance, you can paint the four segments in the elemental colours listed above.

Now that you have made your rune-cards and castingboard you are ready to make your first experiment in runic divination.

Place all your runecards face downwards, so that you can't see the letters, on your castingboard. Shuffle them with your fingers, sliding them about on the castingboard without lifting them from it, so that they are thoroughly mixed up. Then remove, three at a time, making your choice quite at random, 15 of the 24 runecards from the castingboard. Don't look at their lettered faces to see what cards you have removed.

This will leave you with nine rune-cards lying face downwards on your castingboard. Think of the board as a clock with the 12 o'clock position as being exactly in the middle of the outer perimeter of the Air segment. If there is a runecard exactly on the 12 o'clock position, turn it so the lettered face is upward. If there isn't one in exactly this position, which will almost certainly be the case, turn up the first runecard to the right of 12 o'clock. Then, moving clockwise, disregard the next two runecards and turn up the third. Disregard the next two runecards and turn up the third.

This will, of course, leave you with three of the nine runecards on your castingboard turned face upwards. These are indicators of your general situation or that of the person on whose behalf you are casting the runes, and should be read in accordance with the interpretations of the rune in a particular elemental segment, as given on pages 94 to 97.

After you have derived an interpretation from these three, remove them from your runeboard, leaving six runecards behind.

Once again, think of the runeboard as a clock with the 6 o'clock position being exactly in the middle of the outer perimeter of the Earth segment. If

A silver crucifix dating from the early years of Christianity in Sweden, its design retaining certain pagan conventions of the type associated with rune magic.

there is a runecard lying exactly on the 6 o'clock position, turn it lettered side upwards. If not, turn up the first rune-card to the left of this position, i.e. the first runecard to be found in a clock-wise direction from 6 o'clock. Moving clockwise, disregard the card follow-ing the card you have turned up and turn up the next one. Disregard the next card (still moving clockwise) and turn up that which follows.

Once again you have three lettered cards on view. These indicate finances and matters associated with money, and should be read in accordance with the significance of the runes listed below. These are, of course, general interpretations and have to be approached with some care when they are being applied to money and busi-ness matters. Usually, however, their significance in relation to financial matters will be reasonably apparent; if not, you will have to use your intuitive abilities. When you have completed the interpretation of the three rune-cards related to money and associated matters, remove them from the board.

The three remaining runecards should be turned face upwards and read in relation to one's love life and sexual matters, in accordance with their general significance as listed below. Usually the application of these general interpretations to the emo-tional life of the enquirer will be simple and evident enough; sometimes, again, a certain amount of intuition has to be used.

Whether in relation to the general situation, money matters or the emo-tional life, the three runecards must be interpreted in relationship to one another. Usually this is a fairly easy task – the three cards complement one another, the significance of one being made more apparent by that of the other two. On the basis of the three cards you, the fortune-teller, can 'make up' a coherent story, an inter-pretation that makes sense. Some-times, however, there seems to be an element of contradiction between the meanings of two of the cards. Thus, for example, the three runecards that you have to interpret in relation to the enquirer's general situation might be:

FEOH in the Water Segment
SIG in the Water Segment
IS in the Air Segment

The Vikings were metalworkers and artists as well as traders and warriors, as can be seen from this superbly crafted gold ring, engraved with runic letters spelling out the name of its original owner.

The meanings of these, as given below, are:

FEOH in Water: Things are about to improve; you may find yourself get-ting increasingly interested in the occult and things of the spirit.

SIG in Water: Moderate risks taken now will pay off in the future.

IS in Air: Take care, you are walking on thin ice.

Clearly, the meanings of the last two flatly contradict one another – SIG urges you to take risks, IS to avoid them. What is indicated here is a fluid situation in which outside forces play a part and for which the runes can give you no helpful advice or indications at the moment. You must abandon the divination and repeat it after a day or two, by which time the situation should have evolved sufficiently for the runes to be able to give you a sen-sible message.

GENERAL SIGNIFICANCE OF THE RUNES

(FEOH)

In Air Segment: Your desires are about to come true; your longings will at last be fulfilled.

In Fire Segment: Business or other relationships you set up in the next year are likely to prove per-manent. Your life is about to become more stable.

In Earth Segment: Success will be yours; everything you desire will be yours.

In Water Segment: Things are about to improve; you will find yourself getting increasingly interested in the occult and things of the spirit.

(UR)

In Air Segment: You are about to go through a most fortunate period of your life if you grasp the oppor-tunities open to you.

In Fire Segment: Press forward; if you trust in your own abilities and judgment, success will be yours.

In Earth Segment: This is a time when, at all costs, you must avoid taking risks. This is the time for thought, not impetuous action.

In Water Segment: You are likely to receive unexpected visitors or messages from a distance. In either case the results will be surprising.

▷ (THORN)

In Air Segment: This is not the time to take risks or be in any way adventurous. Be patient, however tiresome things may be, and all will come right in the end.

In Fire Segment: This is the time to be thoroughly suspicious of all propositions made to you. Others are trying to exploit you.

In Earth Segment: A time to be careful; on no account antagonize others.

In Water Segment: This is not a lucky time for you. Don't gamble or take risks.

ᚠ (ASS)

In Air Segment: You will find yourself in close and surprising relationships with those of a different generation to yourself. Good fortune will result.

In Fire Segment: Now is the time to listen to good advice and work in co-operation with others.

In Earth Segment: Be careful of the decisions you make; their effects will be felt for a very long time.

In Water Segment: Now is the time to take action – but not by yourself. It is essential that you co-operate with like-minded associates.

ᚱ (RIT)

In Air Segment: You are about to find yourself engaged in an amusing adventure; as long as you don't take it seriously all should be well.

In Fire Segment: This is a time for patience; don't do anything hastily.

In Earth Segment: Be prepared for unexpected surprises. Don't be hasty; don't take chances.

In Water Segment: Be wary. Play life's game in such a way that others don't find out what cards you are holding.

ᚲ (KAON)

In Air Segment: You will either receive gifts or help from others.

In Fire Segment: Your life is about to become much fuller.

In Earth Segment: You will shortly find that your full energies have returned and that life has changed for the better.

In Water Segment: You must grasp the opportunities you will shortly be given.

✕ (GIFU)

In Air Segment: This is not a good time to be on your own. Enlist the support of others.

In Fire Segment: You are about to attain much that you desire.

In Earth Segment: More effort is required if you are to get what you want.

In Water Segment: You must be prepared to take advice and others' help.

ᚹ (WUNNA)

In Air Segment: You are about to achieve considerable happiness.

In Fire Segment: You should discuss matters with friends and partners.

In Earth Segment: Take what is available. Don't yearn for what you can't have.

In Water Segment: Help others if you want to be helped yourself.

ᚻ (HAGAL)

In Air Segment	All segments: for good or ill,
In Fire Segment	events beyond
In Earth Segment	your control
In Water Segment	are about to influence your life.

ᚾ (NAWT)

In Air Segment: All your qualities of tenacious perseverance will soon be called upon.

In Fire Segment: You are about to go through difficult times; be patient.

In Earth Segment: Avoid recklessness. Be purposeful and patient.

In Water Segment: You are soon going to have problems – but these can be overcome.

ᛁ (IS)

In Air Segment: Take care, you are walking on thin ice.

In Fire Segment: Take great care – don't move, the ice is *very* thin.

The oldest surviving Swedish inscription in the runic alphabet of 24 letters. Another runic alphabet had only 16 letters; the complexities of Old English (Anglo-Saxon) were met by a 31 letter alphabet.

Part of a huge Viking hoard found in Northern England in the last century. The hoard, which included silver from places as far apart as Sweden and Byzantium, illustrates the extent of Viking travel – as does the use of runes in the Ukraine.

In Earth Segment: You may shortly experience a disappointment.
In Water Segment: A time for thought, not hasty action.

(YER)

In Air Segment: Be patient. After delays things will go well.
In Fire Segment: Success is coming, but rather slowly.
In Earth Segment: Try to relax; making too much effort is counter-productive.
In Water Segment: Be careful. Look at the possible long-term effects of choices made.

(YR)

In Air Segment: Don't quarrel. Be calm at all costs.

In Fire Segment: You must face up to the problems in your life.
In Earth Segment: Try to be as stable and calm as the yew-tree.
In Water Segment: Remain outwardly calm, whatever your inner emotions.

(PEORTH)

In Air Segment: You are about to experience surprising good luck.
In Fire Segment: Don't be too trustful. Hide your emotions.
In Earth Segment: A time for great care in every aspect of your life.
In Water Segment: Don't gamble or take any chances whatsoever.

(AKZI)

In Air Segment: You must make decisions and let others know your thoughts.
In Fire Segment: This is the time to be thoroughly outgoing and extrovert.
In Earth Segment: Be sharp – someone is trying to use you.

In Water Segment: A time for expansion; cut your way forward through life.

(SIG)

In Air Segment: Relax and restore your energies.
In Fire Segment: Remain calm at all costs.
In Earth Segment: Be calm and consider matters carefully.
In Water Segment: Moderate risks taken now will pay off in the future.

(TIW)

In Air Segment: You must take positive action if you are to fulfil your desires.
In Fire Segment: Don't be afraid of the new. Experiment!
In Earth Segment: Don't keep things back. Let others know your thoughts and feelings.
In Water Segment: This is the time to move on. Don't let yourself stay in a rut.

ᛒ (BIRCA)

In Air Segment: Good news, probably involving a marriage or a birth, is on the way.

In Fire Segment: Take great care over the small details of life – this will pay dividends eventually.

In Earth Segment: Try to take things more easily; don't strive too hard.

In Water Segment: This is a time to take the long-term view; don't worry about the present.

ᛖ (EOH)

In Air Segment: Things occupying your time at the moment will prove transitory.

In Fire Segment: This is a time to be prudent and not to reveal yourself.

In Earth Segment: A new and important person is about to come into your life.

In Water Segment: A time to be very careful while giving an impression of daring.

ᛗ (MAN)

In Air Segment: It is essential you remain calm, however stressful or provoked you may feel.

In Fire Segment: A relationship will deepen and become of major importance.

In Earth Segment: Avoid strain and asking too much to yourself.

In Water Segment: Be wary of others who may be secretly working against you.

ᛚ (LAGU)

In Air Segment: Try hard to understand the real nature, possibly hidden, of what is happening.

In Fire Segment: Learn from past mistakes and try to do things differently.

In Earth Segment: Endeavour to see deeper than the surface of things.

In Water Segment: You are in the dark about what is really going on.

ᛜ (ING)

In Air Segment: Be more flexible; don't stick to the habits of the past.

In Fire Segment: Be more helpful and consider others' feelings.

In Earth Segment: If you want success, you must change your behaviour.

In Water Segment: What happens to you depends on other people's attitudes and actions.

ᛟ (ODAL)

In Air Segment: You must take an unselfish attitude – in the long run you will find this the most rewarding procedure.

In Fire Segment: If you are patient, you will get those things you desire.

In Earth Segment: If you make a big effort you will achieve success.

In Water Segment: Be prepared to take a chance – you'll find it pays off handsomely.

ᛞ (DAG)

In Air Segment: A time for thought, not action – make haste slowly.

In Fire Segment: Things are about to move in the direction you want them to.

In Earth Segment: Take every opportunity open to you if you want to achieve success.

In Water Segment: Actions taken now will prove effective.

Odin and another of the Aesir, Nordic gods believed to be masters of rune magic, sail the world ocean. An occult tradition avers that rune forms were first traced by Odin in his own blood.

THE I CHING

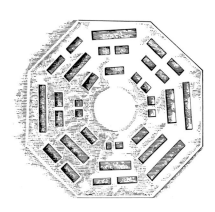

The I Ching *is an oracle book – a book that is consulted in order to obtain advice and answers to questions – which has been studied in China for thousands of years.*

Three centuries ago Jesuit missionaries brought it to Europe where it attracted the attention of a discerning few, among them Leibnitz, the philosopher and mathematician who discovered the differential calculus.

Today a very large number of people regularly consult the I Ching *when they are perplexed. They find the guidance it gives always stimulating and usually helpful, and regard the* I Ching *as a personality in its own right, a wise friend always ready to give of its wisdom to those who seek it.*

Sages contemplate the Yin-Yang symbol, a diagrammatic representation of the 'pairs of opposites' – light and dark, hot and cold, birth and death – which the I Ching *tradition sees as the warp and weft of the universe.*

The *I Ching* of ancient China is the oldest of the world's oracle books – books which are used to 'tell fortunes', answer questions and give general and particular guidance to those who make enquiry of them.

Throughout history there have been many books, reputed to convey supernatural wisdom, some of which were certainly not written for that purpose. For example, from the time of the later Roman Empire until the end of the Middle Ages the *Aeneid*, Virgil's epic Latin poem, was used as an oracle book.

An enquirer would open the book (or unfold the scroll) three times at random, on each occasion letting his finger fall, completely by chance, upon a line of the poem. The three lines indicated would be studied intently and either taken literally, or interpreted symbolically, to provide an answer to a given question. In the Middle Ages the *Aeneid* was so widely thought to give reliable oracles that its author, Virgil, was popularly believed to have been a magician rather than a poet. Tales of his wonder-working occult powers circulated all over Europe and his tomb at Naples acquired a reputation as a site at which miracles took place and to which magicians travelled to pay homage.

After the Protestant Reformation the Bible came to be regarded as the greatest of all oracle books and sincere and intelligent Christians, such as John Wesley, founder of the Methodist Church, would open it at random when they sought spiritual guidance for their perplexities.

The main problem with using either the *Aeneid* or the Bible as an oracle book – quite apart from the propriety of doing so – was that the answers given were often extremely obscure and demanded much interpetation. There seemed to be a need for oracle books which gave easily understandable advice, and a number of these were compiled by occultists of the last century. The most notable among them was *Napoleon's Book of Fate*, a book which is fun to use and has been almost continually in print since the 1820s, though it has no real connection with Napoleon. Its compiler was the astrologer and fortune-teller R. C. Smith, some of whose attributes were described in Chapter One.

The *I Ching* is to *Napoleon's Book of Fate* as vintage Champagne is to a poor, home-made country wine. It is almost an impertinence to call the *I Ching* an oracle book for it seems almost to be alive, to have a personality of its own. So much is this the case

that many of those who have regularly consulted it for advice have come to feel that they are on terms of personal friendship with it. One such is the writer R. L. Wing, who has observed that at times the *I Ching*:

> ... likes to carry on a witty and multi-faceted conversation; and at other times petulantly dwells upon a particular issue or problem. You may find it a wilful book – neither to be put off nor used aimlessly. As your relationship with the *I Ching* becomes ... familiar it may embarrass or frighten you, and will occasionally share a good laugh with you.

A book which 'shares a good laugh with you' is rather difficult for most of us to believe in, but I myself have encountered the *I Ching's* sense of humour – or experienced a very surprising coincidence. An architect I knew had written a question on a piece of paper and, without telling me what the question was, had asked me to make the manipulations required to receive a reply from the oracle.

In the translation of the *I Ching* I was

using at the time the answer I received seemed almost meaningless, containing much curious symbolism and the strange phrase, 'there is no skin on the thigh, walking is very difficult'.

This weird answer was a quite literal and exact one to the question which had been written, 'What is the state of my wife's health?' The enquirer's wife was finding walking very difficult, having just had a skin graft on her foot, the skin having been taken from her thigh.

The architect was amazed by the accuracy of the reply but, being of a sceptical disposition, was convinced that it was a mere coincidence. He decided to repeat his question, this time himself carrying out the processes which indicated the particular passage of the book to be taken as the answer. He received precisely the same answer as before. 'A remarkable coincidence,' he said crossly, before yet again enquiring of the oracle as to the state of his wife's health.

This time a different, but equally pertinent, answer was given. It read, in the particular translation being used, 'At the first question I answer the young fool, but if he asks two or

A detail from the late Ming period painting of 'The Hundred Children of the Duke of Chou'. The Duke and his father, King Wen, were supposedly the compilers of the oldest parts of the I Ching.

three times I refuse to give an answer.'

Now, as then, it seems to me that the *I Ching* was, with rude humour, telling the architect to stop bothering it with redundant questioning.

The Origins of the *I Ching*

The *I Ching* is not only the most ancient of the world's oracle books but also the most venerated. It is consulted from Hong Kong to New York, from Singapore to London; its ancient wisdom is held in great respect by both analytical psychologists and occultists; among some Taoist cults it is revered as though it were a semi-divine being; and in the present day there are many who feel, as Confucius did 2,500 years ago, that, 'if years were added to my life I would devote them to the study of the *I Ching*'.

At the time when Confucius lived and taught, the core of the *I Ching* already existed in a form similar to that used by fortune-tellers today. This core was supposedly compiled, on the basis of much older material, by King Wen, who ruled China in the twelfth century B.C.

The *I Ching* which is used today includes not only the core material from King Wen but additional texts written by his son, the Duke of Chou, and commentaries attributed to Confucius and his disciples. Much later commentaries are also extant and are studied by specialists in the *I Ching* and the spiritual philosophy derived from it.

Consulting the *I Ching*

Both the early textual elements of the *I Ching* and the commentaries upon them can only be used with great difficulty by the ordinary Westerner who wishes to consult the oracle to obtain its advice on his or her everyday life.

This is because, at the time the *I Ching* was compiled and most of the commentaries upon it were written, it was not available for consultation by the common people of China. It was regarded as a peculiarly sacred oracle which could only be used properly by a very small number of people – members of one or the other of two groups.

The first group consisted of the upper strata of the rulers, administrators and bureaucrats of the Chinese Empire – princes of the Imperial House, governors of provinces and large cities, high-ranking soldiers, and so on. The second group was made up of 'superior men', eminent scholars, intellectuals and philosophers: sages who devoted their lives to profound contemplation of the eternal verities.

Inevitably enough, written matter intended for the use of such people included much advice on things that would be of concern to them – military strategy and tactics, for example. The advice given by the *I Ching* on such subjects was no doubt found useful by the soldiers of 500 or 1000 years ago; even in World War Two many Japanese military commanders consulted the *I Ching* and its commentaries, and found inspiration in such passages as 'it furthers one to set armies into retreat with the intention of consolidating forces for attack – no blame'. Those of us who live everyday lives, working in factories and offices, dwelling in suburban houses or inner city apartments, can only apply such advice to our own situations if we interpret it symbolically. This is not always an easy task, and there is always the danger of misapplying the symbolism, distorting it so that we ensure that the *I Ching* gives us the advice we would like to hear.

A further difficulty arises from the fact that the text of the *I Ching* often employs metaphors and symbols derived from the religious, political and social life of the China of 3,000 years ago. Thus, there is a good deal about the *ting*, the sacrificial cauldron of China – not an object commonly found in the homes of most Westerners or even present-day Chinese. Similarly, one is advised that in certain circumstances one should behave as a fox does when it walks upon a frozen lake – not an event many of us have witnessed.

Any dedicated student of the *I Ching* who regularly consults it in one of its many full translations soon becomes accustomed to those symbols and metaphors and is able to interpret them with ease. Nevertheless, the oriental symbolism of the original text of the *I Ching*, with its charming cauldrons, tigers and foxes with wet tails, would be quite out of place in a book such as this. So the *I Ching's* advice on how to handle the situations encountered in everyday life, whether they concern love, money, or anything else, is expressed here in a modified, contemporary way.

Time and the *I Ching*

Before explaining how you can master the simple techniques needed to obtain guidance from the oracle, an important point about the nature of such advice should be considered.

Unlike most oracle books, such as *Napoleon's Book of Fate* mentioned on page 99, the *I Ching* does not make hard-and-fast predictions about the future. Those sages who created and developed the oracle adhered to a spiritual philosophy which asserted that by correct action men and women are capable of making their own destiny. By making proper responses to particular circumstances and events, one can cease being blown hither and thither by the winds of fate and use one's own strength to decide what the future holds.

In other words, as far as the *I Ching* is concerned, your own future does not stretch before you like a single-line railway track, offering only the journey from the station marked Now to that marked Death. On the contrary your future is, so to speak, fan-shaped. Before you at any particular point in time are an infinite number of main highways, small roads, path-

Lao-Tse (Lao-Tzu), the supreme sage of the Taoist philosophy on which the commentaries upon the I Ching *are based, depicted riding a water buffalo, symbol of the Chinese lunar year.*

ways and ill-trodden trails. You can choose which one of these to follow and, by your own free choice of action and conduct, you can at any time turn off the road you are travelling down and take a diversion which will lead you on a quite different journey through the countryside of life.

The future, for those who accept the teachings of the *I Ching*, is always fluid, never fixed and unchangeable. So it is no use asking the oracle such questions as 'Will Peter fall in love with me?' or 'Will Jean marry me?', or 'Shall I get promotion?', for the answers to such questions will depend upon your own actions, on choices and decisions freely made. Instead you should ask questions about the nature of a given situation or problem and seek guidance on how you should behave if you want things to progress satisfactorily.

Examples of such questions might be 'What are so-and-so's feelings towards me and how should I behave if I want him/her to love me?' 'How established am I in my job and what should I do to get promotion or a salary increase?'

In other words, you should phrase your question so that the *I Ching* can, as it were, describe the true nature of a situation or problem and give its advice on how you should handle it. It is essential that you formulate your question as precisely as possible. If you don't, the oracle may answer a quite different question from that which you think it is answering. If, for example, you are in some financial dispute with your bank and want to know what course of action you should follow if the matter is to end in a satisfactory way, ask: 'What should I do to ensure that this dispute ends satisfactorily for me?' If you express your question vaguely, perhaps as something like 'How can I make sure this matter ends satisfactorily?', the oracle might give you advice on how to behave in such a way that the matter ends completely satisfactorily – for the bank.

It is probably best to write your question down, reading it through carefully to ensure that it contains no ambiguities and that its meaning is utterly clear.

Generating a Hexagram

After you have formulated your question in the clearest possible terms the next step is to obtain a *hexagram*, a figure made up of six lines. This may consist entirely of whole lines, entirely of broken lines, or some combination of the two. For example:

A Taoist Immortal drifts over a landscape. Its hills and valleys are, like the whole and broken lines of the I Ching, symbolic of Yin and Yang.

In all, there are 64 possible hexagrams; the simplest method of generating the one which will indicate the oracle's answer to your question is to use a dice. Throw it six times, note the numbers thrown on a piece of scrap paper, and then place them in a vertical column of six *in the reverse order to that in which they were thrown*. That is to say, you write down the *sixth* number you threw at the top of the column and the *first* number you threw at the bottom of the column. So, if you consecutively threw the numbers 5, 4, 2, 6, 5 and 3, you would write down:

3
5
6
2
4
5

Beside each of the six numbers in the column draw a whole line if the num-

ber is an odd one, or a broken line if the number is an even one. For example:

```
3 _____
5 _____
6 ___  ___
2 ___  ___
4 ___  ___
5 _____
```

While this dice method is certainly the quickest way of generating a hexagram, it is of modern origin and has the disadvantage that it contains no *moving lines* – that is, broken lines which change into whole lines and vice versa. These moving lines, which give a more detailed analysis of a particular situation, are, however, to be found in hexagrams generated by a simple technique involving three coins. If you want to follow this method you can, if you wish, obtain three old Chinese coins and use these for your purpose. It is far less trouble, however, and quite as satisfactory, to use three coins in current circulation – perhaps 20p or 25 cent pieces.

Take the three coins and toss them in the air. Make a note of the result – three heads, for example – and repeat the process five times more. Take the results of the six throws and write

them down in a vertical column, once again in reverse order, first throw at the bottom, last throw at the top. For example:

Last throw	Three heads
Fifth throw	Three tails
Fourth throw	Two heads, one tail
Third throw	Three tails
Second throw	One head, two tails
First throw	Two heads, one tail

Count each head as two and each tail as three and make a numerical total of the value of each of the six throws of three coins. Thus:

Last throw	Three heads = 6
Fifth throw	Three tails = 9
Fourth throw	Two heads, one tail = 7
Third throw	Three tails = 9
Second throw	One head, two tails = 8
First throw	Two heads, one tail = 7

At this stage a hexagram is produced by a similar process to that used after throwing a dice six times, i.e. a broken

line is drawn for an even number, an unbroken one for an odd number. But after each unbroken line derived from the number 9, and after each broken line derived from the number 6, a capital letter M is written.

Thus, using our example, the hexagram will be:

```
___  ___  M
_____  M
_____
_____  M
_____
_____
```

The M stands for moving – the line is in a process of change. To see the nature of that change simply take the hexagram you have generated and copy it out with the M lines altered to their opposites: broken lines become whole lines; unbroken lines become broken.

In the case of the hexagram given as an example:

```
_____
___  ___
_____
___  ___
_____
_____
```

In this way, using the coin method,

The prelude to a ceremonial consultation of the I Ching, with the traditional yarrow stalks being venerated as incense smokes in honour of the Immortals.

you get (provided there is at least one M line, derived from 6 or 9, in the original hexagram) not one but two hexagrams which indicate the nature of the guidance given by the *I Ching*. In very general terms, the first hexagram, the one directly derived from throwing the coins, indicates the situation as it is now and the best course of action that the enquirer can adopt. The second hexagram, the one obtained by changing the M lines to their opposites, indicates the situation or problem that is developing and how it should be coped with or approached.

Besides the dice and the coin method there are numerous other techniques for generating hexagrams. The most ancient and notable of these involves the manipulation of 50 thin sticks or plant stalks – yarrow stalks were traditionally used by Chinese fortune-tellers – and, while it is somewhat time-consuming, is favoured by many dedicated students of the *I Ching* and its mysteries. Such students admit that the method is a laborious one, but

they assert that it gives more accurate answers than those obtained by the use of simpler techniques.

Hexagram Generation by Sticks
Take 50 thin sticks (or stalks), remove one of them and put it on one side – it plays no part at all in the operations which follow, and the hexagrams are generated by the use of only 49 sticks. Exactly why one starts with one extra stick is something of a mystery – no one is absolutely sure of the reason although numerous theories have been put forward. One occult scholar has suggested that 49 (which equals 7×7) is a number of such mystic significance that it is positively dangerous to carry about a bundle of 49 sticks for any length of time, so one is added as a sort of safety precaution. This seems somewhat unlikely. All one can say for sure is that fortune-tellers have used 50, not 49, sticks since time immemorial, and that with a divinatory system as ancient as the oracle of the *I Ching* it is probably best to stick to tradition and avoid rash experiment. In this connection it is interesting to note that some *I Ching* devotees claim that if you start with only 49 sticks you *always* get a misleading answer or incorrect guidance.

Take your 49 sticks and place them in front of you. Divide them, without counting, into two roughly equal heaps, one on your right, the other to your left. Next:

1. Take a single stick from the *right-hand* pile and place it between the little finger and the ring finger of the left hand.
2. With your right hand remove four sticks at a time from the *left-hand* pile, putting them together in a heap, until four or fewer sticks remain in the left-hand pile. Put the remaining sticks or stick between the ring and middle finger of your left hand. At this stage you will be holding in your left hand: a) one stick between the little and ring fingers; b) one, two, three or four sticks between your ring and middle fingers.
3. With your right hand remove four sticks at a time from the *right-hand* pile until four or fewer sticks are left. Place these between the middle and first fingers of your left hand.

Because of the mathematics involved in this method, the total number of sticks held in three groups between the fingers of your left hand must *always* total five or nine. If your sticks total any other number you have carried out the process incorrectly, miscounting at some stage, and must start all over again. If you have carried out your countings properly, the various possible combinations of sticks between the fingers of your left hand are:

$$1 + 4 + 4 = 9$$
$$1 + 3 + 1 = 5$$
$$1 + 2 + 2 = 5$$
$$1 + 1 + 3 = 5$$

Place the five or nine sticks held in the left hand apart and gather the rest of the sticks into a single pile. There will, of course, be either 40 or 44 of these. Divide them into two roughly equal piles without counting and repeat steps 1 to 3 as before.

When you have completed these you will, again because of the mathematics involved in the process, be left with a total of either four or eight sticks between the fingers of your left hand. The possibilities are:

$$1 + 1 + 2 = 4$$
$$1 + 2 + 1 = 4$$
$$1 + 3 + 4 = 8$$
$$1 + 4 + 3 = 8$$

Put the four or eight sticks in your left hand into a pile next to the pile of five or nine sticks which you have already put aside.

Take the rest of the sticks and, once again, divide into equal piles and go through steps 1 to 3. When you have completed these you will, once again, be left with either four or eight sticks in your left hand. Put these in a pile next to the first two piles. The three piles in front of you now (if you have carried out the process correctly and without miscounting) are in one of the following combinations:

	Pile One	Pile Two	Pile Three
A	9	8	4
B	9	4	8
C	5	8	8
D	5	8	4
E	5	4	8
F	9	4	4
G	9	8	8
H	5	4	4

If the piles are as in the first three combinations above (A, B or C), you must draw an unbroken line as the bottom of your hexagram.

If they are as in the second three of the above combinations (D, E or F), draw a broken line as the bottom line of your hexagram.

If the combination is that shown as G, the bottom line of your hexagram is drawn as a broken line with a capital M at the end of it – this, of course, is a moving line.

If the combination is as H above, the bottom line of your hexagram is drawn as an unbroken line with a capital M at the end of it – this is another moving line.

You now reassemble your 49 sticks into one pile and repeat the whole process. This will give you the second line of your hexagram, the line immediately above the bottom line.

Another four repetitions are required to give you the entire hexagram. Remember that you complete your hexagram from the bottom; the last time you carry out the process will be to obtain the hexagram's top line. If, as is often the case, the hexagram you have generated by the stick technique contains one or more moving lines, you can derive from it a second hexagram in the way described on pages 103-4.

Kuan Ti, a god concerned with both books and martial arts, was sometimes invoked by Japanese generals of World War Two as a preliminary to consulting the I Ching on questions of strategy and tactics.

此是關聖帝君神像夜讀春秋
側立周倉手持偃月刀軍民人
供之

Which Hexagram?

By using dice, coins or sticks you will have generated either one or two hexagrams. Now comes the time for you to read the oracle's advice.

Look at the table below and run your finger along the eight groups of three lines at the top until you come to the one which corresponds to the top three lines of your hexagram. Then run your finger down the numbered column below until it is opposite the figure in the left-hand column which corresponds to the bottom three lines of your hexagram. The number in the square on which your finger rests will give you the number of the particular interpretation which is relevant to your enquiry. The 64 separate interpretations are printed below and to the end of the chapter. If, of course, you have generated two hexagrams, you look at the meanings of both – the second one is also applicable to your situation and indicates how it is developing and what actions will be appropriate on your part.

■ *Table of hexagrams.*

INTERPRETING HEXAGRAMS

1.

Now is the time to achieve success by pressing forward. Be bold without letting yourself become reckless. It is possible that a powerful and perhaps aggressive person will bring about a resolution of the situation or problem that you are enquiring about, for this is the most strongly masculine of all the hexagrams.

2.

Persistence and endurance are the watchwords of the moment, particularly where financial and other practical situations are concerned. Provided you do not lose heart and let yourself become discouraged, your efforts will bring you success on all levels. According to an ancient Chinese sage, this hexagram indicates that the time has come 'to find friends in the South and West rather than the North and East'. Sometimes this hexagram literally indicates that you should put reliance on those friends who live to the South and West of your home. More usually, however, the injunction must be interpreted in accordance with ancient symbolism; in this case it simply means: 'don't relax; intense and patient effort is called for'. This hexagram is the most strongly feminine of the 64 and sometimes signifies that a subtle and perhaps mysterious person will be the means of solving the problems you are enquiring about.

3.

The beginnings of new relationships, new ventures and new situations are never without difficulties and at times you may feel discouraged. Metaphorically speaking, you sometimes feel as though the sprouting seed corn you have planted is about to be blasted by frost. In spite of this, all your difficulties can be overcome by persistence, 'making haste slowly'. Do not be *too* self-reliant and afraid or unwilling to ask for the assistance and advice of others. Outside help can ensure the success of new projects.

4.

The bold, even headstrong, young person can achieve success. The oracle of the *I Ching* is not asking you a question – it is you who are enquiring of the oracle. The *I Ching* answers any sincere question that has been addressed to it. But if a seeker keeps asking it the same question, the oracle will give foolish and unhelpful answers. The time has come for you to make up your mind, to come to a definite decision.

5.

Sincerity and persistence are called for. If you show both, you will be successful and achieve the ends you desire. You must, however, be decisive in your dealings.

6.

Take care: don't make any sudden and irrevocable decisions; don't act with-

UPPER 3 LINES ▶ LOWER 3 LINES ▼	☰	☳	☵	☶	☷	☴	☲	☱
☰	1	34	5	26	11	9	14	43
☳	25	51	3	27	24	42	21	17
☵	6	40	29	4	7	59	64	47
☶	33	62	39	52	15	53	56	31
☷	12	16	8	23	2	20	35	45
☴	44	32	48	18	46	57	50	28
☲	13	55	63	22	36	37	30	49
☱	10	54	60	41	19	61	38	58

out much consideration. It is the time for caution. Pause and consider all the factors in the situation you are enquiring about. Above all, don't charge recklessly forward. On no account embark on risky ventures or 'trust to luck'.

7.

The crowd, the general run of people one encounters in everyday life, are capable of achieving a lot, provided that they are properly organized. As an individual you are in the same position. You must organize and discipline yourself if you are to get the things you want, achieve the success you desire. There is a time for thought and a time for action – but now is the time for both. Neither unthinking, reckless action nor thought which does not find expression in deeds will achieve anything at the present time.

8.

You must be prepared to give as well as take – you won't get the help you want from others unless you give them your own assistance in their difficulties. But this hexagram can also indicate the advisability of reconsulting the oracle. Go through the process involved in generating another hexagram. The text appropriate to it should tell you whether you have the right qualities to cope successfully with the problems or situation about which you are enquiring.

9.

This is not a favourable time for trying to achieve major successes. Don't take on more than you can safely handle at the moment. Strive for small victories, minor triumphs; be gentle, persuasive and responsive to the needs and wishes of others.

10.

The present situation is not an easy one and you are faced with many problems and with what at times seem insuperable difficulties. Nevertheless, if you are bold, enterprising and fear-

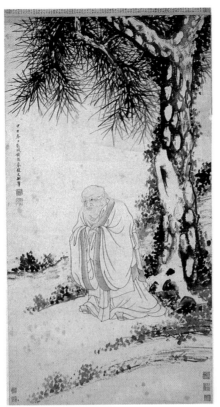

Lao-Tse, the Immortal mystic, rapt in contemplation of the eternal Tao – the harmonious union of the pairs of opposites, Yin and Yang, whose permutations generate the hexagrams of the I Ching.

less, all difficulties will be overcome and success achieved.

11.

This is a most harmonious and lucky hexagram which has the traditional meaning of 'Heaven uniting with Earth' – in other words, good fortune, almost effortlessly achieved, is on its way. A particularly excellent and fortunate hexagram when it appears as the answer to any question involving love, sexual matters and marriage.

12.

This hexagram indicates a confused and puzzling situation where things may not be quite as they seem. It is a time for sticking to your principles and proceeding in the way that you think is right rather than letting your actions be influenced by the advice of others, who may not be as well-disposed

towards you as you believe. In particular, do not be led to involve yourself in actions that may be risky, even dangerous. If you do, you will almost certainly have cause to regret it.

13.

In this situation, or in coming to a decision to solve a particular problem, you must think of others rather than yourself. If you do the outcome will be a fortunate one. This is a time to make the decisions you know must be made. Push on; don't shilly-shally.

14.

The help of those in positions of authority, and advice – even inspiration – from forces superior to your own should help to resolve the situation or problem about which you are enquiring. It is likely that this assistance from above, or inspiration from within, will lead you to understand matters which have puzzled you and others. There is a probability that you will learn something, or find something out, which will cause you considerable surprise.

15.

A calm and peaceful attitude will be advantageous at the present time. If you can remain tranquil, in spite of the storms which rage around you, little harm will come to you. Persist quietly in the course of action you have decided is correct and much good fortune will result.

16.

It is a most favourable and advantageous time to seek the help of other people. If you try to cope with the problem or situation about which you are enquiring without trying to get outside support, things are likely to end unhappily. If, however, you are to obtain the assistance and support you need, it is vital that you ensure that there are no misunderstandings, that others fully appreciate the realities of the situation and understand your point of view.

17.

Don't try to play the leading part in things at the moment. Keep a low profile; be content to play second fiddle and to let others take the decisive first steps. If you disregard this advice and insist on pushing yourself forward, you are likely to find yourself involved in an extremely stressful, tiresome and risky situation.

18.

The situation you are enquiring about and/or the problem with which you are concerned is a very messy and muddled one. The muddle and difficulty have not come about by chance but as a result of human errors – incorrect decisions and foolish actions. But human beings are capable of clearing up messes as well as making them. The damage that has been done can be repaired. The task will not be an easy one, but thoughtful decisions and prudent activity can restore the situation and ensure a happy ending.

19.

Things are beginning to move; good and evil forces are both stirring. Fortune and ill fortune are approaching. It

is important that negative forces are checked before they become too strong and malignant. Let good fortune take its course; it will come of its own accord. But watch out for unhelpful influences and developments, and destroy them before they become really powerful and dangerous.

20.

This is a time for reflection and contemplation, for looking into the depths of your own being rather than being concerned with the outside world. Carefully consider your own thoughts, emotions, desires and possible actions. Do not make hasty decisions; consider matters in all their possible aspects.

21.

Limitation is the key factor in the situation in which you are involved, the problem that you are trying to deal with. You do not have complete freedom of action and there are obstructions upon the path that leads towards your goal. These obstructions must be

In this painting, dating from the early Ming period, the artist combines the features of the landscape, perhaps to express hexagram 12 of the I Ching.

swept aside; you must take decisive action, break through the barriers that hinder you and move forward in the direction you want to go.

22.

There is a time to break the rules and a time to adhere to them with the utmost rigidity. At the moment you should follow the second of these courses. Be thoroughly conventional in your actions and the attitudes which you adopt. In any situation, whether one arising out of work, social activities or emotional matters, behave in the generally accepted way.

23.

At the present time almost any purposeful activity is likely to make things worse. Do not undertake any new projects, however safe they may appear to be, and as far as old ones are concerned, keep them gently ticking over rather than trying to accelerate their progress. This is not the time for expansion or for extending your obligations, whether they be financial, social or emotional. You may be going through difficulties, or be about to encounter them, in a situation that is of great concern to you. The adverse factors which are troubling you should not be met head-on – don't actively attack them at the moment. Remain calm; if you do so, things will improve without any intervention on your part.

24.

'Off with the old, on with the new' is the correct attitude towards what is happening or is about to happen. The time is one for change, for abandoning old habits, worn-out emotions, ways of behaving which have led you astray. As far as your particular situation or problem is concerned, you must realize that you are at a major turning point in life. Don't be afraid to strike out into unknown territory.

25.

Act in accordance with your interior nature – the real desires of your secret self. If you do so, persevering in your efforts to obtain what is right for you, much good fortune will follow. If you take the opposite course (by persistently trying to please others rather than yourself, and frustrating your own needs and desires), the results will be unfortunate.

26. This is not the time for self-analysis and withdrawing into yourself. Don't sit at home brooding about your own and other people's worries. While a certain amount of restraint must be maintained, you should be as outgoing as is compatible with such restraint, enthusiastically throwing yourself into work and social activities. If you do this, not only will good fortune result but you will achieve ambitions which, at the moment, seem almost impossible to attain.

27. Great prudence is required at the present time. Take the utmost care and practise moderation in all your activities. In every aspect of your life – physical, financial, emotional and mental – be temperate. Don't concern youself with trivialities. If everything is to go well, it is essential that you concentrate upon matters of real importance. Put first things first. Don't allow yourself to be distracted.

28. You are living in a quite exceptional period of your life and enormous effort will have to be made if you are to cope fully with the situation in which you find yourself. The efforts you make, however, should be carefully planned so that they produce the maximum effect with the minimum of strain. What the situation requires is a steady, continuous pressure, not intermittent heaves. Sustained effort on your part will produce the desired results.

29. Do not compromise your ideals and principles, however much you may be

A traditional celebration of attainment of manhood, a 'rite of passage', usually involved consultation of the I Ching.

tempted to do so by the difficulties of your present situation. If you stick to your guns, following your principles with sincerity and determination, you will attain your goal and overcome the barriers which obstruct your progress.

30. Like every other human being you are subject to limitations and constraints upon your freedom of action. Some of these come from within – limitations arising out of the nature of your own character and capacities. Others are imposed from without and have their origins in the nature of the society in which you live. There is a sense in which you can only find your personal freedom by understanding and accepting those limitations. You must come to terms with the world in which you live and realize that not everything can be achieved.

31. You are enjoying, or about to enjoy, many of the pleasant things of life. Take pleasure in this, but don't allow yourself to be swept off your feet, to become giddy with excitement. Retain an interior calmness; listen to the

advice of those you know and trust; keep your thoughts clear and your mind unmuddied.

32. This is a time when all your capacities for endurance and persistence must play a full part in your life. It is essential that you should stoically and patiently exert all your powers to resist the storms that threaten to blow you off your feet. Stay put, stand fast, whatever happens. This does not mean that you should obstinately oppose all changes in your life; it is possible to adapt to a situation in a manner that is compatible with adherence to principle.

33. This is the time for a masterly inactivity. You should not take any active steps in matters that concern you, nor should you actively defend yourself against the blows of fate. On the contrary, a carefully thought-out withdrawal is the order of the day. This retreat must be an ordered one, not a disorganized and confused rout. A withdrawal of this type is not an indication of weakness. It is a sign of future strength and provides the needed opportunity for a mobilization of all your forces – your own capacities – which will enable you to advance to the attack at some time in the future.

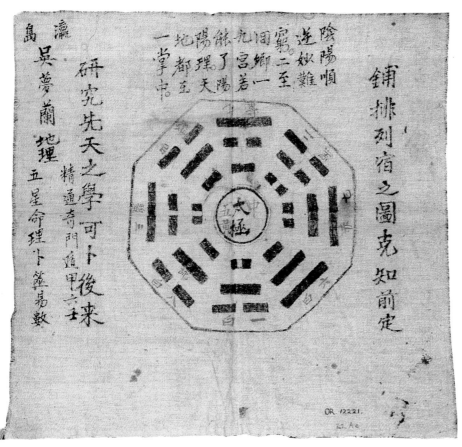

Both the late Manchu block-printed cloth (above) and the Yin-Yang symbol on the opposite page show the eight trigrams from which are derived the 64 hexagrams of the I Ching. The printed instructions (above) apply the trigrams to astrology.

34.

The situation you are enquiring about could prove very favourable to you. Success will be yours provided you keep in mind that it is of the utmost importance that you conduct yourself in the right way. Provided you carry out your obligations towards others they will carry out their obligations to you, and all should end well. Don't just follow your own inclinations: fully consider the interests of others.

35.

You have considerable influence in the matter you are enquiring about. Don't be led to abuse this influence by profiting from it entirely for your own advantage. If you use your influence

for the good of both yourself and those who wish to help you, you will find that you will be even more in command of the situation.

36.

At the present time it is likely that the situation you find yourself in seems most unlucky and you feel rather unhappy. Don't let yourself become depressed or confused. Don't allow yourself to be swept away by the current of events, but keep your head amid the disorder around you. At this stage in your life you must rely upon your 'inner light' – the most essential part of your being, the true you – and make sure it continues to shine out through the gloom.

37.

Loyalty to others, particularly to those with whom you are linked by ties of blood and the emotions, is called for in the present circumstances. This will not always be easy. Nevertheless, it is important for your own well-being that you meet your obligations and

duties, however burdensome they may be.

38.

You are in a situation, or will soon be in a situation, where the opposition and obstruction of others causes you personal difficulty. But both the opposition and the obstructions you encounter are free from malice towards you. They are expressions of genuinely held points of view – your opponent is just as sincere as you. It is best to try to compromise, to come to some form of agreement.

39.

At the present time there are too many obstacles in your path for you to move forward in the way you would wish. It would be no good for you to try to push onwards at the moment. You should draw in your horns, retreat – in the hope of advancing at some time in the future – and avoid all direct confrontations. Your unaided strength will not suffice to overcome the difficulties which hinder your progress. Seek the help of friends and those who are well-disposed towards you. The situation is somewhat similar to that indicated by hexagram 33, and it could prove advantageous to read the interpretation of that hexagram as well as this.

40.

This is the time for boldness. Go on to the attack; face up to the problems in your life; smash the barriers that have cut you off from the attainment of your desires. The future is the important thing, so don't brood about the past or mistakes made by others.

41.

Restraint and control are called for in every aspect of your life. Be prudent. Only move with the utmost care and draw on the inner strengths that are to be found at the core of your personality. If you follow this advice, good fortune and happiness will result.

42. 'To rule is to serve' is one of the fundamental axioms of the sages who compiled the *I Ching*, and this is the time to bear this rule constantly in mind. If you are aware of the need to consider others' requirements you can now successfully engage in bold enterprises and make major changes in your life.

43. Now is the time to be resolute without being rash or foolishly adventurous. You must base all your actions upon an approach which combines strength and determination with goodwill and friendliness. Your resolution must show itself as a peaceful strength, not the sort of determination which manifests itself by disagreeable behaviour and hostility towards others. Concentrate on your own behaviour with the object of eradicating your own faults

and weaknesses. Don't try to reform other people, but always be aware of their interests as well as those that you feel are important.

44. This is a time when you are particularly receptive to advice given you by outsiders and there is some probability that you will be given such advice. However, such advice will not be good – if you act upon it you will find that it is not in your own interests. Rely on your own judgment. Be yourself.

45. At the present time it would be a mistake to be too confident of your own self-sufficiency and exclusively reliant upon your own strength, resilience and capacities. Seek the assistance of others – those who can help you in the situation you find yourself in and help you solve the problem that you are endeavouring to cope with. If you follow this course, good fortune will come to you, possibly in some quite sudden and totally unexpected fashion.

46. The present situation is one which calls for prompt actions and the use of all your capacity for adaptability. Circumstances are likely to change with the utmost rapidity and your responses to these changes must be well thought-out but extremely quick. Don't be afraid to use the advice of others, or to ask those in positions of power and responsibility for their help. Such advice or assistance may well prove invaluable in the resolution of difficulties and problems.

47. You are going through a difficult phase of your life. As far as you are concerned this is a time of adversity. Nothing seems to go right: unexpected difficulties crop up in the simplest piece of business; even social and emotional aspects of life cause problems. But difficulties and the ex-

perience of adversity can be turned to your advantage. What is needed is resilience, a cheerful response to the blows of fate, and a refusal to be downhearted. You must be tough because, at the moment, life is tough. If you can show a persistent and quiet courage in the face of adversity and misfortune, you will come out of this 'bad patch'. Fortune will smile upon you and success will be within your grasp.

48. At the present time you must endeavour to draw strength from the past. Not only your own past – the events, happy and unhappy, you have experienced in life – but the past which is shared by us all. In other words, you must draw upon the ritualized patterns of human behaviour (conventions, ways of feeling, types of reaction to common experiences, etc.) that humanity has developed over thousands of years. Discover and tap the reservoir of strength that lies at the deepest level of your own mind, as it does at the core of the being of each and every one of us.

49. This is a time of change, upheaval and the approach of new situations. The world in which you move is undergoing rapid and great alterations, and you must change with it. Just as your environment is being transformed, so must you be transformed. You must be prepared to change both the way you act and, to some extent, the way you think. Don't struggle against change, adapt to it and thus ensure that you are a survivor.

50. The time is not one to be adventurous, to behave in unexpected ways, or to launch out on new enterprises. Try to keep a low profile, and avoid any sort of action which makes you stand out from the crowd. Behave as dully as you can; appear to be a thoroughly conventional person. In this way your success in the present, unpromising situation will be assured.

51.

The time is one of surprises. The totally unforeseen will manifest itself in your life – and the surprises you receive will not only be pleasant ones. Don't allow yourself to be overwhelmed with astonishment. Instead, think deeply about your life, present and past, examining the nature of the actions you have taken and your true motives for doing so.

52.

This is a time of stillness in your life. It is both the stillness that succeeds energetic movement and the stillness, the tranquillity of power, which accompanies the gathering of forces prior to a bold move forward. In your life some situation or succession of events has either come to its conclusion or is about to do so. You now find yourself, or will soon find yourself, in a new situation or experiencing a new sequence of events. The time has come for you to engage in a calm process of self-examination; this will give you the necessary strength to take the steps that will be required in the situation which is now unfolding.

53.

At the present time hasty actions must be avoided, particularly in relation to any efforts you make to influence others or persuade them of the correctness of your viewpoint and the rightness of your actions. Be prepared to let situations develop slowly and naturally; avoid futile efforts to speed things up. Let the fruit ripen fully before you eat it – otherwise you may find yourself suffering indigestion.

54.

Be tactful and take the utmost care not to give offence to friends, workmates and those to whom you are emotionally attached. Be so cautious that you are, if anything, over-careful. Take a back seat. Don't try to push yourself to the front in either your work or private life. Ensure that your behaviour is acceptable to those with whom you associate; don't do anything that could make you open to hostile criticism. This is not the time to take chances – don't speculate or gamble in either the literal or metaphorical sense of the words.

55.

A horn of plenty, overflowing with all the good things of life, is the appropriate symbol for your present situation or the situation you will soon be in. It is the time of fullness, of abundance, of good luck and of success. Things cannot stay quite as good as this for evermore, but don't waste time worrying about what may happen in the future. Enjoy your happiness and success. Be happy now.

56.

It is possible that at the present time you are feeling fairly relaxed about things, that your personal situation is stable, that there is nothing to be concerned about. If so, you are much mistaken. At the moment nothing in your life is fixed, secure or certain. You are, in a sense, a wanderer upon the face of the earth who can have no certainty about what will happen next. Metaphorically speaking you are an individual 'of no fixed abode'. It is vital that you are prudent and reserved, not exposing yourself to hurtful rebuffs. Be patient and persevering. In this way you can ensure that you will slowly but surely attain the success and happiness you desire, and move towards the stability and security which, whether or not you are aware of it, you so desperately need.

57.

At the moment there is a need to keep in mind the old proverb 'time mends all things'. It would also be well if you held in mind the advisability of careful consideration and planning before embarking upon a course of action – particularly if the move you are thinking of making is an irrevocable one. In order to attain your goals you must be patient and persistent, moving steadily forwards, making what a military correspondent might call 'a slow but remorseless advance'.

58.

It is possible that you don't appreciate just how good things are at the moment. Whether or not you are aware of it, your position is an enviable one. Be relaxed and happy, but don't let your happiness lull you into a complacency which might result in your behaving foolishly. Keep pressing steadily forward. Don't relax your efforts because everything seems to be going rather well.

59.

You are in a situation in which unselfishness and generosity are called for. This is particularly the case in relation to any new activity, enterprise or course of behaviour that you may be considering. You must avoid mental and emotional rigidity; consider new ideas and approaches calmly. If you genuinely want to achieve your goals, you must be prepared to work – and play – in co-operation with others.

60.

You are in a period of your life that can be summed up in the word, 'limitation'. You must accept the fact that, strive and struggle as you may, you cannot have everything you want. There are positive aspects to an acceptance of the limitations that constrain us all. At times it does us good to 'tighten our belts', both literally and metaphorically. While accepting and making the best of unavoidable constraints, which arise out of the nature of life itself, you should not endure any galling restraints that adversely affect either your emotional or your working life. You are at important turning points in both your life and the particular situation or problem you are asking the oracle about. The proper course of action is for you to accept fully those unavoidable limitations on your freedom, doing your best to mitigate their effects so that they become tolerable, but endeavouring to overcome those constraints that can be overcome.

Lao-Tse, the legendary sage whose wisdom transformed him from earthly mortal to heavenly Immortal, in the company of Confucius, to whom many of the early commentaries on the I Ching *were attributed. Confucians and Taoists both venerate the oracle of the* I Ching.

capable of understanding the thoughts and feelings of others with the utmost difficulty. The only way you can get through to such people, communicate properly with them, is to explain your actions and motives persistently and quietly. Such explanations may have to be repeated again and again. It is vital that you adopt the right approach to those with whom you work or otherwise associate. Above all, never lose your temper with such people, however stupid or unfeeling they seem to be.

62.

A time in which you should behave with the utmost correctness and propriety, paying full attention to all the major and minor conventions of the society in which you live. In some ways the time is one of smallness – small beginnings, small upheavals and small endings. Concentrate, therefore, upon the little things of life, while avoiding mere pettiness. It is not a good time to decide to make large alterations in your way of life, or to solve major problems or embark upon ambitious ventures.

63.

It may well be that at the present time everything in your life seems harmonious, peaceful and ordered. But this is not the moment to relax. The reigning harmony could collapse into chaos if you started to feel so secure that you let things slide. However satisfactory and stable the present position may appear to be, it will only remain so as long as you keep up the juggling that is needed to maintain a state of balanced harmony. If you are not careful, events will take you by surprise so be prepared for the unexpected development, the unlikely happening.

64.

Provided you remain cautious and don't behave in a headstrong way your efforts should be rewarded with success and good fortune. Remember, however, that you are treading on thin ice and that taking risks will invalidate all your efforts.

61.

In your work and/or private life you are dealing with people who sometimes behave stupidly and are only

$\mathcal{N}$UMEROLOGY

*A*rithmetic, most children say, is a very dull subject – and yet there is a magic in numbers which has fascinated mankind since ancient times. For example, Pythagoras was excited by the fact that the musical intervals known in his time could be expressed in terms of the ratios 4:3, 3:2, and 2:1, and that these numbers add up to 10 (4 + 3 + 2 + 1 = 10). The fact that ten is the product of the first four numbers suggested that they were the basis of all reality – everything, it was argued, is an expression of number.

Modern numerologists usually eschew such mystical theorizing – but they do believe that the numbers derived from personal names provide a key to the character and destiny of an individual.

Dürer's engraving of the Spirit of Melancholy incorporates symbolism which makes clear the great artist's interest in numerology. The numerological 'magical square of Jupiter' (see pages 121-122) is shown, significantly, in the top right-hand corner of the engraving.

Most of us have heard or read such phrases as 'he thought his number was up' – meaning that the person concerned was in a very dangerous situation – or 'my lucky number had come up'.

These casually used, colloquial phrases refer to a very ancient belief that from any individual's name it is possible to derive a number (or numbers) that will not only be of great significance in that person's life, but will provide a key to unlock the secrets of his or her character and destiny.

These numbers are obtained by giving number equivalents to each letter of the alphabet, and the system of giving such equivalents in popular numerology has usually been based on the following simple table:

1	2	3	4	5	6	7	8	9
A	B	C	D	E	F	G	H	I
J	K	L	M	N	O	P	Q	R
S	T	U	V	W	X	Y	Z	

However, most serious students of numerology find this system unsatisfactory. The letters of the English alphabet, they say, have never had numerical values attached to them, and even in the Roman alphabet, from which English letter forms were largely derived, only six letters

(M,D,C,V,X,I) were of numerical significance. What is needed, so it is argued, is to correlate the vowels and consonants of the English alphabet with the letters, and thus the numerical equivalents, of the twenty-two letters of the Hebrew alphabet. For it was by students of the ancient Hebraic mystical system known as the cabala that 'number-in-your-name' techniques were first developed in the Western world.

The nineteenth-century numerologists who first endeavoured to produce tables of English/Hebraic letter (and thus number) equivalents encountered certain difficulties. Thus, while there are twenty-one consonants and five vowels in the English alphabet, there are only twenty-two letters in the Hebrew alphabet and none of them are vowels. Furthermore, certain Hebrew letters have more than one English equivalent (thus, for example, the Hebrew letter *vau* is roughly equivalent to both V and W) while others have no English equivalent.

The result of all this is that the numerical values of only twenty-one English letters can be derived from Hebrew, leaving five letters (E, I, J, O and X) unaccounted for. Fortunately for numerologists, equivalents to these letters can be derived from Greek letters which, like Hebrew, have a numerical significance:

E is taken as equivalent to the numerical value of the Greek letter *epsilon*, five.

I and **J** are taken as equivalent to the Greek letter *iota*, value ten, which reduces to one (1 + 0).

O is taken as equivalent to *omicron*, value seventy but reducing to seven (7 + 0).

X is taken as equivalent to *xi*, value sixty, reducing to six (6 + 0).

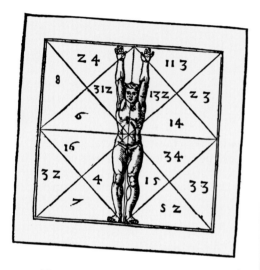

Later developments of the numerological mysticism of the Greek philosopher Pythagoras (above right) inspired the diagram above which appeared in the Occult Philosophy *of Cornelius Agrippa (1486-1535).*

The numerical values of the English alphabet as derived from the Hebrew and supplemented by the Greek is as follows:

1	2	3	4	5	6	7	8
A	B	C	D	E	U	O	F
I	K	G	M	H	V	Z	P
Q	R	L	T	N	W		
J		S			X		
Y							

It will be noted that in giving the numbers derived from the Greek alphabet, the numerical values of ten and above were reduced to single figures by adding together the digits of the number. Thus, for example, sixty has been reduced to six (6 + 0) and seventy to seven (7 + 0). This is a general and important

rule in this sort of name-numerolgy. With two exceptions, described below, all numbers of a name are reduced to a single digit, that is, a number from one to nine. If, for example, a name adds up to 156 you write down the number and add up its digits. Thus:

$$1 + 5 + 6 = 12.$$

But twelve is a double-figure number, so you have to take the process one step further:

$$1 + 2 = 3.$$

So, in the case of a name adding up to 156, you will be concerned with the supposed numerological properties of the number three.

The two exceptions are when the numerical values of the letters of a name add up to (or reduce to) either eleven or twenty-two. Even in these cases, however, a numerologist would also take into account the single-figure number to which these reduce, respectively two and four.

As an example of how number-in-your-name techniques are employed, let's suppose an individual is named Peter Anthony Dalby. In practice his name would probably only appear in that form on official documents, and those whom he knew would probably refer to him as Peter (or perhaps Pete) Dalby. On the other hand, he might be one of those people who prefer to be known by their second forename, in which case the

name used for numerological analysis would be Anthony Dalby, or Tony Dalby.

For the purpose of this example we'll assume he is known as Peter Dalby to both those he works with and those with whom he is only casually acquainted, but is called Pete by his friends.

First of all we'll analyse the hypothetical Peter Anthony Dalby as he is known at work and other formal and semi-formal situations.

Numerical value of letters from the table above:

P	E	T	E	R		
8	5	4	5	2	=	24

D	A	L	B	Y		
4	1	3	2	1	=	11

Adding the numerological value of 'Peter', 24, to that of 'Dalby', 11, we get a total of 35. Adding the 3 and the 5 together, we get the number (8) of the name Peter Dalby. This number of the whole name is usually referred to as the Key Number. The Key Number represents the whole character, inner and outer combined, of 'the bearer of the name from which it has been derived'. It is also held to give an indication of the likely destiny of the individual concerned.

Besides the Key Number of 8 which has been derived from the name Peter Dalby, two other numbers are included in that (and every other) name – the Heart Number which is obtained from the vowels of a name (A, E, I, O, U) and the Personality Number which is derived from its consonants. Thus:

numerical value of vowels from the table above:

P	E	T	E	R		
	5		5		=	10

D	A	L	B	Y		
	1				=	1

The two vowel totals are added together (10 + 1) to give 11. This, it will be remembered, is one of the two double-figure numbers considered significant by numerologists, so the Heart Numbers of Peter Dalby are 11 and 2 (as 11 reduces to 2).

MANDY
41541 = 15

THOMAS
457413 = 24

= 39.

3+9 = 12.   (12

= 1

711 = 8 ≠ 9

4   5   2   1

The total of the consonantal values is 24 (8 + 4 + 2 + 4 + 3 + 2 + 1), which is reduced by a further addition (2 + 4) to 6, the Personality Number of Peter Dalby.

The numerological analysis of the example name can be summarized as follows:

Key Number (the whole person) **8**
Heart Numbers (the inner personality) **11** and **2**
Personality Number (outward impressions) **6**

To find the significance of these and other numbers, look them up in the following list.

One is, as might be expected, a somewhat egotistical number, and One personalities tend to see everything and everybody in relation to themselves. This self-concern has both its strengths and weaknesses, its positive and negative aspects.

Ones display a certain single-mindedness, knowing what they want out of life and, because of their assertive and ambitious qualities, usually getting it. Inevitably, this sometimes ults in Ones behaving selfishly, sidering their own interests to the lusion of other people's. Like most ng individualists they do not make gether satisfactory subordinates, ng a great deal better at giving ers than taking them. They can be y good leaders indeed, provided y do not let their natural tendency ake the dominant part become so verful that leadership degenerates tyranny.

hose who have One as the Key mber of their name should always leavour to be fully conscious of the gers of the character-strengths h which they have been endowed. their relationships with friends, ordinates, partners, lovers and ldren they must always use their assertiveness and ambition in such a y that these traits result in a reputa-n for strength and tough-minded-ness, not selfishness, greed and petty tyranny.

Two is the number of femininity or, more strictly speaking, the psychological qualities traditionally associated with femininity but which have always been possessed by many men – tact, kindness, good nature, a placid temperament, and so on. These are the factors which make for a pleasant home life, and some numerologists find it significant that the Hebrew letter *beth*, which also represents the number Two, has the specific meaning 'house'; Bethel, a common name for a Nonconformist chapel, is derived from the Hebrew words *Beth El*, 'the house of God'.

It is worth emphasizing that while the psychological qualities of the man whose number is Two are characterized as 'feminine', the possession of these qualities in no way implies effeminacy. Soldiers, policemen and others whose occupations are traditionally considered masculine often have names in which the number Two is a dominant influence. Such men, however, tend to be in subordinate, although often important, positions; the essentially retiring nature of the Two personality tends to make him (or her) a better follower than leader.

This does not mean that the typical Two is incapable of leadership or of supervising others; it means that the

Some bingo players are convinced that if the first number called at a session is their personal 'lucky number' they will experience good fortune on the following day.

Two personality who wants to command others has to overcome the natural diffidence which can result in him or her being underestimated by friends, associates and workmates. The Two has to strive to make on others the sort of impression which the One personality makes with almost no effort at all.

The essential weakness of the Two man or woman is summed up in the old phrase 'playing second fiddle'. Twos are so anxious not to give others the idea that they are pushy egoists that there is a tendency to drop into the background even when they should be at the forefront.

Every number has its negative as well as its positive aspects, its vices as well as its virtues, and Two is no exception. The inborn diffidence of Twos can be developed to such an extent that shyness degenerates into a pointless secretiveness in which deceit, sometimes malicious deceit, becomes almost a way of life. Such a person soon gets a reputation as either someone who has something to hide or as a compulsive liar.

Three is a number of wholeness and completion and those who have it as their Key Number are to be envied. Threes are likeable, fast-thinking, versatile and sometimes brilliant. Their outgoing and adaptable personalities, their rich sense of humour and their affability make them popular with almost everyone they encounter, either socially or at work.

Threes tend to do well in all fields of activity which involve contact with others and 'putting on a show' designed to stimulate, inform or entertain. Thus, for example, they have the capacity to succeed in acting, television, salesmanship, and make excellent teachers and demonstrators.

The vices of the typical Three are an excess of the three virtues. A capacity to entertain or amuse becomes boring self-display; a likeable character becomes excessively concerned with cheap popularity; a talent for salesmanship is perverted into the technique of the confidence trickster.

Four is the number of steady application, hard work, determination and a drive to get things done as they should be done. The Four personality reflects all these qualities, and the Four individual usually displays at least some of the characteristics which astrologers have generally associated with the zodiacal sign of Capricorn.

Like typical Capricorns, Fours are inclined to 'make haste slowly' – to progress through life with a steady determination which often results in financial success and emotional happiness in the second rather than the first half of life. The Four personality is like the tortoise of the ancient fable. The slowness with which he or she moves sometimes arouses the derision of others, particularly the young, but in the long run determination leads to success and it is the tortoise, not the exuberant hare, which wins the race.

The negative aspects of the Four personality are, firstly, a tendency to let stoicism degenerate into an immobility and apathy which expresses itself as long-lasting depression and, secondly, a capacity to switch from a seemingly calm state to one of violent rage. These two negative characteristics of the Four are believed to be inter-related; Fours who unduly suppress their natural emotions in the interests of stoic calm are like boilers without a safety valve – all seems under control until an explosion takes place.

Five is the number of the pentagram, the five-pointed star which has traditionally been associated with the strange arts of the occultist and the magician, and Five personalities tend to be drawn towards the mysterious and the unexplained. They are often fascinated by unusual beliefs, whether religious, philosophical or even political, and are drawn towards minority and fringe movements, particularly in

artistic fields. Thus, for example, they are richly represented among those who delight in experimental music and painting, those who belong to obscure cults, and those who belong to societies devoted to 'borderlands-of-science' research like the investigation of psychic phenomena, alternative medicine and supposed contacts with beings from outer space.

They love everything unfamiliar, from strange places and people to unfamiliar types of work and play. When something new comes along they want to be the first to try it.

All this makes Fives very interesting to know; they are lively, questioning, intelligent, adventurous and are always prepared to listen to another point of view, however unusual.

Their vices are an inclination to self-indulgence, notably in their emotional lives; and a tendency to adopt points of view which go beyond the merely unorthodox to the point of extreme eccentricity.

Six personalities are not as phlegmatic as the slow-moving Fours but, on the other hand, are neither as unconventional as the adventurous Fives nor as glitteringly brilliant as the outgoing Threes.

In spite of this they are, in the long run, often more successful in their home, work and love lives than either reckless Fives or flashy Threes. While such successes are sometimes delayed, the Six usually achieves them much earlier in life than the slow-moving Four.

In many ways the Six personality displays exactly opposing characteristics to the Five. While the latter becomes easily bored with the familiar and longs for new sensations and experiences, Six individuals are happiest when they are in places or situations which are familiar to them, and among people they know well. Sixes prefer old friends to new ones, custom to experiment and comfort to adventure. They are loving, kind, reliable and often make life-long emotional attachments in the first part of their adult lives. The Six temperament is essen-

tially a happy one.

The negative aspect of the Six personality is a tendency to become almost too happy – to be complacent and unduly self-satisfied. Sixes in whom these negative characteristics have become predominant are usually looked upon as conceited by those who know them well.

Seven has always been looked upon as a mystic number and folklore and legend tell of its strange powers. Thus, for example, the seventh son of a seventh son was thought to be naturally gifted with second sight, i.e. the ability to foretell the future.

Numerologists assert that there is some truth in these traditional beliefs. Sevens, they say, are drawn towards the occult and the unseen, and enjoy an unusually rich inner life, being both imaginative and capable of deep thought. Their inclinations to esoteric studies, to the philosophical and mystical, are usually more scholarly and profound than those of Five personalities. It is a desire to explore the depths of their own beings, 'inner space', not a craving for the unusual, which most

Apart from the zero a roulette wheel has 36 numbers. Why 36 rather than, say, 34 or 37? Perhaps because classical numerologists divided the circle of the zodiac into 36 'decans'.

generally motivates Sevens who become students of the unknown and the unexplained.

Sevens are sometimes so absorbed with the realities of their interior life that to their families and friends they seem withdrawn, otherworldly or strange. This results from the negative aspect of the Seven personality, which is subject to introversion, a concern with inner thoughts and feelings, to such an extent that it can make for difficulties in communicating with others. A Seven of this type often has a powerful mind which is capable of original thought and real creativity, but is handicapped by difficulties in formulating his or her ideas in such a way that they can be understood by others.

Eight is the number of both material success and material failure. Eight personalities are almost always

anxious to achieve financial security and the things which accompany it, but, alas, they are only able to achieve it at the cost of unremitting struggle. They do not accumulate wealth and material possessions as easily as some of the other numerological types, such as the Threes or even the Sixes, and even when they do at last achieve success in life, they must ceaselessly struggle to hold on to what they have got.

The Eight individual has to be a worker; for him or her nothing comes without effort, and life is a ceaseless battle. Inevitably, this does not make for a carefree and relaxed temperament. The Eight must always be on guard, must always think of the next step, and this sometimes leads others to look upon the Eight as being stand-offish or even hostile. This is the cause of the chief negative aspect of the Eight personality; the Eight knows that others look upon him or her as being rather unfriendly and, as a consequence of this, sometimes becomes twisted, bitter and gains a reputation for being sarcastic and rude.

Nine is the number of completion and success in both material and the emotional life of the individual. Nines are achievers – men and women who usually get what they want out of life. Exactly what they want tends to change over the years, for there is an element of waywardness in the typical Nine. Thus, for example, they are liable to temporary fits of enthusiasm and they tend to fall in or out of love more easily than other numerological types.

The sudden enthusiams to which Nines are subject sometimes lead those who know them to regard them as being impractical visionaries or even eccentrics. Nevertheless, they are generally popular, for their genuine desire to help others as well as themselves usually outweighs their irritable behaviour towards those who do not fully share their enthusiasms.

The negative aspect of the Nine personality is a tendency to nosiness and domination; when this aspect is uppermost in a Nine individual the desire to help others finds expression in a tiresome and interfering way.

Eleven and **Twenty-Two** are the only double-figure numbers which are regarded as important in the numerological analysis of personal names.

Eleven is looked upon as being the number of revelation and inspiration and the Eleven personality possesses all the characteristics of the enthusiastic and visionary Nine – but on a much higher plane. An Eleven is also endowed with all the 'feminine' virtues of the Two, but with none of the vices; Elevens only play second fiddle to those whom they genuinely consider to be their superiors.

Elevens are not, however, without their own faults, and these are the failings of the idealist, the woman or man who has a deep belief in the truth and value of the principles to which she or he adheres. In other words, Elevens can be so deeply in love with their ideals that they disregard the practical needs and desires of their fellow human beings.

All in all, however, Eleven is a desirable and fortunate number and those whose names reduce to it are likely to make their mark on life in a way which will earn the respect and admiration – though not always the love – of those whom they encounter.

Twenty-Two is perhaps the most desirable of the numbers to which a name can be reduced. It is the number of the genuinely great human being and incorporates all the most favourable elements of the other numbers. The Twenty-Two, as has been pointed out by many writers, has the energy of the One, the harmonious and likeable personality of the Two, the brilliance of the Three combined with the Four's capacity for hard work, the adventu-

rousness of the Five along with the reliability of the Six, the richness of the imagination of the Seven, the worldly abilities of the Eight, the idealism of the Nine and the breadth of vision of the Eleven.

If you are a Twenty-Two you may well have felt a certain complacency when you read this list of pleasant and virtuous attributes. A word of warning, however: Twenty-Two is not only the number of the wise and visionary adept; it can also be the number of what has been called 'the master black magician', the human being who takes the road of moral perversion and becomes as great a force for evil as the Twenty-Two generally is for good.

As an example of how the meanings of the numbers can be blended into a numerological analysis of the personality of the holder of a given name, let us return to our hypothetical Peter Dalby. His numbers (see pages 116-17) were found to be:

Key Number	8
Heart Numbers	11 and 2
Personality Number	6

We will take these in reverse order. Peter Dalby's Personality Number – which is an indication of the impression he makes on others – is 6. This shows that he appears to most of those who know him as a kind, loving and reliable man who either has achieved, or will in time achieve, both happiness and material success; a fairly stolid type, but not, perhaps, a person who strikes others as being particularly imaginative, let alone visionary.

However, there seems to be rather more to Peter than outward appearances would indicate. For his Heart Number, the key to his hidden nature, the secret side of his existence, is 11. As an 'inner Eleven' Peter, beneath the worthy but perhaps slightly boring exterior with which he faces the world, is an enthusiast, a visionary idealist who at the same time has all the positive virtues associated with the number 2.

Inevitably, there will be some conflict between Peter's dull outward mask, his love of familiar things, his drive for comfort and success, and his rich inward imaginative life as an Eleven. How this conflict is resolved is, to some extent at least indicated by

his Key Number, 8.

The Key Number of a person's name is also known as the Destiny Number, for it is taken as an indicator of both the overall character of the person in question and the likely course of his or her life.

Eight (see page 119) is the number of hard work, of material success only being achieved as the result of continuous struggle. It seems likely that Peter will be a person torn between his outward 'Sixness' and his inner 'Elevenness', in other words a person who will only achieve material success if he controls his inner desires for the things of the mind and the spirit. Life for him will be a continual struggle against his own inner self, for he will only be, for example, a successful financier if he fights against his own inner wishes to be, perhaps, a poet or a prophet. In real life, such a person often obtains both material success and interior serenity by drawing a sharp dividing line between his public and private lives. In his working hours he might be a conventional banker or tradesman; in his own time he would be an enthusiastic member or leader of an idealistic cult or association, a charity worker, or a writer or painter.

Numerologists assert that the owner of a name can make practical use of his or her Key Number by ensuring that all important decisions are both made and enacted on a day of the month which adds up to the Key Number. If the number is 8, for example, the best days for the person concerned would be the 8th, 17th and 26th days of any particular month. If, on the other hand, it was 2, the best days of the month would be the 2nd, 11th and 20th.

It is also believed that changing one's name so that its numerological values alter can, over a period of time, change both one's luck and one's character. Thus if the hypothetical Peter Dalby decided to change his name by dropping one letter from the first of his names, becoming Pete Dalby, his Heart Number would remain the same – inwardly he would remain a visionary Eleven – but his Personality Number would become 4 and his Key (Destiny) Number would become 6.

If the numerologists are right in their beliefs this would be a far happier and less stressful number combination than that derived from the original name of Peter Dalby.

The outward impression made by Pete would become that of the typical Four – an individual who attains success in life as a result of steady application but seems, perhaps, a little dour and boring. His Key Number would be 6, so his overall destiny would be happiness at home, at work and in his emotional life. As a consquence of this, Pete would not find his interior nature, his Elevenness, in such marked opposition to his Key Number, and would not be torn apart by Peter's eternal struggle between the demands of his exterior life and the desires of his heart.

Besides the three numbers derived from a particular name, one other number is looked upon by some numerologists as being of major significance in an individual's life. This is the Birth Number, which is obtained from the day, month and year of birth. It is derived as follows:

Add together: the day of the month on which birth took place; the number of the month in which birth took place; the individual digits of the year of birth.

Then reduce them to one of the numerologically significant figures; that is, **22, 11** and **1** to **9** inclusive.

If, for example, the date of birth was February 12, 1948 one would write down:

12 (the day of the month on which birth took place)
+2 (February, of course, is the second month of the year)
+1948 (Year of birth)
_____
1962

$1 + 9 + 6 + 2 = 18$
$1 + 8 = 9$ (The Birth Number)

Those numerologists who attach significance to the Birth Number assert that it is, in the words of Richard Cavendish, 'an indication of the stamp . . . impressed on your character and destiny at the moment when you were born'. If it does not harmonize or coincide with either your Heart or Personality Number, you will 'be torn

by inner conflict and . . . seem to be always struggling against fate'.

As it is impossible to change one's Birth Number, those finding themselves in such a situation might be well advised to change their names or, alternatively, resolve to master their own destinies and let the numerologists say what they will.

OTHER NUMEROLOGICAL TECHNIQUES

The idea of finding 'your numbers in your name' is only one small aspect of numerology, an occult art which has fascinated many. One of these was the sixteenth-century artist, Albrecht Dürer, perhaps the greatest engraver of all time, and certainly a man of wide-ranging interests. Dürer seems to have accepted the belief, still held by some present-day occultists, that numerological techniques could be used to induce mood changes – the lifting, for example, of acute depression, the psychological disorder which our ancestors referred to as melancholia.

Magical Squares
Dürer's engraving 'Melancholia', reproduced on page 114, shows the angel of Saturn symbolizing an individual suffering from acute melancholia. On the wall behind the angel is a 'magical square' made up of 16 separate numbers in four rows of four. A 'magical square' is one in which the

A childish fascination with numbers can develop in adulthood into a serious interest in numerology – or a neurosis characterized by obsessive counting of objects like spoons.

numbers in any particular row, whether across, perpendicular or diagonal, add up to the same figure. In the case of the square shown in Dürer's engraving the significant number is 34. If you look at the square below, you will see the reason for this.

The four rows across are:

$4 + 14 + 15 + 1 = 34$
$9 + 7 + 6 + 12 = 34$
$5 + 11 + 10 + 8 = 34$
$16 + 2 + 3 + 13 = 34$

Similarly the four perpendicular rows are:

4	14	15	1
+ 9	+ 7	+ 6	+12
+ 5	+11	+10	+ 8
+16	+ 2	+ 3	+13
=34	=34	=34	=34

And the two diagonals are $16 + 11 + 6 + 1$ (=**34**) and $13 + 10 + 7 + 4$ (=**34**).

The fact that all the rows of figures in this 16-figured square add up to 34 is not the only interesting thing about it from the point of view of the numerologist. Thus, the 16 figures in the square add up to 136, and $1 + 3 + 6 = 10$, which becomes one (1 + 0), the 'number of perfect happiness' and 'personal integrity' according to some occult numerologists. Again, the totals of the four perpendicular, four horizontal, and two diagonal rows add up to 340, which reduces to 7 (3+4+0), which has, for millennia, been thought to possess mystical properties.

The square which has been analysed above and which was incorporated by Dürer into his 'Melancholia' engraving is, in fact, referred to by some numerologists as 'the magical square of Jupiter'. It is believed to be intimately connected with all the attributes which astrologers have traditionally associated with the planet Jupiter: happiness, prosperity, good fortune, a long life, and so on.

Albrecht Dürer included this square in his engraving as a reflection of the belief that its mere presence in the room occupied by a person suffering from depression would help to lift that person's spirits. Similarly – but conversely – it was believed that the magical square of Saturn (significant number, 15), shown below:

4	9	2
3	5	7
8	1	6

would 'bring down to earth' someone suffering from maniacal exaltation.

In the present day the idea that figured squares may possess occult powers seems very odd indeed to most of us, but three or four centuries ago such beliefs were commonplace among those who concerned themselves with the mystic power of numbers. It was not only numerologists who held such beliefs: one seventeenth-century Pope used them in the Vatican in order to counter 'evil astrological influences' which he believed were threatening his life.

The Pope in question, Urban VIII, was a dedicated student of the astrology of his time and had come to the conclusion that the influence of the planetary positions of Mars and Saturn in his horoscope, combined with that of an impending eclipse of the sun, would have to be counteracted in some way or another. He consulted a Dominican friar named Cam-

panella, one of the most learned men of his time, who advised that the benefic planetary effects of Jupiter and Venus should be used to neutralize the harmful aspects of Mars and Saturn.

On the walls of the Pope's private apartments was hung the magical square of Jupiter, as shown above, together with that of Venus (significant number 175) which is:

22	47	16	41	10	35	4
5	23	48	17	42	11	29
30	6	24	49	18	36	12
13	31	7	25	43	19	37
38	14	32	1	26	44	20
21	39	8	33	2	27	45
46	15	40	9	34	3	28

The supposed influences of the squares were supplemented by the Pope listening to music which he believed was of a Jupiterian or Venusian type, scenting his apartments with roses – flowers attributed to Venus – and drinking distilled liqueurs flavoured with aromatic plants which the astrological herbalists of the time believed to be 'under the dominion' of Jupiter and Venus.

Perhaps all this worked; certainly the sun's eclipse took place without the death of the Urban VIII, who lived on for another 16 years, during which he passed a law making it illegal for any subject of the Papal dominions to investigate the probable life spans of Popes on the basis of astrology. Urban also, rather ungratefully, condemned Campanella to prison for practising occult arts.

If you want to make the astrological/numerological experiment of attracting the influences of Jupiter, thought to bring prosperity and happiness, or Venus, bringer of love, by using the magical squares of these planets, it is easy enough to do so. You can, as some present-day occultists have done, have them engraved upon a ring, pendant or bracelet, or – much simpler and cheaper – simply copy them out and either pin them upon the wall of your bedroom or carry them in your purse or wallet. No guarantees of successful results are given!

Using Dice
A number of numerological techniques involve the use of numbers derived from the fall of dice. Some of these are very simple – almost games

The planetary spirits of Venus and Sol, whose influence Campanella invoked by the use of magical squares in the rites employed by him to avert the effects of malefic planetary influences.

rather than serious fortune-telling – while others are more complicated, and many of those who have used them claim that they are capable of providing an uncannily accurate forecast of future events. Before attempting to experiment with the latter it is a good idea to 'play' with the dice. This play, an only half-serious type of fortune-telling, can take two forms. You can either enquire what is to be the most significant event in your life over the next month, or you can use the dice to obtain answers to simple questions.

The procedure for finding the significant event is as follows:

1. Draw a circle about 7 inches across on a piece of paper.
2. Throw three dice on the piece of paper, aiming at the drawn circle.
3. Total up the numbers thrown, disregarding the numbers on any dice which have fallen outside the drawn circle.
4. Interpret the total in accordance with the following list.

Total Number Thrown

0. (Note. This total will, of course, only be encountered in the highly unusual circumstance of all three dice falling outside the drawn circle.) The next month of your life will be remarkably uneventful, dull in the extreme. You should also endeavour to improve your dice-throwing techniques.

1. (Note. Only encountered when two dice fall outside the circle.) In spite of your lack of skill in aiming dice at a circle, the next month of your life will be one in which you have a stroke of good fortune which will fill your life with happiness.

2. (Note. Only encountered when one or two dice fall outside the circle.) At some time in the next month an important event will take place in your life which will fill you with gloom, but which you will subsequently realize is a blessing in disguise.

3. You are going to get a very pleasant surprise.

4. Something you have felt very sure about won't go quite as you have planned.

Urban VIII, Pope from 1623 to 1644, practised astrology, and with the help of the Dominican friar Thomas Campanella employed numerological white magic.

5. A new person will come into your life who will either become one of your closest friends or, perhaps, a more intimate acquaintance.

6. Unless you are very careful indeed you will lose something of great value. This may be something concrete, like a piece of jewellery, or it may be something abstract, like friendship.

7. You will be disappointed by the treatment you receive from someone whom you have hitherto regarded as a friend or ally. It is likely that a distorted account of your actions, and the motives for them, will be put into circulation. Take steps to ensure that everybody who matters knows the facts.

8. You must be careful, for you are in danger of making a serious mistake. If you do so, you will get all the blame, even though others may have been partly responsible.

9. Either you, or someone very close to you, is about to make a definite step towards a long-term relationship.

10. News of a birth, or perhaps a pregnancy, will cause you much surprise and some pleasure.

11. The coming month will be one of partings. At least one friend or close associate will take temporary leave of you, and there is a possibility of a longer-term parting from someone else.

12. News of immense importance to you or your partner will soon be received through the post.

13. An unpleasant surprise is likely. Try not to be too upset about this: things are not going to be as difficult as may seem likely at first.

14. Someone new will come into your life who clearly wants to become your friend or form an even closer relationship. You may not feel the same way at all.

15. The next month will be a difficult one, both in relation to your feelings and financial matters. Take great care! You must be prudent if you are to avoid major difficulties.

16. Travel – possibly planned quite a long time ago but more probably something which has suddenly come up – will be a feature of your life over the next month. The consequent experiences and adventures will be much more enjoyable and exciting than you might expect.

17. News from afar will be received. It will almost certainly be news you will be very happy to receive and may well be to your financial advantage.

18. Something totally unexpected is about to take place. In the long run it will certainly be the cause of much happiness.

A technique for obtaining answers to a variety of questions also involves the use of three dice thrown into a circle. You can formulate simple questions of your own to be answered by this method and, provided the question has been properly phrased, you will usually obtain a meaningful and often accurate reply. Some of the questions you can ask are:

Will I soon meet a new partner?
Will I become financially prosperous or wealthy?
Will I inherit money or acquire it by some stroke of good luck?
Will I get from life the thing I most desire?

Will I achieve my immediate object?

Will I ever get over my present unhappiness?

Am I going to receive good news?

Will the letter I'm expecting tell me what I hope?

Will I change my job soon?

Will I ever be an accomplished fortune-teller?

Does my partner really love me?

Am I being misled?

Can I trust X?

Should I move to a new home?

Should I take the chance offered to me at the moment?

To get your answers proceed as in the previous technique: aim your three dice at the circle when you throw them and add the numerical values of the dice together, but don't count any dice which have fallen outside the circle. Look below and take as your answer the reply listed opposite the number corresponding to the total obtained.

0. The matter is not yet resolved. Ask again in a week's time.

1. Yes.

2. The probabilities are too finely balanced for a definite answer to be given at the present time. Repeat your question in two or three week's time.

3. The next lunar month will decide fate's throw. Ask your question again exactly four weeks from today.

4. Yes, provided you are not too self-centred in your approach.

5. No, unless you approach things with more care than in the past.

6. Yes, but don't worry about things so much.

7. Yes, if you rely upon your own inner strengths.

8. Yes, provided you are prepared to be co-operative.

9. Only if you do your best and are really persistent.

10. Not if you are always worrying about unreal problems.

11. Nothing is certain at the moment, it's all a matter of chance.

12. Yes, provided that you are serious.

13. Only if you look before you leap and don't believe everything you are told.

14. Of course – as you are inwardly well-aware.

15. Only if you behave decisively, or are quite sure of the facts.

16. Only if you are true to your inner nature.

17. Not if you are unprepared to take risks.

18. No at the moment, but wait for a sign, message or information which will make things clear.

As was said above, this half-playful method of obtaining an answer to a simple question usually gives a meaningful answer. Sometimes, however, the answer to your question is not altogether clear and has to be interpreted symbolically. In this case a minute or two's thought should enable you to interpret the nature of the answer you have received. If, even after a little consideration, you cannot perceive any straightforward or symbolic meaning which makes the answer relevant to the question, don't strain after a meaning. All that you will achieve is a distortion – your unconscious mind will twist the meaningless phrase into an answer that it would like to get.

It is held that if you get a nonsensical answer to a simple question by using this technique, it is a strong indication that the situation is too fluid for a definite answer to be given. So you should put your question aside for the moment; consult the dice again in a week or ten days' time.

A slightly more elaborate method of numerological fortune-telling with dice involves the use of an astrological horoscope outline as the circle in which you throw your dice.

Draw a circle between 6 and 9 inches across and divide it into 12 numbered segments as shown in the diagram above right. Now:

A. Take a piece of scrap paper and note down in sequence the same numbers as those which appear in the circle, that is, 1-12 inclusive.

B. Throw the three dice into the circle. Unless one or more of the dice has landed outside the circle (in which case the throw should be disregarded and repeated until all three dice have fallen within the circle) there will be one or more dice in either three, two, or one of the segments. Add up the total number shown by the dice contained in any particular segment of the circle and

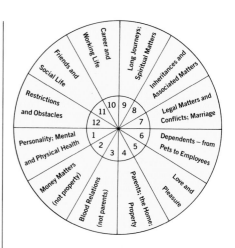

← 15 cms (6″) or 23 cms (9″) diameter →

note that number down on your scrap paper opposite the number of that segment. For example, if two of the three dice, showing numbers 5 and 4, were in segment 2, and the third of them, showing a 6, was in segment 7, you would note down '9' opposite the number 2 on the list and '6' opposite the number 7.

C. Pick up the three dice and make another throw. Disregard any dice which fall into segments for which you already have a dice total. Total up the numbers of the dice in the 'new' segment or segments (that is, any segment on which dice have fallen at the second throw but did not fall on the first throw) and enter the total or totals against the number of the segment(s) on your piece of scrap paper.

D. Repeat C. (above) as many times as necessary until you have a figure against each of the numerals 1-12 on your piece of paper.

E. Interpret these 12 totals in accordance with the following meanings:

1. As far as the relevant aspect of your life is concerned things are likely to go very well for you over the next 12 months. Some set-backs may be experienced, but the overall position will be one of general improvement.

2. Things are likely to go well over the next year in this field, provided you are prepared not only to avoid disputes but to co-operate fully with others.

3. Compared with the past, things are going to go very well indeed for you over the next year or so. If the situation has been unsatis-

factory, it will become satisfactory; if it has been good, it will become very good.

4. Things are unlikely to be very satisfactory in relation to this aspect of your life over the next year. Great care must be taken and no course of action embarked upon without a full consideration of the possible consequences.

5. As far as this aspect of your life is concerned there is likely to be considerable improvement soon. This may come suddenly – there is a possibility of a very pleasant surprise.

6. It is uncertain how this aspect of your life will develop over the next year. It will be dependent on both the actions of others, which are out of your control, and on your own responses, sensible or foolish, to those actions.

7. Major problems and obstacles, some totally unexpected, will crop up in your life over the next 12 months. These will not prove insuperable provided that you do not despair, and show energetic persistence in endeavouring to overcome them.

8. Unless you take great care and avoid all thoughtless and reckless action over the next 12 months this area of your life is likely to be a troubled one.

9. This whole aspect of your life will be influenced in the next 12 months by an impending – or already existing – marriage, long-term emotional partnership, or romantic attachment. You yourself will not necessarily be one of the two people directly involved in this matter, but someone very close to you, friend or opponent, will be.

10. There will be new and surprising developments in this area of your life. Expect the unexpected!

11. Travelling and journeyings will influence this aspect of your life over the next year. Don't be too alarmed – whether it bodes good or ill largely depends upon your own attitudes.

12. What the old fortune-tellers called 'news from afar' will greatly influence this aspect of your life in the first half of the year to come. Expect an important letter or long-distance telephone call.

13. This aspect of your life is likely to be full of problems over the next year. If you adopt a common-sense attitude and remain calm and ordered in your life, these will prove only temporary and will have no harmful, long-term effects.

14. Problems are likely to be encountered in this area of your life, but with assistance from others they will almost certainly be overcome. Those who give this help will include friends and close associates, but some of it will come from a quite unexpected and surprising source.

15. Great care on your part is required if there are to be no troubles in this area of your life over the next few months. Tread very delicately – you are on thin ice.

16. This aspect of your life will, in all probability, involve a certain amount of travelling over the next year or so. The outcome of these journeys should be satisfactory – indeed, they may bring great happiness.

17. In this area of your life a matter in which you have been greatly involved, perhaps worryingly involved, is about to come to a satisfactory and beneficial conclusion.

18. In this area of your life you will have nothing to complain about over the coming 12 months. Everything will go smoothly and even things which start badly will end well. Great good fortune will be yours.

When making your interpretations you must apply each in accordance with the attribution of the segment in which the relevant number fell. For example, suppose that the totals put down beside the first of the six segment numbers listed on your piece of paper were:

1. **6**
2. **8**
3. **3**
4. **4**
5. **11**
6. **12**

You would apply the interpretation given for the number **6** to the area of your life pertaining to segment 1 – your physical and mental health, how your personality is likely to develop, and so on. Similarly, you would apply the interpretation given for the number **8** to the aspects of your life pertaining to segment 2 – money matters, general financial problems and allied concerns. You must carry on round the segments like this, applying the meaning of the number **12** to the area of life pertaining to segment 6, which is dependents – from pets to employees. So your relationships over the coming year with both your dog and your butler (if you are very rich) will be affected over the coming year by 'news from afar'. Perhaps you will get an angry letter informing you that your dog persistently barks, or someone will telephone you to tell you that your butler has a criminal record.

So when using the numerical meanings for the numbers 1 to 18, as shown above, remember that you should always interpret those meanings in relation to the particular segments to which they relate. Also remember that you may well have to apply the meaning of a particular number to more than one segment; theoretically (but very improbably) you might have to apply the meaning of just one of the numbers to all 12 segments. As an example of applying the same meaning to more than a single segment let us suppose that the number 2 applies to segments 1, 2 and 10.

In this case:

a) The number **2** as the dice total for segment 1 means that your mental and physical health will be good over the next year, 'provided you are prepared not only to avoid disputes but to cooperate fully with others'. In the context of your personal health – the dominion of segment 1 – this can be taken as urging you to maintain your health by adopting a life-style generally thought to be advantageous by the medical profession. You should 'cooperate' with the medical profession by, for example, not stuffing yourself with large quantities of animal fats, and avoiding excessive drinking and smoking.

b) The number **2** also relates to segment 2 – money matters. The same meaning (as given on page 124) applies, but this time you should interpret that meaning in a different way. You are being urged to cooperate with others who also have an interest in your financial affairs – perhaps your business or marital partner, perhaps those you work with, or perhaps even your insurance broker, or bank manager.

c) The number **2** is finally related to segment 10 which, as you will see from the diagram on page 124, is concerned with your working life and your career. Clearly, the information being given is that all should go well in these areas of your life provided that you don't quarrel with work colleagues and are fully cooperative with them.

There is another interesting method of using dice to get a numerological reading in relationship to the general situation of the enquirer, his or her emotional and love life, and his or her financial affairs. The procedure for generating the numbers is simple: just throw one dice three times, at each throw noting the number indicated.

The number of the first throw is taken as pertaining to the general situation; that from the second throw to the emotional life; and that of the final throw to money matters.

The Numbers 1 To 6 In Relation To A General Situation

1. It is likely that, in the very near future, fate will provide you with an opportunity to solve a problem that has been troubling you for some time. Grasp this chance with the utmost eagerness. Also ensure that you live your social life to the full.

2. The time for action has arrived. If you act now, not letting yourself be discouraged by small difficulties, you will get what you have long desired. This is the time when, if you are bold, you can turn the stuff which dreams are made of into real life. Some welcome news should shortly arrive, perhaps by post.

3. Recently, you have been displaying altogether too much energy and activity in relation to a matter which has been causing you some concern and is, as you must realize if you are honest with yourself, largely beyond your control. Don't try to do more than is possible. Think carefully about this and don't make any move which has no real hope of success.

4. You have been thinking about the past, regretting past errors and mournfully dreaming of what might have been. But there is nothing you can do to alter what has already happened. You can, however, do your best to mitigate the harmful effects of past actions – you can learn the lessons of old mistakes and make sure that you do not repeat them. Do this and the future will be as good as the past might have been.

5. You are a far more ambitious person than most of those who know you are aware, and you are determined to get what you want out of life. This is fine, but you are unlikely to succeed unless you talk less about your plans and simultaneously make more effort to put them into effect. Quiet, firm, purposeful action is called for.

6. It may seem to you that others – family, friends and those you work with – are acting as a brake on your progress. If so, you will be feeling thoroughly irked, for at the present time you are in a mood to forge ahead. However, it will do no harm at all if you do slow down for a bit: from the best and most understandable of motives you have taken on more than you can handle.

The Numbers 1 To 6 In Relation To Emotional Life

1. It is likely that at the moment, or in the very near future, you will be trying to get out of an entanglement with someone who takes your relationship with him or her as something far more important than you your-

The novelist Ian Fleming chose '007' as the number of his hero, James Bond. By a curious coincidence this was the code number by which the occultist John Dee (see page 14) was sometimes referred to.

self consider it to be. To escape from this trying situation will be difficult and will involve more complications than you expect. Seek the advice and help of someone who has been in an almost identical situation.

2. If you are not involved in a long-term relationship you will find that change is in the air. Either someone new is coming into your life or someone you have known for a long time is going to assume a much greater importance as far as your emotions are concerned. If, on the other hand, you do have a permanent partner, you can be sure that your relationship with him or her is going to become much better and deeper. Happiness is at hand.

3. At the present time you are probably feeling somewhat restless – dissatisfied with life, wondering if all the effort you put into things is really worth it, and feeling that you may have been moving in the wrong direction for some time. To whatever extent you may have these feelings, you must endeavour not to let them adversely affect your relationships with loved ones in general, and your partner in particular. Without being unduly secretive, try to keep worries to yourself for the time being and don't let them become problems for others.

4. If everything is going well at the moment as far as the emotional aspects of your life are concerned, good. Relax and enjoy the situation. If, as is more likely, things are in muddle and turmoil and you are not sure what you should do next, relaxation is still the best course of action. There is nothing much to be achieved at the moment by even the most decisive moves. Time, without much effort on your part, will eventually resolve your problems.

5. Difficulties with your partner may be experienced over the next few months unless you are very careful indeed. Don't drag other factors and outside influences into your relationship. If you do, the effects are

By the nineteenth century the real Cornelius Agrippa, greatest numerologist of the Renaissance, was forgotten; he had become a bogeyman to frighten naughty children.

likely to be unfortunate. Try to avoid discussing either money matters or your partner's friends and relations in anything but the friendliest way.

6. A really excellent period is beginning as far as your emotional life is concerned. You will experience new pleasures and much happiness. If you already have a partner, your life together will become far more satisfying and complete. If you are still on your own, it is time to think of a permanent relationship – it should be blissful.

The Numbers 1 To 6 In Relation To Finances

1. You have a money problem, perhaps one that has arisen very recently, more probably one that is long-standing and is now a 'chronic complaint'. There is no point in trying to pretend the problem doesn't exist; you will find that you can't forget it for very long. On the bright side, however, is the fact that your problem is not insoluble. With careful planning, economy and determination, your trouble can be reduced to the point at which it vanishes away.

2. The time has come for you to consider seriously your financial position and make both short- and long-term plans in relation to money matters. Once you have made your plans, act upon them – although first ensure that you have taken into consideration all the factors involved. Action now will pay off ten or a hundredfold in the months and years to come.

3. This is probably one of the times when you feel that you are not entirely in control of money matters. It may well seem to you that every time things are going as you would wish them to go, some outside factor interferes with your plans. Don't worry unduly; all will turn out well in the end, provided that you are prepared to be prudent.

4. It is time to stop worrying about money matters which are entirely beyond your personal control. All you can do at the present time is conduct your personal finances as carefully as you can and make every effort to avoid reckless expenditure. It is no use letting your mind dwell on past financial mistakes or disasters; plan for the present and the future.

5. This is not a good time to speculate, gamble or enter into chancy business deals. Do not do so yourself and endeavour to get those to whom you are close to follow a similarly prudent course. While the coming months are not a period in which risks should be taken, they are not going to be impoverished either. The indications are that there will be a very considerable improvement in your finances, and that in a year's time you will feel able to relax your efforts slightly.

6. If your current financial position is a difficult one, don't despair – there is going to be a notable (and probably unexpected) improvement in the near future. If, on the other hand, your present financial state is stable or good, be prepared to celebrate, for you are about to experience one of the most fortunate episodes in your financial life.

SAMPLE NUMEROLOGICAL ANALYSES

Napoleon Bonaparte

Everyone has heard of Napoleon Bonaparte, the obscure officer of artillery who became, firstly, a General whose exploits astonished Europe, then First Consul of the French Republic, then Emperor of the French, virtual ruler of all continental Europe, and finally, an exile on the remote island of St Helena.

If one asked a random selection of ordinary Americans or Europeans to name the most famous Frenchman of all time, it is a virtual certainty that the overwhelming majority would reply 'Napoleon'.

Yet Napoleon's ancestry was Italian, rather than French, and until after the spring of 1796 he and his family normally spelt their names Buonaparte – all of them were descendants of Francesco Buonaparte, a man from the Italian town of Sarzana who emigrated to Corsica in the middle of the sixteenth century.

Even after the spring of 1796 most members of Napoleon's family still thought of themselves and their increasingly distinguished relative as being 'Buonaparte' not 'Bonaparte'. This particularly applied to the older members of the family, such as Napoleon's mother, Letizia, who on occasion wrote the surname of her sons in its older form long after the second of them had, from being a supremely successful soldier, become Emperor. The numerological analysis of Napoleon's original name is:

N A P O L E O N
$5+1^*+8+7^*+3+5^*+7^*+5+$
B U O N A P A R T E
$2+6^*+7^*+5+1^*+8+1^*+2+4+5^* = 82$

(* indicates a vowel)

$\quad 8+2 = 10$

$\quad 1+0 = 1$ (the Key Number of the original name).

The vowels of the name, indicated by asterisks, add up to 40, and reduce to 4, thus:

$\quad 1+7+5+7+6+7+1+1+5 = 40$

$\quad 4+0 = 4$ (the Heart Number of the original name).

The consonants of the name add up to 42 which reduces to 6, thus:

$\quad 5+8+3+5+2+5+8+2+4 = 42$

$\quad 4+2 = 6$ (the Personality Number of the original name).

Thus the numbers in Napoleon's original name can be summarized as:

Key Number	1
Heart Number	4
Personality Number	6

The Key Number, One, indicated a splendid future for the young artillery officer from Corsica, who seems to have been regarded with some contempt by the more aristocratic of his fellows. In reality, of course, there was nothing to be contemptuous about – quite apart from the fact that he was a soldier of genius, Napoleon's family tree could be traced back to the eleventh century, a good deal longer than those of the comparative upstarts who slighted him.

The young Napoleon was unique – in his talents, in his determination, and in his capacity for being in the right place at the right time. This led to him being looked upon as an excep-tionally lucky person. He himself attributed this luck to what he called his 'star'; he felt that he had been singled out by history to achieve greatness and in a sense, he was right. For it was the great upheaval of the Revolutionary epoch that enabled Napoleon to transform himself from a junior officer to an Emperor.

Napoleon was, then, quite exceptional. Yet in some ways the young Napoleon was a typical One – and he retained some of his Oneness long after he had changed his name.

Like all Ones he was egotistical, seeing everything and everybody in relation to himself and often using others for his own private ends, giving little consideration to the feelings of those

The future Emperor Napoleon as a young General who still spelt his surname in the Corsican manner – Buonaparte.

he used. Napoleon was also possessed, to the highest degree, by the One ambitiousness, the burning desire to excel.

After his change of name, Napoleon retained most of his One characteristics – a numerologist might say because in his heart he still considered himself, as his older relatives certainly considered him, a Corsican Buonaparte rather than a Gallic Bonaparte. There is no doubt, however, that as the years went by Napoleon also displayed more and more of the qualities, particularly the negative qualities, numerologically associated with the new spelling of his name, which is analysed as follows:

N A P O L E O N
5+1*+8+7*+3+5*+7*+5+
B O N A P A R T E
2+7*+5+1*+8+1*+2+4+5* = 76
 7+6 = 13
 1+3 = 4 (the Key Number of the name).

The vowels of the name, indicated by asterisks, add up to 34, and reduce to 7, thus:
 1+7+5+7+7+1+1+5 = 34
 3+4 = 7 (the Heart Number of the name).

The consonants of the name add up to 42, which reduces to 6:
 5+8+3+5+2+5+8+2+4 = 42
 4+2 = 6 (the Personality Number of the name).

Thus the three numbers contained in Napoleon's new name can be summarized as:

Key Number	4
Heart Number	7
Personality Number	6

Four, the Key Number of the name of Napoleon in its later version, has been called 'the number of failure'. Not many numerologists would agree with this without qualification; there have been many Fours who have made great successes of their lives, usually as a result of steady application and unremitting effort. To use an athletic metaphor, successful Fours have generally tended to be long-distance runners rather than sprinters.

Napoleon kept much of the sprinting capacity of his original Oneness, as witnessed by his daring escape from Elba in 1814 – but the negative qualities of the Four displayed themselves prior to and during the Battle of Waterloo, the decisive defeat which ended the

brief Napoleonic restoration which had resulted from that escape.

The negative qualities of the Four can be summed up as depression, apathy, a switching between over-hasty action and a profound immobility – an inability to make a decision even when the situation is such that to make almost any definite move is probably better than to make no move at all. The calm philosophy of the positive Four degenerate s into systematic lassitude.

Military history as such is outside the scope of this book. Nevertheless, it is worth saying that some students of Napoleon's life have argued that his defeat at Waterloo was not inevitable; that if he had made a quick decision to attack the British and Belgian forces under the Duke of Wellington's command, instead of being torn by indecision for many hours, he could have

Napoleon as Emperor – torn, think some numerologists, by indecision arising from a conflict between Fourness and Oneness.

destroyed Wellington before the Prussians under Blücher had had a chance to reinforce him.

It has been suggested that Napoleon's indecision prior to Waterloo resulted from illness, that he could think of nothing save the violent stomach pains which he was suffering. But a similar fatal indecision marked the 1812 retreat from Moscow. If the retreat had started earlier then it is probable that far more of Napoleon's decimated troops would have survived.

Perhaps if Napoleon had not been torn between his Fourness and his Oneness he would not have ended his life in exile.

Marilyn Monroe

'What's in a name? That which we call a rose
By any other name would smell as sweet.'

Romeo and Juliet (Act II, Scene 2)

No doubt all of us would agree with Shakespeare's Juliet that the name of a flower does not affect its odour – but in fact, many of us feel that there is a great deal in a name, quite apart from any occult significance attached to the numerical significance of its vowels and consonants. There is little doubt that, for most of us, names become psychologically associated with a certain type of personality. We are surprised, for example, if we meet a man who is exceptionally weak and whose first name is Rocky. One cannot help thinking that Juliet might have found Romeo slightly less attractive if his name had been, say, Morbido, or that the late Diana Dors might not have been quite so successful in show business if she had stuck to her original surname of Fluck.

The young Marilyn Monroe – still, from the point of view of the name-numerologist, Norma (Jean) Baker, Key Number either Four or Seven.

A far more successful film star who changed her name was 'Marilyn Monroe', born Norma Jean Baker and known in childhood and adolescence as both 'Norma' and 'Norma Jean'.

Each version of Marilyn Monroe's original name would be considered significant by those who attach importance to name/number equivalents and accordingly, both should be analysed.

As 'Norma Jean Baker' the name is analysed as follows:
N O R M A J E A N
$5+7*+2+4+1*+1+5*+1*+5+$
B A K E R
$2+1*+2+5*+2 = 43$

(* indicates a vowel)

$4+3 = 7$ (the Key Number of Norma Jean Baker).

The vowels of the name, marked by asterisks, add up to 20 and reduce to 2, thus:

$7+1+5+1+1+5 = 20$
$2+0 = 2$ (the Heart Number of Norma Jean Baker).

The consonants of the name add up to 23, which reduces to 5, thus:

$5+2+4+1+5+2+2+2= 23$
$2+3 = 5$ (the Personality Number of Norma Jean Baker).

Thus the numbers contained in the original name can be summarized as:

Key Number	7
Heart Number	2
Personality Number	5

A very different result is obtained by using 'Norma Baker', the shorter form of the film star's original name:
N O R M A
$5+7*+2+4+1*$
B A K E R
$2+1*+2+5*+2 = 31$

The Key Number of the shorter name is $(3 + 1)$ 4. The vowels of the name, which provide the Heart Number, add up to 14 $(7+1+1+5)$, which reduces $(1+4)$ to 5, while the consonants total $(5+2+4+2+2+2)$ 17, reducing $(1+7)$ to 8, the Personality Number of 'Norma Baker'.

Putting the results of the numerical analysis of the two original versions (the longer and the shorter) of Marilyn Monroe's name side by side we get:

	Longer Version	Shorter Version
Key Number	7	4
Heart Number	2	5
Personality Number	5	8

This presents, from the point of view of the numerologist, a 'number picture' which is perhaps confusing.

Let us start with the two Key Numbers, Seven and Four, which as was said on page 116, 'represent the whole person'. A 'whole person' who, like the future film star, is simultaneously a Seven and a Four, is a walking contradiction. Fours tend to be practical, hard working, pressing steadily forward to their objectives and keeping in hand the task of mastering the outside world as it affects their lives. Sevens, on the other hand, tend to have a rich interior life but find difficulty in adjusting to reality. In terms of the probably over-simple psychological classification of human beings into extroverts and introverts – those who are outgoing and those who are inward looking – the Four is an extrovert and the Seven is an introvert. It is likely that anyone whose 'whole self' is both Four and Seven will live a muddled life, making decisions in a 'Seven fashion' which the 'Four self' will subsequently regret and vice versa. It could well be that the pattern of Marilyn Monroe's early life – frequent changes of job, early marriage, hasty divorce, and so on – was reflected in her being both a Seven and a Four.

Certainly as either a Seven or as a Four the future Marilyn Monroe was very untypical. Her early life was, to say the least, a muddle – most people would have used a stronger phrase. In fact she seems to have combined all the negative features of the Four and the Seven, which reinforced one another, with hardly any positive features of those same numbers.

Similar contradictions are to be seen in the opposition between the two Heart and Personality Numbers of Norma (or Norma Jean) Baker.

Now for an analysis of the new name, Marilyn Monroe, under which Norma Jean Baker became famous.

M A R I L Y N
4+1*+2+1*+3+1+5+
M O N R O E
4+7*+5+2+7*+5* = 47
    4+7 = 11
    1+1 = 2 (the Key Number of Marilyn Monroe).

The vowels of the name, indicated by asterisks, add up to 21, and reduce to 3, thus:
    1+1+7+7+5 = 21
    2+1 = 3 (the Heart Number of Marilyn Monroe).

The consonants of the name add up to 26 and reduce to 8, thus:

    4+2+3+1+5+4+5+2 = 26
    2+6 = 8 (the Personality Number of Marilyn Monroe).

The fact that Marilyn Monroe's Key Number – expressing her whole self – was Two, fits in exactly with her career in show business, for Two is 'the number of femininity', and for Monroe's fans she was the archetypal expression of the feminine principle.

Twos, however, tend to be somewhat shy and unsure of themselves. Marilyn Monroe was both – but this was certainly not the impression she made other than on those who knew her extremely well, such as her psychotherapist. The general impression she gave to the world in general was indicated by, and in accordance with, her Personality Number – Eight. This is the number of both material success and material failure, and to outsiders

Marilyn Monroe at the height of her career, successful but inwardly unhappy, demonstrating all the negative aspects of the Three.

Marilyn Monroe seemed to have undoubtedly achieved the first of these, and in a financial sense she had done so. She also achieved material success in her marriages to wealthy and successful men – but not emotional happiness.

Possibly this was because her Heart Number was Three. Certainly she displayed in her private life all the negative aspects of the Three. A tendency to be overly entertaining; always seeking to be the centre of attention; a determination to be liked with such intensity that it could result in imprudent behaviour; and a certain capacity for deception.

Woody Allen

We all have our own opinions about comedians. Some of us find the wise-cracking humour of the Marx Brothers greatly to our taste while others – myself among them – would prefer ten minutes of Laurel and Hardy to a marathon showing of Groucho and his brothers.

There is at least one comedian today, however, who seems to unite those of us who adore the wisecrack and those of us who prefer slapstick: most of us, in our different ways, are amused by Woody Allen. He is a comedian of universal appeal.

Like a great many other show business personalities, Woody Allen has changed his name. Originally he was 'Allen Stewart Konigsberg', known by most people as Allen Konigsberg – a Five name. The analysis of it is:

A L L E N
1*+3+3+5*+5+
K O N I G S B E R G
2+7*+5+1*+3+3+2+5*+2+3 = 50
(* indicates a vowel)

5+0 = 5 (the Key Number of the original name).
The vowels of the original name, indicated by an asterisk, add up to 19, which reduces to 1, thus:

1+5+7+1+5 = 19
1+9 = 10
1+0 = 1 (the Heart Number of the original name).

The consonants add up to 31, which reduces to 4, thus:

3+3+5+2+5+3+3+2+2+3 = 31
3+1 = 4 (the Personality Number of the original name).

Now let us analyse the adopted name, Woody Allen.

W O O D Y
6+7*+7*+4+1+
A L L E N
1*+3+3+5*+5 = 42

4+2 = 6 (the Key Number of the adopted name).
The vowels of the name add up to 20 and reduce to 2, thus:

7+7+1+5 = 20
2+0 = 2 (the Heart Number of the adopted name).

The consonants add up to 22 and reduce to 4, thus:

6+4+1+3+3+5 = 22
2+2 = 4 (the Personality Number of the adopted name).

In other words, Allen Konigsberg was a Five, and Woody Allen is a Six.

The brilliant Woody Allen, probably the world's most popular comedian, was originally named Allen Stewart Konigsberg.

Woody Allen is not only a comedian of great talent, he is also a film director and actor with a genius for sympathetic communication with his fellowmen. All of us who have seen Woody Allen perform feel that we know him as well as we know ourselves – that we have participated in his emotional triumphs and disasters. Yet clearly none of us can know the real Woody Allen, the man whose face lies behind the mask with which an actor must face his public. The numerologist can do his best to guess what is underneath the mask by contrasting the original Key Number, Five, with the adopted Key Number, Six.

One can sum up the difference between Fives and Sixes by an astronomical metaphor – Fives are comet-like, tending to outshine the other heavenly bodies, but for only a brief time; Sixes are stars, shining steadily, week after week, month after month, year after year.

I know nothing of the character of the young Allen Konigsberg – but if numerological ideas are correct we can surmise a great deal about it.

He would have been a bouncy, adventurous young man, prepared to try his hand at anything, confident of his own abilities and inspiring confidence in others. A typical Five, in fact.

Not all Fives are exactly the same, say numerologists – the essential Fiveness of any particular individual being modified by the combination of his or her Heart and Personality Numbers, environmental factors and the way in which a particular Five uses the qualities associated with the number.

These points are of some importance and apply, say numerologists, to all the number characters derived from names, not just to Fives. For example, the tendency to introversion of the Seven character can manifest itself as a selfish concern with his or her own affairs and feelings that results in a total lack of interest in the inner feelings of others.

From the fact that the future Woody Allen developed into a likeable and successful person the numerologist would deduce that his environment and his strength of will resulted in him manifesting the positive rather than negative characteristics of Fiveness.

In other words, he would have been an outgoing person who was always prepared to experiment with the untried technique, to listen to new and unfamiliar points of view and to give them serious consideration, and to take a chance. On the other hand he would not have been one of those Fives who is so enamoured of the new and unusual that he would have rejected everything that is associated with the past – one of those tiresome people who have been called 'neophiliacs'. Similarly, he would have been prepared to take risks, but not foolish risks. He might have taken a chance which, in case of failure, would have resulted in major difficulties , but he would not have embarked on a venture so risky that failure would have ruined the rest of his life.

As a 'Six by adoption', that is to say as a person who has taken a new name which has changed his Key Number, Woody Allen has, quite obviously, manifested in his career all the positive and few, if any, of the negative characteristics of Sixness.

That is to say he is loving, kind, reliable and possessed of an essentially happy temperament – a very likeable person indeed. Sixes are, however, sometimes a little stick-in-the-mud, preferring the familiar to the unfamiliar, safety to risk, comfort to adventure. Clearly Woody Allen could not have made quite such a success of his career in show business if he had become that sort of Six – although he might well have become an eminent, if conservative, investment adviser or manager of a pension fund.

What some numerologists would deduce is that Woody Allen combines the best qualities of Fiveness and Sixness. The adventurousness of the Five, which sometimes verges on recklessness, has blended with the foresight and prudence of the Six; the Five's admiration for the new has survived but is combined with that respect for the past which is often a characteristic of the Six; and the Five's brilliance is driven on by the Six's capacity for sustained effort.

Woody Allen's adopted Key Number is Six, but his original Key Number, as Allen Konigsberg, was Five.

CHAPTER 9

WESTERN ASTROLOGY

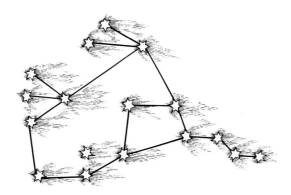

In ancient Chaldea wise men observed the motions of sun, moon and planets and, on the basis of what they saw, prophesied the futures of kings and emperors. At that time astrologers concerned themselves only with the destinies of monarchs and believed that the nature of the lives of ordinary people was not influenced by celestial events.

Today astrologers adopt a very different point of view. They believe that the character and destiny of every individual is influenced by the quality of the moment of time at which he or she was born.

A medieval illustration which pertains to both astrology and the earth-centred astronomy which was once closely related to it. The 28 'Mansions of the Moon', shown beyond the zodiac, were considered to possess great astrological importance.

Most people know which sign of the zodiac they were 'born under' – in other words the sign of the zodiac in which the sun was positioned on the day of their birth – and will occasionally glance at the astrology column in a newspaper or magazine to see what is forecast for the day, the week or the month ahead.

While the position of the sun in the zodiac at a particular birth date is of great importance to astrologers, it is not considered to be the most important single factor in an individual's horoscope. That factor is the ascendant or 'rising sign', i.e. the sign of the zodiac that is on the horizon at the time of birth.

At whatever date a person is born it is possible for him or her to have any one of the 12 zodiacal signs as the ascendant. So, for example, it is possible for a Libran, a person born with the sun in Libra, to have an Aries or a Capricorn ascendant. This is a very important and insufficiently understood point, because it means that only a few of us (less than three-quarters of one per cent) are 'pure' zodiacal types, i.e. individuals born with the same ascendant as their sun sign. So, if someone is, for example, born with the sun in Aries and a Libran ascendant, it is likely that his or her characteristics will

be a blend of those regarded as 'typically Libran' and 'typically Arian'.

On pages 150 to 155 it is explained how you can calculate both the appropriate ascendant for your own or someone else's birth, and another very important zodiacal position, the midheaven. The midheaven (sometimes referred to as MC from the initials of the Latin words meaning 'in the middle of heaven') means the sign of the zodiac which is highest above the horizon at the moment of birth.

First, however, is a description of the 12 pure zodiacal types, from Aries to Pisces. Remember that these individual descriptions only apply with total accuracy to those rare people who have the same sign of the zodiac as the ascendant and sun sign. Most of us will be a blend of two of the signs.

Aries *(The Ram)*
March 21 to April 20

SUMMARY

Aries has always been looked upon by astrologers as a fiery and masculine sign. Consequently, those dominated by its influence were described by

her emotional life by a need to express a burning sexual drive. This can lead to an emotional selfishness which, at its worst, can amount to an arrogant disregard for the inner needs and feelings of partners and close associates. Often, however, the sexual egotism of the Arian is tempered by a more romantic side; this largely prevents him or her from indulging in a selfishness which would inflict emotional trauma on others.

General Character 'Choleric' is the word which would have been used by the physicians of three centuries ago to express the typical Arian psychology, in other words, 'fiery', pugnacious and, on occasion, extremely bad-tempered and dangerously impulsive.

The choleric psychology of the Arian often begins to find expression in early childhood, sometimes in temper tantrums, more often in a precocious adventurousness and spirit of enquiry. This last is more usually directed towards practical rather than theoretical ends; an Arian child is more inclined to take a clock or radio to bits in order to see 'what makes it work' than to bother his parents with questions about the nature of clockwork or electricity.

In later life these childish characteristics take the form of an 'outgoing practicality' – a concern with the nuts-and-bolts aspects of reality rather than its theoretical concepts. In other words, the Arian is concerned with tactics rather than strategy. This does not mean that the Arian is not an intellectual; but Arian intellectualism is rarely divorced from the world of everyday things. Thus, for example, the Arian intellectual is more likely to be drawn towards applied rather than pure mathematics; more likely to be an engineer than a theoretical physicist; more likely to be a sculptor or a painter than one who makes a profound study of the philosophy of aesthetics.

The same practicality is apparent in every aspect of the Arian personality. The Arian judges others by their deeds, not their words; is concerned with the effects of others' actions, not their purposes; and is determined to influence what actually happens, not to analyse it.

Life Style The Arian wants to control reality – not to be controlled by it or even to understand it. Careers which are not in some way concerned with

Raphael, a key astrologer in the last century's revival (see page 23), as being 'commanding, choleric and violent'.

Contemporary astrological practitioners tend to use politer language – perhaps because they do not wish to offend their Arian clients unduly – but, in essence, they are in agreement with Raphael, describing the typical Arian personality (whether biologically male or female) as having all the virtues and vices traditionally associated with masculinity.

Thus, the Aries woman tends to dominate a relationship, to take the lead in joint activities, and to be both boisterous and extrovert. Similarly, the Aries man is outgoing, confident of his own virility and, on occasion, the archetypal male chauvinist.

Success in career matters is as important to the Arian personality as it is

A symbolic representation of the planet Mars and its astrological attributes. The animals to the left and right of the warrior figure symbolize Scorpio and Aries, traditionally ruled by Mars.

in his or her emotional life. The Arian wants to get to the top – and he or she is usually very good at doing so in any field which calls for plenty of energetic activity, physical or mental.

Men and women of note in whom Aries characteristics have been predominant have included Marlon Brando, Bette Davis, Louis Armstrong; the painter Vincent Van Gogh; the novelists Emile Zola and Georges Sand; and conductor Leopold Stokowski.

IN DETAIL

Sexuality and the Emotions The typical Arian tends to be dominated in his or

material reality provide little satisfaction to the Arian. His or her job must be concerned with the control of natural things and/or other people.

Manipulation, whether of things or people, is an Arian characteristic. Thus, for example, they make adequate social workers but not social workers of genius. In other words, they are good at moulding clients to the Arian pattern and setting them on the right path – in Arian terms. They are, though, rarely able to achieve the goal of the outstanding social worker – to bring out the fundamental nature of a client, to enable him or her to express their inner nature successfully in the social environment. The pure Arian, for the same reason, makes a better leader than a follower; he or she is not an ideal team-worker because Arians are incapable of understanding the need for self-expression in anyone but themselves.

In general, Arians make better innovators than administrators. They are better at starting a project off than keeping it running; better at – metaphorically speaking – launching a ship than sailing it.

In work, as in all aspects of their lives, they are forceful, finding it difficult to cope tactfully with either active opposition or the passive opposition of inertia.

Taurus *(The Bull)*
April 21 to May 21

SUMMARY

Pure Taureans tend to be earthy – 'slow but sure'. Their 'bullishness' can under extreme pressure be expressed in violent outbursts of rage, but more usually they are like oxen, plodding forward steadily, strongly and surely.

Taurus is an 'earthy' sign of the zodiac and material things are of major importance to the typical Taurean. He or she is no ascetic, dining on dry bread and water, but revels in all the appetites, loving the pleasures of the table, physical contacts with the opposite sex, comforts and luxuries of every kind. Material possessions are of great importance to the Taurean.

All this may sound unattractive, and so it would be if that was all there was to the Taurean. But with the strong physical appetites goes a generous nature, an astonishing capacity for hard and painstaking effort, and, rather unexpectedly, a tendency to generate brilliantly imaginative ideas. It is probably this last characteristic, allied with a stubbornness that refuses to admit defeat, which has resulted in some strongly Taurean personalities, such as Ulysses S. Grant, becoming outstanding soldiers.

Characteristically Taurean men and women have included Catherine the Great, Karl Marx, Sigmund Freud, Greta Garbo, Bing Crosby, Orson Welles, Fred Astaire and Barbra Streisand.

IN DETAIL

Sexuality and the Emotions Taureans value their possessions, and as far as they are concerned their partners are the most valued possession of all. Consequently, an emotional characteristic of many Taureans is a tendency to jealousy: a rival is not just a rival, but a thief who is trying to steal the Taurean's rightful property. Taurean jealousy is often nursed for a long time before it is outwardly expressed. Anger smoulders away for weeks or months, even years, until it flames up into a rage which transforms the placid Taurean ox into a mad bull or – just as frightening – a mad heifer.

The positive side of Taurean sexual possessiveness finds expression in a

Venus, astrologically associated with luxury and romance, shown as the queen of all lovers and the ruler of Taurus and Libra, The Bull and The Balance.

caring attitude towards partners. The husband or wife of the Taurean is cared for with devoted constancy.

In spite of this, Taureans are capable of outbursts of intense physical passion which can be almost as alarming as their rages.

General Character 'Phlegmatic' was a word often applied to the Taurean by the astrologers of old, and it is true that a stolid practicality, a certain earthiness, is the most notable trait of the pure Taurean. But this earthiness is a fertile field on the slopes of a volcano rather than a placid meadow. Taurean children, hard-working at school and usually 'biddable' at home, are capable of rare outbursts of rage – usually jealous rage – which are even more alarming than the temper tantrums of the Arian child because they are so totally unexpected and, so it seems, 'out of character'.

In adulthood the Taurean's goals are security, comfort and lack of anxiety. The Taurean hates to be worried; he/she will cope with almost anything except anxiety about the unexpected and the inexplicable. When anxiety is inflicted on Taureans by the surrounding environment or those who live in it, their tendency is to 'move away' – in both the literal and the metaphorical senses. This, in fact, is almost the only circumstance in which a Taurean will voluntarily move; usually they wish to stick with what they know well, even if doing so makes others regard them as dull and boring.

Taureans' patience, their determination, their quiet affection and their occasional flashes of inspiration more than make up for their occasional outbursts of rage, their possessiveness and their tendency to be a little dull. They are pleasant people to know as acquaintances or close friends.

Life Style The Taurean does best in a career environment in which he or she can feel secure. A plodding job in which one can slowly advance towards (if not quite to) the very top, with a guaranteed, inflation-proof pension, is the ideal. The worst job for a Taurean is one in which he or she is unsure what money, if any, will be coming in at the end of the month. So Taureans rarely find satisfaction in, for example, freelance journalism or selling insurance on a commission-only basis. On the other hand, they are extremely good at accountancy and

other jobs involving money, provided that no risk-taking is involved. They are good at almost all jobs which involve a patient application to practical matters and make, for example, excellent farmers.

With all this practicality there is a streak of imaginative artistry in many Taureans and they are often interested in music, painting and sculpture. Sometimes this Venusian element in the Taurean personality is dominant and a surprisingly large number of sculptors, singers and other artists are Taureans or have Taurean ascendants.

The planet Mercury, traditionally the ruler of the zodiacal sign of Gemini, is associated with travel, communications and, oddly, theft. He is shown here bearing the staff of Hermes, messenger of the gods.

But the Taurean artist is usually a prosperous artist, not the sort of talented individual who would be happy to starve in a garret so long as he or she is practising their art.

II

Gemini *(The Twins)*
May 22 to June 22

SUMMARY
Gemini is a double sign and a certain duality is apparent in the pure Geminean. There is an ambivalence, a shifting outlook, which makes Gemineans delightful in their unexpectedness, but irritating in their inconsistency. Gemineans are often exasperating – but they can be relied upon not to be

boring. A pure Geminean is a person with whom it is almost impossible to argue for any length of time. His/her mind is so subtle, moving ahead like quicksilver, that one can never be quite sure what one is arguing about. Gemineans have golden tongues as well as quicksilver minds; like the monkeys of Chinese Astrology, they can charm the birds off the trees, induce others to follow courses of action which they don't really think advisable, and fascinate almost anyone they wish.

At its worst, this makes the strongly Geminean person capable of being the archetypal confidence-trickster; at its best, it makes him or her a communicator of genius – an individual capable of conveying complex ideas in a simple way and of inspiring others.

But even the most idealistic Geminean is not altogether trustworthy or completely reliable. This is not because of any deliberate disloyalty, dishonesty or deceit – it is because he or she is extremely apt to change his/her mind and, being intellectual as well as versatile, can put forward excellent arguments for the newly adopted point of view. Well-known Gemineans have included Judy Garland, Marilyn Monroe, Errol Flynn and Ian Fleming.

IN DETAIL

Sexuality and the Emotions The Geminean man or woman is always very liable to fall suddenly in (or out) of love. This characteristic persists throughout life (although it is particularly noticeable in young adulthood) and it applies to emotions of friendship as well as to those of a more romantic nature. Even an elderly Geminean is quite likely to introduce you to 'a very close friend' with whom, in fact, he or she has only recently become acquainted. This can make life rather confusing for others, particularly if they take Geminean lovers or friends seriously. A Geminean's love-making and expressions of affection are sometimes more ardent than his/her true feelings. As partners, though, pure Gemineans are reasonably reliable – if their affections stray, it is not for long.

General Character 'Airy' is rather an old-fashioned word but it admirably describes the character of the pure Geminean. He or she has all the

unpredictability of a feather or a soap bubble bobbing about in ever-changing air currents. With this unpredictability goes an astonishing buoyancy and resilience. A Geminean may seem, metaphorically speaking, to be about to fall to earth, but almost always an unexpected breath of wind comes along and he or she is shooting up again.

Gemineans are often noted for their intellectual qualities – they quickly grasp the essence of a situation, a process or an argument. Usually, however, they fail to understand things in depth; they tend to have a somewhat superficial approach. This is not because they are inherently incapable of deep thinking. It is because their interests are very wide indeed and they are interested in things in general rather than one thing in particular.

Life Style The Geminean will never be happy unless there is some change or variation in his/her life. No Geminean can satisfactorily do a job which varies little from day to day, nor one in which he or she is not expected to take an interest in the activities of others, nor one in which a certain amount of amiable sociability is not involved. In other words, the Geminean temperament, mercurial in every sense of the word, must be fully allowed for. Any job in which the Geminean can talk or communicate with others is ideal: Gemineans make superbly gossipy taxi drivers, wonderful journalists, magnificent sales representatives, and so on. In short, the pure Geminean has all the qualities of the successful politician (although rarely those of a statesman) and must ensure that his/her lifestyle is appropriate to those qualities.

Cancer *(The Crab)*
June 23 to July 23

SUMMARY

The psychological nature of the pure Cancerian is rather like the physical nature of the crab and other crustaceans: a hard outer shell conceals an interior that is soft and vulnerable to injury. To outsiders Cancerians present a hard appearance, giving the impression that they are rough and unsympathetic; to those who know

them well they are gentle and compassionate. A sea crab is totally attached to its home, in the most literal way, and the pure Cancerian is, in metaphorical terms, equally attached to his/her home – his/her life is centred on partners, parents, children and their surroundings.

A Cancerian is a loyal and devoted friend, an even more devoted parent or child, and one who can be relied upon in all circumstances – Cancerians would rather betray themselves than those who are close to them. As they are themselves so loyal, Cancerians are badly wounded if others are disloyal to them. Their reaction is almost always to withdraw, like a crab into its shell, rather than to attempt to revenge themselves on those who have hurt them. Cancerian individuals include and have included the poet Byron, the writer and artist Jean Cocteau, the painter Chagall, the movie star Gina Lollobrigida, and that extraordinary novelist and confidence trickster 'Baron Corvo'.

IN DETAIL

Sexuality and the Emotions Beneath an outward aspect which suggests coolness to the point of frigidity, Cancerian men and women are often highly sexed. The Cancerian type was attributed to the Element of Water by the astrologers of old, but as far as the emotions are concerned the Water of the pure Cancerian is that which erupts from volcanic depths rather than that which is found in ice-cold mountain lakes. The strong physical urges of at least some Cancerians are modified by their attachment to the home and those they know well. In a sense Cancerians never leave their parents: the female Cancerian will seek a lover who is also a father figure; the male will rarely value a partner who does not have some maternal qualities. On the whole Cancerians make good long-term relationships. These, however, are sometimes marred by an emotional moodiness which can be trying to those who have to cope with it. Cancerians tend to swing between extremes of attraction and repulsion, elation and depression, optimism and pessimism. Only someone who is prepared to accept such swings of temperament should marry a Cancerian.

General Character The first, and even

it would be hard to find a more rewarding friend or associate than a Cancerian whose trust has been won.

Life Style Home is the most important aspect of the pure Cancerian's life, and if he/she is to be happy at work the workplace must acquire some of the characteristics of home. That is to say, the Cancerian must feel secure in his/her work and feel that workmates are all part of some enormous family. Any type of enterprise which demands the utmost loyalty from its staff and, in turn, endeavours to protect them from the harshness of the outside world provides an admirable work environment for the pure Cancerian – a university, an old-established school or a traditional financial concern, for example. Nevertheless, a Cancerian's work life must not be too humdrum: Cancerians are often imaginative, in spite of their sometimes pedestrian outward aspect, and they also tend to be shrewd and intelligent. Any successful Cancerian career must provide some scope for these qualities. Provided the home environment is right, Cancerians do not care whether that home is in the depths of the countryside or the midst of the city.

♌

Leo *(The Lion)*
July 24 to August 23

SUMMARY

Of a sunny disposition, the pure Leo nevertheless has a commanding personality and always stands out from the crowd. He or she either dominates or, if resisted, endeavours to dominate, not being afraid to try a little bullying. A Leo is the pure extrovert, outgoing, sociable and determined to be the life and soul of the party. If there isn't a party, or the party wants to go its own way and avoid being bossed about by the Leo who wants to take it over, that Leo will either become bad-tempered or withdraw into a sulk. Once they are in a dominating position pure Leos find it difficult to step out of the limelight. They are the politicians who cling on to office long after their day is done, the industrialists who refuse to hand over to younger successors, even though their companies suffer as a

Luna (the Moon) shown as straddling the symbol of Cancer, The Crab, of which she is traditionally the ruler. She bears a hunting horn and is thus identified with Diana, Roman goddess of the chase.

the second, impression made by a Cancerian is often an unfavourable one. He/she strikes others as ultra-logical, a person who does not fully appreciate the feelings and problems of others, who adopts a sternly practical attitude lacking in sympathy and empathy. Nothing could be more erroneous; whatever their outward aspects, Cancerians are the kindest, most generous and most protective of human beings.

They are also the most sensitive and are extremely easily hurt. Cancerians respond very badly to criticism and such criticism rarely has good results,

for Cancerians do not respond to it by making greater efforts but by running away. However good the motives of the critic, the Cancerian feels under attack and goes into retreat, withdrawing into the crab-like shell which feels familiar and utterly safe. Thus, for example, the Cancerian child who is told that his painting is attractive but that his perspective is defective will respond, not by concentrating on improving his/her perspective, but by giving up painting in favour of metalwork. Similarly, the adult Cancerian will retreat from anyone who does not enthusiastically respond to a kindly action or an agreeable word. There is no doubt that this causes more extrovert types to find considerable difficulty in establishing good relationships with Cancerians. If they persist, however, it is well worth the effort, for

140

result, and the ageing actors who still insist on playing the juvenile lead. In his or her heyday, however, a strongly Leonine type lives in a blaze of glory, leading others and illuminating their dull existence. Leos and Leonine types have included Louis XIV (the Sun King), the Emperor Napoleon; Bismarck; Robert Burns, Scotland's national poet; the dancer Isadora Duncan and the opera singer Maria Callas; and the novelist Aldous Huxley.

IN DETAIL

Sexuality and the Emotions It is rare for two Leos to establish a really satisfactory relationship with one another, unless they come to some sort of demarcation agreement by which they map out their respective areas of authority. If they don't do this, they spend much of their time disputing which of them should be the decision-maker. Usually, Leos make loving and loyal partners, particularly if they are allowed to make all the important decisions. In general, the Leo likes to be the 'sun' of any emotional relationship, with the partner being the moon, reflecting the Leonine light.

General Character It is difficult for a Leo not to take command or, at least, to endeavour to take command, for he/she is genuinely convinced that his/her capabilities are superior to those of almost everybody else. If you know someone who tastes a dish which you cook superbly and immediately tells you how much it would be improved by the addition of some particular herb, or someone who when given a lift rewards you by pointing out what an unsuitable route you have chosen, you are almost always dealing with a pure Leo. The infuriating thing is that more often than not they are right: the casserole is improved by the herb that has been suggested; the alternative route does save time and is scenically more attractive. The plain fact is that Leos are not only convinced that they should make the decisions, but that they are also very good at it. Even when they have made decisions which seem to have been manifestly incorrect, the extraordinary good fortune of the typical Leo – Leo is perhaps the luckiest of all the signs – transforms the situation, and disaster is turned to triumph.

As they are so good at commanding and directing others, it is not surprising that Leos regard it as almost perverse for others to attempt to command them. They resent such attempts and, if the attempt persists for long, can become extremely angry (and regally Leonine).

Normally this is the only occasion when a Leo will lose his/her temper. Usually they take a generous view of the faults and oddities of others and can be quite remarkably forgiving. This capacity for forgiveness allied with a warm and affectionate nature makes the average Leo a very pleasant person to know – provided, of course, you allow him/her always to stand in the limelight.

Life Style Leos have ambitious and energetic natures. On occasion, however, they will wish to relax and, like great cats, bask in the warm sunshine of life. If they don't get the opportunities to relax when they want to, they become irritable, apt to unsheathe their claws and scratch those nearest and dearest to them. So the ideal occupation for the Leo is one in which great energy is called for, but in which there are intervals for rest and recuperation. If such a job also allows a Leo to be the permanent centre of attention, then this is all to the good – acting, teaching and professional sports are all archetypal Leo occupations. Leos need the same sort of environment for their home lives: an admiring circle of friends and relatives.

Sol (the Sun) shown as a crowned but naked monarch. Between his calves is the sign of Leo, ruled by the sun. The virile sports illustrated, such as fencing and wrestling, were in the Middle Ages looked upon as being ruled by Leo.

Virgo *(The Virgin)*
August 24 to September 23

SUMMARY

Common sense, intelligence, precision and an insistence on 'doing it right' are the outstanding characteristics of the pure Virgo. There is an emphasis on technique which makes the Virgoan approach to life almost chilling in its efficiency. One astrologer has claimed that even in their sex lives Virgoans are more notable for the clinical perfection of their techniques than for genuine enthusiasm. The Virgoan love of order extends into almost every aspect of life: a holiday is planned, almost hour by hour, long before it has begun; a Virgoan in his/her twenties enters into complex saving schemes which will ensure a prosperous retirement; a Virgoan home-owner will ensure that everything is in its right place. Even in childhood Virgoans tend to behave in an ordered way. They are the pupils whose exercise books are a model of neatness, who like the dull routine of school life and the pattern of rules and discipline, and are described as being 'no trouble at all'. At home they are equally neat and ordered – a Virgoan child never has to be told to tidy his or her room.

At its worst, the qualities with which the pure Virgoan is endowed lead to a certain 'dryness' – he or she begins to take on some of the characteristics of a well-programmed computer. If, on the other hand, the Virgoan can retain tolerance for the foibles and fecklessness of others, he/she can use the Virgoan capacity for imposing order on chaos to the advantage of friends, partners, and workmates, and become both popular and prosperous in the process. Virgoan personalities have included Albert the Good, the tiresomely virtuous husband of Queen Victoria; the writers Charlotte Brontë and D. H. Lawrence; and the comedian Peter Sellers.

IN DETAIL

Sexuality and the Emotions Pure Virgoans find it almost impossible to let themselves go fully. They keep a tight rein on their own emotions and, if possible, those of their associates. This is not because they don't have strong feelings, but because they fear them – if emotional guards are let down, there is a risk that the unplanned and the unpredictable may manifest themselves in Virgoan life. In a certain sense Virgoans are right to do so, for there is nothing less controllable than the passions of a Virgo who gives full vent to them. In a long-term relationship pure Virgos are rarely happy with partners who neither possess their own perfectionist outlook on life and its problems nor are prepared to let the Virgo partner make all the rules. If, however, they find partners who are prepared to accept their own exacting standards, Virgoans are affectionate, loyal and supportive.

General Character With Virgo's energy and foresight goes a concentration upon detail – even the smallest and least significant aspect of a planned event is usually taken into account by a Virgoan. This frequently means that the Virgoan moves smoothly forward along his or her chosen path through life – neither literally nor metaphorically is the Virgoan likely to go on a camping trip without carefully packing both a corkscrew and a tin-opener. It is possible, however, for Virgoans to become so obsessed with detail that they stop seeing the broad picture – to go camping, so to speak, with two corkscrews, but to pitch their tents in a spot liable to flooding.

The sort of over-precise Virgoan who does this, who becomes almost obsessive in his/her concentration upon detail, is rarely able to relax and becomes nervous and edgy. This seems to increase the obsession with detail and, at worst, the Virgoan becomes trapped in a vicious circle in which he/she expends more and more energy on unimportant matters and less and less on things of real importance. This applies in only a minority of cases; most Virgos manage to keep their obsessions under control, to relax

A fifteenth-century illustration of Virgo from a Book of Hours – a prayer book for private devotional use – showing a peasant threshing with a flail. This was the characteristic activity of the time during which the sun was in Virgo.

occasionally and to be considered delightful – if fussy – people.

Life Style Provided that they can manage to see life and career as a whole, without excessive concentration on unimportant minutiae, Virgoans are successful and happy in almost any sort of work and can live with equal ease in city, suburbia or countryside. What they cannot stand is mess and muddle: they like to work in a systematic way to a carefully planned routine. If they are allowed to do this, they are not only happy themselves, they make others happy by providing a stabilizing influence in both the home and the workplace. Work and routine home life are rarely quite enough for the pure Virgoan, who is a great hobbyist. Virgoan elements are usually a strong feature of the horoscopes of philatelists, print collectors and other dedicated amateurs. Sometimes this interest in hobbies takes the form of a concern with unusual dietary theories, alternative medicine, and so on; many Virgoans display a more than ordinary interest in their own physical health and that of others.

Libra (*The Balance*)
September 24 to October 23

SUMMARY

For the Libran almost everything has to be 'weighed in the balance' – no astrological type has a stronger sense of justice and fair play. Sometimes this can result in a Libran behaving in a positively miserly way. He or she will work out, almost to the penny, the cost of a birthday present which has been received so that he/she can reciprocate exactly when the giver's birthday comes along. This tendency to balance everything, to believe that something is wrong if one side of the scales that symbolize the Libran personality is more heavily weighted than the other, extends beyond money values. Librans tend to have balanced and moderate political and religious views, to like pleasure and luxury but to reject debauchery and greed, to eat enough to be neither fat nor thin, to take a moderate amount of exercise, and so on. If, however, the psycholog-

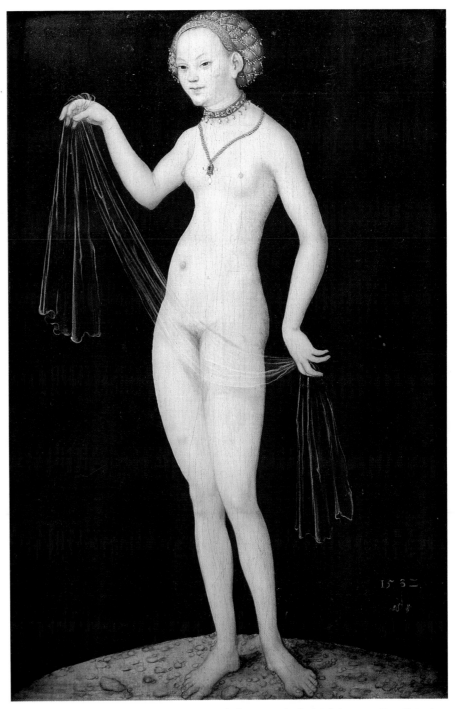

A medieval painting of the goddess Venus, many of whose traditional attributes, such as seeking the pleasures of the flesh, are associated with the zodiacal sign of Libra.

ical balance of a pure Libran is tipped strongly to one side or the other of the scales, he/she can become very extreme indeed. When this happens it is as a result of persuasion by others – Librans are easily influenced.

Libran personalities include and have included Mahatma Gandhi; the writers Graham Greene, T. S. Eliot and William Faulkner; the composer Franz Liszt; the actress Brigitte Bardot and – an example of the Libran balance decisively tipping in a particular direction – the occultist Aleister Crowley.

IN DETAIL

Sexuality and the Emotions Libra is a sign of the zodiac ruled by the planet Venus, and pure Librans, male or female, tend to have many supposedly feminine qualities – gentleness, a

143

romantic nature, a taste for beautiful objects, and so on. This sometimes results in a strongly Libran man being regarded as slightly effeminate when this is not, in fact, the case. Librans of either sex have a great charm which arouses feelings of affection and love in many of those they encounter. Their main fault is to be too romantic – to let their hearts rule their heads. Once Librans are fully involved in an emotional relationship their sense of balance comes into full play. They give back precisely the same amount of warm affection and sexual passion as they receive.

General Character The pure Libran sometimes gains a reputation for laziness and, certainly, few individuals are more likely to procrastinate than the Libran. He/she will write to that old friend who is in a difficult situation tomorrow, not today; something will be done about getting someone to repair the roof next week, not this; next year, not this, he/she will decide whether to take out a new insurance policy . . . Usually this procrastination results not from laziness but from a chronic inability to make decisions, due to the fact that a Libran is always able to see all the pros and cons of a given course of action, and to him or her they seem very finely balanced.

When Libran indecision is allied with the Libran love of comfort, good food and pleasant surroundings, the impression of laziness is increased – a typical Libran can seem almost pathologically idle. Nevertheless, when a Libran does at last act the action is usually energetic and decisive and achieves, sometimes to the surprise of others, exactly the desired result. A notable characteristic of the pure Libran is an intense dislike of disputes, quarrels and. arguments. He/she will sometimes so sedulously avoid these that an impression of weakness is given – but the person who attempts to take advantage of the Libran's gentleness, courtesy and seeming weakness will often regret it. An iron hand often lies concealed within the Libran velvet glove.

Life Style Librans are rarely happy in a career which involves constant decision-making. It is not that they are invariably unsuccessful in such jobs – when Librans have to make decisions they usually make the right ones – but that the processes involved cause

them real mental agony. Provided that no frequent decisions are called for, Librans are happy working at almost anything so long as it is in pleasant surroundings; if the job involves the Libran using his/her artistic flair and design sense, so much the better. Whatever their occupations, however, Librans must avoid being too gentle and agreeable, otherwise they will find that they are doing others' work as well as their own. Librans enjoy living in almost any pleasant home environment, but they are particularly happy if their homes are set in rich and verdant countryside.

Scorpio *(The Scorpion)*
October 24 to November 22

SUMMARY
The seventeenth-century astrologer John Gadbury, whose own horoscope was strongly Scorpionic, wrote a pamphlet endeavouring to prove that pure Scorpios were not, as tradition averred, quarrelsome, treacherous, drunken and sexually debauched. Present-day astrologers tend to agree with Gadbury rather than ancient tradition and to interpret the Scorpio nature by concentrating upon the positive aspects of the sign. They argue that only a small number of pure Scorpios have characters of the violent and irrational nature traditionally attributed to them, and that most individuals born with both a Scorpio ascendant and with the sun in Scorpio are honest, rational and not exceptionally quarrelsome or debauched. Nevertheless, it has to be admitted that a good number of pure Scorpios are more secretive, abrupt, strong-willed and fiercely erotic than most people. Provided that these characteristics are modified by a certain amount of self-control, they are, however, a source of strength for the Scorpio, who can use them to get what he/she wants out of life. Scorpionic personalities have included Indira Gandhi, Marie Curie, Edith Piaf, and – the dark side of Scorpio – Nazi leaders Goering and Goebbels.

IN DETAIL
Sexuality and the Emotions Pure Scor-

pios have strong emotions, ardent passions and a physical eroticism which greatly exceeds that of other zodiacal types. A pure Scorpio will find it difficult to 'forget about it' if his/her sex life is unsatisfactory. No one is less able to transmute sexual energies and desires into, for example, artistic creativity than the Scorpio. If Scorpios love ardently, they also love long; they can develop an almost obsessive relationship with the object of their desires. As a consequence, they can be extremely jealous, and to be on the receiving end of Scorpionic jealousy is not a pleasant experience.

General Character No one could legitimately accuse the pure Scorpio of being dull and pedestrian. He/she possesses tremendous energy and, often, ambition. The old astrologers taught that some of the characteristics of this zodiacal sign were best symbolized by the eagle. Scorpios, they said, have all the fleshly appetites of the carnivorous eagle, liking to tear and rend the prey that they snatch from earth and then to fly high, hovering far above the rest of us, and to detach themselves from the boredom which lies below, In other words, however concerned with their strong appetites Scorpios may be, they are also likely to turn out to be high flyers, men and women whose inner strength can overcome all the problems of everyday existence – including, it is worth adding, those that arise as a direct consequence of indulgence in the delights of the flesh.

There are strong relationships between the sign of Scorpio and the planet Mars and (if modern astrologers are to be believed) Pluto, and pure Scorpios display many of the good and bad characteristics associated with these planets. Thus, they are authoritative, brave, energetic, innovative and creative. If, on the other hand, a Scorpionic personality manifests some of the more negative aspects of the planets, he or she can be cruel to the point of sadism, a brutally destructive individual who says 'evil be thou my good' (the Nazi leader Hermann Goering, founder of the Gestapo, provides a chilling illustration of the type). Even their best friends would be unlikely to refer to pure Scorpios as 'instantly likeable' or 'full of charm', yet their energy and drive make them useful – although dangerous – friends and allies. Better to avoid Scorpios than to

abuse their friendship by disloyalty.
Life Style Pure Scorpios only find satisfaction in a life-style which allows them both to satisfy their strong physical and emotional appetites and to provide an outlet for their drive to success. What is unacceptable to the pure Scorpio is triviality and pettiness: he/she could be happy auditing the accounts of large companies, but to devote his/her life to checking the petty cash would be unendurable. The Scorpionic personality thinks big, wants to act big, and usually needs a great deal of money to satisfy his/her desires. At its worst, this can lead to crime: the big-time bank robber usually has a horoscope in which Scorpionic elements are prominent. At its best, the pure Scorpio can become an immensely capable, although utterly ruthless, industrialist, business person, or military leader. At home the Scorpio is unfussy about his/her surroundings, as long as they satisfy his/her physical and emotional appetites.

Sagittarius *(The Archer)*
November 23 to December 22

SUMMARY

All pure Sagittarians have enormous potential, but by no means all of them fulfil the promise they display in early life. This is because one of the characteristics of the sign is a happy-go-lucky attitude, a carelessness about the consequences of actions, which some-

times results in the pure Sagittarian throwing away success when it is in his/her grasp. If, for example, you meet a brilliant young student who suddenly stops doing any work a few months before finals, there is a strong probability that he/she is a pure Sagittarian. The sudden and unexpected failure of a Sagittarian in some enterprise or activity in which he/she seemed destined to succeed is not always conclusive. Sagittarius is a lucky sign and destiny usually seems to afford pure Sagittarians more than one opportunity of achieving success; for them the old saying about 'as one door closes another opens' usually proves to be true.

With the Sagittarian carelessness goes a freedom-loving personality and an open and generous-hearted attitude towards life. Curiously enough, this seems to repel some people; even the most agreeable Sagittarian finds that some people try to pick quarrels with him or her. The natural talents of the Sagittarians, combined with their tendency to throw chances away, result in pure Sagittarians usually achieving either great success and popularity or ending their lives as rather pathetic 'might-have-beens'. Sagittarian personalities include and have included Winston Churchill, Abraham Lincoln, Noel Coward, John Osborne, and performers Frank Sinatra and Gipsy Rose Lee.

IN DETAIL

Sexuality and the Emotions Strongly Sagittarian men and women are both lovable as friends and desirable as

Botticelli's portrayal of Mars, god of war and ruler of Scorpio, seduced by Venus. Medieval astrologers regarded the planet Venus as a neutralizer of malefic Martial influences.

long-term partners. As a consequence, they are much sought after by the opposite sex. And yet, paradoxically, they often only establish satisfactory long-term emotional relationships in the second half of their lives. This is because they have a tendency to reject, kindly but firmly, the love that is offered to them. This is not because they do not wish to take on responsibilities for others – they will shoulder them uncomplainingly – but because they set an enormous value on their emotional freedom. Once they do settle down, however, Sagittarians make devoted husbands, wives and parents. In spite of this devotedness, Sagittarians are quite remarkably lacking in jealousy and possessiveness.
General Character Sagittarius is a lucky sign, but in youth Sagittarians need every bit of their inherent ability to fall on their feet, both literally and metaphorically. For they are continually taking chances in a way that most people would regard as thoroughly reckless. They drive fast, engage in dangerous sports, are careless with money – pure Sagittarians like gambling and speculation – and seek every type of excitement, physical, emotional and intellectual. All these activities are spin-offs, as it were, from their search for personal freedom – an endeavour to escape from the restraints which bind us all to

A symbolic representation of Jupiter, traditionally regarded as the ruler of both Sagittarius and Pisces. Modern astrologers depart from tradition and consider Neptune as ruling Pisces.

tarian's progress through life, rarely end a friendship definitively – charm, genuine niceness and a certain amount of Sagittarian luck usually result in reconciliation.

Life Style Sagittarians are always versatile and it is quite common for them to change from one career to another that, on the face of it, calls for quite different qualities. But both careers will have in common freedom from dull routine work and will give the Sagittarian a chance to use his/her versatility and intelligence. Challenge is important to the Sagittarian, and a job which does not offer problems will never be totally satisfactory to him/her, however well paid it may be.

Capricorn (*The Goat*)
December 23 to January 19

SUMMARY

The pure Capricornian has many earthy qualities but, alongside them, a surprising capacity to behave in a thoroughly capricious manner – on rare occasions. When a Capricornian does behave in this way, friends and associates are astonished and, subsequently, the Capricornian feels some shame, wondering why he/she behaved in such an uncharacteristic way. Normally, however, pure Capricornians are very predictable indeed, plodding steadily forward along life's road in a way more suggestive of a carthorse or an ox than of a leaping, headstrong goat. There is no doubt at all that the first impression made on others by a strongly Capricornian personality is one of docility, even dullness. 'One does not invite Leo and Capricorn to dinner upon the same occasion,' said one astrologer, and certainly their outward behaviour contrasts sharply, the lively Leo personality (see pages 140-1) being ill-matched to that of the pure Capricornian, who is introverted, submissive and placid to the point of self-effacement.

Yet there are Capricornians who are just as ambitious and keen to dominate as any Leo. The difference is that Capricornians tend to keep their ambitions to themselves, being rather secretive people by nature, and do not indulge in dramatic attempts to get to

a greater or lesser extent. In later life this recklessness is usually somewhat diminished (although even elderly Sagittarians are ready to take risks which might make younger people blanch), and the Sagittarian quest for personal freedom assumes a more thoughtful and intellectual form. They seek a philosophy of life which sees each and every individual as unique and solely responsible for his/her own destiny.

The free-and-easy attitude of the Sagittarians extends to others as well as themselves. A Sagittarian is rarely the sort of bogus libertarian who

expresses deep concern for his/her own freedom of thought and action but fails to defend the liberties of others or, even worse, endeavours to impose his/her standards of behaviour upon them. With the Sagittarian's love of personal liberty goes a certain unconventionality which, quite unwittingly, can cause deep offence – it is the Sagittarian who blithely assumes that it is quite acceptable to wear casual clothes at a formal social gathering or to take an uninvited guest to a party. It is, to some extent, the annoyance produced in others by the Sagittarian's free-and-easy manners that probably accounts for the fact that, in spite of his/her friendliness, the pure Sagittarian finds that others insist on picking quarrels. These quarrels, which are sometimes responsible for unexpected reverses in the Sagit-

the top at all costs. In fact they usually do get what they want out of life, their solid worth and patient strivings ensuring that, at some time, usually not until they are in middle age, they achieve their desires. One should not underestimate the pure Capricornian; more often than not the leaden exterior conceals, if not a heart of gold, at least a hidden mercurial temperament and an acute mind. Strongly Capricornian personalities have included the Soviet dictator Joseph Stalin; Immanuel Kant, the eighteenth-century philosopher; Mary Tudor; Isaac Newton; Helena Rubinstein (who made an enormous fortune out of beauty products); and the multi-millionaire Howard Hughes, a man whose later life admirably illustrates a Capricornian tendency to melancholia and excessive worrying about physical health.

IN DETAIL

Sexuality and the Emotions Power, wealth and sexuality are, for the pure Capricornian, three aspects of one reality. The archetypal Capricornian marries for money and prestige as well as for love. This does not mean that he/she does not feel deep affection for his/her partner, but that it is difficult for him/her genuinely to love someone who does not contribute in any way to the prestige and worldly well-being of the Capricornian concerned. Capricornian men usually command the respect and admiration, rather than the passionate devotion, of their partners. Their female counterparts often seem extremely glamorous – but this is usually no more than a veneer which conceals a shrewd and money-conscious personality. In spite of these somewhat unlovely characteristics, pure Capricornians of either sex make loyal and reliable partners who develop a deep affection, although rarely a passionate concern, for those with whom they live for any length of time.

General Character If, upon arriving at a party, you see someone surrounded by a circle of admiring listeners you can be reasonably sure it is not a Capricornian. He or she is probably not even one of the listeners. The most likely place to find a Capricornian is in a quiet corner, carefully observing everything that is going on, but not fully participating in it. This capacity to watch and wait explains two things:

firstly, the difficulty some find in getting close to a Capricornian; and, secondly, the fact that Capricornians, while they move slowly, progress steadily forward and eventually reach their goals. To do so they are quite prepared to remain quietly in the background for most of the time, to carry out the plodding routine tasks which Sagittarians would find contemptibly boring, and to accept the fact that a lot of people find them dull.

As a matter of fact the genuinely dull Capricornian is something of a rarity. It is surprising how much time the

The planet Saturn portrayed, in accordance with ancient tradition, as the ruler of both Aquarius and Capricorn. At the present day most astrologers regard Uranus as ruler of the former sign.

Capricornian will devote to thinking out better ways of doing everyday things and how quickly his/her mind works when it is called upon to do so. There is no doubt that Capricornians are more concerned with accumulating wealth for its own sake, rather than for what it will buy, but they are rarely miserly – they are careful rather than grasping people – and, as a result, they often attain great prosperity in middle and old age. If they do become rich, Capricornians are apt to give full expression to their latent capriciousness by, for example, making large donations to eccentric causes and unlikely charities. Such expressions of unpredictability rarely afford much pleasure to their younger relatives.

Life Style Security is of great importance to the pure Capricornian and

Aquarius, the Water Carrier, is a sign traditionally associated with a love of personal liberty. The typical Aquarian personality desires to run as freely as flowing water.

almost any career which provides that and a chance to make steady progress through methodical effort will prove acceptable. If, in addition, it gives the Capricornian a good opportunity to apply his/her intellectual powers – an analytical and logical cast of mind which is occasionally electrified by a flash of inspiration – all to the good. But security is the main requirement; if the Capricornian is to be, for example, a research scientist, he/she will want to ensure that the research is adequately funded. Home life is of great importance to the Capricornian. The home does not have to be beautiful, nor in beautiful surroundings. It must, however, be comfortable – and a good investment.

Aquarius (The Water Carrier)
January 20 to February 19

SUMMARY
Aquarians have in common with Sagittarians a love of liberty – the personal freedom for themselves and others – and an unconventional approach to life. Rarely, however, do they possess the Sagittarian's inbuilt 'luck factor', the capacity almost always to come out on top, even in the most adverse circumstances. And their humanitarian concern for the freedom and welfare of others sometimes lands them in difficult positions and works against their own interests. The Aquarian is always both idealistic and unconventional and he/she is sometimes a very difficult person. The problems that others find in dealing with pure Aquarians in either social or work situations arise from the Aquarian virtues – their idealism, their concern for others, and their freedom from stuffy conventions.

The trouble with Aquarians is that they never know when to stop. They are the sort of people who begin by demanding that there should be less discrimination against minorities and end by expressing their indignation that there are no job opportunities in piano tuning for the tone deaf. Not only are the pure Aquarian's opinions idealistic to the point of eccentricity, they are often expressed with extreme tactlessness and without regard for others' feelings. Sometimes this disregard for common sense goes to lengths which make it difficult to believe that there is not a desire to shock and surprise: the writer Frank Harris, whose horoscope was strongly Aquarian, was apt to lecture such friends as Oscar Wilde on the lives of medieval saints and then to recite improper rhymes to clergymen. If pure Aquarians can keep their enthusiasms within reasonable bounds – perhaps by working in co-operation with others whose feet are more firmly planted on the ground – they are delightful people who are loved by many and leave the world a better place than they found it. Notable Aquarian personalities include and have included the scientists Galileo and Charles Darwin; the writers Charles Dickens and Somerset Maugham; the philosopher Francis Bacon and the actress and political activist Vanessa Redgrave.

IN DETAIL
Sexuality and the Emotions A good long-term relationship with a pure Aquarian is both stable and worthwhile – but not altogether easy to achieve. The Aquarian is usually happy if living alone, making his/her emotional forays when he/she wishes to do so and avoiding the restrictions, however pleasant, which are imposed by permanent relationships. When he/she does enter into longer-term relationships it is essential that there should be no feeling of being trapped, of being compelled to conform to convention and the pressures of family life. Provided that the Aquarian retains a sense of freedom, he/she makes an excellent partner for anyone who can cope with a certain amount of unpredictability and impracticality. An Aquarian is more likely to be concerned with the problems of the Bolivian tin mining industry than with digging the garden or unblocking the kitchen sink.

General Character Most people take immediately to pure Aquarians. They may find their ideas a little too idealistic and impractical, but the personalities are so likeable, the approaches so friendly, that they cannot look upon them as other than thoroughly nice people. And yet, somehow or other, it is difficult to feel close to an Aquarian. However friendly the Aquarian may be – and Aquarians are almost invariably amicable – an impression of distance, of a barrier which cannot quite be demolished, always remains. The barrier is a very real one. Aquarians are never in quite the same world as the rest of us, for at least parts of their minds are always withdrawn from the reality around them and living in the world of their ideals. None of us sees the world exactly as it is – we all view the reality that surrounds us through the distorted lenses of our prejudices and misconceptions – but the pure Aquarian is more subject to defects of intellectual vision than anyone else.

All too often the Aquarian sees the world as he/she would wish it to be, with everyone concerned about each other's welfare and anxious to do good. This sometimes leads to disillusion and a conviction that wickedness is abroad in the world – the Aquarian is genuinely incapable of understanding the ruthless ambition of Aries and Scorpio or the financially prudent ways of Capricorn. The disillusioned Aquarian can be a very dangerous individual – the terrorist who tries to bomb the world into virtue, the cynic who feels that good is inevitably doomed to defeat. If, however, the Aquarian can use his/her very considerable intellectual abilities to apprehend the world as it is, rather than as it might be, he/she can be a tremendous force for good – a reformer of things great and small, a person who transforms others' ways of looking at things. The pure Aquarian, whether he/she operates in only a small field of activities or in the greater world of politics and economics, is never an easy friend. But he/she can be a valued and very worthwhile one.

Life Style Aquarians are not the people to do things in the way they have always been done, to be satisfied with tried and trusted methods. Tell an Aquarian that something has been done in such-and-such a way since 1742 and that no one has ever complained about it before, and he/she will immediately start pointing out the shortcomings of the system. This can be tiresome. Even more tiresomely the Aquarian will suggest a new system which, to the astonishment of all, often turns out to be an improvement on the old one if it is actually tried out. In fact it very rarely is tried out, which causes the Aquarian frustration and annoyance. To avoid this unhappiness it is essential that the Aquarian should seek his/her living in a field of activity which is open to new ideas and innovation. Radical administrations, both local and national, are always filled with pure Aquarians busily engaged in efforts to transform the lives of others for the better. Other fields in which Aquarians excel include social and charitable work, town planning, psychotherapy, economics, sociology, and anything else in which they feel they are making the world either a better place to live in or, as a cynical Capricornian might say, making a tiresome nuisance of themselves.

Pisces *(The Fishes)*
February 20 to March 20

SUMMARY

Pisces is sometimes described as 'the poet's sign'. In reality very few poets have been pure Pisceans, but there is an element of vague dreaminess about some Pisceans which some people associate, almost certainly wrongly, with artistic and literary creativity. At best, the pure Piscean can be an artist, albeit one who is somewhat unworldly; at worst, he/she is an arty drop-out, enthusiastically seeking grants and subsidies from public bodies. Most pure Pisceans come somewhere between these two rather alarming extremes. They are amiable, kindly and, on occasion, a little devious, twisting and turning to find the easy way out of difficult situations. No one could legitimately accuse them of being self-centred – quite the opposite. For some strongly Piscean individuals hardly seem to have a centre at all: their attitudes are always changing as the wind blows, and they are only consistent in that they always oppose 'spiritual' or 'aesthetic' values to the crass materialism which they believe to dominate others.

This sounds rather tiresome but, as a matter of fact, most Pisceans are immensely kindly and loving people. They give generously of their affections, sometimes unwisely so, and they thoroughly deserve the affection and regard they earn. The most strongly negative aspect of the Piscean personality is a tendency to be excessively influenced by others. If you meet an unpleasant Piscean (almost a contradiction in terms), he or she is almost certainly a tool of someone else. The Piscean is intrinsically a thoroughly decent person, and if he/ she behaves in a cruel or unpleasant way, you can be reasonably sure that the Piscean in question is being manipulated and is not acting in accordance with his/her basic feelings. Outstanding Pisceans have included the painter Renoir, the dancer Nijinsky, the composer Chopin, the poet Elizabeth Barrett Browning, and the novelist John Steinbeck.

IN DETAIL

Sexuality and the Emotions The Piscean woman who displays the characteristics of her sign in their purest form is the Victorian ideal of femininity – loving, shy, submissive and anxious to please her partner. The Piscean male shares at least some of these characteristics and, if his partner is a person who enjoys a dominant role, can become that old comic butt, the henpecked husband. Pisceans of either sex tend to take a romantic approach to life and see virtues in those they love which are not always apparent to others. Sometimes this romanticism is difficult to reconcile with the practicalities of a long-term relationship, in which case the Piscean may concen-

The planet Neptune, discovered in 1846 and named after the Roman god, is thought by modern astrologers to rule Pisces, traditionally believed to be ruled by Jupiter.

trate his/her romantic longings on an outsider.

General Character All pure Pisceans are kindly, caring and considerate people. There is nothing at all wrong in that, of course, but with all the Piscean sensitivity to the feelings, or supposed feelings, of others there goes a tendency to unworldliness and impracticality which is sometimes carried to foolish lengths. The combination of immense sensitivity, real kindness and lack of realistic common sense can be a very dangerous one. The pure Piscean always runs the risk of being exploited by those who would influence his/her delicacy of feeling and use it for their own ends. Pisceans must endeavour to avoid being treated in this way by being willing to consult others before uncritically accepting the truth of any and every sob story they are told.

There is a sense in which the Piscean wants to be the victim of the confidence-trickster; any individual whose horoscope is dominated by Piscean influences finds it difficult to take too much reality, and the conman's tale often provides a temporary escape – illusory but valuable to the pure Piscean – from harsh realities. The Piscean's flights of fantasy and torrents of emotion can, and often do, result in a rejection of everyday life and a withdrawal into a private world in which ambition and other material considerations play very little part. There can, however, be a positive side to the other-worldliness of the Piscean: all the Piscean faults become virtues; all the weaknesses are transformed into sources of strength. In such cases the pure Piscean channels his/her emotions and fantasy into creativity and becomes a poet, a painter, a musician or – Pisceans can be healers of genius – a psychotherapist or a mystic.

Life Style Pisceans are rarely motivated by either greed or ambition and they are happy in any field in which they are subject to neither rigid discipline nor major onslaughts on their emotions – no Piscean would wish to work as a prison officer or a slaughterer in an abattoir, for example. Pure Pisceans are happiest in any job which is even vaguely connected with the arts – anything from being a ballet dancer to selling theatre programmes or acting as caretaker at an art gallery. Anywhere is home to a Piscean, as long as those with whom it is shared pay due regard to Piscean sensitivities.

FINDING YOUR ASCENDANT

In reading through the characteristics of one or more of the 12 zodiacal types, it is important to remember that the descriptions given are of the archetypal personalities – the pure Capricornians or Pisceans, for example. Very few people are, in fact, 'pure' zodiacal types, and the person born with the sun in Pisces but a Capricorn ascendant will be a more realistic man or woman than the pure Piscean.

What is needed to get an overall impression of a personality is not only knowledge of what sign the sun was in at the birth date of that person, but his or her ascendant – the sign on the horizon at the actual time of birth. The following step-by-step procedure enables you to calculate this with reasonable accuracy.

Step One Note down the local time – the time as shown on the clock – at birth, the date of birth, and the place of birth.

Step Two Adjust this clock time for any seasonal variations, such as Daylight Saving Time or British Summer Time, which were in force at the date of birth. Thus, for example, for a birth in Britain during the summer you would normally deduct an hour from the clock time to allow for the fact that in summer the clocks are put forward an hour.

Step Three Look up and note down the Star Time (Sidereal Time) at midnight on date of birth from either Table 1 (opposite) or, if the birth took place in a leap year, Table 2 (opposite).

Step Four Take the clock time of the birth as adjusted for seasonal variations (see Step Two) and calculate how many hours it took place after midnight – a birth at an adjusted time of 11.30 pm, for example, is 23 hours 30 minutes after midnight. Write down the number of hours and minutes after midnight below the Star Time you have noted down.

Step Five Allowing 10 seconds for each hour after midnight calculate a total in minutes and seconds and write it down below the other two times. For example, if the birth took place 23 hours 30 minutes after midnight, you would write down '3 minutes 55 seconds' ($23\frac{1}{2} \times 10$ seconds = 235 seconds = 3 minutes 55 seconds).

Step Six Look up your place of birth in Table 3 (page 152). Beside it you will find a plus or a minus figure, expressed in minutes. If it is a plus figure, note it down below your other three times – making sure you put it in the minutes, not the hour, column. If it is a minus figure, just note it on a scrap of paper for the moment. If your place of birth (or a place near it) is not listed, see the *Supplementary Note* below.

Step Seven Add up the four or (if your place of birth had a minus figure beside it in Table 3) the three figures you have listed.

Step Eight (Only applicable if your place of birth had a minus sign beside it in Table 3.) Subtract your minus number of minutes from the total in Step Seven.

Step Nine If, and only if, the birth took place in Australia, New Zealand, South Africa or some other place south of the equator, add a further 12 hours to your total.

Step Ten If your total at the end of Step Seven (or, where applicable, Step Eight or Step Nine) is more than 24 hours, deduct 24 hours from that total. The final total is the Star Time of the birth.

Supplementary Note (See Step Six): The figure in Table 3 (page 152) is a time adjustment which allows for the longitudinal distance between the place of birth and the degree of longitude from which Greenwich Mean Time (GMT) is calculated. If the place of birth, or a place near it, is not included in Table 3 you will have to work out this adjustment for yourself with the aid of a good gazetteer (there is sure to be one in your local reference library).

To do this, look up your place of birth, or if this is not listed, the nearest place to it included in the gazetteer. In the gazetteer you will find listed the longitude of the place in degrees and minutes East and West – for example, 2° W.20' or 12° E.30'. Note down the longitude and turn it into time on the basis of 1° of longitude = 4 minutes of

	Jan.	Feb.	Mar.	April	May	June	July	Aug.	Sept.	Oct.	Nov.	Dec.
1	6 39	8 41	10 31	12 34	14 32	16 34	18 32	20 35	22 37	0 35	2 37	4 36
2	6 43	8 45	10 35	12 37	14 36	16 38	18 36	20 38	22 41	0 39	2 41	4 39
3	6 47	8 49	10 39	12 41	14 40	16 42	18 40	20 42	22 45	0 43	2 45	4 43
4	6 51	8 53	10 43	12 45	14 44	16 46	18 44	20 46	22 49	0 44	2 49	4 47
5	6 54	8 57	10 47	12 49	14 48	16 50	18 48	20 50	22 53	0 51	2 53	4 51
6	6 58	9 1	10 51	12 53	14 52	16 54	18 52	20 54	22 56	0 55	2 57	4 55
7	7 2	9 5	10 55	12 57	14 55	16 58	18 56	20 58	23 0	0 59	3 1	4 59
8	7 6	9 9	10 59	13 1	14 59	17 2	19 0	21 2	23 4	1 3	3 5	5 3
9	7 10	9 12	11 3	13 5	15 3	17 6	19 4	21 6	23 8	1 7	3 9	5 7
10	7 14	9 16	11 7	13 9	15 7	17 10	19 8	21 10	23 12	1 11	3 13	5 11
11	7 18	9 20	11 11	13 13	15 11	17 13	19 12	21 14	23 16	1 14	3 17	5 15
12	7 22	9 24	11 15	13 17	15 15	17 17	19 16	21 18	23 20	1 18	3 21	5 19
13	7 26	9 28	11 19	13 21	15 19	17 21	19 20	21 22	23 24	1 22	3 25	5 23
14	7 30	9 32	11 23	13 25	15 23	17 25	19 24	21 26	23 28	1 26	3 29	5 27
15	7 34	9 36	11 27	13 29	15 27	17 29	19 28	21 30	23 32	1 30	3 32	5 31
16	7 38	9 40	11 30	13 33	15 31	17 33	19 31	21 34	23 36	1 34	3 36	5 35
17	7 42	9 44	11 34	13 37	15 35	17 37	19 35	21 38	23 40	1 38	3 40	5 39
18	7 46	9 48	11 38	13 41	15 39	17 41	19 39	21 42	23 44	1 42	3 44	5 43
19	7 50	9 52	11 42	13 45	15 43	17 45	19 43	21 46	23 48	1 46	3 48	5 47
20	7 54	9 56	11 46	13 48	15 47	17 49	19 47	21 49	23 52	1 50	3 52	5 50
21	7 58	10 0	11 50	13 52	15 51	17 53	19 51	21 53	23 56	1 54	3 56	5 54
22	8 2	10 4	11 54	13 56	15 55	17 57	19 55	21 57	24 0	1 58	4 0	5 58
23	8 5	10 8	11 58	14 0	15 59	18 1	19 59	22 1	0 4	2 2	4 4	6 2
24	8 9	10 12	12 2	14 4	16 3	18 5	20 3	22 5	0 7	2 6	4 8	6 6
25	8 13	10 16	12 6	14 8	16 6	18 9	20 7	22 9	0 11	2 10	4 12	6 10
26	8 17	10 20	12 10	14 12	16 10	18 13	20 11	22 13	0 15	2 14	4 16	6 14
27	8 21	10 23	12 14	14 16	16 14	18 17	20 15	22 17	0 19	2 18	4 20	6 18
28	8 25	10 27	12 18	14 20	16 18	18 21	20 19	22 21	0 23	2 21	4 24	6 22
29	8 29		12 22	14 24	16 22	18 24	20 23	22 25	0 27	2 25	4 28	6 26
30	8 33		12 26	14 28	16 26	18 28	20 27	22 29	0 31	2 29	4 32	6 30
31	8 37		12 30		16 30		20 31	22 33		2 33		6 34

Table 1 (left)

This table gives, in simplified form, Star Time for each day of every year that is not a leap year. (To calculate a full horoscope, a detailed table for the year of birth should be used.)

Use this table as it stands for the years: 1914, 1918, 1922, 1927, 1931, 1935, 1939, 1943, 1947, 1951, 1955.

Add one minute to the times given for the years: 1913, 1917, 1921, 1925, 1926, 1930, 1934, 1938, 1942, 1946, 1950, 1954, 1959, 1963, 1967, 1971, 1975, 1979, 1983, 1987.

Add two minutes to the times given for the years: 1929, 1933, 1937, 1941, 1945, 1949, 1953, 1962, 1966, 1970, 1974, 1978, 1982, 1986, 1991, 1995, 1999, 2003, 2007.

Add three minutes to the times given for the years: 1961, 1965, 1969, 1973, 1977, 1981, 1985, 1989, 1990, 1994, 1998, 2002, 2006, 2010.

Add four minutes to the times given for the years: 1993, 1997, 2001, 2005, 2009.

Deduct one minute from the times given for the years: 1911, 1915, 1919, 1923, 1957, 1958.

time. As there are 60 seconds of longitude in one degree this means that every second of longitude equals four seconds of time. So, if the longitude in the gazetteer was 2° W.20′ (2 degrees and 20 seconds West), one would convert it into time as:

2° of longitude = 8 minutes 0 seconds of time
20′ of longitude = 1 minute 20 seconds of time
Total = 9 minutes 20 seconds of time

If the place of birth normally operates on the same time as London (that is, GMT, not British Summer Time), this total would be the correction – a plus correction if the longitude was an Eastern (E.) one; a minus correction if it was a Western (W.) one. So for any place in Britain which, as in the example, had a longitude of 2° W. 20′ one's time correction would be 'minus 9 minutes and 20 seconds'; for the sake of simplicity one would deduct 9 minutes when carrying out Step Eight.

Obviously enough, most places in the world do not operate on London time – they use a Zone Time which allows for most of the longitude adjustment. So you have, in the cases of all the places which don't have a Zone Time identical with Britain, to adjust your longitudinal time.

	Jan.	Feb.	Mar.	April	May	June	July	Aug.	Sept.	Oct.	Nov.	Dec.
1	6 38	8 40	10 34	12 37	14 35	16 37	18 35	20 38	22 40	0 38	2 40	4 39
2	6 42	8 44	10 38	12 40	14 39	16 41	18 39	20 41	22 44	0 42	2 44	4 42
3	6 46	8 48	10 42	12 44	14 43	16 45	18 43	20 45	22 48	0 46	2 48	4 46
4	6 50	8 52	10 46	12 48	14 47	16 49	18 47	20 49	22 52	0 50	2 52	4 50
5	6 54	8 56	10 50	12 52	14 51	16 53	18 51	20 53	22 56	0 54	2 56	4 54
6	6 57	9 0	10 54	12 56	14 55	16 57	18 55	20 57	22 59	0 58	3 0	4 58
7	7 1	9 4	10 58	13 0	14 56	17 1	18 59	21 1	23 3	1 2	3 4	5 2
8	7 5	9 8	11 2	13 4	15 2	17 5	19 3	21 5	23 7	1 6	3 8	5 6
9	7 9	9 12	11 6	13 8	15 6	17 9	19 7	21 9	23 11	1 10	3 12	5 10
10	7 13	9 15	11 10	13 12	15 10	17 13	19 11	21 13	23 15	1 14	3 16	5 14
11	7 17	9 19	11 14	13 16	15 14	17 16	19 15	21 17	23 19	1 17	3 20	5 18
12	7 21	9 23	11 18	13 20	15 18	17 20	19 19	21 21	23 23	1 21	3 24	5 22
13	7 25	9 27	11 22	13 24	15 22	17 24	19 23	21 25	23 27	1 25	3 28	5 26
14	7 29	9 31	11 26	13 28	15 26	17 28	19 27	21 29	23 31	1 29	3 32	5 30
15	7 33	9 35	11 30	13 32	15 30	17 32	19 31	21 33	23 35	1 33	3 35	5 34
16	7 37	9 39	11 33	13 36	15 34	17 36	19 34	21 37	23 39	1 37	3 39	5 38
17	7 41	9 43	11 37	13 40	15 38	17 40	19 38	21 41	23 43	1 41	3 43	5 42
18	7 45	9 47	11 41	13 44	15 42	17 44	19 42	21 45	23 47	1 45	3 47	5 46
19	7 49	9 51	11 45	13 48	15 46	17 48	19 46	21 49	23 51	1 49	3 51	5 50
20	7 53	9 55	11 49	13 51	15 50	17 52	19 50	21 52	23 55	1 53	3 55	5 53
21	7 57	9 59	11 53	13 55	15 54	17 56	19 54	21 56	23 59	1 57	3 59	5 57
22	8 1	10 3	11 57	13 59	15 58	18 0	19 58	22 0	0 3	2 1	4 3	6 1
23	8 5	10 7	12 1	14 3	16 2	18 4	20 2	22 4	0 7	2 5	4 7	6 5
24	8 8	10 11	12 5	14 7	16 6	18 8	20 6	22 8	0 10	2 9	4 11	6 9
25	8 12	10 15	12 9	14 11	16 9	18 12	20 10	22 12	0 14	2 13	4 15	6 13
26	8 16	10 19	12 13	14 15	16 13	18 16	20 14	22 16	0 18	2 17	4 19	6 17
27	8 20	10 22	12 17	14 19	16 17	18 20	20 18	22 20	0 22	2 21	4 23	6 21
28	8 24	10 26	12 21	14 23	16 21	18 23	20 22	22 24	0 26	2 24	4 27	6 25
29	8 28	10 30	12 25	14 27	16 25	18 27	20 26	22 28	0 30	2 28	4 31	6 29
30	8 32		12 29	14 31	16 29	18 31	20 30	22 32	0 34	2 32	4 35	6 33
31	8 36		12 33		16 33		20 34	22 36		2 36		6 37

Table 2 (above)

This table gives Star Time as applicable to leap years. (To calculate a full horoscope, a detailed table for the year of birth should be used.)

Use this table as it stands for the years: 1924, 1928, 1932, 1936, 1940, 1944, 1948, 1952, 1956.

Add one minute to the times given for the years: 1960, 1964, 1968, 1972, 1980, 1984, 1988.

Add two minutes to the times given for the years: 1976, 1992, 1996, 2000, 2004, 2008.

Deduct one minute from the times given for the years: 1912, 1916, 1920.

Table 3

City		City		City		City	
		Chicago, Illinois	+ 9	Lincoln, Nebraska	−27	Regina, Saskatchewan	+ 2
		Chichester, England	− 3	Lisbon	−37	Reno, Nevada	+ 1
		Cincinatti, Ohio	−38	Little Rock, Arkansas	− 8	Richmond, Virginia	−10
Albany, New York	+ 5	Cleveland, Ohio	−27	London	0	Riga	−24
Algiers	+12	Columbia, South Carolina	−24	Los Angeles, California	+ 7	Rio de Janeiro	+ 7
Amarillo, Texas	−47	Columbus, Ohio	−32	Louisville, Kentucky	+17	Roanoke, Virginia	−20
Amsterdam	−40	Copenhagen	−10	Madrid	−15	Rome	−11
Athens	−25	Dallas, Texas	−27	Manchester, England	− 9	Sacramento, California	− 6
Atlanta, Georgia	+22	Delhi	−21	Manchester,		St. John, New Brunswick	−25
Atlantic City, New Jersey	+ 2	Denver, Colorado	0	New Hampshire	+14	St. Louis, Missouri	− 1
Baghdad	− 2	Derby, England	− 6	Memphis, Tennessee	0	Salt Lake City, Utah	−28
Baker, Oregon	+ 9	Des Moines, Iowa	−15	Mexico City	−36	San Antonio, Texas	−34
Baltimore, Maryland	− 7	Detroit, Michigan	−32	Miami, Florida	−21	San Diego, California	+11
Bangor, Maine	+25	Dublin	−25	Milwaukee, Wisconsin	+ 8	San Francisco, California	−10
Bedford, England	− 2	Dubuque, Iowa	− 3	Minneapolis, Minnesota	−13	Santa Fe, New Mexico	− 4
Belgrade	+22	Duluth, Minnesota	− 8	Mobile, Alabama	+ 8	Santiago	−43
Berlin	− 6	Durham, England	− 7	Montevideo	−15	Savannah, Georgia	−24
Berne	−30	El Centro, California	+18	Montgomery, Alabama	+15	Scranton, Pennsylvania	− 3
Birmingham, Alabama	+13	El Paso, Texas	− 6	Montpelier, Vermont	+10	Seattle, Washington	− 9
Birmingham, England	− 8	Eugene, Oregon	−12	Montreal, Quebec	+ 6	Shreveport, Louisiana	−15
Bismarck, North Dakota	−43	Fargo, North Dakota	−27	Moscow	+30	Sioux Falls, South Dakota	−27
Bogota	+ 3	Fresno, California	+ 1	Nashville, Tennessee	+13	Singapore	−34
Boise, Idaho	−45	Glasgow, Scotland	−17	Newcastle, England	− 6	Spokane, Washington	+10
Bonn	−32	Gloucester, England	− 9	New Haven, Connecticut	+ 8	Springfield, Illinois	+ 1
Boston, England	0	Grand Junction, Colorado	−14	New Orleans, Louisiana	0	Springfield, Massachusetts	+10
Boston, Massachusetts	+16	Grand Rapids, Michigan	+17	New York, New York	+ 4	Springfield, Missouri	−13
Brussels	+17	Halifax, Nova Scotia	−14	Nome, Alaska	− 2	Stockholm	+12
Bucharest	−16	Helena, Montana	−28	North Platte, Nebraska	−43	Syracuse, New York	− 5
Budapest	+16	Helsinki	−24	Oklahoma City, Oklahoma	−30	Tampa, Florida	−30
Buenos Aires	+ 7	Hereford, England	−11	Oslo	−17	Taunton, England	−13
Buffalo, New York	−16	Honolulu, Hawaii	−31	Ottawa, Ontario	− 3	Tokyo	+19
Bury St. Edmunds, England	+ 3	Huntingdon, England	− 1	Oxford, England	− 5	Toronto, Ontario	−18
Cairo	+ 5	Idaho Falls, Idaho	−28	Paris	+ 9	Vancouver,	
Calgary, Alberta	−36	Indianapolis, Indiana	+15	Peking	−14	British Columbia	−12
Cambridge, England	0	Ipswich, England	+ 5	Philadelphia, Pennsylvania	− 1	Victoria, British Columbia	−13
Canberra	− 3	Jackson, Mississippi	− 1	Phoenix, Arizona	−28	Vienna	+ 5
Cape Town	−47	Jacksonville, Florida	−27	Pierre, South Dakota	−41	Wakefield, England	− 6
Caracas	+ 2	Jerusalem	+21	Pittsburgh, Pennsylvania	−20	Warsaw	+24
Cardiff, Wales	−13	Kendal, England	−11	Port Arthur, Ontario	−57	Warwick, England	− 7
Carlsbad, New Mexico	+ 3	Key West, Florida	−27	Portland, Maine	+19	Washington, D.C.	− 8
Carlisle, England	−12	Knoxville, Tennessee	+24	Portland, Oregon	−11	Watertown, New York	− 4
Charleston, South Carolina	−20	La Paz	−32	Prague	− 2	Wellington	−21
Charleston, West Virginia	−27	Las Vegas, Nevada	+19	Providence, Rhode Island	+14	Wichita, Kansas	−29
Charlotte, North Carolina	−23	Leeds, England	− 6	Quebec, Quebec	+15	Wilmington, Delaware	− 2
Chelmsford, England	+ 2	Leicester, England	− 5	Quito	−14	Winnipeg, Manitoba	−29
Chester, England	−12	Lima	− 8	Raleigh, North Carolina	−15	Worcester, England	− 9
Cheyenne, Wyoming	+ 1	Lincoln, England	− 2	Reading, England	− 4	Yakima, Washington	− 2

Let us take an actual example: Toronto, Canada. Its longitude is 79° W.27'. Turning this into time:

79° = 316 minutes = 5 hours 16 minutes
27' = 108 seconds of time = (to nearest minute) 2 minutes
Total 5 hours 18 minutes

As Toronto has a Western (W.) longitude one would make a minus correction of 5 hours 18 minutes if Toronto time was the same as London's – but, of course, it isn't. The clocks in Toronto are normally five hours behind those of London, so the minus correction is only 18 minutes, the correction listed in Table 3. If the clocks in Toronto were normally six hours behind those in London the correction would of course be plus 42 minutes (six hours minus five hours 18 minutes) in spite of the fact that Toronto has a Western longitude.

The rule can be summarized in the following way:

a) If normal (i.e. not Daylight Saving) Zone Time is the same as GMT, turn longitude into time (1° = 4 minutes) and use as a minus figure if W. longitude, plus if an E. longitude.
b) If Zone Time is not GMT, subtract or add longitude correction plus or minus difference between Zone Time and GMT.

If all this sounds a little complex, an actual example will show how very simple it is. We'll suppose a birth taking place in London at 1.31 a.m. on August 11, 1987.

Step One is simply to note down the above facts.
Step Two is to deduct one hour from the time of birth, making it 12.31 a.m. to allow for the fact that the birth took place in the summer months, when the clocks in Britain are put forward an hour.
Step Three is to look up the Star Time for the day of birth. As 1987 is not a leap year, Table 1 applies and the Star Time for midnight on August 11 is noted down – 21 hours 14 minutes.
Step Four is to add the hours and minutes after midnight of the birth,

as adjusted for seasonal variations, and to write it below the Star Time for the date of birth. Thus:

Star Time at midnight on day of birth: 21 hours 14 minutes

Hours and minutes after midnight of time of birth: 00 hours 31 minutes

Step Five Allowing 10 seconds for every hour of birth after midnight only results in an adjustment of 5 seconds. To the nearest minute (accurate enough for the purposes of this calculation) this is zero, so we write down 0 hours 0 minutes as our third figure, below the other two.

Step Six is to look up the place of birth (or a nearby place) in Table 3 and check whether our correction is a plus or minus number of minutes. As the birthplace in this case is London, the correction is zero minutes.

Step Seven The numbers listed are added up:

Star Time at midnight on day of birth (Step Three): 21 hours 14 minutes

Adjusted time of birth after midnight (Step Two): 00 hours 31 minutes

Ten second to hour correction (Step Five): 0 hours 0 minutes

Longitude correction (Step Six): 0 hours 0

Total (Star Time of birth): 21 hours 45 minutes

From the Star Time of any birth north of the equator the important zodiacal midheaven position is very quickly calculated by Table 4. This gives the midheaven (to the nearest degree) for each quarter-of-an-hour interval of Star Time. In the example that has been given, the Star Time of the birth was 21 hours 45 minutes, which gives a midheaven of 24° Aquarius. (The significance of an individual's midheaven sign is described in detail on pages 154-5.)

The same table can be used for calculating the midheaven of a birth taking place south of the equator. For any Star Time take the exactly opposite degree and sign of the zodiac to that shown as being the midheaven. For easy reference the opposing signs of the zodiac are:

Table 4 (Star Times and Midheavens)							
S.T.	**M.C.**	**S.T.**	**M.C.**	**S.T.**	**M.C.**	**S.T.**	**M.C.**
00 00	0 ♈	06 00	0 ♋	12 00	0 ♎	18 00	0 ♑
00 15	4	06 15	4	12 15	4	18 15	4
00 30	8	06 30	7	12 30	8	18 30	7
00 45	12	06 45	10	12 45	12	18 45	10
01 00	16	07 00	14	13 00	16	19 00	14
01 15	21	07 15	18	13 15	21	19 15	18
01 30	25	07 30	21	13 30	25	19 30	21
01 45	28	07 45	24	13 45	28	19 45	24
02 00	2 ♉	08 00	28	14 00	2 ♏	20 00	28
02 15	6	08 15	2 ♌	14 15	6	20 15	2 ♒
02 30	10	08 30	5	14 30	10	20 30	5
02 45	14	08 45	9	14 45	14	20 45	9
03 00	17	09 00	13	15 00	17	21 00	13
03 15	21	09 15	17	15 15	21	21 15	17
03 30	25	09 30	20	15 30	25	21 30	20
03 45	28	09 45	24	15 45	28	21 45	24
04 00	2 ♊	10 00	28	16 00	2 ♐	22 00	28
04 15	6	10 15	2 ♍	16 15	6	22 15	2 ♓
04 30	9	10 30	6	16 30	9	22 30	6
04 45	13	10 45	10	16 45	13	22 45	10
05 00	16	11 00	14	17 00	16	23 00	14
05 15	20	11 15	18	17 15	20	23 15	18
05 30	23	11 30	22	17 30	23	23 30	22
05 45	27	11 45	26	17 45	27	23 45	26
06 00	0 ♋	12 00	0 ♎	18 00	0 ♑	24 00	0 ♈

Aries ♈	Libra ♎
Taurus ♉	Scorpio ♏
Gemini ♊	Sagittarius ♐
Cancer ♋	Capricorn ♑
Leo ♌	Aquarius ♒
Virgo ♍	Pisces ♓

Note: abbreviations employed in the above table are

Aries ♈	Libra ♎
Taurus ♉	Scorpio ♏
Gemini ♊	Sagittarius ♐
Cancer ♋	Capricorn ♑
Leo ♌	Aquarius ♒
Virgo ♍	Pisces ♓

So, in the case of a southern hemisphere birth, if the midheaven was given in Table 4 as '12° Leo' you would note it down as '12° Aquarius'.

The ascendant, the most important factor in an individual horoscope (see page 135), is also calculated from the Star Time, although the approximate latitude of the place of birth has also to be taken into account.

Table 5 on pages 154-5 gives, to the nearest degree, the ascendant for intervals of from 8 to 20 minutes of Star Time for a number of important northern latitudes. Use the one which is nearest to the place of birth; for example, the one for 51° N. 32' can be used for the whole of Southern Britain. Any good atlas will show you the latitude of a particular birthplace.

Continuing with the example that has been used – a child born in London at 1.31 a.m. on August 11, 1987 – we use Table 5 for latitude 51° N.32'. As the Star Time at birth was 21 hours 45 minutes, we get an ascendant of 29°Gemini – if the birth had taken place a little later the child would have had a Cancer ascendant.

For births in southern latitudes take the equivalent nearest northern latitude to that shown in Table 5, but reverse the signs as was done in calculating the midheaven (see above).

To interpret a particular person's character read the zodiacal outlines, as given on pages 135 to 150, of both the sun sign and the ascendant and try to blend them into one composite picture. Remember that the influence of the ascending sign is stronger than that of the sun sign, so a person born with the sun in Pisces but with a Capricorn ascendant is likely to tend more towards the pure Capricornian than the pure Piscean – which does not mean that he or she will not have plenty of the emotionality and artistic flair of the Piscean. At first you will find it difficult to make a composite character picture based on two of the zodiacal signs, particularly if the signs in question are contrasting ones (Leo and Capricorn, for example). In time, however, you will become adept at the technique.

Once you have made your composite interpretation you must modify it by taking into account the zodiacal sign on the midheaven, as calculated by the technique outlined on page 153. The midheaven sign has particular bearing on work and career matters. The exact significance of the zodiacal signs on the midheaven follow.

Aries Midheaven An intense and somewhat ruthless ambition is indicated. Almost certainly a person whose energy will ensure that he/she will get what is wanted out of life – but others may well have their feelings hurt in the process.

Taurus Midheaven A successful and prosperous life in both work and social life. A talent to get on well with other people and a capacity to enjoy life fully is indicated.

Gemini Midheaven A somewhat restless mind, although rather a brilliant one, is indicated. It is essential that enough intellectual stimulation is received in relationships with others, particularly in a career context. A person who will do well in any sphere of life involving communication with other people.

Cancer Midheaven A personality which tends to seek the limelight, to work in the sight of others and to want always to shine. His/her career is likely to be a chequered one – sometimes right on top of things, sometimes the reverse.

Leo Midheaven A person who will get to the top in life, but will be considerably more popular with workmates and friends than most achievers. For while such a person has a driving ambition and is something of a show-off, he/she will display much generosity and will be free of ruthlessness.

Virgo Midheaven A questing and analytical mind is indicated, but one which can be too jumpy, moving from one thing to another and never properly concentrating upon the matter in hand. If this can be controlled, a successful career is indicated.

Libra Midheaven A happy and diplomatic personality is indicated – a man or woman who will find life and work pleasant and, perhaps more importantly, will make it pleasant for others.

Scorpio Midheaven An intensely forceful and ambitious personality

Table 5										
S.T. h. m.	13 N 0	19 N 0	31 N 46	39 N 54	45 N 0	48 N 50	51 N 30	53 N 25	55 N 53	60 N 0
0 00	5♋	8♋	14♋	18♋	22♋	25♋	27♋	28♋	0♌	5♌
0 08	7	10	16	20	23	27	28	29	2	6
0 20	10	12	18	22	26	29	0♌	2♌	4	8
0 40	14	17	22	27	29	2♌	4	4	7	11
0 52	17	19	25	29	2♌	4	6	7	9	13
1 00	19	21	27	1♌	3	6	7	8	10	14
1 08	21	23	28	2	5	7	9	10	12	15
1 20	23	26	1♌	5	7	9	11	12	14	17
1 40	28	0♌	5	9	11	13	14	16	17	20
1 52	1♌	3	7	11	13	14	16	17	19	22
2 00	2	5	9	12	15	17	18	19	20	23
2 08	4	6	11	14	16	18	19	20	22	24
2 20	7	9	13	16	18	20	21	22	24	26
2 40	12	13	18	20	22	24	25	25	27	29
2 52	14	16	20	23	24	26	27	28	29	1♍
3 00	16	18	22	23	26	27	28	29	0♍	2
3 08	18	20	23	26	27	29	29	1♍	2	3
3 20	21	22	26	28	29	1♍	2♍	3	4	5
3 40	26	27	0♍	2♍	3♍	5	5	6	7	8
3 52	29	29	3	4	6	7	7	8	9	10
4 00	1♍	2♍	4	6	7	8	9	9	10	11
4 08	2	4	6	8	9	10	10	11	11	13
4 20	5	6	9	10	11	12	12	13	13	14
4 40	10	11	13	14	15	15	16	16	17	18
4 52	13	14	15	16	17	18	18	18	19	19
5 00	15	16	17	18	19	19	19	20	20	21
5 08	17	18	19	20	20	21	21	21	21	22
5 20	20	21	21	22	22	23	23	23	25	24
5 40	25	25	26	26	26	26	26	27	27	27
5 52	28	28	28	28	28	29	29	29	29	29
6 00	0♎	0♎	0♎	0♎	0♎	0♎	0♎	0♎	0♎	0♎
6 08	2	2	2	2	2	1	1	1	1	1
6 20	5	5	4	4	4	4	3	3	3	3
6 40	10	9	9	8	8	7	7	7	5	6
6 52	13	12	11	10	10	9	9	9	9	8
7 00	15	14	13	12	11	11	11	10	10	9
7 08	17	16	15	14	13	12	13	12	11	11
7 20	20	19	17	16	15	15	14	14	13	12
7 40	25	24	21	20	19	18	16	17	17	16
7 52	27	26	24	22	22	20	20	19	19	17
8 00	29	28	26	24	23	22	21	21	20	19
8 08	1♏	0♏	27	26	24	23	23	22	21	20
8 20	4	3	29	28	27	25	25	24	23	22
8 40	9	8	4♏	2♏	0♏	29	28	27	26	25
8 52	12	10	7	4	3	1♏	0♏	29	28	27
9 00	14	12	8	7	4	3	2	1♏	29	28
9 08	16	14	10	7	6	4	4	2	1♏	29
9 20	18	17	12	10	8	6	6	4	3	1♏
9 40	23	21	17	14	12	10	9	8	6	4
9 52	26	24	19	16	14	12	11	10	8	6
10 00	28	25	21	18	15	13	12	11	10	7
10 08	29	27	23	19	17	16	13	13	11	8
10 20	2♐	29	25	21	19	17	16	14	13	10
10 40	7	4♐	29	25	23	21	19	18	16	13
10 52	9	7	2♐	28	25	23	22	20	18	15
11 00	11	9	3	29	27	24	23	22	19	16
11 08	13	11	5	1♐	28	26	24	23	21	17
11 20	16	13	8	3	0♐	28	26	26	23	19
11 40	20	18	12	7	4	1♐	0♐	28	26	22
11 52	23	20	14	10	7	3	2	1♐	28	24

S.T. h. m.	13 N 0	19 N 0	31 N 46	39 N 54	45 N 0	48 N 50	51 N 30	53 N 25	55 N 53	60 N 0
12 00	25	22	16	12	8	5	3	2	29	25
12 08	27	24	18	13	10	7	5	3	1♐	27
12 20	0♑	29	21	16	12	9	7	5	3	29
12 40	4	1♑	25	20	16	13	11	9	6	2♐
12 52	7	4	28	23	19	16	13	11	9	4
13 00	9	6	29	24	21	17	15	13	10	5
13 08	10	8	1♑	26	22	19	16	14	12	6
13 20	13	11	4	29	25	20	19	17	14	8
13 40	18	15	9	4♑	29	26	23	21	18	12
13 52	21	18	12	6	2♑	28	25	23	20	14
14 00	23	19	15	8	4	1♑	27	25	22	15
14 08	25	22	16	10	6	2	29	27	23	17
14 20	28	25	19	13	9	5	2♑	29	24	19
14 40	3≈	1≈	24	19	14	10	6	4♑	0♑	23
14 52	6	4	27	22	17	13	10	7	3	25
15 00	8	6	29	24	20	15	12	9	5	27
15 08	10	8	2≈	26	22	18	15	12	7	29
15 20	14	11	5	0≈	25	21	18	15	10	1♑
15 40	19	17	11	6	2≈	27	24	21	16	6
15 52	22	20	15	10	6	1≈	27	25	20	10
16 00	25	23	18	13	8	4	0≈	27	23	12
16 08	17	25	20	15	11	7	3	0≈	25	14
16 20	0♓	29	24	20	16	12	8	5	0≈	19
16 40	6	5♓	1♓	27	24	20	16	14	9	27
16 52	10	8	5	2♓	29	25	22	19	15	3≈
17 00	11	11	8	5	2♓	29	26	23	19	7
17 08	14	13	11	8	6	3♓	0♓	29	24	12
17 20	18	17	15	13	11	9	7	6♓	1♓	21
17 40	24	24	23	21	20	19	18	18	15	9♓
17 52	25	27	27	27	26	26	25	25	24	21
18 00	0♈	0♈	0♈	0♈	0♈	0♈	0♈	0♈	0♈	0♈
18 08	5	3	3	3	4	4	5	5	6	9
18 20	6	6	7	8	10	11	13	12	15	21
18 40	12	13	15	17	19	21	23	24	29	9♉
18 52	16	17	19	22	24	27	29	1♉	6♉	18
19 00	19	19	22	25	28	1♉	4♉	6	11	23
19 08	20	22	25	28	1♉	5	8	11	15	27
19 20	24	25	29	3♉	6	10	14	16	21	3♊
19 40	29	1♉	6♉	10	14	18	22	25	29	11
19 52	3♉	5	10	15	19	23	27	29	5♊	16
20 00	5	7	12	17	22	26	29	3♊	7	18
20 08	8	10	15	20	24	29	3♊	5	11	20
20 20	11	13	19	24	28	3♊	6	9	14	24
20 40	16	19	25	29	5♊	9	13	15	20	29
20 52	20	22	28	3♊	8	12	17	18	24	1♋
21 00	22	24	0♊	6	10	15	18	22	26	3
21 08	24	26	3	8	13	17	20	23	27	5
21 20	27	29	6	11	15	20	23	26	29	7
21 40	28	5♊	11	17	21	25	29	1♋	6♋	11
21 52	5♊	8	14	20	24	28	1♋	4	7	13
22 00	7	11	15	22	26	29	3	5	8	15
22 08	9	12	18	24	28	2♋	5	7	10	16
22 20	12	15	21	27	1♋	4	7	9	12	18
22 40	16	19	26	1♋	5	10	11	13	16	22
22 52	19	22	29	4	8	11	13	16	18	24
23 00	21	24	1♋	6	9	13	15	17	20	25
23 08	23	26	2	7	11	14	17	19	21	27
23 20	26	29	5	10	14	17	19	21	23	28
23 40	29	1♋	9	14	18	21	23	25	27	1♌
23 52	3♋	6	11	17	20	23	25	27	29	3
24 00	5♋	8♋	14♋	18♋	22♋	25♋	27♋	28♋	0♌	5♌

A Babylonian boundary stone portraying a royal couple basking beneath the benefic influence of the goddess Ishtar, the planet Venus, the Sun and the Moon.

which, provided it can control its tendency to express itself brutally, thus alienating others, will probably get all it wants out of life.

Sagittarius Midheaven A jovial and benevolent personality – sometimes exaggeratedly so – which pleases most people and generally results in success and prosperity.

Capricorn Midheaven A painstaking, accurate and stolid personality whose patience and slightly boring worthiness and reliability usually ensure that success and prosperity are achieved – although rarely until the second half of his or her life.

Aquarius Midheaven A personality which dislikes the dull routine of everyday life and thoroughly enjoys decision-making. A good leader, although one who tends to dominate others, but one who sometimes suddenly and inexplicably loses interest in what remains to be achieved and abruptly changes course.

Pisces Midheaven An idealistic and enthusiastic personality which sometimes lacks staying power. If this tendency to change course, or to abandon the race suddenly, can be controlled, he/she will sail effortlessly and successfully through life.

A SAMPLE HOROSCOPE

The information given in this chapter will not enable you to construct a complete horoscope for either yourself or an individual whose time, date and place of birth are known to you. To construct such a complete horoscope you would need to have ephemerides – lists giving the position of the sun, moon and planets on each day of a particular year – covering the years from, say, 1900 to 2000. Considera-

Judy Garland, a strongly Geminean personality liable to sudden changes of mood and emotional upheaval. It is likely that Nicky, with a Gemini ascendant, will also rather easily fall in or out of love.

tions of space make it impossible for such enormously lengthy tables to be included in this book.

What you can do from the information which has been included is to work out the two most important features in the horoscope of someone whose time, date and place of birth are known to you. These are 1) the rising sign, that is the sign ruling the ascendant – the sector of the zodiac which is coming up on the horizon at the moment of birth, and 2) the zodiacal sign ruling the midheaven, in other words, the sign which is highest in the heavens at the moment of birth.

From the combination of these two features, together with a consideration of what sign the sun was in at birth, it is possible to work out a far more detailed picture of the character and likely destiny of a given individual than it is from a consideration of the sun sign alone.

Take, for example, the imaginary 1987 birth described on page 152 – that is, a child born in London at 1.31 a.m. (British Summer Time) on August 11.

Obviously the child is what is generally called a Leo – i.e. he was born between July 24 and August 23, the time of the year when the sun is in that sign. But more important than the sun's position in the zodiac on the date of birth is the child's ascendant – his or her rising sign – which depends on the star time of birth on that date.

As was shown on page 153 the imaginary child in question – we'll call him or her 'Nicky', a name which can be that of either a boy or a girl – had a Gemini ascendant. This means that although Nicky will be referred to as a Leo, and will certainly have some of the qualities associated with that sign, he or she will in many ways be more of a Geminean. Nicky's character will be that of a Geminean, but one who will also have Leonine qualities.

Before trying to describe Nicky's blended Geminean/Leonine characteristics let us consider the zodiacal sign of his or her midheaven. As was said on page 153 Nicky has an Aquarius midheaven, which tends to indicate a

decisive nature – a personality which is dominating and possessed of qualities which make for leadership, but is bored by routine and apt to make sudden changes of direction, particularly where career matters are concerned.

These midheaven zodiacal characteristics will modify in one way or another Nicky's Geminean/Leonine nature and must always be kept in mind.

Emotional life

We'll start by considering Nicky's future emotional life. With his or her Gemini ascendant Nicky will always be liable to fall suddenly in love or make new and very close friendships. But love affairs and friendships will be liable to end as quickly as they have begun. Such sudden emotional changes are characteristic of the pure Geminean, but in Nicky's case they are likely to be even more abrupt than normal if he or she feels that a friend or lover is not providing enough attention. This is because Nicky will have the Leonine determination to be the 'sun' in any relationship; a partner will have to be the 'moon' and shine with Nicky's reflected glory.

Once Nicky does settle down with the right partner, however, the relationship is likely to prove a permanent and happy one; the Geminean tendency to fickleness will be tempered by Leonine loyalty. It will be noted that I have said 'the *right* partner' – it is unlikely that anybody would make a satisfactory lasting relationship with Nicky who was not prepared to be the subordinate partner.

Professional life

Nicky, being blessed (or cursed) with the qualities of a Geminean ascendant will show all the 'airiness' of that sign. He or she will be quick-witted, versatile, and likely to take an interest in a large number of subjects, to which a creative approach will be adopted. If, for example, in later life Nicky took an interest in financial matters it is likely that he or she would be drawn to 'creative accounting' as applied to balance sheets, rather than to the minor details of double-entry bookkeeping in 'bought ledgers'. The wideness of Nicky's interests, resulting from a disinclination rather than an inability to concentrate the mind on one particular field of activity, will

almost inevitably result in some difficulties during the course of life.
Nicky's 'airiness', sudden changes of
direction, loss of interest in something
or somebody, will be bound to cause
annoyance to others, who will consider him or her 'unreliable'. This may
well lead to Nicky experiencing setbacks and disappointments in life –
frustrations imposed by those who
consider Nicky not entirely reliable.

However Nicky will overcome any
setbacks or frustrations – for he or she
will not only have all the resilience of
the Geminean, the capacity to 'bounce
back', but also the Leonine drive, the
ability to achieve success and – most
important of all – sheer luck.

Nicky's Leonine capacity for leadership is also likely to display itself in the
way in which he or she approaches all
those activities which require direct involvement. So Nicky may become, at
one and the same time, a salesperson,
an enthusiastic stamp collector, and an
individual who is actively engaged in
local politics. But it will not be long before Nicky is well on the way to
becoming Sales Manager of his or her

*Charles Dickens displayed Aquarian
characteristics in his dislike of the
routine tasks of editing and proof
correction. It is likely that Nicky, with
his/her Aquarius midheaven, will be
similarly bored by routine work.*

company; a leading authority on, say,
the perforations on Victorian stamps;
and the leader of his or her party on
the local council.

Life style
Nicky's Geminean qualities would
ensure that only unhappiness could
result from following a career which,
however well paid, is rather dull and
varies little from day to day. Nicky's
unhappiness in a routine job, however
highly skilled, would be even greater
if it did not provide a chance to meet
people, to indulge in a certain amount
of friendly contact with others during
the course of work.

This desire for contact with people,

*Louis XIV, who employed the
astrological services of Morinus, author
of the monumental* Astrologia Gallica,
*was known as the 'Sun King'. He, like
Nicky, possessed a strongly Leonine
solar personality.*

combined with the Geminean ability
for communication and the Leonine
capacity for leadership, could make
Nicky an exceptionally good journalist
or politician – but he or she will excel in
any field requiring versatility.

Such are the Leonine/Geminean
characteristics of the hypothetical
Nicky. Now try combining your own
zodiacal ascendant, sun sign and midheaven in the same way.

CHAPTER
10

CHINESE ASTROLOGY

The British Library contains literally hundreds of printed books dealing with the subject of Chinese astrology. The oldest of these is an almanac, printed from wooden blocks, which dates from the eighth century – twelve hundred years ago. Even when this almanac was published the origins of Chinese astrology were so old as to be lost in the mists of antiquity.

Today Chinese astrology is regarded as 'a relic of the feudal past' in Communist China. But in both Taiwan and Hong Kong new editions of the ancient almanac are published each year, and in the West the ancient wisdom expressed in Chinese astrology is studied, used and revered by many thousands of non-Chinese people.

Strictly speaking, this chapter should be called 'Chinese calendarism' or 'Chinese chronologism' and not 'Chinese astrology'. For, unlike Western or Indian astrology, both based on the movements of the sun, moon and planets through the zodiac, Chinese 'astrology' is concerned only with the ancient agricultural calendar, based upon complex lunar cycles, and a sixtyfold sun/moon cycle.

This last cycle is based upon rotations of the five Elements of traditional Chinese philosophy (wood, fire, earth, metal and water) in the Positive and Negative aspects, and 12 symbolic year-animals (the Rat or the Monkey, for example).

The effect of the tenfold elemental rotation of the years (five Elements in both their Positive and Negative aspects) means that after ten years the elemental cycle is completed. Thus, for example, the Chinese year which ran from February 7, 1978 to January 27, 1979 had the elemental attribution of Positive Earth, and the same elemental attribution applies ten years later, to the Chinese year running from February 17, 1988 to February 5, 1989.

The effect of the cycle of the 12 animal-years obviously leads to a twelvefold recurrence: the Chinese year which began on February 17, 1988 is a Year of the Dragon, and the Chinese year beginning in February 2000 is also a Year of the Dragon.

The 12- and 10-year cycles coincide every 60 years. Thus, the Chinese year from January 29, 1987 to February 16, 1988 was a Year of the Negative Fire Rabbit. The previous Year of the Negative Fire Rabbit ran from February 1927 to January 1928; the next one will run from February 2047 to January 2048.

The elemental and animal symbol attributions of the Chinese years between 1912 and 2012 are given in table form on pages 160-61.

It should be noted that each of the years shown in this table is attributed not only to an animal symbol but also to one of the five Elements of Chinese cosmology in either its Positive (+) or Negative (–) aspect.

These Elements are not, of course, the elements with which chemists are concerned. They are qualities of mind, modes of behaviour, and so on. Thus, for example, warfare or competitive sport would probably be considered as pertaining more to the Elements of Metal and Fire than to Wood and Water to which some art forms might be attributed. Similarly, banking or insurance, and probably most money matters, would be attributed to Earth.

Sages contemplate the Yin-Yang symbol, gift of Heaven, which expresses the conceptual essence of Chinese astrology as much as it does that of the I Ching. See illustration on page 98.

Thus, an Earth Boar or an Earth Rooster would probably be better at dealing with practical matters, notably financial ones, than a Water Boar or a Fire Rooster.

It will be seen that each of the Elements manifests itself in, first, its Positive and then its Negative aspect. Thus, the year which runs from February 17, 1988 to February 5, 1989 is the Year of the Earth Dragon, which pertains to the Positive aspect of Earth; the year which follows, that of the Earth Snake, pertains to Earth in its Negative aspect.

Westerners must beware of thinking that the Positive aspect of an Element should be equated with goodness, the Negative aspect with evil. In Chinese cosmology, from which Chinese astrology is derived, the Positive (Yang) and Negative (Yin) aspects of reality are not seen as opposing one another, like two wrestlers, but supporting each other, like the left and right sides of an arch. Just as, by definition, an arch cannot exist without having two sides, so reality cannot exist without both its Positive and Negative aspects. In the ancient Positive/Negative (Yang/Yin) Taoist philosophy, everything is classified as pertaining to one of these two aspects of interdependent duality. Thus, night is Negative, day is Positive. Female sexuality is Negative, maleness is Positive. Form is Negative, force is Positive. Sugar is Negative, salt is Positive, and so on.

From the table you will see that 6 of the 12 animal symbols of Chinese astrology are always Positive and that the other 6 are always Negative. This does not mean that people born in a year attributed to one of the Positive symbols (Rat, Tiger, Dragon, Horse, Monkey and Dog) are in any way superior to those born in a year pertaining to one of the Negative animal symbols. It does mean that these Positive people will be happier in their lives generally, and more successful in their careers, if they pursue an active,

thrusting policy in which they strongly influence things rather than being influenced by them. Similarly, those born in Negative years are likely to be more prosperous and happy if they try to avoid approaching life (and other people) in too combative a spirit.

From the table you can quickly see the animal and elemental attribution of the year in which you were born. If, for example, you were born on August 12, 1970, you will see that you were born in the Chinese Year of the Metal Dog. Don't forget that the Chinese year, which is based on the moon not, as is the Western year, on the sun, does not entirely coincide with the Western calendar. So while most people born in 1970 can consider themselves Metal Dogs, anyone born in 1970 at a date prior to February 6 will be an Earth Rooster.

It is not only whole years which are attributed to the animal symbolism of Chinese astrology. Each year is divided into 12 periods, very roughly coinciding with the time the sun is in a particular sign of the zodiac, and each of these periods is attributed to one of the symbolic animals. Similarly, each day is divided into 12 2-hour periods, each attributed to a particular symbol.

These attributions are as follows:

Animal Symbol	Hours of the Day and Night	Zodiacal Month
Rat	11 pm to 1 am	Sagittarius
Ox	1 am to 3 am	Capricorn
Tiger	3 am to 5 am	Aquarius
Rabbit	5 am to 7 am	Pisces
Dragon	7 am to 9 am	Aries
Snake	9 am to 11 am	Taurus
Horse	11 am to 1 pm	Gemini
Sheep	1 pm to 3 pm	Cancer
Monkey	3 pm to 5 pm	Leo
Rooster	5 pm to 7 pm	Virgo
Dog	7 pm to 9 pm	Libra
Boar	9 pm to 11 pm	Scorpio

From the above table you will see that the hypothetical Metal Dog born on August 12, 1970 – which means his/her zodiacal sun sign would be Leo – was, although born in the Chinese Year of the Metal Dog, born in a zodiacal month attributed to the Monkey. If the individual in question was born at 6 o'clock in the evening, he or she would have come into the world in one of the 'Hours of the Rooster'.

When working out the character traits and personal abilities of someone on the basis of Chinese astrology, one usually gets a better result if one considers the zodiacal month and the time, if known, of that person's birth as well as the year in which it took place.

Thus, while someone born at 6 pm on August 12, 1970 will be primarily a Metal Dog, he or she will also have some Monkey elements, because of the zodiacal month of birth, and some Rooster elements, because of the time of birth. Never forget, however, that it is the year of birth that is of the most importance; don't cheat and try to turn a dog into a Rooster just because you prefer the traits of the latter to those of the former.

THE TWELVE ANIMAL SYMBOLS

THE RAT

Key Words
Likeable, hard-working, sociable and thrifty.

General Character
The Rat is both hard-working and careful with money. Sometimes, in fact, the Rat is so economical that thriftiness degenerates into miserliness. Rats only spend money lavishly in three particular circumstances. Firstly, if they are deeply in love or regard someone with great affection – in which case they may behave with quite extraordinary generosity. Secondly, they will spend money if they are collectors (and many Rats are) of books, art objects, postage stamps or anything else usually regarded as collectable. Finally, Rats will spend money like water if they believe that doing so will either further their career or help them achieve their long-term professional ambitions.

This last trait illustrates an important point about Rats. They are almost always ambitious and know precisely what they want out of life. Most Rats not only know what they want, but eventually succeed in getting it; their capacity for hard work, allied with their shrewd practicality and their ability to get on well with others, usually ensures this.

Emotions and Love Life
Rats are so good at hiding their true

ANIMAL AND ELEMENTAL ATTRIBUTIONS

Sign		Element
Rat	February 18, 1912 to February 5, 1913	Water (+)
Ox	February 6, 1913 to January 25, 1914	Water (−)
Tiger	January 26, 1914 to February 13, 1915	Wood (+)
Rabbit	February 14, 1915 to February 2, 1916	Wood (−)
Dragon	February 3, 1916 to January 22, 1917	Fire (+)
Snake	January 23, 1917 to February 10, 1918	Fire (−)
Horse	February 11, 1918 to January 31, 1919	Earth (+)
Sheep	Febuary 1, 1919 to February 19, 1920	Earth (−)
Monkey	February 20, 1920 to February 7, 1921	Metal (+)
Rooster	February 8, 1921 to January 27, 1922	Metal (−)
Dog	January 28, 1922 to February 15, 1923	Water (+)
Boar	February 16, 1923 to February 4, 1924	Water (−)
Rat	February 5, 1924 to January 24, 1925	Wood (+)
Ox	January 25, 1925 to February 12, 1926	Wood (−)
Tiger	February 13, 1926 to February 1, 1927	Fire (+)
Rabbit	February 2, 1927 to January 22, 1928	Fire (−)
Dragon	January 23, 1928 to February 9, 1929	Earth (+)
Snake	February 10, 1929 to January 29, 1930	Earth (−)
Horse	January 30, 1930 to February 16, 1931	Metal (+)
Sheep	February 17, 1931 to February 5, 1932	Metal (−)
Monkey	February 6, 1932 to January 25, 1933	Water (+)
Rooster	January 26, 1933 to February 13, 1934	Water (−)
Dog	February 14, 1934 to February 3, 1935	Wood (+)
Boar	February 4, 1935 to January 23, 1936	Wood (−)
Rat	January 24, 1936 to February 10, 1937	Fire (+)
Ox	February 11, 1937 to January 30, 1938	Fire (−)
Tiger	January 31, 1938 to February 18, 1939	Earth (+)
Rabbit	February 19, 1939 to February 7, 1940	Earth (−)
Dragon	February 8, 1940 to January 26, 1941	Metal (+)
Snake	January 27, 1941 to February 14, 1942	Metal (−)
Horse	February 15, 1942 to February 4, 1943	Water (+)
Sheep	February 5, 1943 to January 24, 1944	Water (−)
Monkey	January 25, 1944 to February 12, 1945	Wood (+)
Rooster	February 13, 1945 to February 1, 1946	Wood (−)
Dog	February 2, 1946 to January 21, 1947	Fire (+)
Boar	Janury 22, 1947 to February 9, 1948	Fire (−)
Rat	February 10, 1948 to January 28, 1949	Earth (+)
Ox	January 29, 1949 to February 16, 1950	Earth (−)
Tiger	February 17, 1950 to February 5, 1951	Metal (+)
Rabbit	February 6, 1951 to January 26, 1952	Metal (−)
Dragon	January 27, 1952 to February 13, 1953	Water (+)
Snake	February 14, 1953 to February 2, 1954	Water (−)
Horse	February 3, 1954 to January 23, 1955	Wood (+)
Sheep	January 24, 1955 to February 11, 1956	Wood (−)
Monkey	February 12, 1956 to January 30, 1957	Fire (+)
Rooster	January 31, 1957 to February 17, 1958	Fire (−)
Dog	February 18, 1958 to February 7, 1959	Earth (+)
Boar	February 8, 1959 to January 27, 1960	Earth (−)

Rat	January 28, 1960 to February 14, 1961	Metal (+)
Ox	February 15, 1961 to February 4, 1962	Metal (−)
Tiger	February 5, 1962 to January 24, 1963	Water (+)
Rabbit	January 25, 1963 to February 12, 1964	Water (−)
Dragon	February 13, 1964 to February 1, 1965	Wood (+)
Snake	February 2, 1965 to January 20, 1966	Wood (−)
Horse	January 21, 1966 to February 8, 1967	Fire (+)
Sheep	February 9, 1967 to January 29, 1968	Fire (−)
Monkey	January 30, 1968 to February 16, 1969	Earth (+)
Rooster	February 17, 1969 to February 5, 1970	Earth (−)
Dog	February 6, 1970 to January 26, 1971	Metal (+)
Boar	January 27, 1971 to January 15, 1972	Metal (−)
Rat	January 16, 1972 to February 2, 1973	Water (+)
Ox	February 3, 1973 to January 22, 1974	Water (−)
Tiger	January 23, 1974 to February 10, 1975	Wood (+)
Rabbit	February 11, 1975 to January 30, 1976	Wood (−)
Dragon	January 31, 1976 to February 17, 1977	Fire (+)
Snake	February 18, 1977 to February 6, 1978	Fire (−)
Horse	February 7, 1978 to January 27, 1979	Earth (+)
Sheep	January 28, 1979 to February 15, 1980	Earth (−)
Monkey	February 16, 1980 to February 4, 1981	Metal (+)
Rooster	February 5, 1981 to January 24, 1982	Metal (−)
Dog	January 25, 1982 to February 12, 1983	Water (+)
Boar	February 13, 1983 to February 1, 1984	Water (−)
Rat	February 2, 1984 to February 19, 1985	Wood (+)
Ox	February 20, 1985 to February 8, 1986	Wood (−)
Tiger	February 9, 1986 to January 28, 1987	Fire (+)
Rabbit	January 29, 1987 to February 16, 1988	Fire (−)
Dragon	February 17, 1988 to February 5, 1989	Earth (+)
Snake	February 6, 1989 to January 26, 1990	Earth (−)
Horse	January 27, 1990 to February 14, 1991	Metal (+)
Sheep	February 15, 1991 to February 3, 1992	Metal (−)
Monkey	February 4, 1992 to January 22, 1993	Water (+)
Rooster	January 23, 1993 to February 9, 1994	Water (−)
Dog	February 10, 1994 to January 30, 1995	Wood (+)
Boar	January 31, 1995 to February 18, 1996	Wood (−)
Rat	February 19, 1996 to February 7, 1997	Fire (+)
Ox	February 8, 1997 to January 27, 1998	Fire (−)
Tiger	January 28, 1998 to February 15, 1999	Earth (+)
Rabbit	February 16, 1999 to February 4, 2000	Earth (−)
Dragon	February 5, 2000 to January 23, 2001	Metal (+)
Snake	January 24, 2001 to February 11, 2002	Metal (−)
Horse	February 12, 2002 to January 31, 2003	Water (+)
Sheep	February 1, 2003 to January 21, 2004	Water (−)
Monkey	January 22, 2004 to February 8, 2005	Wood (+)
Rooster	February 9, 2005 to January 28, 2006	Wood (−)
Dog	January 29, 2006 to February 17, 2007	Fire (+)
Boar	February 18, 2007 to February 6, 2008	Fire (−)
Rat	February 7, 2008 to January 25, 2009	Earth (+)
Ox	January 26, 2009 to February 13, 2010	Earth (−)
Tiger	February 14, 2010 to February 2, 2011	Metal (+)
Rabbit	February 3, 2011 to January 22, 2012	Metal (−)

feelings that they sometimes find it hard to communicate their emotions to others, even when they wish to do so. This leads people who take thing at face value to assume that Rats are cool customers who are not easily hurt and whose emotions are not easily roused. This is not, in fact, true. The exterior calm of the typical Rat often conceals a seething cauldron of emotions. When treated badly by those they love, Rats are as deeply hurt as anyone else, even if they are better than most of us at camouflaging emotional scars.

The animal symbol least likely to establish a successful and long-lasting relationship with a Rat is the Horse. The animals which the Rat is most likely to be happy with are the Dragon and the Monkey. Other combinations are usually reasonably satisfactory, although in a Rat/Rat relationship the partners are often too alike for real ease. Rat/Tiger and Rat/Dog combinations are often also subject to strain, but with a certain amount of goodwill on both sides the relationship can still be a successful one.

The Five Elemental Rats
(All Elemental Rats are Positive.)

The Metal Rat is more emotional than other Rats and more likely to be a person who expresses negative emotions; jealousy of the material success of others is a fault to which Metal Rats are peculiarly liable. At their best, Metal Rats are more idealistic and less self-seeking than other Rats; at their worst, they disguise greed and selfishness by a loud expression of idealistic beliefs which are not genuinely held. In either case a certain tendency to flashy showiness and a desire to dominate others will be apparent.

The Water Rat is the most intellectual of the Rats; he or she is drawn to books, learning and deep thinking. The essential practicality of the Rat personality ensures that this thinking is strongly linked to real life. Even the most intellectual Water Rat is more likely to be an applied rather than a pure scientist, an economist rather than an abstract philosopher. Water Rats are not only thinkers, they are also adept at communicating their thoughts in both written and spoken form. They get on even better with other people than do most Rats, although some find their tendency to

be ultra-conventional in their behaviour a little tiresome.

The Wood Rat is the least conventional of the Elemental Rat types, tending to seize on the new and unorthodox with an almost excessive enthusiasm. Paradoxically, this love of all that is new is often accompanied by a fear of the future – the Wood Rat is a great warrior, but is always afraid of things going wrong, however successful his or her achievements may seem at the time. This inner fear is hidden from all save those to whom the Wood Rat is very close; to everyone else the Wood Rat seems confidence itself.

The Fire Rat has a character that is in accordance with his or her fiery nature. Fire Rats are enthusiastic, ready to respond to challenges (which they seize as flames do a piece of dry wood), and tend to be quarrelsome. A Fire Rat 'flares up' if he/she feels put upon or badly treated. The Fire Rat is an independent creature, liable to make unexpected moves more frequently than other types of Rat – to change jobs or houses, for example.

The Earth Rat is the most imperturbable of the Rats, liking security and stability in all aspects of his/her life. Earth Rats are great home-lovers, getting very attached to familiar places and anxious to stick to what they know well. Material success is important to them and usually they achieve it. Sometimes, however, their desire to avoid change leads to their getting stuck in a rut, with the result that they do not achieve all they should.

Good and Bad Years for Rats to the Year 2010

1999 A calm and pleasant year, but caution is still called for where finances are concerned.

2000 A very good year for both love, and money. Career prospects are also good – but beware of new friends whose motives aren't quite what they seem.

2001 A year in which luck is not all that good. Best to avoid taking risks, particularly where money is concerned.

2002 Not a fortunate year for Rats, both money and love being in short supply. Avoid all risks in any aspect of your life.

2003 A good year for both money and work matters, but not all that good as far as romance is concerned. There may be some unexpected change in the life of the typical Rat during the first part of the year.

2004 A splendid year for Rats, but avoid doing anything which might result in the breakup of old friendships.

2005 An even better year than 2004 for Rats. Pleasant surprises will be the order of the day and there will be plenty to celebrate.

2006 By no means as pleasant a year as 2005 or even 2004. Considerable prudence is called for and the unexpected should be guarded against.

2007 A year of standstill; there will be no great improvement over the previous year.

2008 The name year of the Rat – and one in which prosperity and happiness are there for the taking.

2009 A reasonably good year of rather unremarkable happiness.

2010 Again, a reasonable year, but taking risks in money matters could result in serious losses.

THE OX

Key Words
Patient, courageous, constant, conventional.

General Character
The patience of the Ox is proverbial, as is its capacity for hard work. It is also an animal which can be as stubborn as the proverbial mule. Humans who are born in Years of the Ox share these qualities. They will work until they are almost fit to drop, particularly if all this effort will help those whom they love and cherish. Not only will they work hard, but they will do so quite uncomplainingly. It is almost as though they feel that their rightful function in life is to labour while others play.

The patience of the Ox is matched only by his or her traditionalism – a preference for doing things in the way they have always been done – and the stubbornness with which change is resisted. Just as the Oxen which pull the plough are apt to object to a new way of being harnessed or the unfamiliar voice of a new ploughman, so men and women born in Years of the Ox find it difficult to work in unaccustomed ways. The plough-ox will passively refuse to obey the commands of the new ploughman; the human Ox will pretend that he or she does not understand the new ways.

It is a mistake to assume that the stolidity of the human Ox is an indication of stupidity. On the contrary, Oxen are very intelligent indeed – although they do not always make it apparent to others. The purposeful, logical intelligence of the Ox man or woman, combined with his or her reliability and industriousness, usually ensure that they overtake their flashier contemporaries in the race that is life, and reach the winning post well before those who, in youth, strike others as 'brilliant' or young people who are 'sure to reach the top'.

Emotions and Love Life

Oxen are unlikely to make passionate declarations of love, write poems in praise of loved ones, or gain reputations as Don Juans or Casanovas. However, anyone who assumes that Oxen are neither racked by sexual desires nor capable of deep and abiding love is very much mistaken.

The passions of the Ox man or woman are not easily aroused and it is most unusual for the Ox to experience 'love at first sight'. It is equally unusual for the Ox to fall suddenly out of love. Their love grows steadily over the months and the years and, once it has reached its peak, is unlikely to diminish, even under considerable provocation. Ox men and women are extremely loyal to their partners; it is rare for them to cheat on their husbands, wives or lovers.

The person least likely to establish a long-lasting and harmonious relationship with the Ox man or woman is the Sheep. In spite of the fact that they both appear to be placid, pasture-grazing types, the Ox and the Sheep have so little in common that they find it almost impossible to relate to one another. Oddly enough, the Ox/Ox relationship is also a difficult one, and here it is the similarities between the partners that makes for difficulties – it is very hard to serve and work for someone whose only object in life is to serve and work for you. In other words, Oxen are better at giving than receiving. Ox men and women establish particularly satisfactory relationships with the Snake and the Rooster. Other relationships are likely to be reasonably satisfactory except the Ox/Dog and Ox/Tiger ones, which can be very difficult indeed.

The Five Elemental Oxen
(All Elemental Oxen are Negative.)

The Metal Ox is eloquent, clever and frequently artistic. These valuable qualities are accompanied by a conviction that his/her personal views are the only right ones, and an even more hard-working temperament than other Oxen. This tends to make the Metal Ox an argumentative creature who, particularly where career matters are concerned, is never afraid to express his/her point of view very loudly indeed. Consequently, the Metal Ox is often a difficult colleague – but always a reliable one.

The Water Ox is more prepared to listen to the opinions of others than the Metal Ox. This does not mean that Water Oxen are keen on innovation – they are as traditionally minded as the whole Oxen clan – but they are very open to reasoned argument. If it can be demonstrated that the new is better then the old, they will abandon time-honoured methods of doing things. They will, however, insist on hard evidence of the superiority of the new and will not be prepared to change for the sake of it. Water Oxen demand the utmost of themselves and expect others to do the same. This can lead to a refusal to make allowances for the weaknesses of others.

The Wood Ox is better at working with others than most Oxen and is also more conscious of other people's feelings. Wood Oxen have the same willpower for making tremendous effort as all their clan, but are not as stubbornly obstinate. Consequently, they are the Elemental Oxen most likely to achieve prominence in life.

The Fire Ox has all the biting quality of flames in his/her dealings with others. This can mean that Fire Oxen are sarcastic in their speech, drawing

attention to other people's faults, and are outspoken to the point of rudeness. This rudeness is, at least, tempered by a strong sense of fair play – the Fire Ox is always prepared to apologize if he/she realizes that unjustified criticisms have been made by him/her. In many ways the combative nature of Fire Oxen makes working life difficult for them; they are hardly suited to any job calling for diplomacy and the social graces. They are often, however, good in careers which require a certain amount of fighting instinct – the law and the army, for example.

The Earth Ox is the most stolid of all the Oxen. He/she has many virtues such as loyalty, sincerity and utter reliability, but neither imaginative creativity nor sensitivity of soul are among them. Nevertheless, Earth Oxen usually get what they want out of life, pushing steadily and quietly forward, utterly patient, until they reach their goal.

Good and Bad Years for Oxen to the Year 2010

1999 A fair year in which there is some progress, but in which the possibility of financial loss should be guarded against.

2000 Not a particularly good year for Oxen, but not a particularly bad one either. There will be more surprises in life than Oxen care for, and all their industrious patience will be required to deal with them. On the other hand, Oxen should be pleasantly surprised to receive unexpected help.

2001 A good year, particularly where money matters are concerned. There is a risk of misunderstandings with lovers, friends or colleagues and it is important that Oxen should sort these out by talking frankly, but avoiding rudeness.

2002 Not a fortunate time for either love or money matters – all the prudence and patience of the typical Ox will be called for. The second half of the year should be much better than the first, but all Oxen should still be very cautious.

2003 Not quite as difficult a year as 2002, but still a year of problems, particularly ones concerned with money and/or work. The emotional life of the typical Ox should, however, be placid enough. Towards the end of the year a piece of good news may be expected.

2004 The bright dawn at the end of 2003 keeps its promise – an absolutely splendid year for Oxen in which all goes well. There will be good news in relation to both the emotional and working lives of many Oxen.

2005 A very good year by general standards, but not quite as good as 2004. There is some possibility of an unexpected event which may be of a strange – almost uncanny – nature.

2006 A year of problems – but ones which can, with effort, be solved.

2007 A fair year, and a very busy one. Work done this year should pay off in the future.

2008 A good year in which all goes well. At work, Oxen can expect above average recognition of their efforts, and promotions are a distinct possibility. Home life will be full of joy.

2009 In spite of minor difficulties, most probably involving tiresome journeys, a good and prosperous year for Oxen.

2010 Not a good year for Oxen – a time for patience and avoiding risks.

THE TIGER

Key Words
Lucky, dynamic, restless, daring, unpredictable, life-enhancing and life-loving.

General Character
The Tiger is a 'chancer' – a person who is daring to the point of recklessness and who continually behaves in unexpected ways. No one is ever bored in the company of a Tiger; quite a lot of people, however, long for a bit of boredom after they have spent an extended period of time with one. This is because they typical Tiger is not only dynamic but hasty – he or she has a tendency to rush into things without fully considering the consequences. Tigers are often captured by sudden enthusiasms and tend to neglect other things for whatever their current enthusiasm is. At their best, Tigers are warm-hearted individuals, responding to the needs of others with great sympathy and understanding. At their worst, they are selfish and so unpredictable that they alienate their friends. They are often extremely successful in career and money matters, although their recklessness sometimes results in an up-and-down sequence of success/failure/success.

Emotions and Love Life
Tigers are almost always strongly emotional and have a powerful sexual drive which is usually combined with a certain amount of sensuality – liking the pleasures of love for their own sake. As a consequence, both male and female Tigers are more inclined to 'sow wild oats' than the rest of us. Usually, however, Tigers become more placid as the years go by, and make thoroughly satisfactory husbands and wives – although always retaining a strain of wildness which makes for exciting and eventful long-term relationships.

The animal symbol least likely to make a satisfactory partner for the Tiger is the Monkey; they tend to share few interests or attitudes and to bicker and quarrel. The animal symbols most likely to establish a long-lasting and happy relationship with a Tiger are the Dog and the Horse. The Boar and the Dragon also make very satisfactory partners for the Tiger. Other animal symbols are only fair to moderate in relationships with Tigers; that with the Rabbit is usually poor to fair at best.

The Five Elemental Tigers
(All Elemental Tigers are Positive.)

The Metal Tiger is even more extrovert, outgoing and optimistic than other Tigers. He/she is often both reckless and extremely selfish, happy to exploit others on the way to the top. If this tendency can be controlled, Metal Tigers are both likeable and successful; if not, they are just successful.

The Water Tiger has the elemental qualities of the waters of a large lake – usually placid but capable of being very rough indeed when disturbed by the strong winds of destiny. When rough, the Water Tiger can be a very wrathful animal. Usually, however, Water Tigers are calm, reasonable, and more concerned with the feelings and thoughts of others than most Tigers. The Water Tiger's combination of reasoned calmness and feline energy can result in a successful career and a happy home life.

The Wood Tiger is as friendly and agreeable as a contented domestic cat. Like such a cat, the Wood Tiger is loved and admired by those who know him/her well. But he/she is a wary of strangers and and does not care for them to 'take liberties'; if they do, they find that Wood Tigers can bite and scratch as well as purr.

The Fire Tiger is a born leader and flames with an enthusiasm which he/she is capable of transmitting to others. Fire Tigers are both the most generous and the most resourceful of Tigers and, as such, are usually as popular at work as they are socially. A very likeable Tiger – and a very brilliant and commanding one.

The Earth Tiger is, literally, more down-to-earth than the rest of the Tiger clan. He/she is perhaps the least brilliant of the Tigers, but any lack of sparkle is more than made up for by the Earth Tiger's capacity for persistence and considered thought. Earth Tigers are generally less flamboyant than other Tigers; being less subject to sudden enthusiasms, they tend to take a more objective view of things.

Good and Bad Years for Tigers to the Year 2010

1999 An absolutely splendid year for money matters – and almost as good for love.

2000 A bad year for Tigers financially; speculation and gambling should be avoided at all costs. Also not a good year on the emotional level; care must be taken not to antagonize loved ones.

2001 A moderate year of small successes – provided Tigers are cautious.

2002 A splendid year for both love and money.

2003 A year of problems which the Tiger can cope with as long as he/she takes a relaxed attitude.

2004 A year in which quarrels and disputes are in the air – Tigers must be cautious.

2005 A moderately good year in which problems are solved with the help of others.

2006 A year in which Tigers are unexpectedly lucky, but also have to make a great effort to enjoy the benefits of this.

2007 A good first half to the year – but caution is called for in the second half.

2008 A moderately good year. Tigers should take no risks involving money or emotional life.

2009 A fair year – problems should be nearly resolved by the autumn.

2010 A reasonably good year provided no undue risks are taken.

THE RABBIT

Key Words
Lucky, generous and kind, quietly intelligent, artistic, sensitive.

General Character
The Rabbit is one of the luckiest of the animal symbols and can come unscathed through adversities which would devastate most of us. Rabbits tend not to be fighters – they prefer negotiation and compromise to head-on collision with those with whom they disagree. This readiness to seek the peaceful way out of a problem should not be mistaken for docility. If Rabbits have to fight, they do so with the utmost courage and fierceness. The Rabbit's love of peace is complemented by an interest in music and the arts, and a generous consideration for the interests and feelings of others. The more negative characteristics of the Rabbit are a tendency to sudden mood changes, which others find disconcerting, and a certain deviousness that usually arises from a wish to avoid outright confrontation.

Emotions and Love Life
Rabbits are pleasure-loving creatures

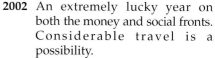
who like the physical excitements of love and marriage. But they like their comforts even more, and the Rabbit's desire for ease – even luxury – usually outweighs all other considerations. Thus, while Rabbits will seek temporary relationships with those who appeal to their physical passions, they rarely enter into a long-term relationship or marriage with anyone they don't believe will provide comfort and ease. The animal least likely to enjoy a satisfactory relationship with the Rabbit is the Rooster. Tigers also rarely get on well with Rabbits, and relationships with Monkeys and Horses are also difficult. Boars and Sheep are excellent partners for Rabbits. Relationships with other animals are usually reasonably good, that with Dogs often notably so.

The Five Elemental Rabbits
(All Elemental Rabbits are Negative.)

The **Metal Rabbit** is more devious than other Rabbits. He/she is extremely artistic and sensitive – but also subject to very dark moods in which life seems almost too much to bear. The Metal Rabbit is also much more of a passionate romantic than most of the Rabbit clan, and tends to be swept away by emotional forces.

The **Water Rabbit** has such an

intense desire for a peaceful life that he/she is sometimes rather withdrawn and introverted – afraid to show emotions which are, nevertheless, still there and apparent to the discerning observer. The Water Rabbit's meditative and thoughtful nature sometimes leads to an excessive concern with past events.

The **Wood Rabbit** is the most generous and considerate of all the Rabbits. Sometimes this generosity is excessive and in such cases Wood Rabbits don't look after their own interests as they should. Wood Rabbits are enormously kind and likeable – but for their own good it is essential that they should not be too kind and considerate to others.

The **Fire Rabbit** is extremely emotional and is not afraid to express his/her emotions, making others aware of them. Fire Rabbits, however, still tend to be secretive and a little devious – although not to the same extent as other Rabbits. As a consequence of his/her ability to speak out boldly if necessary, the Fire Rabbit is more of a leader than most of the clan.

The **Earth Rabbit** is more serious and steadfast than most Rabbits – and even more comfort-loving!

Good and Bad Years for Rabbits to the Year 2010

1999 A year of standstill in which Rabbits must have 'safety first' always in mind.

2000 A moderately good year in which new friends make a strong impact on Rabbit lives.

2001 Not a disastrous year, but not a good one. Rabbits may experience financial strains.

2002 An extremely lucky year on both the money and social fronts. Considerable travel is a possibility.

2003 Another fortunate year – but no hasty financial decisions should be made.

2004 Only a moderately good year and one in which financial difficulties are a possibility.

2005 A difficult year for both money and home life or affairs of the heart.

2006 A fairly good year, but one in which some unexpected obstacles are encountered.

2007 At best only a moderately fortunate year. Unexpected problems are likely to be encountered.

2008 A better year than last, but by no means a marvellous one.

2009 A bad year in which decisions should not be made hastily. Problems and disappointments abound.

2010 A better year than the previous one, but still not without difficulties.

THE DRAGON

Key Words
Energetic, strong, a power broker, prosperous.

General Character
In pre-revolutionary China the Dragon was a symbol of the power of the Emperor and that of the great Mandarins who served the Celestial Empire and ruled its peasant subjects. Those born in a Year of the Dragon have a great many of the characteristics which were considered desirable to Emperors – burning zeal, boundless enthusiasm, an ability to inspire others, and so on. In legend, Dragons vomit fire, and human Dragons, metaphorically speaking, do the same, particularly at those who are seen as hostile or in any way threatening. In other words, Dragons are powerful and resolute opponents of people who challenge them – a Dragon is a dangerous enemy. Fortunately, Dragons are as helpful and considerate in friendship as they are resolute and dangerous in enmity. They make good friends, but not easy friends: they insist on imposing their own standards and ideas on those with whom

they associate and they always insist on taking the lead in every activity. Dragons are usually successful in their chosen careers and are almost invariably prosperous. It is almost as though each individual Dragon incorporated in his/her being a magnet endowed with the remarkable power of attracting money; Dragons, however, have the capacity to spend money almost as easily as they earn it. Dragons rarely come to grief, but if they do, it is usually because they have underestimated the strength of the forces opposed to them. They can, in fact, be oversure of their own abilities. If Dragons can control this arrogant and cocksure strain in their psychological make-up, they are invariably successful and happy.

Emotions and Love Life

There is an element of the loner in almost every Dragon. Paradoxically, young Dragons also seem to have a strong desire to enter into long-term emotional relationships. As a result of this, Dragons tend either to marry at a rather early age – usually such marriages prove stable – or to remain single throughout life, either being utterly chaste or engaging in a large number of short relationships. Dragons are least likely to find satisfactory partners among members of the Dog clan, with whom they seem incompatible. They get on only moderately well with Horses and Sheep and very well with everyone else, particularly Rats, Monkeys and, rather surprisingly, other Dragons.

The Five Elemental Dragons

(All Elemental Dragons are Positive.)

The Metal Dragon is the hardiest and toughest of the Dragon clan. He/she is also the most energetic, the most strong-willed, the most efficient, and the most attacking. Metal Dragons are so capable and intelligent that they find it impossible to suffer fools at all, let alone gladly. They also find it difficult to understand – less still tolerate – either idleness or dishonesty. Metal Dragons are honest, brave, reliable and convinced of the rightness of their beliefs and actions. They make wonderful friends or partners – and terrible opponents.

The Water Dragon has all the energy of other Dragons, but finds it

difficult to concentrate that energy. As a consequence of this diversion of effort, it is hard for the Water Dragon to realize fully his/her very considerable potential. Nevertheless, Water Dragons almost always fulfil their desires, although not as quickly as they would like. This type of Dragon is more prepared to consider compromise than most of its fellows.

The Wood Dragon is more open to new ideas than other Dragons. He/she is also more capable of genuinely creative thinking. While not quite as ruthless with opponents as most Dragons – and considerably less vindictive – the Wood Dragon is, nevertheless, quite as capable of looking after him or herself, and is destined to find success and happiness.

The Fire Dragon flames! Other Dragons may be harder or more energetic, but none more nearly resembles a volcano in eruption than the Fire Dragon. He/she roars into action, even when there is no real need to take any action at all. The Fire Dragon makes a very good leader – provided followers and associates are prepared to believe that he/she is always right.

The Earth Dragon is perhaps less combative than other Dragons – or perhaps just better at administering with an iron hand concealed in a velvet glove. The Earth Dragon is seemingly more stable than other Dragons; certainly he/she is less given to explosive outbursts. Like all Dragons,

however, the Earth Dragon never forgets an injury.

Good and Bad Years for Dragons to the Year 2010

1999 A calm year, and a fortunate one, in which last year's troubles are forgotten.

2000 A magnificent year of success, prosperity and general happiness.

2001 A very good year, although not as splendid as 2000.

2002 Not a good year; unpleasant shocks abound. Provided Dragons remain calm these can be coped with.

2003 A moderately good year – pleasantly dull rather than pleasantly exciting.

2004 A good year for money matters, although not an outstanding one. But emotional problems arise.

2005 A splendid year with everything going as Dragons want it to go.

2006 A year of tiresome problems in which all the Dragon energies are called upon.

2007 Most of last year's problems are resolved. On the whole a happy year.

2008 A good year for the emotional side of life. Money flows in –

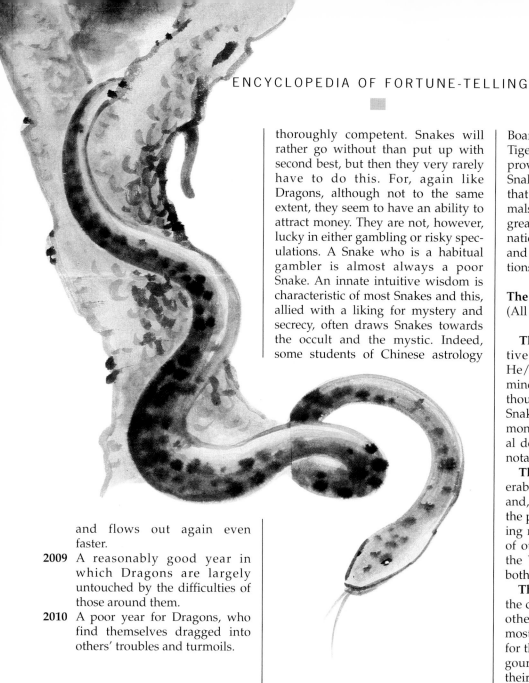

thoroughly competent. Snakes will rather go without than put up with second best, but then they very rarely have to do this. For, again like Dragons, although not to the same extent, they seem to have an ability to attract money. They are not, however, lucky in either gambling or risky speculations. A Snake who is a habitual gambler is almost always a poor Snake. An innate intuitive wisdom is characteristic of most Snakes and this, allied with a liking for mystery and secrecy, often draws Snakes towards the occult and the mystic. Indeed, some students of Chinese astrology

and flows out again even faster.

2009 A reasonably good year in which Dragons are largely untouched by the difficulties of those around them.

2010 A poor year for Dragons, who find themselves dragged into others' troubles and turmoils.

THE SNAKE

Key Words
Mysterious, inscrutable, wise, self-reliant, tenacious.

General Character
Snakes, like Dragons, radiate power, energy and boundless self-confidence. They are, however, more subtle than Dragons, making their moves less openly; and more sybaritic: they are lovers of the luxuries in life and take pleasure in good food, good drink and elegant living. Snakes are, in fact, epicurean in their taste for luxuries; a Snake may be happy to dine on bread and cheese, but will want the cheese to be a good one, exactly at the proper stage of ripeness, and the bread to be home-baked. Similarly, the Snake will be prepared to sit in a cheap seat at the theatre – as long as the play is really worth watching and the actors are

claim that a substantial proportion of Snakes have the capacity to develop psychic abilities. Snakes are almost always successful in both their careers and private lives. Those who aren't tend to fail spectacularly. Snakes are rarely mediocre; they are either at the top of the pile or right at the bottom.

Emotions and Love Life
Snakes are sexually passionate and sometimes give the impression that they are promiscuous. This impression is usually false; the secrecy with which many Snakes like to cloak their activities often gives other people the idea that clandestine affairs are being hidden from them when, in reality, everything is perfectly legitimate and above board. In their romantic lives Snake men and women display their characteristic insistence on having 'only the best'. If they can't get the partners they yearn for, they will remain alone. The

Boar, the Monkey, the Horse and the Tiger are the least likely animals to provide satisfactory partners for the Snake; but a lot of Snakes are so subtle that they get on well with these animals, even though they don't have a great deal in common. The best combinations are Snake/Snake, Snake/Ox, and Snake/Rooster; other combinations are reasonably satisfactory.

The Five Elemental Snakes
(All Elemental Snakes are Negative.)

The Metal Snake is the most secretive and mysterious of the tribe. He/she also has a sharply logical mind which operates like a computer; thought is untinged by emotion. Metal Snakes are sometimes interested in money matters to an almost obsessional degree, and their love of luxury is notable.

The Water Snake combines considerable intelligence with artistic flair and, perhaps surprisingly, a genius for the practical. They are good at managing money, their own lives, and those of other people. The negative side of the Water Snake is a tendency to be both jealous and vengeful.

The Wood Snake is the kindliest of the clan and is far more considerate of others' feelings and interests than most Snakes. Wood Snakes are notable for their discernment – they tend to be gourmets rather than gluttons – and their interest in good writing, music, the theatre and the plastic arts (e.g., sculpture, pottery, etc.).

The Fire Snake is a suspicious animal, avoiding exposing him or herself to the slightest possibility of being harmed by others. Fire Snakes often express their supposed convictions very strongly but the only thing they are convinced of is the importance of power and money. This conviction, allied with an ability to influence the thought and feelings of others, ensures that Fire Snakes make successful politicians, company directors and trade union leaders.

The Earth Snake is slower in mind than other Snakes and usually less ruthless and more likeable than any other Snake save the Water Snake. Their likeability, combined with a practical common sense, usually outweighs the effects of mental inertia, and Earth Snakes almost always get what they want out of life.

Good and Bad Years for Snakes to the Year 2010

1999 A good year and an active one – but it is essential not to over-spend.

2000 A poor year, particularly where money is concerned, by the worst should be over by the autumn.

2001 A year of slight financial gains and some emotional upheavals. Patience and coolness are required.

2002 A highly successful year in which problems are encountered but overcome.

2003 A moderate year in which Snakes must make calm preparations for the future.

2004 On the whole a good year, but one in which Snakes must avoid being drawn into quarrels.

2005 An excellent year for Snakes in every aspect of their lives.

2006 A reasonably good year, although not as outstanding as 2005.

2007 Only a moderate to poor year, and one in which Snakes must avoid getting into money troubles.

2008 A good year as far as work is concerned, but one in which Snakes should not lend money.

2009 A moderate year in which Snakes must be prepared to compromise.

2010 An eventful year in which small but irritating problems continually manifest themselves.

THE HORSE

Key Words

Adventurous, cheerful, sociable, popular, changeable.

General Character

The Horse is a temperamental but usually cheerful animal and human Horses share these characteristics. They are liked by most people they meet and loved by those who know them well. The love and regard which others feel for Horses is sometimes subject to considerable strain – human Horses are not only high-spirited but are hot-tempered and liable to fits of erratic and often trying behaviour. Their unpredictability ensures that

Horses are regarded as a trifle odd by their more unimaginative acquaintances. Freedom is all-important to the Horse – or rather his or her own freedom, for Horses are essentially self-centred and tend to forget that others also desire a certain amount of unshackled liberty. The selfishness of the typical Horse is not calculated selfishness, and therefore does not usually extend to money matters – indeed many Horses are generous to a fault. In spite of their unpredictability, and their inability to keep to schedules which inconvenience them, Horses usually do well in their chosen careers. Their likeability, plus an almost uncanny power to come to the correct decision on the basis of inadequate evidence, provides them with enormous personal strength.

Emotions and Love Life

Horses fall in love easily. They fall out of love with equal facility. Their unpredictable natures make them exciting (but often exasperating) partners, and Horses are reputed to change their mates more than most of us. This is said to be particularly true of Fire Horses – in ancient China male Fire Horses were regarded as the human equivalents of stud bulls, and female Fire Horses as being far more passionate than other women. The animal symbol least likely to establish a good relationship with the Horse is the Rat; also Horse/Snake and Horse/Rabbit combinations are frequently difficult and rarely satisfactory. Best relationships are with the Dog and the Tiger; Sheep, rather surprisingly, also get on well with Horses. Other relationships vary from moderately poor to moderately good – neither outstandingly miserable nor deliriously happy.

The Five Elemental Horses
(All Elemental Horses are Positive.)

The Metal Horse is more egotistical, adventurous and liberty-loving than most Horses. He/she is almost incapable of following a fixed routine, of keeping to schedules, or working in a controlled and supervised fashion. Such a Horse is always seeking new experiences in every aspect of his/her life. Metal Horses find it difficult to make long-lasting emotional relationships as they are afraid that if they do so their liberty will be restricted.

The Water Horse is noted for his/her sense of humour, the ability to amuse others, and adaptability to his/her environment. They are just as unpredictable as any of the Elemental Horses and often display an almost pathological inability to make serious plans for the future or to consider the consequences of their own actions.

The Wood Horse has the same qualities of inconsistency as other Horses, but is better at controlling them, having a more disciplined mind and being more amenable to reasoned argument then other Horses.

The Fire Horse is highly intelligent, excitable, and hot-blooded in every sense of the phrase – liable to indulge in outbursts of bad temper and explosions of sexual passion. A dangerous Horse, but one that many find extremely intriguing and exciting.

The Earth Horse is a less temperamental Horse than most of the clan. By no means the most exciting of Horses, but perhaps the most dependable and certainly the least exasperating.

Good and Bad Years for Horses to the Year 2010

1999 A splendid year, particularly where money matters are concerned.

2000 An up-and-down year in which Horses should keep a low profile.

2001 A demanding year in which Horses have to run hard in order to stand still.

2002 An excellent year for Horses provided that they do not break off old friendships and connections.

2003 A moderately good year in which only minor problems are encountered.

2004 An excellent year for the Horse, who experiences some remarkable good fortune.

2005 A moderate year in which Horses move forwards – but only slowly and with effort.

2006 A very good year for Horses of an intellectual bent. Otherwise only fair to moderate.

2007 A year of troubles, particularly money troubles. These diminish towards the end of the year.

2008 A year of upheavals – and not particularly pleasant ones. Horses must try to be prudent and calm.

2009 A great improvement on 2008. Far fewer problems and the financial situation improves.

2010 A happy year for Horses who can curb their hot tempers and emotional outbursts.

THE SHEEP

Key Words
Good, kind, sensitive, artistic, emotional, gloomy.

General Character
The Sheep is the archetype of genuine goodness and consideration for others. They are gentle and their ready sympathy for the troubles of the less fortunate sometimes leads them to be

exploited by unscrupulous individuals who play on their feelings. They expect from others a kindliness equal to their own; as a consequence, they react badly to criticism and rebuke, taking a fairly mild piece of criticism as a woundingly heartless personal attack. As a result of this, some Sheep become gloomy, even depressed. Sheep tend to be lucky, to be the recipients of unexpected strokes of good luck, and have the knack of being, quite by chance, in the right place at the right time. According to some ancient Chinese writers, this is because the essential goodness and gentleness of the Sheep's nature attracts the favours of the Immortals. The Sheep's good fortune is sometimes offset by the fact the he/she will only fight for his or her own interests if absolutely necessary, in which case he/she turns into a berserk warrior – there is nothing more terrifying than a battling Sheep. Only extreme provocation, however, will make Sheep fight and, as a consequence, they do best in the work, business, and financial aspects of life when they are teamed up with a more outgoing and bad-tempered animal, the Horse for example.

Emotions and Love Life

Sheep do best in marriage and other long-term relationships when they have partners who complement them rather than resemble them; in other words, Sheep need partners who are less gentle and trusting than themselves and can supply the qualities that Sheep are deficient in. It might be thought from this that the Sheep/Sheep combination is a difficult one, but this is not so – the combined weaknesses of two Sheep seem to blend into a peaceful strength. The worse partner for a Sheep is the Ox. Relations with Rats, Tigers, Monkeys and Roosters are sometimes almost as difficult. The Sheep/Boar and Sheep/Rabbit pairings are ideal, and the Sheep/Horse combination is almost as good. With other animal symbols relationships are usually satisfactory.

The Five Elemental Sheep

(All Elemental Sheep are Negative.)

The Metal Sheep protects his/her inner gentleness and kindliness in an armour-like skin and, as a result, often gives a quite false impression of hardness, even brutality. In reality, however, the character of the Metal Sheep is summed up in the familiar phrase 'very rough but with a heart of gold'.

The Water Sheep is the softest and weakest of the Sheep clan – or, at least, the one who most impresses others with his/her helpless gentleness and need for assistance. As a consequence, Water Sheep are never in trouble for very long; people rush to their assistance whenever they are in difficulties. If they don't, the Water Sheep becomes very gloomy indeed.

The Wood Sheep also gets assistance from others; but he/she is not so passive as the Water Sheep and gives as well as receives.

The Fire Sheep is more outgoing, active and combative than other Sheep and is usually less reliant on the support of others.

The Earth Sheep is a notably hard worker – he/she actually enjoys work and is usually a success in life. This animal, however, reacts even more badly to criticism than other Sheep.

Good and Bad Years for Sheep to the Year 2010

1999 A moderate year, but one in which Sheep can be successful if they make the necessary efforts.

2000 A moderate year in which Sheep should avoid gambling and speculation.

2001 Quite a good year in which Sheep receive much help from others.

2002 A good year in which old problems no longer seem very important.

2003 A year which begins well but ends rather badly. Sheep should be cautious, especially in relation to money.

2004 A very good year in almost all aspects.

2005 A good year, but one in which caution in money matters is essential.

2006 An unpleasant year in which much goes wrong. Sheep must avoid taking on more than they can handle.

2007 A moderate year by general standards, but one that is brilliant compared with 2006.

2008 A very good year of business success, strokes of good luck, and romance.

2009 A moderate to poor year in which caution will be needed to avoid financial problems.

2010 A rather poor year in which money troubles may be experienced.

THE MONKEY

Key Words

Clever, flexible, capable of deceit, resourceful, conceited, charming.

General Character

There is a classic Chinese novel called *Monkey* which recounts the adventures of a monkey who journeys from China to India in search of – rather improbably – Buddhist scriptures. The novel's hero has all the characteristics of the Monkey of Chinese astrology, being adaptable, ingenious, humorous, intelligent and, on occasion, an unscrupulous trickster. The most evident characteristic of the human Monkey is his or her charm. Monkeys are liked by almost everybody. Even those who do not take to a Monkey at first acquaintance usually succumb eventually. This is particularly so if the Monkey bothers to exert his/her beguiling charm – almost every Monkey has the power of 'charming the birds from the trees' if he or she makes the effort. There is far more to the Monkey than mere charm and general affability. Monkeys are far more quick-witted than most of us, they are capable of original thought and invention, are fast learners, and can adapt to almost any situation, however difficult. On the other hand, it has to be admitted that Monkeys can sometimes be remarkably devious, being prepared to bend the truth if that is the only way they can get what they want. At its worst this Monkey guile can degenerate into outright fraud – the Monkey makes a very good confidence trickster. Some Monkeys are so guileful that, without prompting, they cheerfully tell lies for the purpose of helping their friends. This is sometimes a cause of difficulty; an individual who has no desire to deceive is virtually forced to support Monkey-lies told on his or her behalf. In general, however, Monkeys keep their deceptiveness within reasonable limits and are as admirable as they are charming and capable.

Emotions and Love Life

Because Monkeys get on well with almost everyone they sometimes find it difficult to get on with a particular person, their long-term partner. The problem is that it is difficult for the Monkey to display more warmth and be more charming towards a specific individual than he/she does to other friends. Nevertheless, once a relationship is properly established the average Monkey makes a splendid partner. The animal least likely to be a satisfactory partner for the Monkey is the Tiger, who finds the Monkey tricky and 'too clever by half'. Monkey/Snake relationships are sometimes strained. Monkeys establish excellent relations with other Monkeys, with whom they form a mutual admiration society, being overcome with wonder at each other's cleverness and charm, and with Rats. With other animal symbols, Monkeys establish relationships which are always tolerable and sometimes very good.

The Five Elemental Monkeys

(All Elemental Monkeys are Positive.)

The Metal Monkey is rather more combative than most of his/her fellows. He/she is markedly good at making money, particularly when self-employed – Metal Monkeys do not take kindly to receiving orders from others.

The Water Monkey is more secretive and more sensitive than the rest of the clan – less outgoing and much more easily hurt.

The Wood Monkey is the most communicative of this very outgoing tribe. He/she has a tremendous drive towards material success and usually achieves it.

The Fire Monkey is extraordinarily outgoing. He/she is also much more reckless than other Monkeys – most of whom are prepared to take certain risks – and a tendency not to look before leaping sometimes get Fire Monkeys into trouble.

The Earth Monkey is calmer and less outgoing than other Monkeys – and a lot less egotistic and self-seeking.

Good and Bad News for Monkeys to the Year 2010

1999 A very good year, although not so good as 1996, particularly where money is concerned.

2000 Not a good year financially and a very bad one for gambling or speculation. A time for patience.

2001 A moderately good year in which some problems and unexpected obstacles manifest themselves.

2002 A reasonably good year for Monkeys provided they don't take too many risks.

2003 On the whole a good year, but one in which Monkeys should be cautious.

2004 A splendid year for love, money and success. The only risk is that of exhaustion.

2005 A moderately good and rather uneventful year.

2006 A bad year, particularly where money is concerned. Monkeys should neither speculate nor lend money.

2007 An energetic year in which Monkeys will find themselves in dispute with others and should rely only on themselves.

2008 A splendid year on every front. Good fortune and luck continually manifest themselves.

2009 A moderately good year in which Monkeys should not over-extend themselves, financially or romantically.

2010 An unpleasant year for Monkeys, who should keep a low profile and not be too outgoing.

THE ROOSTER

Key Words

Odd in behaviour, critical in stance, tactless, funny and witty, efficient, good performers.

General Character

The Chinese word for this animal symbol means 'chicken', but as the characters of humans ruled by it more nearly resemble those tradtionally associated with the cockerel than the hen, it is here called the Rooster, following

standard Western practice. Human Roosters are good with money (they can manage other people's even better than they can their own), have highly disciplined minds and enjoy organizing people and things. They do this very well, and know as much, and want others to know it too: as a consequence, they tend to boast about their own abilities, to 'crow like a barnyard cock'. Their crowing is less monotonous than that of their avian namesakes, however, as they are usually amusing and informative conversationalists – the sort of people who entertain others at a party, over a drink or at a dinner table. There is a distinctly theatrical element in most Roosters; they enjoy performing, they welcome applause and they adore being the centre of attention. There is, however, a strain of oddness in many Roosters – although with a Rooster one can never be quite sure whether his/her eccentricity is genuine or just another way of attracting attention. With this oddity goes a tendency to indulge in tactless criticism and tell others how they should manage their lives. Nevertheless, most Roosters are pleasant people to know, their virtues outweighing their vices.

Emotions and Love Life

Emotionally the Rooster, male or female, is subject to erratic surges of mood. He/she is usually either very happy or extremely miserable, rarely anything in between. The Rooster either likes or dislikes someone very much; indifference is not a characteristic emotional stance. The animal least likely to make a good partner for the Rooster is the Rabbit; the two animals are completely incompatible. Partnerships between the Rooster and either the Dog or the Monkey are often subject to severe strains. Rooster/ Rooster relationships are also strained; each partner is incapable of understanding why the other does not spend more time admiring him/her. The Snake and the Ox are the ideal mates for the Rooster. Other relationships are reasonably successful.

The Five Elemental Roosters
(All Elemental Roosters are Negative.)

The Metal Rooster has strong beliefs and is so convinced of their rightness that he/she has difficulty in

believing that anybody could conceivably oppose them. As a result of this, the Metal Rooster finds compromise extremely difficult.

The Water Rooster is the most intellectual of the clan, although his/her real talent is sometimes constrained by a tendency to concentrate on small detail to the exclusion of larger, more pressing matters.

The Wood Rooster tries to control the Rooster tendency to criticize, although not always with complete success. He/she is a kindly creature and more concerned about others' feelings and problems than most Roosters.

The Fire Rooster hardly ever stops crowing and makes an exhausting, albeit exciting, companion. The Fire Rooster's burning enthusiasm is never far from the surface and is sometimes combined with an inflexibility which can lead to conflict and frustration.

The Earth Rooster is less flamboyant than most Roosters, but is an even more fanatical organizer of other people, whom he/she constantly urges to follow his or her excellent example.

Good and Bad News for Roosters to the Year 2010

1999 A moderately good year, but one in which Roosters should take no chances with money.

2000 An excellent year for Roosters, particularly where money matters are concerned.

2001 Also a good year, but not quite as fortunate as 2000.

2002 A poor year in which unforeseen problems are encountered, and things that begin well end badly.

2003 A good year in which the troubles of 2002 are largely forgotten.

2004 A moderate year in which problems abound, but prove not as serious as they first seemed.

2005 Only a moderate year, but slightly better than 2004.

2006 A good year, but one in which some domestic or emotional difficulties arise.

2007 Not at all a good year. The Rooster is plagued by bad luck and must be cautious.

2008 A very bad year, particularly for finances. Roosters must be very cautious.

2009 A year in which the difficulties of 2007 and 2008 are overcome and some progress is made.

2010 A good year in which Roosters prosper and experience strokes of luck, but must avoid undue risks.

THE DOG

Key Words
Honestly affectionate, open-mindedness, objective, fair, intelligent.

General Character
The Dog is friendly, kindly, altruistic, and will never abandon a friend who is in trouble or any sort of difficulty. The Dog is the most fair-minded of the animal types of Chinese astrology, and his/her sense of fairness is such that an injustice to another is resented quite as bitterly as an injustice that has been personally experienced. The Dog's concern for righteousness and justice sometimes leads him or her to view the world in a rather simplistic way. Everything – and everybody – is seen as black and white; there are no shades of grey. People and institutions are seen as good or bad, nice or nasty. The Dog is almost incapable of appreciating that most of us have mixed motives for our actions, that there is some good in the worst of us, some original sin in even the most virtuous of saints.

Their rather colour-blind attitude to the world around them does not mean that Dogs are unintelligent. On the contrary, they have powerful, logical minds and often display considerable astuteness. Sometimes this astuteness is coloured by distrust. Dogs have a certain suspicion of strangers and they tend to be unduly worried about the motives of those whom they do not know well. While Dogs can be very combative indeed, particularly when they feel they are opposing injustice, they are not normally or constitutionally aggressive; they only fight when they feel that they or their friends are under attack. All in all, Dogs are admirable people; if one has a Dog as a close and trusted friend, one is fortunate indeed.

Emotions and Love Life
Dogs, as mentioned above, are suspicious of strangers and slow to make friends. They are even slower to give their affections and are alarmed by those who display them too openly; nothing is more offputting to the Dog of either sex than someone he/she does not know well suddenly announcing their affection or regard. Once, however, a Dog does give his/her love to another it is usually for life or, at least, until driven away by blows and kicks – Dogs are quite extraodinarily loyal to their partners, even in very trying circumstances. Dogs are least likely to establish satisfactory relationships with Dragons, with whom they are incompatible: each is incapable of seeing the other's point of view. The Dog/Rooster combination is also a difficult one. Horses and Tigers provide the best partners for Dogs, and there are no great problems with other combinations.

The Five Elemental Dogs
(All Elemental Dogs are Positive.)

The **Metal Dog** is an inflexible character who applies his/her unbendingly stern principles to him or herself and to others. Metal Dogs make good friends – but woe betide those who oppose them.

The **Water Dog** is more contemplative and easy-going than most of the clan – but, if the need arises, can be a doughty fighter.

The **Wood Dog** is more flexible than the Metal Dog, has a warmer and more generous nature, and is consequently better liked.

The **Fire Dog** is a born leader, possessing strong personal magnetism. Many Dogs, like their animal namesakes, like to go about in packs and establish close relationships with the members of a group. Fire Dogs tend to head such groups.

The **Earth Dog** moves rather slowly when thinking is involved but is prudent, considered, extremely good with handling money, and gives excellent advice on practical matters.

Good and Bad Years for Dogs to the Year 2010

1999 A fairly favourable year, particularly where money matters are concerned.

2000 A bad year in which all the terrier-like qualities of Dogs are called upon.

2001 A very good year, a complete contrast to 2000. Dogs will prosper and enjoy happiness.

2002 An even better year for Dogs than 2001. Everything goes splendidly.

2003 A moderate year in which unexpected problems produce anxiety.

2004 Another moderate year, but one in which social/romantic matters go very well.

2005 A rather poor year in which Dogs are beset by financial worries.

2006 Not a wonderful year, but one in which Dogs make progress.

2007 A moderate year in which Dogs are likely to make new and useful friends.

2008 An absolutely splendid year for Dogs provided they don't lend money.

2009 A year in which quarrels and disputes are likely. Dogs must muzzle their jaws.

2010 A fairly good year, but one in which Dogs have to concern themselves with others' troubles.

THE BOAR

Key Words
Honest, decent, popular, merry, pleasure-seeking.

General Character
'A rough diamond' is the rather hackneyed phrase which best sums up the character of the typical Boar. His/her manner may give the impression of slightly cynical toughness, even rudeness, but beneath the hard exterior is an utterly decent, rather soft-hearted, individual. Boars make loyal, discreetly trustworthy and very generous friends. Their generosity, however, is two-sided; they will happily share their last penny with a friend, and they expect friends to be prepared to do the same. If a Boar's generosity to a friend is not reciprocated he/she will rapidly bring that particular friendship to an end. Boars are notable for their general good humour and cheerfulness. This is particularly evident after or during a good meal, and at parties and other social gatherings. The sociability and pleasantness of Boars usually ensures that they are popular with friends and successful in their careers. Rarely, however, will a Boar succeed in any field that requires diplomacy. Tact is not one of the Boar virtues.

Emotions and Love Life
The emotional temperature of the Boar is easily raised and is only reduced by, metaphorically speaking, large quantities of ice-cold water. Boars, male or female, have strong sexual desires and the physical side of love is of great importance to them; at their worst, Boars become lecherous and debauched. Normally, however, they are loyal and loving. The worst partner for a Boar is the Snake – neither can communicate with the other or understand the nature of his/her ways of thinking or feeling. The Boar/Boar and Boar/Monkey combinations are also subject to strain. The best partners for Boars are Rabbits and Sheep. Other combinations are tolerable to good.

The Five Elemental Boars
(All Elemental Boars are Negative.)

The Metal Boar is iron clad, and is pushy, energetic and even more outgoing than most of the Boar clan. Outsiders rarely penetrate the iron jacket; those who do so will encounter gold.

The Water Boar is an extremely persuasive creature who finds it difficult to keep his/her appetites under control – particularly if someone else is paying the bill, literally or metaphorically.

The Wood Boar has all the good-heartedness of his/her general type, but is a little more devious and somewhat subtler in his/her thought and ways of putting thought into action.

The Fire Boar is sensual, energetic, reckless and determined to the point of – suitably enough – pig-headed obstinacy. He/she takes so many chances that he/she is either outstandingly successful or fails miserably.

The Earth Boar is a contented, friendly and usually successful animal, very good at practical matters and fond of the good things in life.

Good and Bad Years for Boars to the Year 2010

1999 A reasonably good and happy year.

2000 A good year for Boars in which problems, obstacles and general anxiety are overcome.

2001 A busy year, but unpleasantly so. Boars are beset by problems, particularly financial ones.

2002 A pleasant and lucky year for those Boars who do not engage in speculation or gambling.

2003 Only a moderate year; money problems, resulting from extravagance, may arise.

2004 Another moderate year in which finances may be difficult unless Boars are prudent.

2005 A good year for Boars who act with persistence and energy.

2006 A disappointing year in which Boars are liable to be unlucky.

2007 A fairly good year in which steady progress is made and last year's problems solved.

2008 A tiresome year in which anxieties loom continually. Overall, though, some progress is made.

2009 An excellent year in which Boars continually experience strokes of good fortune.

2010 A poor year, particularly where money is concerned. Boars should not be trustful.

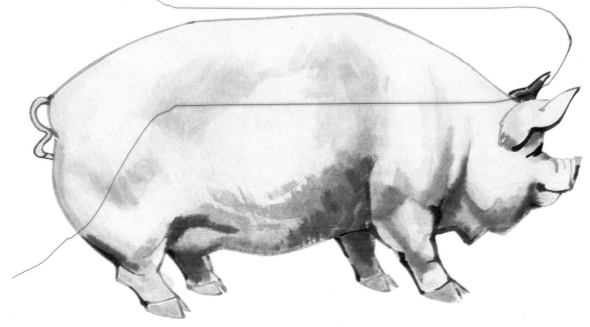

OTHER FORTUNE-TELLING METHODS

Over the centuries many different methods of fortune-telling have been employed by seers. The livers of sacrificed animals have been examined, the flights of birds observed, the markings on the shells of mountain tortoises scrutinized, and conclusions about future events derived from all of these.

It is likely that all these methods produced satisfactory results if the seer was possessed of that intuitive faculty which distinguishes the great from the merely competent fortune-teller. Few of them can be practised today: most of us would find the sacrifice of a sheep disagreeable and mountain tortoises are rarely encountered.

There are, however, many little-known methods of divination which can be practised by anybody with access to, for example, a teacup or a set of dominoes.

A nineteenth-century photograph of a seer 'reading the coffee grounds'; the patterns were interpreted in a similar way to those made by tea leaves.

READING TEA LEAVES

Telling fortunes by means of tea leaves, popular since the early nineteenth century, has suffered something of a decline in recent years. This is not because it is a particularly difficult technique, but because so few present-day tea cups have any tea leaves in them, as a result of the ubiquity of the tea bag.

So the first thing to do if you want to tell fortunes from tea leaves is to abandon the use of tea bags and revert to the old formula of 'one teaspoonful for each person and one for the pot'. This will not only enable you to read the tea leaves but will give you a cup of tea free from the characteristic tang of infused paper.

If you are serving tea to friends and think you may be asked to read the tea leaves, it is best to use plain white cups or mugs as it is surprisingly difficult to pick out leaf patterns against a dark or patterned background. You must not, of course, use a strainer, and it is best to use a type of tea blend which contains at least some fairly large leaves.

Each person who is going to have his/her fortune told should leave about a quarter of an inch of tea at the bottom of the cup. This should be swirled around so that the tea leaves are in a

state of suspension and then gently poured off leaving the tea leaves on the bottom and sides of the cup.

If you look at the tea leaves after this has been done, it is unlikely that you will find that any of the leaf-groups are immediately recognizable as a clear picture of anything – an anchor or a clock, for example. You have to squint, as it were, at the leaves through half-closed eyes, letting your imagination roam at will. After a time you will see resemblances to particular things in precisely the same way that someone who looks at ink blots or cracks on a plaster ceiling will begin to sort them into patterns, shapes and pictures. Make a mental note of the symbols/shapes/patterns you see; if any leaf or leaves suggests more than one object or symbol (both a triangle and an anchor, for example) make a note of both and combine meanings.

Interpret the symbols in accordance with the following meanings:

Airliner A little surprisingly, this is not usually taken as an indication of travel, but of 'going up in the world' – an increase in prosperity, perhaps as a consequence of inheriting wealth. In tea-cup interpretations of a century or more ago, a balloon was given the same meaning.

Anchor A journey which will end in happiness.

Arch The person whose fortune is being told will meet someone who will become an important influence upon his/her life.

Bell Good news is on the way.

Bird A reliable indication of good fortune.

Book This is taken as a sign that the person whose fortune is being told should seek advice on a matter which is causing concern.

Bottle A rather active social life is in store.

Butterfly An indication that someone in the life of the person whose fortune is being read is not serious as they might be about an emotional tie.

Chain An indication that more effort should be made in a work matter.

Clock An important meeting will shortly take place.

Crescent Moon Financial good fortune is on its way.

Cross Some unpleasant news is likely to be received. The matter which it concerns can be forecast from the nature of the symbol nearest to it. If it is near to a bottle, for example, it could be about the enquirer's social life; if near to a bird, it might be about a reversal of good fortune.

Crown A promotion at work or some desired appointment.

Dart A happy love affair.

Dice A warning not to take chances.

Envelope Good news is on the way.

Fish Splendid news is on the way, though probably from a considerable distance.

Flag A sure sign of coming good fortune.

Foot Good news will be delayed.

Gate A sudden change of circumstances will come about.

Hammer (or a mallet) The enquirer must make more effort in life.

Harp A very fortunate symbol of worldly prosperity and emotional happiness.

Hat A very minor misfortune is on its way.

Hatchet (or either axe or saw). This is a warning to be very careful where both money and emotional matters are concerned.

Heart Exciting things are in store where the emotions are concerned.

Key A matter which has appeared mysterious will soon be explained.

Knife A coming quarrel.

Ladder Things are about to improve.

Mountain(s) Problems lie ahead.

Ring Emotional good luck.

Road (i.e. two lines of leaves parallel to one another) If straight, things are going to go well. If crooked, the opposite.

Rocks Small problems lie ahead.

Roof A change in home life is imminent.

Scales The enquirer must try to take a more balanced view of things.

Ship Good luck will be experienced as the result of a journey.

Trees This suggest everything is going to flourish.

The above list is not, of course, all-inclusive. Nor does it give much indication of the time-scale involved – whether, for example, the problems indicated by the appearance of mountains in the cup are likely to arise next week, in the distant future, or at some intermediate time.

For symbols which don't appear in the list you will have to depend upon your own intuitive abilities. Doing this, you must endeavour to make a personal interpretation of a symbol go beyond a merely literal significance. So, for example, you might well interpret a tea leaf which looks, to you, like a coffin as an indication of a loss of some type, not as a specific forecast of death. In the same way a shape which, in your mind's eye, is that of a standard lamp, might be interpreted as an indication that light is about to be thrown on some obscure problem, or that the enquirer is about to undergo an illuminating experience. It would be a mistake to take the symbol literally and assume that the enquirer will acquire new electrical apparatus.

There is a traditional – which in this case implies a tradition not going back more than two centuries – interpretation of the time-scale involved in reading the tea leaves. Any symbol near the rim of the cup indicates something that is going to happen within the next month or so; a symbol at the bottom of the cup indicates a situation or event that lies two or more years in the future; the distance between the rim and the cup shows a time interval of 18 months. So, for example, something half-way down the side of the cup is an indicator of how the situation will develop in a year's time.

GEOMANTIC QUESTIONS

Geomancy is an ancient system of fortune-telling which seems to have been derived from the sand divination of ancient Arabia. Originally, it involved making marks in the desert sand with a pointed stick but, after it had reached Europe in the Middle Ages, it developed into what has been called 'shield numerology'. A shield, similar to that employed in the complex quarterings of heraldry, was filled with figures derived from the throws of dice or the random marks made by a pen.

Geomancy, which literally means 'fortune-telling by earth', is a fascinating and complex system of divination which is described at length in Stephen Skinner's remarkable books *Terrestrial Astrology* (Routledge & Kegan Paul) and *The Oracle of Geomancy* (Element Books). The following system for obtaining favourable or unfavourable responses to questions is derived from one of the many techniques described in these.

Throw a dice four times, noting down the numbers thrown in consecutive order. Opposite each odd-numbered throw write down a single cross; opposite each even-numbered throw write down two crosses (see diagram above right).

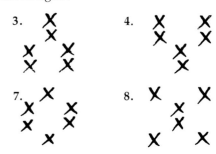

1st Number Thrown 6
2nd Number Thrown 1
3rd Number Thrown 4
4th Number Thrown 3

Count up the total number of crosses in the resulting figure. If that total is an odd number, the matter is 'not yet ripe for judgment' and the question should be left unanswered and not asked again for a week. If that total is an even number, the crosses will form one of the eight figures shown in the diagram below left. Take the significance of your figure as follows:

Figure 1. The matter cannot yet be decided. Ask again tomorrow.
Figure 2. The matter will end neither well nor ill.
Figure 3. The matter will end favourably; things will go as you wish.
Figure 4. The matter will go very well for you and you will experience great good fortune.
Figure 5. The answer to your question is favourable if it concerns love and romance; otherwise it is very unfavourable indeed.
Figure 6. A favourable answer is indicated, particularly so if your question concerns money and finance.
Figure 7. The answer is unfavourable.
Figure 8. The answer is neither bad nor good. A neutral situation is indicated.

DOMINOES

There are two very simple methods of telling fortunes using dominoes. The first of these involves the use of an entire set of dominoes and is designed to indicate the dominant influence over the next week in the lives of one or more people.

The dominoes are placed face down upon a flat surface and shuffled well. Each person participating in the divination selects one domino, interpreting its significance in relation to the events of the next seven days in accordance with the following cookbook meanings:

Six-Six An extremely lucky week lies ahead in which money arrives from an unexpected source as a

Dominoes are usually associated with undemanding games – but they can also be employed in an equally undemanding mode of divination.

result of a surprising stroke of good fortune.
Six-Five You are likely to be surprised by news of an engagement, a marriage or a birth.
Six-Four A legal matter, or one relating to an agreement of some sort, will cause concern to either you, a partner or a close friend. This may drag on for rather a long time, but with patience and prudence the matter should be satisfactorily resolved.
Six-Three Social life could be exciting. Make sure you play a full part in everything that is going on.
Six-Two You will receive an unexpected and perhaps slightly embarrassing gift. Try not to make your surprise too apparent.
Six-One You will meet an old friend who will probably ask for your help. Don't promise more than you can deliver.
Six-Blank You will find someone whom you have always looked upon as a friend behaving in rather an unpleasant way – perhaps spreading gossip about you.
Five-Five A week of change; you may find yourself seriously considering moving home or taking a new job.
Five-Four A week in which luck

will be with you. A modest gamble or speculation should turn out well.
Five-Three A week in which work takes up more of your time than you would wish, but you will find that this pays off in the end.
Five-Two An exciting week in which you will visit new places.
Five-One Romance, perhaps only temporary, is in the air.
Five-Blank A rather gloomy week lies ahead; you may find yourself involved in a parting, either permanent or of long duration.
Four-Four A long journey should result in happiness. Don't refuse invitations to parties, even if some trouble and expense is involved in getting to them.
Four-Three You will encounter, rather unexpectedly, someone with whom you were emotionally involved in the past. This could lead to exciting developments.
Four-Two A week in which everything, notably finance, gets better.
Four-One A week of worry, particularly over money matters. Avoid disputes at all costs, and remember the old saying that 'a soft answer turneth away wrath'.
Four-Blank You are likely to receive an unpleasant letter. Remain calm – don't be rude or lose your temper because someone else has done so. If you can remain cool, in spite of provocation, the rift will be healed and the matter brought to a satisfactory conclusion.
Three-Three Someone else's emo-

tional life will cause you worry and annoyance.

Three-Two Not a week in which you can afford to take any chances at all. Don't act without careful consideration and, above all, don't gamble or speculate – this is not your lucky week.

Three-One Matters that have been puzzling you will be clarified. A surprising piece of information will throw sudden light on the motives and actions of someone well-known to you.

Three-Blank You will be told a scandalous tale about someone you know well. Don't believe it unless it is confirmed beyond reasonable doubt. As a matter of fact, scandal is in the air – be wary of gossip about yourself, as there may be someone who is spreading unfounded rumours about you.

Two-Two A pleasant week, with lots of jollity, but you may find your enjoyable week arouses the jealousy of an associate.

Two-One Not a week to borrow or lend money.

Two-Blank A week of irritating delays in which everything takes longer than expected. Try to remain calm – irritation will not speed things up.

One-One An exciting week, particularly if you spend as much time as possible in the open air.

One-Blank A very boring week indeed. The following one should be an improvement – it could hardly be duller unless you draw:
Blank-Blank.

The second method is even simpler and is designed to give an indication of the most important trends in your life during the coming year.

Remove all the dominoes with blank halves from the set. Shuffle the remainder and draw three of them, interpreting their significance in the following way:

Six-Six A year of unexpected strokes of good fortune.

Six-Five Good luck lots ahead in career matters.

Six-Four Good luck lies ahead in money matters.

Six-Three Lucky in love.

Six-Two An enjoyable social life.

Six-One Fortunate journeys, happy holidays.

Five-Five A year of hard work, but rather enjoyable.

Five-Four A prosperous year.

Five-Three Possibility of romance with someone you know at work.

Five-Two Workmates will soon become friends.

Five-One Work will involve much more travel than previously.

Four-Four Money matters will dominate much of the year.

Four-Three Love life will prove expensive.

Four-Two Your friends will involve you in much expenditure.

Four-One You will spend rather a lot on your holidays.

Three-Three A year of romance.

Three-Two Love and money will be yours.

Three-One Travel and holidaying may lead to unusual emotional involvements.

Two-Two A year of prosperity.

Two-One A year of financial good fortune and much travelling.

One-One A restless year in which you will travel more than you wish.

Sixteenth-century German prospectors used 'divining rods' to find metallic ores. 'Radiesthesia' is a modern development of this.

THE MYSTIC PENDULUM

The use of the pendulum for the purposes of fortune-telling, usually called radiesthesia, is a fairly modern derivation of the ancient art of dowsing, in North America sometimes referred to as 'water witching'.

Classical dowsing is a fairly energetic technique, usually involving long periods of tramping about in muddy fields holding some sort of implement – a hazel twig, a wire coat-hanger twisted into the shape of a capital Y, or two strips of whalebone taped together. The dowser walks across the land beneath which he or she believes water, minerals, concealed tunnels or even buried treasure may be hidden, and by the twists and dips of the dowsing implement comes to conclusions about what lies beneath.

Radiesthesists employ a pendulum for much the same purposes, but most of them practise their art in the comfort of their homes using a large-scale map of the area in which they are interested instead of walking across it.

A pendulum can be a very elaborate and expensive object indeed, made of rare woods and suspended from springs which amplify its movements. Most radiesthesists, however, find that almost any object can be used as a bob (a weight) for a pendulum. A wedding ring suspended from a foot or 18 inches of cotton or silk thread usually makes a very satisfactory pendulum for the apprentice radiesthesist.

The simplest experiment in radiesthesia is to try to obtain replies to simple questions that can be answered yes or no.

Write YES and NO on a piece of paper – the YES directly ahead of you, at the top of the paper, the NO about half-way down the right-hand side of the paper. Hold your improvised pendulum in your hand and suspend it over the middle of the paper. After no more than a minute, usually no more than a few seconds, the pendulum bob will begin to move. At first this will probably be in small circles, or in directions which continually change. After a time, however, it should adopt a definite swing towards either YES or NO. Take this as your answer.

A development of this is to obtain answers to more complex questions. Write all the possible answers to your question in a circle. Hold the pendulum over the middle of the circle and note, once a definite swing is established, which answer is indicated.

Many amateur radiesthesists use the pendulum as a means of finding objects which have been lost in home or garden. If you want to do this, draw a rough map of your garden, and/or the various rooms of your home, and suspend your pendulum over each in turn. The missing object should either be: a) at one of the extremes of the swing of the bob; b) in the middle of the swing; or c) where the pendulum describes a small circle.

A development of this is to use a rough diagram of your garden to find out the whereabouts of pipes and drains or to decide where a particular bush, tree or plant is best suited.

If you become a very accomplished radiesthesist, you can employ large-scale maps to investigate what lies beneath the surface of the earth. You might detect an Anglo-Saxon or Viking grave, a Roman villa or even a hoard of pirate gold.

To dream of either a young baby or of a birth is traditionally supposed to be an omen of good fortune which will take place in the near future.

DREAMS

Quite apart from the significance which psychoanalysts and practitioners of other schools of depth psychology attach to dreams, there is an ancient lore which interprets them prophetically, as forecasts of the future of the dreamer and those he or she knows well. Here are some traditional interpretations of dreams:

Accidents Dreams of these forecast a happy surprise or surprises.
Babies A smiling baby prophesies good fortune; a crying baby is an indication of a forthcoming disappointment.
Banquet (or large dinner) Good news is on the way.
Bathing If the water is deep, something is going to happen which will be a cause of satisfaction to the dreamer. If shallow, a disappointment or some frustration will be experienced.
Beds To dream of buying a bed indicates a likely change of residence. To dream of yourself in bed is a forecast of a long-awaited romantic involvement.
Bird(s) Coming good luck if the birds are flying. If roosting, however, this indicates the opposite.
Birth A surprising piece of good fortune is imminent.
Blood A friend is going to ask for help. Giving it will be the cause of a good deal of effort and worry, but the request should not be refused.
Boat Time for the dreamer to get out of the rut and launch a new enterprise.
Cat If jet black, good luck is on the way. Any other colour signifies that someone is practising deceit and wishes the dreamer no good.
Climbing Financial affairs are about to take a turn for the better. The higher the object which the dreamer is climbing, the better the good fortune. A dream of a mountaineering expedition is particularly fortunate.
Clock Now is the time to take chances. The dreamer should not be afraid to seize all the opportunities open to him or her.
Coffin News of a marriage or an engagement is on the way.
Cup If full, some pleasant, small windfalls; if empty, some annoying frustrations.
Dancing An improvement in relationships with others.
Danger To dream of a dangerous situation is taken as an indication that the dreamer should be careful about health and money matters.
Darkness Something perplexing is about to happen.
Death As for 'Coffin': news of some imminent and far-reaching change.
Fainting If the dreamer is fainting, financial losses are indicated. If someone else faints, a quarrel may be on the way.
Falling A nasty disappointment is in the offing.
Flowers A minor illness or indisposition is prefigured.
Flying A warning not to be over-ambitious.
Funeral As for 'Death' and 'Coffin'.

To dream of a black cat is an indicator of approaching good luck, but cats of other colours are omens of 'cattiness'.

To dream of golden objects is a warning against judging things by appearance, an indicator that reality is deceptively masked from sight.

Ghosts A disappointment or a minor illness.

Gifts If the dreamer is the giver, financial good fortune. Otherwise the reverse.

Gold A warning to be careful – things may not be all that they seem.

Grass News of a birth.

Hair A minor accident. To dream of sudden baldness signifies unexpected good fortune.

Illness An unexpected journey.

Jewels An extremely prosperous year lies ahead.

Keys Losing keys means the dreamer should brace him or herself for many troubles. Finding keys means the possibility of a new emotional relationship.

Kissing An unexpected gift.

Ladders A warning to be prudent and beware of false friends.

Letters Receiving letters means good news is in the offing. Writing one suggests this is the time to take a small gamble.

Marriage Someone else's marriage suggests good fortune on the way. Dreaming of your own marriage indicates a serious quarrel with a loved one.

Mirror A danger of serious quarrels with friends and loved ones.

Money Finding money indicates that something pleasant and totally unexpected is in the offing.

Moon A splendid augury as far as the dreamer's sex life is concerned.

Music Gloomy news will be received before long.

Nakedness A sign that false friends are gossiping about the dreamer's private life.

Numerals Emotional difficulties lie ahead.

Pain An unexpected financial windfall.

Prison To dream of being in prison indicates a forthcoming sexual adventure.

Purse Losing a purse is an intimation of coming money problems. Finding one suggests a surprising and delightful adventure is in store.

Quarrels An unexpected visitor.

Railways A financial setback, probably as the result of a friend's incompetence.

Ring When the dreamer receives a ring as a gift, he or she may expect an unpleasant surprise. When the dreamer loses one, or gives one away, excellent news is suggested.

Singing Hearing others sing in a dream is a sign of a year of prosperity; hearing oneself singing is an indication of unexpected setbacks.

Snow An extremely important letter or other communication will be received in the near future.

Stairs A dream of ascending these is a sign that the dreamer's ambi-

To dream of railways is inauspicious as far as money matters are concerned – an indicator that there is risk of coming off the rails' financially.

It has long been believed that there is a symbolic link between the moon and sexuality; to dream of the moon is a general omen of emotional excitement.

tions will be realized. Descending a flight of stairs is an indication of difficulties in work and business.

Strangers To dream of meeting complete strangers signifies major upheavals, for better or worse, in the dreamer's life. Nothing will be quite the same after this dream.

To dream of twins has traditionally been regarded as a very favourable augury, particularly in relation to material prosperity.

Tears To dream of weeping is a forecast of unexpected happiness.

Twins To dream of twins is a sign of coming good fortune and financial prosperity.

Umbrella An unexpected but welcome gift will be received.

Voyage (air or sea) Either good news from afar or a successful speculation.

Walking Tiresome news concerning a friend.

Washing Of clothes – a change of dwelling or a new job. Taking a wash oneself indicates a risky circumstance which must be dealt with carefully.

Water Drinking – good fortune to the dreamer's partner. Looking into water – a sign that no hasty actions should be engaged in.

Zoo (or any dream involving animals/birds in cages) The dreamer should be careful; others – perhaps apparent friends – are working against his/her interests.

PHYSIOGNOMY

Physiognomy is the art of reading character and temperament from facial appearance. It is, in a sense, the most widely practised method of fortune-telling. For even people who express scepticism about all forms of the divinatory arts are apt to use such phrases as 'He has a lecherous look about him' or 'She has an honest face'. Judgments based on such considerations are often very accurate indeed. For while we inherit our features – the actual physical structure of our faces – there is no doubt that the lives we live give a particular cast to those features. Thus, for example, perpetual worries give a drawn and anxious form to the face, and a lot of smiling produces what are sometimes called 'laughter lines'.

Physiognomists divide the face into three sections:

1. **The forehead.**
2. **The middle of the face,** approximating to the area that is occupied by the nose.
3. **The remainder of the face.**

If these three sections of the face are equal in length to one another, it is an indication of an exceptionally well-balanced personality, but perhaps not a particularly interesting one. A person, in short, who will neither excel nor do spectacularly badly in any aspect of his or her life.

If the longest of the three sections is the forehead, a character in which thought dominates the emotions and the physical aspects of life is indicated. If the central section of the face is dominant, a temperament with a great capacity for physical endurance and an underlying common-sense approach to life is shown. A dominant lower section of the face is associated with several different characteristics which are believed to be determined on the basis of chin shape. The physiognomists of three and more centuries ago classified human chins into more than 20 different categories, some of them so similar that it was easy to confuse them. The main characteristics, however, depend upon two factors: width, and shape apart from width (that is, whether the entire chin area is square, pointed, oval or dimpled).

A broad chin supposedly denotes physical and psychological strength coupled with reliability and determination. A narrow chin is taken as a sign of less energy and a certain ten-

An oval and slightly pointed chin would be taken by some physiognomists as an indicator of a restless and sometimes discontented artistry.

dency to introspection. Those who have it are believed to make better followers than leaders.

These qualities will be modified according to how the shape of the chin is seen when looked at full face:

Square A certain obstinacy and tendency to reject advice.
Pointed A grumbling, discontented nature.
Oval Artistic tendencies and a pleasure-loving temperament.
Dimpled Rather overconcerned with relationships with members of the opposite sex.

If one of the three sections of the face is much shorter in length than the other two, this is also regarded as a significant feature.

A very short forehead is an indication of an impulsive personality – the sort of person who sets his or her mouth in motion before ensuring that the mind is in gear. If the forehead is also narrow, this impulsiveness is likely to be confined to speech – a certain physical timidity in the face of dangers or threats being denoted by this formation.

A very short middle section of the face is thought to denote a lack of practicality and a tendency to be easily deceived by others. It is also asso-

A broad, strong chin, in harmony with the rest of the face, is believed by physiognomists to denote a strong character and a balanced personality.

ciated with a lack of staying power and determination – an inability to see things through.

A very short lower third of the face is associated with difficulty in communicating with others and expressing deeply-felt emotions. It is also believed to indicate a somewhat cold and calculating temperament and a less than usual interest in members of the opposite sex.

While there is no need to take this sort of thing too seriously, it is worth adding that some physiognomists have attached great importance to the shape of the ears. It has been said that:

Large ears denote a driving and ambitious personality.
Medium-sized ears denote an average sort of person.

Phrenology, satirized in this caricature, was a pseudoscience of character interpretation, involving the examination of the 'bumps on the head'.

Small ears denote a retiring personality, a timid disposition and a lack of ambition.

Physiognomy provides a great deal of amusement to those who practise it, but, as with any form of fortune-telling, its insights need to be interpreted in context rather than taken literally. Surviving portraits of Casanova show that he had features which, strictly following the rules laid down by one physiognomist of his own time, indicated an ascetic personality totally lacking in any sort of sexual drive.

FURTHER READING

(Note: this list is by no means a complete bibliography; it is simply intended to give readers of this book a guide to some of the books which are either in print or easily available through public libraries which will enable them to enlarge their knowledge of fortune-telling and its history.)

Agrippa, Cornelius, *Fourth Book of Occult Philosophy*, Askin Publishers, London, 1977 (a photographic reproduction of the London edition of 1655).

Case, Paul Foster, *The Tarot*, Macoy Publishing, Richmond Va., 1947.

Cavendish, Richard, *The Magical Arts*, Arkana Books, London, 1984.

Cavendish, Richard, *The Tarot*, Chancellor Press, London, 1986.

Cavendish, Richard, (edited by) *Encyclopedia of the Unexplained*, Routledge, London, 1972.

Cavendish, Richard, (edited by) *Man, Myth and Magic*, (7 vols.), Purnell, London, 1972.

Cheasley, C. W., *Numerology*, Rider, London, 1926.

Clodd, Edward, *Magic in Names*, Dutton, New York, 1921.

Deacon, Richard, *The Book of Fate*, Muller, London, 1976.

Douglas, Alfred, *The Tarot*, Gollancz, London, 1972.

Fitzherbert, Andrew, *Hand Psychology*, Angus and Robertson, New South Wales, 1986.

Gettings, Fred, *Palmistry Made Easy*, Wilshire Books, Hollywood, 1973.

Gettings, Fred, *The Book of the Hand;* Hamlyn Books, London, 1965.

Hall, Angus, and King, Francis, *Mysteries of Prediction*, Aldus Books, London, 1978.

Hall, Manly Palmer, *The Philosophy of Astrology*, Philosophical Research Society, Los Angeles, 1943.

Hartmann, Franz, *Principles of Astrological Geomancy*, Rider, London, 1913.

Hone, Margaret, *Modern Textbook of Astrology*, L. N. Fowler, London, 1975.

Huson, Paul, *The Devil's Picture Book*, Sphere Books, London, 1972.

Jung, C. G., *Mysterium Coniunctionis*, Routledge, London, 1963.

King, Francis, *Palmistry*, Orbis, London, 1979.

King, Francis, *Witchcraft and Demonology*, Hamlyn Books, London, 1987.

King, Francis, and Kingston, Jeremy, *Mysterious Knowledge*, Aldus Books, London, 1978.

Lau, Theodora, *Handbook of Chinese Horoscopes*, Souvenir Press, London, 1979, Arrow Books, London, 1987.

McIntosh, Christopher, *Eliphas Levi and the French Occult Revival*, Rider, London, 1972.

Mathers, S. L. MacGregor, *Astral Projection, Ritual Magic and Alchemy*, Aquarian Press, Wellingborough, 1987.

Mathers, S. L. Macgregor, *The Tarot*, London, 1888 (currently available as a paperback reprint, Occult Research Press, New York, n.d.)

Parker, Derek and Julia, *The New Compleat Astrologer*, Mitchell Beazley, London, 1984.

Raphael (i.e. Smith, Robert Cross), *The Philosophical Merlin*, London, 1822 (most easily found in Skinner's *Oracle of Geomancy*, in which it was reprinted as an Appendix).

Regardie, Israel, *The Golden Dawn* (4 vols.), Aries Press, Chicago, 1937-40 (currently available as 4 vols. in 1 from Llewellyn Publications, Minnesota).

Skinner, Stephen, *Oracle of Geomancy*, Prism Press, Bridport, 1986.

Skinner, Stephen, *Terrestrial Astrology*, Routledge, London, 1978.

Thorndike, Lynn, *Michael Scot*, Nelson, London, 1965.

Tilley, Roger, *Playing Cards*, Octopus Books, London, 1973.

Waite, A. E., *Pictorial Key to the Tarot*, Rider, London, 1910 (numerous reprints have been issued over the years).

Wilhelm, Richard, *I Ching*, Routledge, London, 1951 (numerous reprints have been issued over the years).

Yeats, W. B., *Autobiographies*, Macmillan, London, 1926 (numerous reprints have been issued over the years).

Zain, C. C., *Predicting Events*, Church of Light, Los Angeles, 1934.

INDEX

Bold numerals indicate captions to illustrations.